Digital Computer Fundamentals

Digital Computer Fundamentals

JEFFERSON C. BOYCE

Allan Hancock College

PRENTICE-HALL, INC., Englewood Cliffs, New Jersey

Library of Congress Cataloging in Publication Data

BOYCE, JEFFERSON C
   Digital computer fundamentals.

   Bibliography: p.
   Includes index.
   1. Electronic digital computers. I. Title.
TK7888.3.B69   001.6'4'044   76–11768
ISBN 0–13–214114–0

© 1977
by PRENTICE-HALL, INC.
Englewood Cliffs, New Jersey 07632

10 9 8 7 6 5 4 3 2 1

Printed in the United States of America

PRENTICE-HALL INTERNATIONAL, INC., London
PRENTICE-HALL OF AUSTRALIA, PTY., LIMITED, Sydney
PRENTICE-HALL OF CANADA, LTD., Toronto
PRENTICE-HALL OF INDIA PRIVATE LIMITED, New Delhi
PRENTICE-HALL OF JAPAN, INC., Tokyo
PRENTICE-HALL OF SOUTHEAST ASIA PTE. LTD., Singapore

To my mother,
whose life has been dedicated
to helping others

Contents

Preface

Electronic digital computers, the subject of this book, show promise of providing solutions to many of today's problems. Man's muscles were extended by machines as a result of the industrial revolution. Now man's intellect is being extended by computers in an "intellectual" revolution. Computer techniques, for example, provide the mechanism for storage of untold billions of pieces of information. Consider how an attorney might be able to use computer-stored libraries of rulings, laws, regulations, procedures, and the like. The time formerly spent scanning such voluminous data could be more effectively spent in creative thinking, advancing the legal profession. The engineer, whose design activity typically consists of short periods of creative thought followed by long periods of systematic analysis, can relegate the analysis tasks to the computer. Similarly the doctor, airline pilot, teacher, almost anyone, can benefit from a computer's abilities to store large amounts of information and process such information in very short periods of time. All of these possibilities hinge on the electronic digital computer and man's developing capability to use it. The doorway to the future is via the electronic digital computer; this book attempts to open that door for the reader.

Certain deviations from conventional approaches to the digital computer are used in *Digital Computer Fundamentals*. Although Chapter 1 follows common introductory processes to orient the reader toward the world of the digital computer, Chapter 2 deviates from traditional presentation sequences. The author feels that it is highly desirable to establish a "talking knowledge" of digital computers very early in the reader's experience. Therefore Chapter 2 contains considerable detail concerning each conventional functional section of the computer. The reader should not feel overwhelmed at this detail. Consider that it is presented so that information

in subsequent chapters can be more adequately assimilated, and so that communication with others interested in digital computers can be established
very early.

Chapter 3 develops the basic circuits and shows how to describe them
in preparation for detailed discussion of each of the functional units of the
computer. The mathematics of the computer—Boolean algebra—is presented in Chapter 5 by use of basic logic circuits and logic simplification
(both algebraic and map methods). The basic circuits of Chapter 3 and the
Boolean algebra of Chapter 4 are combined in Chapter 5 to explain many
complex computer functions such as counting, decoding, multiplexing, etc.
and the like. Chapter 6 discusses information coding and how it is applied to
the digital computer.

The Control function introduces a detailed coverage of the computer's
functional sections in Chapter 7. Basic timing and data flow for the remainder
of the computer is also discussed in this chapter. Computer memories con-
stitute the contents of Chapter 8, where the complete range of memory
devices from high-speed semiconductor memories to high-volume magnetic
tape memories is developed. Chapter 9 presents simple computer arithmetic
operations and the logic circuits that are used to implement them. Input
functions and devices are the subject of Chapter 10, and Chapter 11 discusses
output functions and devices.

In Chapter 12 the very basic fundamentals of computer programming
are shown. Machine language, assembly language, high-level language, and
operating system terminology are developed, and simple examples are covered. Chapter 13 integrates the operation of the five basic functional units,
and explains their applicability to the increasingly-popular bus-organized
concepts. Finally, for those readers desiring details concerning the internal
operation of logic circuits, Appendix C discusses diodes and transistors, and
Appendix D covers implementation of logic functions with various logic
families.

As a result of understanding and applying the concepts presented in this
book, the reader should be adequately prepared to discuss computer operation at the functional level. He or she should be able to follow the flow of data
in digital computers, explain the operation of the five functional sections of
the computer, and recognize the requirements for various levels of programming. As computer technology advances, the reader should be adequately
prepared to advance with it, and apply related concepts as they appear.

Preparation of this book would have been impossible without the aid
of many people. First has been the cooperation of the many manufacturers in
the computer and digital fields. Their unselfish sharing of technical information has made possible the inclusion of much of the detailed coverage
presented here. Credit lines accompanying illustrations throughout this text
identify the manufacturers whose assistance has contributed so much to the

technical detail. Secondly, the experience gained from so many people at Prentice-Hall, Inc. during publication of the predecessor to this book, *Digital Logic and Switching Circuits,* was invaluable. Margaret McAbee, perhaps, was most influential in motivating this author during some rather trying times. Without her encouragement, perhaps this book might have never reached publication. Finally, and not at all last in order of importance, has been the cooperation of my wife and family. Without their unselfish dedication to the details of day-to-day operations of a household, the many thousands of hours required to prepare this book would not have been available.

JEFFERSON C. BOYCE

Digital Computer Fundamentals

1

Introduction to Digital Computers

1–1 INTRODUCTION

What is a Digital Computer?

An answer to the question what is a digital computer is not very difficult if one is willing to accept the broad dictionary type of definition. The class of machines called *computers* are devices that accept information, apply predetermined processes to the information, and supply the results of the processes. When more strictly classified, *digital computers* perform these functions by representing information in a discrete or discontinuous form and operate with symbols expressible as digits in some number system.

Dictionary definitions are complete and accurate but do not really reflect the manner in which different people view digital computers. Today's students often see computers as a tool that can extend their abilities and save large amounts of time when routine tasks must be accomplished. Many have been introduced to computers early in life by using computer-operated learning devices. In school computers prepared report cards, scheduled classes, cut calculating tasks and allowed more time for creative thinking, and even made large libraries of educational materials available at the touch of the "inquiry" button. Colleges and universities are even more progressive in their applications of computers, and most modern college graduates are well versed in computer usage. Today's students, and tomorrow's leaders, are being prepared for the computer-assisted world.

How is the computer regarded by the average citizen? Many different opinions exist, of course, based on individual experience. Consider the factory production line worker's image of the computer. New machines are moved into the factory, and attached to the new machines are electronic devices called computers. The worker sees the new machine performing routine production jobs and is told that the computer is directing the machines. Thus the computer becomes a threat to the factory worker and his job.

The person who has been harassed by an improperly programmed computer billing system obviously has negative opinions and considers the computer as an impersonal, unyielding, "stupid" machine. When that same computer makes and confirms airline and hotel reservations almost instantaneously, the negative opinions are forgotten. Suddenly the computer becomes a warm, obedient, and wise helper. Fortunately the "good" aspects of the computer overshadow the "bad," and the general populace is beginning to become aware of the computer's great positive impact on society.

The true effect of the computer on society is of such great magnitude that it cannot accurately be measured. Past contributions are well documented, and are discussed in this chapter. Present contributions are easily observed all around us. Manned trips to the moon, automatic computer-controlled spaceships to the planets, instantaneous credit-card verification in department stores, roadway traffic signals operating according to computer direction, election results being accurately forecast by computer, and so forth. There should be no doubt that future computer uses will be limited only by the imagination of society.

The communications media are largely responsible for the avid interest of the average citizen in computers. Newspapers, magazines, radio, and television all publicize the computer and its attributes. One can hardly live in today's world without being reminded that computers exist. When a criminal is apprehended, credit is given to the computer-stored information that helped identify and locate the culprit.

Pictures of planets taken by spacecraft yield highly usable photographs by computer techniques. Data gathered from both manned and unmanned spacecraft is stored in computer memories and reduced by computer techniques to provide the scientific community with the latest information. Practically all manned and unmanned space explorations are computer controlled. Human intervention is available as backup and is used only if necessary. It is highly doubtful that the objectives of many of the space exploration activities could be accomplished *without* the computer.

Thus the definition of "digital computers" is both technical and non-technical. For the technical individual, a technical definition is most meaningful, while for the general populus a less stringent definition (one which describes what it does) may be more useful. In this book the technical definition, tempered by the many application definitions, is used to guide the readers' progress from general to specific knowledge about the computer.

What Does the Digital Computer Do?

Implicit in all of the digital computer's applications is the *processing of information*. Whether controlling a space vehicle or verifying a credit card number, the computer is performing some kind of operation on information. It is constantly accepting new information, storing that information, performing mathematical operations determined by the information, routing the information to the required parts of the computer, or making processed information available to the user. Each of these functions is discussed in detail in this and succeeding chapters.

1–2 THE PAST

Pre-1940

One of the earliest devices built to aid man in his intellectual pursuits was the *abacus*. This digital device finds mention in history prior to the birth of Christ. The example of the abacus shown in Figure 1–1 is a modified

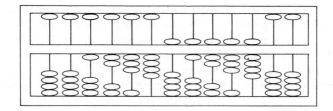

Figure 1–1 Japanese abacus, or soroban

form of the early abacus and was used extensively in the Japanese and Chinese civilizations. A skilled abacus operator can still successfully compete with mechanical desk-top calculators, although the electronic calculator easily outstrips either the abacus or the mechanical calculator. There was very little additional progress in the field of mechanical aids to mathematics until the appearance of Blaise Pascal's desk calculator in 1642. Pascal's device used simple gears to add and subtract. Other mathematicians improved Pascal's early machine by achieving multiplication, but the lack of mechanical precision hampered progress.

The next major milestone associated with the development of digital machines occurred in the early 1800s. Charles Babbage envisioned a mechanical device which incorporated many of the principles of the modern digital computer. His "Difference Engine" was developed to calculate and print mathematical tables. Again, imperfect materials, a shortage of precision tools, withdrawal of government support (after 1843), and a lack of understanding among his associates resulted in abandonment of his project after several incomplete models had been constructed.

Post-1940

As scientists developed techniques for application of electrical and electronic principles to the record storing, account handling, and book-keeping processes, new and versatile machines appeared. The early 1940s saw the development of an electromechanical computer. Pulse techniques which evolved in connection with World War II radar development were wedded with increased use of applied mathematics. Automation requirements to meet wartime production needs resulted in machines which could perform routine tasks without human intervention. Electronics took over, and soon the production machines were programmed to make decisions concerning quality, quantity, and so forth. The general development of vacuum tube electronic computers in World War II was soon followed by increased activity in design and application of "intelligent machines."

While the application of vacuum tubes resulted in a tremendous increase in computer speed of operation over the electromechanical computer, the instructions to the machine still tended to be stored external to the actual computer and fed in sequentially as needed. In addition, the high electrical power requirements of the vacuum tube computer began to restrict its capability. Two important events occurred in the mid-1940s that were to shape the future of the digital computer. In 1946, Dr. John von Neumann made a now-classic proposal for computer design. He proposed placing the program of instructions for the computer in storage internally with the data being processed. This was to shape the entire future architecture of digital computers. In 1947 the work of Drs. William Shockley, John Bardeen, and Walter H. Brattain culminated in the demonstration of a solid-state amplifying device—the transistor. In a very small fraction of the space and requiring an even smaller fraction of the operating power, the transistor removed the barrier of physical size and power requirements. Soon computers which formerly required *rooms* to house their components shrank to desk size, and computers which were beyond comprehension during vacuum-days began to appear.

Knowledge gained by developing and using the smaller and more powerful computers further expanded the field. Requirements for larger capacity memories soon resulted in improved technology to meet the requirement, and physical size once again shrank. Techniques which were used to develop and manufacture transistors were applied to other solid-state achievements, and multifunction solid-state devices appeared. Soon complex computer functions were built into packages no larger than a common transistor.

Perhaps one of the easiest ways to demonstrate the development of the digital computer is to show examples of the evolution of these powerful machines. Figure 1–2 shows an early electromechanical computer. It had a storage capacity of 132 words, and it took three seconds to add two num-

Figure 1–2 Automatic sequence controlled calculator, Mark I, circa 1940s (courtesy of International Business Machines Corporation)

bers. The next generation machines were constructed with vacuum tubes. The example shown in Figure 1–3 could add two 10-digit numbers in 1/5000 of a second, quite a jump from the earlier three-second add time (storage capacity was still limited, however). Occupying 15,000 square feet of floor space, weighing 30 tons, and containing approximately 18,000 vacuum tubes, this behemoth ushered in the era of electronic computers.

Transistor-based digital computers greatly reduced space and power requirements, and the early transistorized computer of Figure 1–4 could easily perform additions in mere microseconds.* Storage capacity was in the general range of 1000 to 4000 words internally. Peripheral (external) storage devices, such as the magnetic tape units shown in Figure 1–4, greatly

---

*A microsecond is a millionth of a second.

Figure 1–3 ENIAC, one of the first all-electronic computers, circa late 1940s (courtesy UNIVAC Division, Sperry Rand Corporation)

extended the storage capacity of second generation and all later digital computers. The development of integrated circuit techniques again reduced the size and power requirements, and the digital computer in Figure 1–5 is representative of today's so-called minicomputer. Mini describes size only, because this machine possesses the following characteristics: (a) operating times in nanoseconds,* (b) storage capacity up to 31,000 words internally, and (c) a full system weight of only 110 pounds.

Finally, the modern large-scale computer of Figure 1–6, with a capability of nanosecond operating times, a storage capacity limited only by the imagination, and a multi-million dollar price tag, shows the results of less than half a century of technological advances in the digital computer field. As new techniques and devices appear, speed of operation is decreasing, price is decreasing, and storage capacity is increasing. Is it any wonder that even professionals in the field are sometimes awed by such progress?

---

*A nanosecond is a billionth of a second.

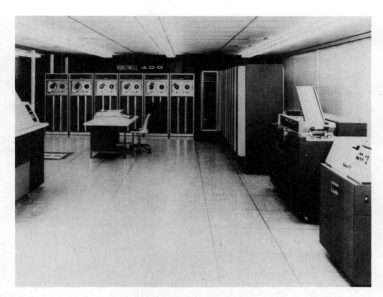

Figure 1–4 The HONEYWELL 400, a transistorized medium-scale second-generation computer system (courtesy HONEYWELL)

Figure 1–5 Modern minicomputer (courtesy Lockheed Electronics Co., Inc., Data Products Division)

Figure 1-6 The Burroughs B6500, a very large scale, modern computer (courtesy Burrough Corporation)

1–3 THE PRESENT

Construction of Modern Digital Computers

Figures 1–5 and 1–6 are representative of the "mini" and the "maxi" of today's computers. Minor variations in construction methods exist, but today's hardware consists generally of components (integrated circuit assemblies, transistors, resistors, etc.) mounted on plug-in circuit cards. Interconnection of components is by means of printed circuit conductors, with an absolute minimum of wiring required. A printed circuit board from a modern minicomputer is shown in Figure 1–7.

Functional Organization and Timing

Understanding the digital computer necessitates recognition of two major factors. First, the computer can be approached from a *functional* viewpoint, with the emphasis on what operations the machine performs. Second, it must be recognized that the digital computer is time-oriented.

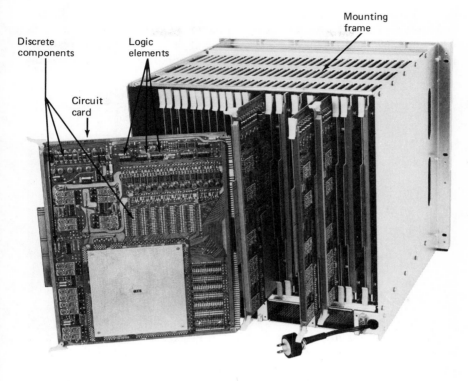

Figure 1–7 Printed circuit board used in minicomputer (courtesy Lockheed Electronics Co., Inc., Data Products Division)

The inter-relationships of the functions performed and the time it takes to achieve that performance are of utmost importance.

The five basic functions performed by the digital computer are as follows.

1. The INPUT function interfaces between the outside world and the computer.
2. The OUTPUT function interfaces between the computer and the outside world.
3. The STORAGE (MEMORY) function stores information and instructions about what to do with the information.
4. The ARITHMETIC-LOGIC function performs the mathematical operations of the computer.
5. The CONTROL function sequences and controls the complete computer.

These are *functional* categories only and in many cases are not directly equitable to actual hardware. Often a function shares hardware locations with a number of different physical sections of the computer. For example, in the functional block diagram of a digital computer (Figure 1–8), the

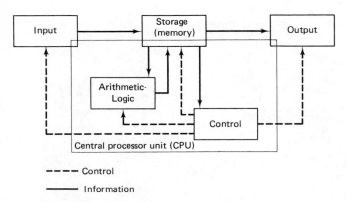

Figure 1–8   Digital computer functional block diagram

functions *inside* the division labeled Central Processor Unit (CPU) are commonly located within a physical part of the computer so labeled. Note that the INPUT and OUTPUT functions are only partially contained within the CPU. Other portions of these functions are located in other pieces of hardware that also provide INPUT and OUTPUT functions. However, because of the complexity of the computer, it is usually advantageous to learn its operation from the functional standpoint before becoming completely hardware oriented.

The flow of information within the computer may be seen in Figure 1–8. Except in special cases, all information that the computer possesses must be entered via the INPUT function. Depending on the type of information, it may be used either to tell the computer what to do (instructions) or it may be used as data in arithmetic-logic operations (data). As an instruction, the information tells the computer where the next information is stored or it tells the computer what to do with the next information called up. As data, it will be routed to the ARITHMETIC-LOGIC function for processing and then back to STORAGE to await its next use. The OUTPUT function displays the results of the internal processing of information when called upon by the CONTROL function. The flow of information throughout the computer is from INPUT to STORAGE to OUTPUT, with detours along the way to the ARITHMETIC-LOGIC function for processing operations and to the CONTROL function to determine what is to be done next.

Control signals, occurring at the proper time and in the proper sequence, are developed by the CONTROL function. There is no need, for
example, to have the ARITHMETIC-LOGIC function operating when it is
not needed. Therefore it is *enabled* only during the time it is required, as
are all other functions of the computer. The *timing diagram* of Figure 1–9
shows a very simplified version of the major control signals required to
enable and disable the basic computer functions of Figure 1–8. It should be
understood that these timing signals are very broad in coverage and that
they will be modified greatly as more is learned about the computer.

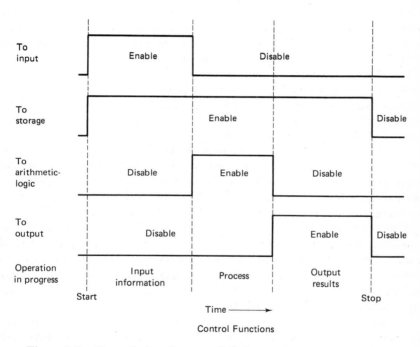

Figure 1–9 Gross timing diagram, digital computer

Communicating with the Computer

All methods of communication depend on the use of symbols, and
communicating with the computer is no exception. The symbols used must
be of a form that is mutually understandable to all parties involved. As an
example, when correspondence is exchanged between English-speaking
people, the punctuation marks, letters, and numerals of the English language
are used. These "symbols" mean the same to both writers and receivers
(assuming similar educational backgrounds) and communication is estab-

lished. If, however, an English-speaking person using English-language symbols attempts to communicate with a non-English-speaking person (one who is of Oriental background, perhaps), difficulty is encountered. English-language symbols may have no meaning in the Oriental language and vice-versa, and communication is not established.

The same difficulty exists when it becomes necessary to communicate with a digital computer. In order to take advantage of the speed and accuracy of electronic circuits, the computer represents all information in terms of two-state (binary) symbols. Zero (0) and one (1) are the two symbols most often used, and it should be apparent that a communication problem exists if it becomes necessary to "converse" with the computer in English language. With only two symbols available in computer language, some means must be developed to represent the many letters, numerals, and punctuation marks of the English language. This is usually accomplished by using *groups* of ones and zeros, arranged in unique combinations for each English-language symbol to be represented. It is shown in subsequent chapters that a group of seven ones and zeros provides 64 unique combinations, which is adequate to represent all English-language symbols. If capital letters are also required, a group of eight ones and zeros is used.

Conversion from English-language symbols to computer language symbols is often accomplished by input devices. A simple example is the punched paper tape used to feed information into computers. The tape consists of many rows of holes (1s) and no holes (0s). A typewriter-like device punches the holes, row by row, as each key on the keyboard is depressed. The conversion to computer language thus is accomplished directly by the keyboard-controlled tape punch. When the tape is fed into the computer, a tape reader converts the holes and no holes to electrical impulses which may be directly used by the computer. Punched paper tape and many other input devices are discussed in subsequent chapters. A sample of a typical punched paper tape is shown in Figure 1–10.

Thus communicating with the computer is done in the computer's language with the assistance of some type of translating device that converts English-language symbols into computer language symbols. The rationale

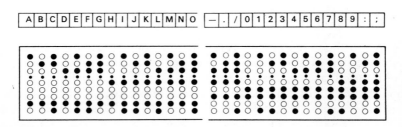

Figure 1–10 Punched paper tape

for using two-state symbols in the computer becomes more apparent as the hardware used to implement the computer is discussed in later chapters.

Applications

It is difficult to know where to begin discussing the applications of digital computers. Most readers are aware of such applications as computer billing, airline reservation control, and spacecraft navigation. Television, radio, and newspapers do not hesitate to keep the general public well informed on such applications. But where else is the computer performing? Consider some less common but tremendously important uses for the computer.

One major automobile manufacturer uses a computerized information system to increase its production capacity. Its entire parts inventory is calculated by the system each night. Orders on hand are analyzed to determine which vehicles are to be built; then optimum production schedules are calculated. The computer thus furnishes the plant manager with his order condition, inventory condition, and his best production schedules with alternatives for each day's planning.

A digital computer is studying how a child's learning capacity develops. Computer "models" of a child at various levels of development are built using computer programs that include all of the stored information and processing routines a child needs to perform a specific task. Researchers compare the models of different performance levels to determine what is needed to stimulate a child to move from one development stage to the next.

A minicomputer helps engineering students during performance of complex experiments. Photographic slides explain the experiment and introduce the associated equipment. Another group of slides discusses the theory of the experiment, asking questions as the program progresses. Incorrect answers by the student result in the computer issuing review material until the theory is completely understood. During performance of the experiment the student is kept informed of what to expect so that he may repeat procedures if necessary. In addition, potentially dangerous situations are terminated automatically. Complete computer control of the experiment from beginning to end assures maximum educational value and safety.

In a midwestern hospital the position and dosage delivered by a radiation therapy machine used to inhibit or destroy cancerous tissues are controlled by a minicomputer. A magnetic tape casette containing the patient's medical record is loaded into a reader when the patient enters the therapy room. Safeguards prevent any activation of the therapy machine if the patient's identification number does not match the record number, or if machine adjustments are improper, or if the total dosage exceeds accepted tolerance or other criteria. Reduced setup time, less chance of human error, lower cost per patient, and a permanent, absolutely accurate and detailed record are but a few of the advantages of computer control of radiation therapy.

The digital computer is even aiding the farmer. A fungus disease that affects potatoes is known to be related to the following factors: (a) relative humidity equal to or greater than 90% for over ten hours, (b) relative humidity equal to or greater than 90% for over four hours during specific phases of fungus growth, (c) temperature independent of moisture, and (d) relative humidity less than 70%. Mathematical models have been developed that relate these factors. Measurements from about 50 standard weather reporting stations are combined with the mathematical model in the computer, and critical dates in the growth of the fungus are predicted and calculated. Farmers are then advised of the existence of critical conditions and the need for application of control measures. Thus the computer contributes to the task of raising food for a hungry world.

The dramatic increase in shipping goods by ship, the appearance of supertankers rated at up to 400,000 deadweight tons, and the focus on pollution controls from oil leaks have resulted in design and application of computerized collision-avoidance systems. These systems relieve the ship operators of the somewhat inadequate radar plotting duties, plus providing for automation of many of the other shipboard functions. With adequate programming, a general-purpose digital computer can use inputs from navigation receivers, radars, sonars, gyrocompasses, shipboard sensors, and preprogrammed course data to safely guide a ship from departure to arrival with maximum safety and minimum time and cost. Such systems are becoming as necessary to modern-day shipping activities as the wireless was early in this century.

Electric utilities are installing computer control centers to provide improvements in both system operation and reliability. With the proper combination of *equipment* (hardware) and *programming* (software), the computer control center can collect and compute data, monitor system status, provide alarm indications when out-of-tolerance conditions are about to or do exist, plan and schedule operations, automatically locate and compensate for failed equipment, etc. Present installations are aimed at assisting power system operators during normal operating conditions and, as such, are of the preventive control type. As more confidence is gained in the capabilities of the computer control system, more and more of the functions mentioned above will be provided directly under control of the computer without intervention of the human operator.

1-4 THE FUTURE

Today's computers range afar in capability and application. Machines that perform operations at the rate of more than a million per second are used to serve the needs of science, industry, and business. Storage capacity in the range of millions of computer words maintains data files on individuals, banks, scientific experiments, etc. Hand-held special-purpose computers are replacing slide rules on the small end of the spectrum, while rooms full of computing equipment are used to monitor and record the efforts of all nations in space activities.

The future holds great promise in the digital computer field. Technological advances are increasing the speed of computer operations so that hundreds of millions or perhaps billions of operations per second are not inconceivable. New techniques in storage methods are resulting in shrinking of the space requirements and a dramatic decrease in the time necessary to recover the stored information. All of these advances promise to reduce size, increase capability, and reduce cost of digital computing equipment in the future.

QUESTIONS

1. What is *your* definition of a digital computer?
2. What do *you* think a digital computer does?
3. Trace the history of "aids to calculation" from the abacus to modern digital computers.
4. List the five basic functions performed by a digital computer and explain each function.
5. Draw a functional block diagram of a digital computer and show the interconnections and flow of information.
6. Why is it important to understand the timing relationships existing within a digital computer?
7. Discuss the task of communicating with a digital computer.
8. List ten modern applications of digital computers.
9. Speculate on the future of digital computers.

2

Digital Computer Operation

2–1   BASIC CONCEPTS

When one initially investigates digital computer operation, a number of conceptual questions may arise. Foremost are the concepts of sequential operation, information representation and storage, and stored programs of instruction.

Sequential Operation

A very simplified introduction to sequential operations was seen in the timing diagram of Figure 1–9. Information is accepted from the INPUT device(s) during the period T_0 to T_1, when the INPUT device(s) and STORAGE section are enabled. It is during this time that the list of instructions (the program) is given to the computer. The computer is helpless without direction to tell it what to do and how to do it. The list of instructions informs the computer of the actions to be performed and gives the sequence in which they are to be performed.* The information to be processed may also be presented to the computer during this time. Instructions and information are placed in STORAGE (Section 2–3) and called upon as needed during the T_1-T_2 time period. With both the STORAGE and ARITHMETIC/LOGIC sections activated, instructions and information are processed as required by the *stored program*, and intermediate/final results are returned to STORAGE. Upon completion of information processing, the ARITHMETIC/LOGIC section is disabled and the OUTPUT section is enabled. The stored program then controls transfer of results to the output device

---

*Preparation of the program is the task of a *programmer*, who, in conjunction with a *systems analyst*, prepares a *detailed*, *sequential list* of steps which direct the operations necessary to perform the information processing.

$(T_2\text{-}T_3)$. All functional sections are disabled upon completion of the stored program. As the computer is examined in greater detail, more complete sequential timing operations will be shown.

Information Representation

One of the biggest stumbling blocks to understanding the digital computer is the concept of how information is represented. The use of symbols to represent information is an abstract concept. However, if it is understood that a symbol is *not* the real thing but merely a convenient representation, the concept becomes clearer. Highway warning signs are good examples. The actual curve in the roadway, with its guard rails, roadside trees, and scenery, in no way is the same as the pictorial symbol advising the motorist of the impending hazard. Yet the sign performs the required function; that is, it causes the motorist to visualize the roadway curving in the direction shown on the sign. Representation of more than one piece of information may also be accomplished by combinations of symbols. A rough-surfaced curve in the roadway is represented by a "curve" sign *and* a "rough road" sign. The only important requirement is that the user of the symbols recognize their meanings. In other words, symbols *communicate* information between originator and user, or vice-versa.

Each instruction to the computer must be presented to and stored within the memory of the computer in a form that the computer understands. The symbols used in digital computers are the binary (base 2) numbers (1 and 0). It may seem impractical to use only two symbols for information representation, but electrical/electronic implementation of computer functions is difficult with more than two symbols. Therefore all information presented to and stored within the computer is in binary form. In addition, the information must be in a format that is easily and unambiguously interpretable by the computer. These problems are attacked during initial design of the computer, and the solutions vary from computer to computer. In all cases, of course, binary symbols are used. The format of the information generally consists of selection of *a fixed number of binary symbols* (called a computer word) to be presented to the memory of the computer for each instruction in the program. *Information to be processed* (commonly called data) is also arranged in a similar format. Formats vary from extremely simple to quite complex.

The computer is given information in groups of binary symbols called *computer words*. If the information is data to be processed, such as letters, numbers, or symbols, the package of information is called a *data word*. If the computer is being told what to do, then the package of information is called an *instruction word*. Figure 2–1(a) is a simplified representation of a data word and an instruction word that could be used with a computer that handles information in groups of 16 binary symbols.

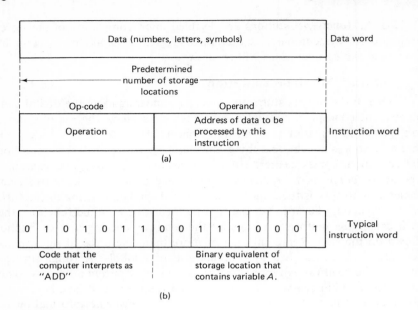

Figure 2–1 Computer words

Note that the instruction word consists of two parts: the operation and the operand. The *operation* portion of the word (*op-code*) *informs the computer what to do*, and the *operand* supplies a coded indication that *tells where any data to be operated upon is located in memory*. Computer words are supplied in the order in which they are to be used, and the computer automatically selects the next computer word in sequence unless told to do otherwise. The basic cycle of operation is one of retrieving the computer word from memory, evaluating it, obtaining the information at the indicated operand location, performing the operation with the obtained information, and progressing to the next computer word for another instruction.

Information Storage

The concept of a computer information storage device may be seen in a modern "jukebox." As many as 100 phonograph records are placed in separate storage locations inside the machine. Each location is assigned an arbitrary address, usually a combination of row and column as shown in Figure 2–2. Selection of a particular record merely requires depression of the appropriate row and column pushbuttons. The mechanism of the jukebox then travels to the proper location, retrieves the information (the record) at that location, and moves it to the record player for output.

In like manner, information is stored in computer memory. A package of information (the computer word) containing a given amount of intelli-

Figure 2–2 A modern "juke-box," showing use of "computer-like" storage of records at assigned "addresses" (courtesy Seeburg Corporation)

gence is assigned an identifiable location in memory and may be retrieved by "addressing" that location. It should be pointed out at this time that there is no way of knowing whether the information is instruction or data except by knowledge of its assigned location. Assignment of memory locations is primarily the job of the programmer, and the computer must be told where to go for instructions and where to go for data. The actual mechanism of information storage is discussed in Section 2–3 and again in considerable detail in Chapter 8.

Stored Program Capability

This section has already shown the inter-relationship of timing (sequential operations), information representation, and storage. By combining these concepts, the major attribute of the computer may be seen, that is, the *stored program capability*. If the computer is considered as a device to perform arithmetic calculations, the major advantages over a simple calculator or hand calculations become apparent.

A simple calculator, capable of performing addition, subtraction, multiplication, and division, does not have the advantages of the computer. The calculator (Figure 2–3) responds to the wishes of the operator by mechanizing the basic arithmetic operations. Multiplication of the sum of two num-

Figure 2–3 A simple pocket calculator (courtesy Sharp Electronics Corp.)

bers $(A + B)$ by the difference of two other numbers $(C - D)$ is a good example.

Example 2–1.

Solve $(A + B)(C - D)$, where $A = 1$, $B = 2$, $C = 5$, and $D = 3$.

Solution:

Step 1. Operate CLEAR key.
  2. Enter A.
  3. Operate $+$ key.
  4. Enter B.
  5. Operate $=$ key.
  6. Store sum.
  7. Operate CLEAR key.
  8. Enter C.
  9. Operate $-$ key.
  10. Enter D.
  11. Operate $=$ key.
  12. Operate X key.
  13. Enter stored sum.
  14. Operate $=$ key.
  15. Record the product.

Note that all of the steps performed by the calculator could have been performed by paper and pencil. The simple calculator can add accuracy and speed to hand calculations while obtaining the same result.

The "stored program" computer, however, solves the problem of Example 2–1 without the requirement for multiple operations by the operator. A "program" is developed by the programmer that causes the computer to perform each of the required operations in sequence *without* operator intervention. Each of the operations in the calculator solution has an equivalent step in the program. Of course, each step in the program is coded in binary form and stored in the memory in that form. A typical example is the step which enters A. Actually, this step is accomplished by adding the value of A to zero, since in the previous step the computer was "cleared" of all previous data in the arithmetic circuits. So the "enter A" step and the "operate $+$ key" step are combined into a single step.

Thus the command to the computer is one that identified the "ADD" operation *and* the location of the quantity A. If the simplified computer word of Figure 2–1(a) is considered, then the operation section is the code for ADD and the operand is the code for the address (location) of A. Figure 2–1(b) is a possible 16-bit (binary digit) computer word that may be fed to and stored in computer memory to cause A to be retrieved and added into the arithmetic circuits.

Each of the steps is coded in a manner similar to the example of Figure 2–1(b) and entered *in sequence* into the memory. Values for A, B, C, and D are entered next at locations called out in the respective sections of the computer words. It is only necessary then to select the address of the first word in the program; the computer *sequentially* performs the steps necessary to obtain the solution to the problem and, if the program is so written, makes the solution available to the user.

The "stored program" capability, then, relieves the operator of anything more than mechanical functions and supplies problem solutions in much shorter times. Example 2–1 is a relatively simple problem, yet the advantages of stored program operations are quite apparent. When a complex problem, such as space travel trajectories which require the interactions of many variables, is encountered, there is no doubt that the stored program digital computer is a welcome addition to science, industry, and the community.

Computer Operation

With this added information, computer operations can now be explored in more detail. By viewing the functional sections of the computer in a slightly different manner, the constant action of the control function is quite apparent. Figure 2–4 separates the storage function into three blocks for the purpose of establishing a "straight-line" flow of information from input to output. This is *not* to imply that the results of processing data are stored in different parts of STORAGE (MEMORY), since in many cases instructions, data, and results are intermixed. It should also be noted that data and instructions are separated during the input and storage functions. Such an arrangement

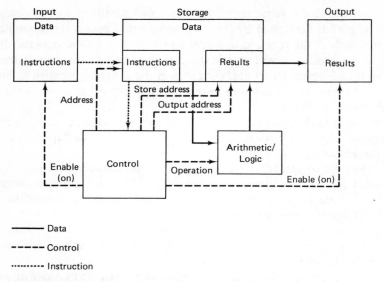

Figure 2-4 Computer operation—functional diagram

is to be expected, since the sequential nature of computer operations requires each step of the program to immediately follow the preceding one. (There are ways around this problem, but they will not be discussed until more details of computer operation are developed.) In a similar manner, instructions are shown being routed *only* to the CONTROL section. More detailed discussion in subsequent chapters shows occasional trips by instructions to and from the ARITHMETIC/LOGIC section.

Control lines extend from the CONTROL section to all other sections in the diagram of Figure 2-4, just as they did in the conceptual diagram of Figure 1-8. Note, however, that more detail is provided in the expanded diagram, especially in the STORAGE section. The addition of just these few extra control lines materially expands the coverage of the diagram.

Generally instructions are "loaded" into the computer first, followed by data. The CONTROL section provides the "enabling" command to the INPUT section and maintains the input device(s) in an active state until all information is loaded.

The list of instructions (*program*) which has been prepared by the *programmer* includes address assignment for each instruction so that the computer operator knows the location of each instruction. Within the CONTROL section are circuits which allow selection of *any* memory address. When the operator selects the address of the first instruction in the program and activates the computer (operates the START control), the memory is enabled and the information present at that address is made available to the

CONTROL section. The information is examined within the CONTROL section and decisions made as to what action is to follow.

If the CONTROL section determines that the information requires an operation to be performed (addition, store results, etc), the address of the data to be operated upon is routed to STORAGE and the ARITHMETIC/LOGIC section is told what operation to perform. The CONTROL section, meanwhile, retains the address of the original instruction for later use. The data to be operated upon is routed to the ARITHMETIC/LOGIC section; and since it has been previously set up to perform the operation, it proceeds with the task. While the operation is being performed, the CONTROL section increases the original instruction address by one and prepares to obtain the next instruction upon completion of the operation required by the first instruction.

This cycle is repeated over and over again until the STOP instruction is received. Each cycle results in a trip to STORAGE either to obtain data to be processed or to store the results of an operation. If output of total results (or intermediate results) is required, these instructions are also included in the program. The CONTROL section interprets the output instruction, enables the output device(s), and locates the results in STORAGE to be made available for output.

The timing diagram of Figure 1–9 can now be expanded to show the control functions more accurately (Figure 2–5). For the purpose of simplicity, it is assumed that all input operations are conducted at one time, as are the output operations. As will be noted in subsequent chapters, it is not necessary to input *all* instructions and data at one time. Once initial instructions are provided and stored in memory, those instructions may also include frequent excursions to the input devices for additional instructions or data. Output operations are similarly controlled, so that output does not have to occur all at one time, but intermediate results may be obtained as the program is progressing.

To obtain the detailed operating timing diagram of Figure 2–5, it is necessary to vastly expand the processing time scale. Actually, since the input and output functions remain the same for the purposes of this discussion, they are not shown in detail on the expanded diagram but are assumed to be present.

2–2 THE CONTROL SECTION

Requirements

As pointed out earlier, the digital computer operates in a sequential manner as determined by a stored program of instructions. But the program by itself is not enough. For example, the computer must know where in

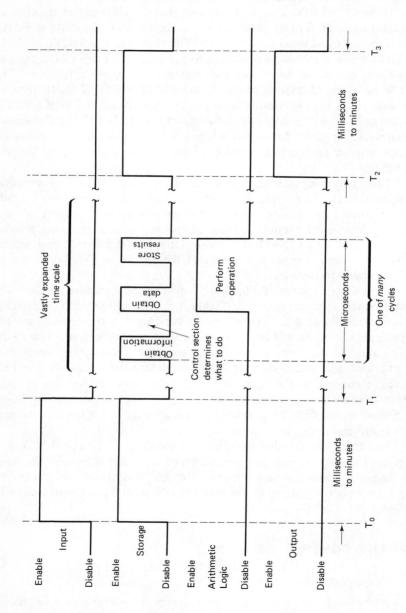

Figure 2-5 Computer operation—timing

memory to go to obtain the first instruction of the program. It must develop the control signals that obtain this instruction and then determine what action the instruction calls for. The STORAGE, INPUT/OUTPUT, and ARITHMETIC sections must be enabled at the proper time to perform the decoded instruction and in the proper order so that their operations do not interfere with each other. These requirements define the need for the CONTROL section.

In short, the *control section is the nerve center of the computer, providing the timing, decoding, and enabling operations for all of the other parts of the computer*. Figure 2–6 is a functional block diagram of a CONTROL section.

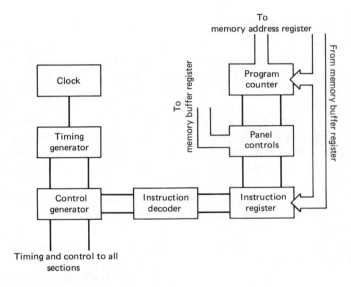

Figure 2–6   CONTROL section—functional block diagram

Timing

Sequential operations not only exist for the loading of information into the computer but a specific sequence is required to retrieve information from memory, evaluate that information, and to act upon the results of the evaluation. At an even greater level of detail (in later chapters) it is found that far more precise timing requirements appear. It is one of the requirements of the CONTROL section to furnish the overall timing of the computer.

Timing requirements vary from relatively long durations (seconds) to very short durations (nanoseconds). The nature of the timing signals is such that they may exist for only the required time, or they may be repeated at some predetermined rate, or they may be required "on demand," etc. In many cases a requirement for synchronous operations (where multiple operations occur simultaneously, in step with each other) may even exist. The basic source of all of the timing signals is a precise and accurate electronic circuit called a *clock*.

The *clock* operates in such a manner that the *shortest duration* timing signal is its basic output. All other timing signals which require synchronous characteristics are then developed from the basic timing signal. Bistable electronic circuits called flip-flops (Chapter 3) are used in the timing generator to divide the basic timing signal into greater duration timing signals to be made available at the required times.

Decoding and Control

The instruction decoder determines what actions are required. In Section 2–1 it was stated that an instruction word was stored in a format that separated the required operation and the address of the data to be operated upon. The operation portion of the instruction word (*op-code*) is used by the instruction decoder in the CONTROL section to determine the required actions. As a result of a previous CONTROL section sequence, the op-code portion of the instruction word has been transferred to the *instruction register*.* The instruction register is used to store the op-code while it is being decoded so that the memory may be freed to perform other duties during the decoding time.

The *instruction decoder* is made up of electronic circuits called gates (Chapter 3), which are connected to recognize only specific combinations of binary symbols. A separate combination of gates is used for recognition of each of the op-codes, and the output of the instruction decoder is a separate enabling signal to the *control generator* for each of the op-codes.

The *control generator* is also composed of gates which combine the outputs of the instruction decoder with timing divider outputs to supply all required timing signals in the proper sequence to the remainder of the functional units of the computer.

2–3 THE STORAGE (MEMORY) SECTION

Requirements

One merely needs to consider why the computer is capable of its fantastic operating speeds to understand the need for information storage. For example, if during the solution of a problem it were necessary to obtain problem data from the input function every time new data was required,

---

*A register is a group of flip-flops connected to act as a temporary storage device.

the computer would be speed-limited by the input device. Storage of problem data allows *immediate* access (at least five or six orders of magnitude faster) to the data. Without data storage capability the computer would obviously be operating much slower. Furthermore, if it were necessary to physically record intermediate results each time a portion of the problem was solved, speed of operation would again suffer.

Consider what would happen to the speed of operation if the computer had to be told what to do each time an operation were to be performed (as with a hand calculator). The difference between the slow speed of the hand calculator and the high speed of the digital computer is the storage capability of the computer. Storage of instructions and data, whether it be initial problem information or intermediate results, defines the requirements for the storage function of the digital computer.

Concepts of Information Storage

But how is it possible to store such a large volume of information in the computer? Due to the nature of the electronic circuits used, it has been necessary to employ binary symbols (1 and 0) throughout. Numbers, letters, punctuation marks, special symbols, etc are all assigned a specific combination of binary symbols for use with the computer. Information is supplied to the computer, in the example already discussed, in groups of 16 binary symbols, and may be either instructions or data. Such information, to be stored, must then have available a device with 16 separate storage "cells," one "cell" for each of the binary symbols in the computer word.

Single bit (binary digit) storage is relatively simple to visualize, since a device which is capable of only two separate conditions (states) is all that is required. Consider a simple switch such as is used to control a light in a room. It may be either OFF (binary 0) or ON (binary 1). In fact, the light to which it is connected provides an indication of its state. If the light is illuminated, the switch may be considered to be in the 1 (ON) state, while if the light is not illuminated, the switch is in the 0 (OFF) state. The switch, then, is storing either a binary 1 or a binary 0, and the light indicates which. Examples of electrical and electronic devices with two easily identifiable states are almost without end. Electromechanical devices called *relays* (they are used in automobiles, telephone systems, etc.) may be either energized or de-energized to cause electrical contacts to close and open in the same manner as switch contacts. Electronic circuits called flip-flops (Chapter 3) are stable in either one of two possible states, which may be identified by voltage/current relationships within the circuit. Common implementation of flip-flops is with semiconductor devices (transistors, diodes, etc.) or, more recently, with integrated circuits (IC) technology. Magnetic devices may be used to store binary information, either by the presence or absence of a magnetic charge or the direction of a magnetic field. Electrical devices called capacitors may be either charged with an electrical field or not charged, giving rise to a binary condition. Optical techniques, where a beam of light (or perhaps a laser beam) causes electrical circuits to respond or not to respond, depending on the existence or non-existence of an optical path, are also binary in nature. Many of these techniques are discussed in Chapter 8, but for now only the concepts of storing binary information are investigated.

Memory Operation

A practical memory, in addition to storing information, must have the means to identify the storage location (address) and circuitry to provide a means for moving the input data into the memory or the extracted data from the memory to external circuits (see Figure 2–7). The address signals are derived from the address portion of the instruction word, which contains the binary equivalent of the location of the data to be used in the present operation. The address information is temporarily stored in a register (*memory address register*) so that the rest of the computer may go on about its business while the memory is obtaining the data required.

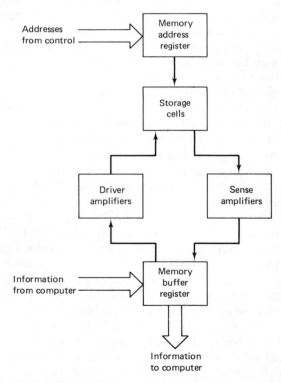

Figure 2–7   STORAGE section—block diagram

Another register, called the *memory buffer register*, provides input and output temporary storage. If the information is to be written into storage cells, it is temporarily stored in the memory buffer register until it is time for the WRITE operation. Electronic circuits (driver amplifiers) that match the power requirements of the memory to the buffer register route information into the storage medium (*memory*). Similar action occurs when information is to be taken from storage. The information at selected cells is provided to a circuit called a *sense amplifier* and, when the READ operation is initiated, this information is stored in the buffer register for routing to other circuits in the computer.

In one common memory configuration, storage cells are arranged in a matrix form as shown in Figure 2–8. Each horizontal row contains as many storage cells as there are bits in the computer word—that is, in a 16-bit word,

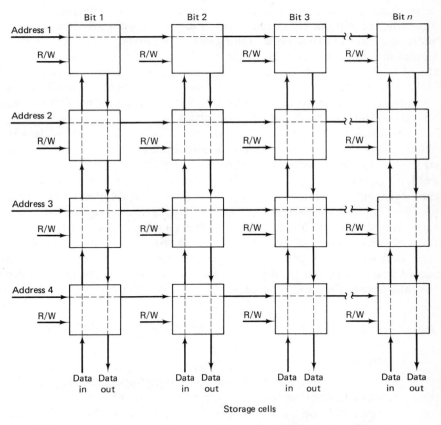

Figure 2–8 Multi-bit memory organization. All R/W are connected together; *n* equals the number of bits in a computer word

16 storage cells in each row. All cells in a row possess the same address, so that when the information stored at an address location is desired, all storage cells at that address are selected. There are as many rows as there are words storable in the memory. A read/write input is provided to all cells in the memory simultaneously. However, unless the cell is addressed, the read/write input is ineffective; therefore only the addressed cells in the memory are activated. Each cell also has provision for feeding data in and reading data out. All cells in a given column are supplied the same data to be stored, for example. Only the addressed cell, however, will store the data. The data outputs of all cells in a column are also connected together, but once again only the addressed cell will provide any information on the data output line. Since each column represents one bit in the computer word, there must be n columns, where n represents the number of bits in the word.

A practical 16-bit memory, then, supplies a complete 16-bit computer word each time an address is selected and the READ command is valid. Similarly, the WRITE command stores a complete 16-bit word when properly addressed. Thus information is handled in groups of bits, or computer words. Complete lists of instructions, made up of many computer words, may be stored in the type of memory just described. It is necessary, of course, to make available thousands of words of storage, but it should be apparent by now that this is easily accomplished merely by increasing the number of cells and expanding address decoding capability.

In this section it has been shown that it is possible to store data in either original input form or modified, calculated form, along with the instructions that tell how the data is to be manipulated. This information is available in such a manner that it is not destroyed when used, and may be used over and over again. This capability allows the solution of repetitive problems without the need to "reload" the instructions every time they are used. The requirement to furnish the problem's data one package at a time is overcome, as is that of storing intermediate results and the list of instructions that tell the computer how to perform the problem solution. There should be no doubt that the digital computer, properly used, possesses many advantages over the hand calculator.

2–4 THE ARITHMETIC/LOGIC SECTION

Introduction

The data manipulation, arithmetic, and logical operations required by the computer's instruction repertoire are performed within the part of the computer commonly called the ARITHMETIC, or ARITHMETIC/LOGIC section. As with the other sections already described, the actual hardware that makes up the ARITHMETIC/LOGIC section may be physically located throughout the computer. The analytical approach of considering the functional operations required, however, allows grouping of the arithmetic/logic functions into an easily understandable section.

Also, as within the other functional sections of the computer, information is handled in binary form in the ARITHMETIC/LOGIC section. Performance of arithmetic operations using binary numbers is discussed in Chapter 9, where it is seen that all arithmetic operations are easily implemented in the binary number system. By this time it should be realized that *all* of the computer operates binarily because of the ease and non-ambiguity of information representation when only two different symbols need be represented.

Implementation of the data manipulation, arithmetic, and logical operations may be accomplished completely by built-in hardware or by a compromise between built-in hardware and programmed instructions. When it is considered that such operations as arithmetic addition, subtraction, multiplication, division, root finding, exponentiation, differentiation, integration, plus data manipulations which include movement of binary information, comparison of data, and logical operations must be performed, it should be apparent that the pure hardware implementation approach may be out of the question. Individual hardware circuits are possible for each of these operations, or they may be constructed from existing hardware, but considerable space and expense are required for this type of approach. The basic advantage, however, is that speed of operation is maximized with the pure hardware implementation of the operations.

When programmed instructions are used, the ARITHMETIC/LOGIC section contains, usually, a device capable of performing arithmetic addition and data storage and manipulation, and the other operations are performed by the use of a number of instructions. This method requires minimum hardware, but, since each instruction requires time to execute, speed of operation is reduced. The degree of compromise between speed of operation and hardware requirements is a choice to be made by the designer of the computer system.

An ever-increasing approach to arithmetic/logic operations is that of *microprogramming*, where a single instruction from the programmer results in performance of a number of computer operations at a much higher rate of speed. Separate *control memories* contain the *microprogram*, which responds to the programmer's general instructions and guides the ARITHMETIC/LOGIC section through a sequence of steps to perform the required operations.

ARITHMETIC/LOGIC Section Operation

From an introductory standpoint, however, the arithmetic/logic operations can be performed with the functional units shown in Figure 2–9. (It

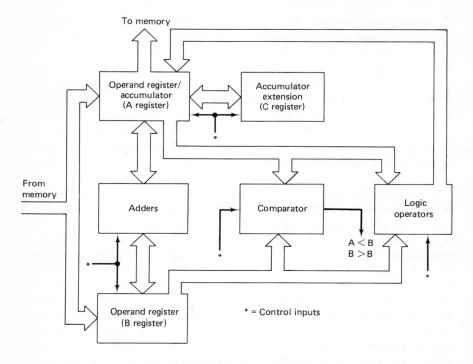

Figure 2–9   ARITHMETIC/LOGIC section—block diagram

will be shown in Chapter 9 that all arithmetic functions can be performed with the binary adder and properly controlled registers.)

The data that the ARITHMETIC/LOGIC section must work with is stored in memory and is a result of program steps requiring arithmetic/logic operations. Reviewing the operation of the STORAGE and CONTROL sections aids in understanding the operation of the ARITHMETIC/LOGIC section. Recovery of a computer word containing the code defining the operation to be performed and the address of the information to be operated upon is the first step in the process. Decoding the operation to be performed results in a signal to the ARITHMETIC/LOGIC section from the CONTROL section that enables the required functional units.

The data is then extracted from the memory address found in the computer word and supplied to the ARITHMETIC/LOGIC section. The operation to be performed is executed, and the CONTROL section obtains the next instruction, which will ultimately result in extraction of the next package of data to be operated upon. This cycle continues under control of the program until another type of operation is required.

Most ARITHMETIC/LOGIC sections contain the functional devices shown in Figure 2–9. The arrangement of devices and interconnections may vary from computer to computer, but fundamentally the following devices must exist.

1. An *adder* to perform the basic arithmetic operations.
2. An *operand register* to store one of the numbers to be operated upon.
3. An *accumulator/operand register* to store the other number to be operated upon and to accumulate the results of the operation.
4. An *accumulator extender* to accommodate the extra digits that result during multiplication and division, etc.
5. A *comparator* to look for magnitude relationships between the numbers placed in the operand registers.
6. A *logic operators unit*, which performs logical operations (see Chapter 4) on numbers placed in the operand registers.

For ease of explanation, the registers in the ARITHMETIC/LOGIC section are given letter-designation names. Actual assignment of designations is arbitrary, although an attempt is often made by some computer manufacturers to provide mnenomic designators. For example, the accumulator register is often called the AC register, the accumulator extension register the MQ register (due to its use during multiplication), and so on. In Figure 2–9 the accumulator/operand register is designated *A* register, the operand register is called the *B* register, and the accumulator extension register is named the *C* register.

The operation of each functional device shown in Figure 2–9 is detailed in Chapter 5, but a simplified explanation of a simple arithmetic addition operation follows. All information in the registers is removed (the registers are "cleared") as the first step. A memory cycle is initiated then, and one of the numbers to be acted upon is placed in the accumulator. The second memory cycle loads the other number to be acted upon, and the ARITHMETIC/ LOGIC section is ready to accomplish its task. The adder is enabled, and the number in the operand register is added to the number in the accumulator, with the sum of the two numbers replacing the number that was initially in the accumulator. A simplified waveform diagram describing these operations is shown in Figure 2–10. If additional additions or arithmetic operations are to take place, the sum in the accumulator is retained, and the information to combine with the sum is entered into the operand register for processing. If not, the sum is routed from the accumulator to memory under orders from the CONTROL section. ARITHMETIC/LOGIC sections may operate in either the serial mode or the parallel mode. In the serial mode one bit from the *A* register and one bit from the *B* register are examined in the adder and the sum is obtained before examining the next bit in each register. Thus, in the simple computer that is being examined, each of the 16 bits in each of the

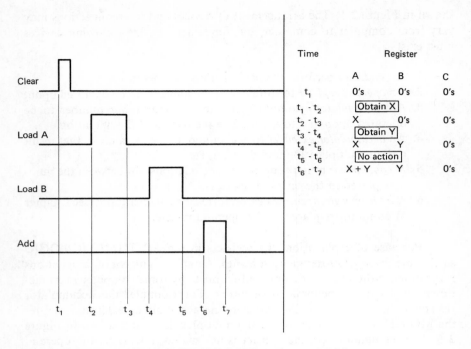

Figure 2–10   ARITHMETIC/LOGIC section—controls

registers must be examined. Obviously, this is fairly time consuming, although only one adder is required. More commonly, an adder is provided for each of the bits in the data word, so that simultaneous addition, subtraction, etc. may be performed. Although more costly, the parallel method is much faster. In both cases, however, each register must have sufficient stages to store the complete computer word (in the example case, 16 stages). Comparison operations or logic operations are accomplished in a similar manner, with the appropriate functional device enabled as required.

2–5 THE INPUT SECTION

Introduction

From a strictly practical standpoint, the computer is *initially* incapable of *any* useful function. The memory has no information stored; and since all computer instructions and data must come from memory, those instructions and data must be *loaded* via the INPUT section. A knowledge of computer codes (Chapter 6) is vital to an understanding of the input process, but an explanation using simplified terms follows.

Perhaps the simplest input device is available at most computer control panels. A group of switches, one for each bit in the computer word, is provided. Each switch can be positioned to generate a binary 0 or a binary 1 (Figure 2–11). When all switches are properly positioned, the information

Figure 2–11   Typical computer control panel (courtesy Hewlett-Packard)

may be loaded into memory (usually via an intervening storage register). Addresses, instructions, or data may thus be entered *directly* into the computer by means of panel controls. The programmer merely arranges the required information in the proper order, and word-by-word, at selected addresses, the instructions and data are loaded. Manual entry of information by use of console switches is, however, an inefficient means of loading the computer.

Any input device that does not provide information in direct binary computer word format provides a challenge. Attempts to make digital computers user oriented have, unfortunately, resulted in input devices that are *not* binary computer word formatted, and conversion methods must be provided to make them so. The common method of providing this capability is to write a computer program that will accept the input information in the format of the input device and convert it, within the computer, into binary computer word format. Details of computer programming are discussed in Chapter 12. At this time it is considered that no matter what form the input information assumes, the computer program is capable of converting it directly to binary form for use and storage in memory.

Another convenient, though still relatively slow, method of inputting information to the computer is via a keyboard that closely resembles the electric typewriter. Numerous keyboard devices are in use, but a common example is the Teletype* (see Figure 2–12). When used as an input device, its speed is limited to that of the operator and is relatively slow therefore in

---

*Trademark registered by Teletype Corporation.

Figure 2–12   A keyboard input device, TELETYPE Model 33 ASR
data terminal (courtesy Teletype Corporation)

terms of internal computer speeds. (The use of the Teletype as an *output*
device is discussed in Section 2–6.)

Input Devices

The most common methods of information input to the computer are
of an indirect nature. Direct input devices, such as the console switches and
keyboards, are severely limited by operator speeds and can make computer
use ineffective. Indirect methods of input are characterized by recording of
information on some medium that the computer can rapidly read. In addition, indirect input may be prepared "off-line," that is, without the computer
operating. Input may thus be prepared at the same time the computer is performing other tasks.

One of the most common indirect input media is punched cards. A
card punch (Figure 2–13) prepares precut cardboard cards by punching
holes in specific locations and combinations for each character to be fed to
the computer. Figure 2–14 shows a typical punched card and the code
used with this type of card. Each card can contain up to 80 characters, and

Figure 2–13 Modern punched card reader (courtesy HONEYWELL)

card readers (a typical card reader is shown in Figure 2–13) may process up to 2000 cards per minute, although 500 cards per minute is more common. This equates to approximately 670 characters per second.

The Teletype keyboard (Figure 2–12) often has a paper tape punch associated with it. Again, a specific combination of holes and spaces in a column corresponds to a character to be entered into the computer. The reader station on the Teletype processes the punched tape, entering the information into computer memory as the tape is read. A typical piece of punched paper tape was shown in Figure 1–10. Tape punching capabilities exist at speeds up to 300 characters per second, while readers process punched paper tape up to 1000 characters per second.

Still higher input speeds may be achieved by the use of magnetic tape-recorded information. Instead of combinations of holes and spaces as in the paper tape, combinations of magnetized and non-magnetized locations in columns on the magnetic tape are used. Very high density of information is obtainable with this method, and up to 1600 characters per inch are not unusual. When it is considered that magnetic tape is read at speeds up to 75 inches per second, it can be seen that readings of many thousands of char-

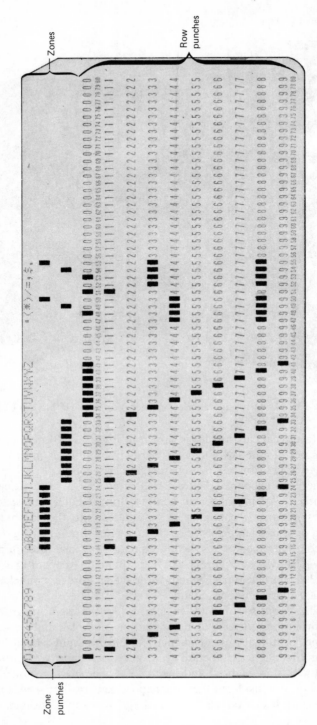

Figure 2–14 Hollerith coded punched card

38

acters per second are easily obtainable. A typical magnetic tape transport is shown in Figure 2–15. Magnetic tape may be directly recorded as an output of the computer, or direct key-to-tape systems (Figure 2–16) are available.

Reel-to-reel magnetic tape systems are supplemented by casette systems (Figure 2–17) which operate on the same principle. However, the casette is easier and more convenient to use and is finding widespread use. Speeds are similar to reel-to-reel systems. Numerous other input methods exist; these are examined in detail in Chapter 10.

Consideration of only the bare minimum needs for an input device shows that the following elements are required.

1. A device to convert the recorded information into electrical signals, such as a reader.
2. A means of temporarily storing the information from the reader until a computer word is composed.
3. Timing and control to synchronize the input element with the rest of the computer.

Figure 2–15 Typical magnetic tape transport (courtesy PERTEC Peripheral Equipment Division)

Figure 2–16 Honeywell Keytape device. Information is transcribed directly onto magnetic tape from the keyboard without the usual punched card intermediate step (courtesy HONEYWELL)

A block diagram shows these requirements [Figure 2–18(a)], while the gross timing for a hypothetical INPUT section is shown in Figure 2–18(b).

2–6 THE OUTPUT SECTION

Introduction

Once the concepts of input operations have been mastered, it is relatively simple to explain output operations. Whereas the INPUT section was the interface between man and the computer, the OUTPUT section interfaces between the computer and man. This requires conversion of the binary

Figure 2–17 Digital magnetic tape cassette recorder /reader (courtesy REMEX Division of EX-CELL-O Corp.)

computer word to a format that is acceptable to the output device in use. A typical simplified OUTPUT section closely resembles the INPUT section except that the flow of data is in the reverse direction [Figure 2–19]. Timing requirements are similar.

Output Devices

OUTPUT sections also have devices similar in concept to INPUT sections. Direct information output is obtainable at the operating console of the computer in the form of indicator lights (Figure 2–11). Complete computer words may be examined, bit by bit. The electrical condition of important control operations may be displayed. Individual register contents are accessible by the use of console display lights. In other words, the complete operation of the computer is available to the operator with the indicators provided on the console of most computers. Once again, however, this manual method of obtaining output is very slow and most often is used only for troubleshooting purposes.

Output may also be obtained by the use of printing devices which furnish a "hard-copy" of the output information. The complexity of the printing mechanism also dictates the amount of information conversion that must take place. For example, use of the printing portion of the Teletype (Figure 2–12) furnishes a printed record of the information and requires a minimum of conversion effort. Of course, the information in the computer word must be converted into the code that is recognized by the Teletype, but that is true of all output devices other than the indicator lights. Writing speeds on the order of 100 to 150 words per minute may be expected from the Teletype.

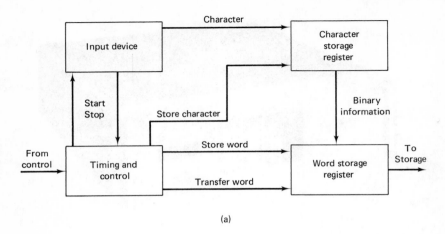

(a)

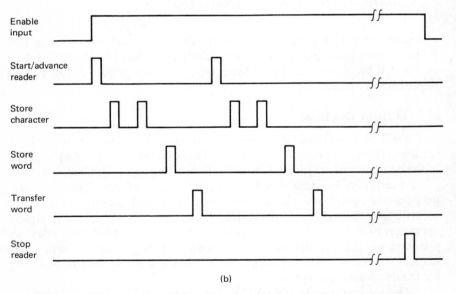

(b)

Figure 2–18 INPUT section—functional block diagram and timing

Many printing-type output devices do not print a single character at a time. The line printer (Figure 2–20), for example, includes intermediate storage capability (usually called buffer storage) which accumulates all of the information necessary to print a complete line before actually printing that information. Since information transfer between the computer memory and the buffer storage may take place at speeds much greater than the printing

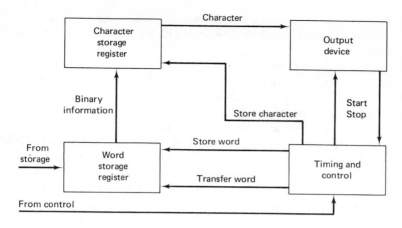

Figure 2–19 OUTPUT section—functional block diagram

Figure 2–20 Typical line printer (courtesy Mohawk Data Sciences Corp.)

mechanism can use, actual information output speed is much greater. Line printers with speeds of up to 1400 lines per minute, 120 characters per line, are available.

Once again the emphasis on making the operation of the computer user-oriented is resulting in numerous innovative output devices. Equipment complexity usually increases in such instances, but the user of the computer realizes much greater results. Many different printing devices are in use, and the most common of these are discussed in detail in Chapter 11.

The cathode-ray tube (CRT) is also used widely as an information display device. Operating on the same principles as the television picture tube, the CRT makes available such information as letters, numbers, special symbols, graphical portrayal of information, electrical schematics, etc. The electronic circuitry required for operation of this type of display device is extremely complex, but once again the need usually justifies such cost. A typical CRT display device is shown in Figure 2–21 and discussed further in Chapter 11.

Figure 2–21   Cathode-ray tube (CRT) display device combined with keyboard input device (courtesy Beehive Terminals)

Expanding use of digital computers is resulting in the need for both input and output capability at locations removed from the main computer. The Teletype and the CRT display device represent this trend. A keyboard allows input to the computer, while either the printed output or the displayed output provides immediate response. Programming, of course, is somewhat complex to allow the quasi-conversational operations that exist, but once again the need justifies the complexity. Numerous examples of this type of operation are encountered throughout this book.

2–7 SUMMARY

Considerable detail concerning digital computer operation has been furnished in this chapter. As each subsequent chapter is studied, it can be approached with the knowledge of what must be performed by the section of the computer being viewed. In addition, a rough idea of the inter-relationships between each section has been provided to keep an image of the overall computer operation in mind. At this time the reader should refer to Figure 2–4 and review the functions of each of the five basic sections of the digital computer.

QUESTIONS

1.   What is a computer program?
2.   Describe the functions of a computer program.
3.   Discuss the differences between an instruction word and a data word.
4.   How does the computer know the difference between an instruction word and a data word?
5.   What is meant by the term "stored program"?
6.   Explain how stored programs are used in digital computers.
7.   Discuss the flow of information and sequence of operation of a digital computer using the diagram shown in Figure 2-4.
8.   List the functions of the CONTROL section.
9.   What is the purpose of the instruction register; the instruction decoder; the control generator?
10.   List the functions of the STORAGE section.
11.   How is information stored in the STORAGE section?
12.   What is the purpose of the memory address register; the memory buffer register; the sense amplifier?
13.   List the functions of the ARITHMETIC/LOGIC section.
14.   What is the purpose of the accumulator; the adder; the comparator?
15.   List the functions of the INPUT section.
16.   List five input devices. Describe their functions and general characteristics.
17.   List the functions of the OUTPUT section.
18.   List five output devices. Describe their functions and general characteristics.

Basic Computer Circuits

3–1 COMPUTER CIRCUIT CONCEPTS

Logic Circuits in General

The electronic circuits that make up the hardware of digital computers are not commonly encountered in non-digital devices. Special types of circuits are needed to accommodate the *binary-oriented* operations of the digital computer. Actually, the electronic makeup of the circuits is unimportant to most of the users/maintainers of the computer. As long as the basic operations can be performed, the mechanics of their performance need not enter into the understanding of system functions.

It may be recalled from Chapter 2 that two general types of operations are required in the digital computer: decision-making and storage/timing. Circuits that perform decision-making operations are categorized as *combinational* circuits and are generally known as *gates*. In combinational logic circuits the output depends only on the particular input combination present when the output is examined.

Storage/timing operations are performed by *sequential*, or time-dependent, circuits. The term *flip-flop* (FF) is commonly applied to logic circuits that perform sequential operations. Sequential logic circuit outputs depend not only on the inputs present when the output is examined but also on the *entire input history* of the circuit.

It will be shown in subsequent chapters that all functions of the digital computer can be performed using these two basic operations. In the meantime, it is necessary to investigate the hardware that performs these operations.

The hardware that performs digital operations appears in many different forms. In early digital computers, electromechanical relays performed the digital operations. Vacuum tube circuits are still occasionally found in older equipment, although semiconductor and integrated circuit devices have replaced practically all vacuum tubes and relays in recent years. *Discrete component* assemblies, consisting of individual transistors, diodes, capacitors, resistors, etc., have been a feature of digital devices for a number of years, and these are found in many different sizes and shapes.

Semiconductor technology advances resulted in development of sub-miniature assemblies which contained all of the active and passive functions of a logic device on a single *chip* of silicon less than 0.05 inch square and 0.006 inch thick. These assemblies, called *integrated circuits* (ICs), allowed packaging of complex logic functions into a space no larger than a discrete transistor. Even more recently, much larger scale integration of logic functions into single assemblies has been accomplished, and complete arithmetic/logic units, control units, and memories have been incorporated into single assemblies. Figure 3–1 shows the evolution of digital logic packaging from the vacuum tube circuit to the complex function IC. More examples of complex interconnected logic assemblies are shown as they are encountered elsewhere in this book.

Numerous different physical packages are used to contain digital integrated circuits. The generally accepted standard industry packages are shown in Figure 3–2. As logic operations become more complex, more and more connections are required. It is not at all uncommon to see 50 or more connecting leads emanating from the specially designed and packaged multi-function logic packages. An example of this type of package was seen in Figure 1–7.

Representing Logic Circuits

In the next chapter each of the logic circuits will be examined from a mathematical viewpoint using the mathematics of logic—Boolean algebra. Initial discussion of logic circuits does not require extensive mathematics, however. All that is required is the recognition that a number, value, quantity, etc. may be represented by an alphabetic character for the purpose of mathematical manipulation or ease of handling.

Logic circuits used to perform computer operations may be described not only in physical form but also in functional form. The symbols used to represent logic circuits are summarized in Section 3–5. These symbols also describe the circuits *functionally*. Symbolic representation allows functional diagrams to be constructed to show the complex operations resulting from interconnection of individual logic circuits. Although many different groups of symbols exist, MIL-STD-806B tends to be the standard governing a majority of the digital computer diagrams in use by the military and many commercial organizations. (MIL-STD-806B is one of many standards developed by U.S. government agencies to assure commonality in equipment

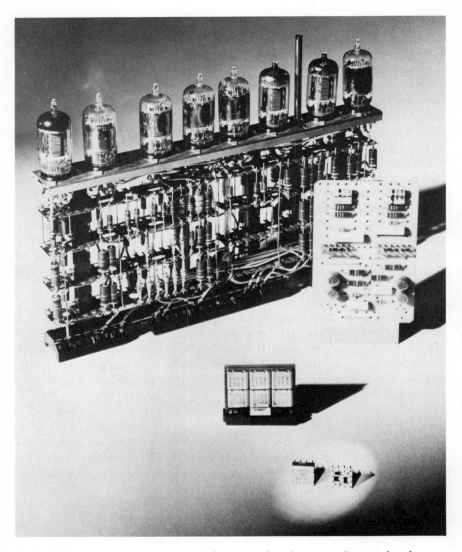

Figure 3–1a Evolution of logic packaging (courtesy International Business Machines Corporation). The original vacuum tube circuit assembly

developed by various manufacturers.) Such symbols can be directly related to electrical and electronic gate and inverter circuits. With such close correlation to actual hardware, it is much easier to understand the operation of digital computers.

Figure 3–1b   The tiny silicon chip, or IC (courtesy IBM Corporation)

Other methods of representing the logic circuits are also in use. When mathematical manipulations are to be performed, or when a compact representation of the circuit is desired, the substitution of letter variables for English-language input descriptions is used. In addition, tabular descriptions called truth tables are employed to investigate and depict logic operations and functions.

In digital computers logic circuits perform specified operations on the inputs and provide outputs that are related to the inputs in accordance with predefined rules. For example, one of the logic circuits used is called an AND gate. The AND gate provides a *useful* output only when *all* of its inputs are in *useful* form simultaneously.

AND gates are used extensively in digital computers to perform logical, arithmetic, and control operations. Applications such as the routing of information from the ARITHMETIC section to the MEMORY section

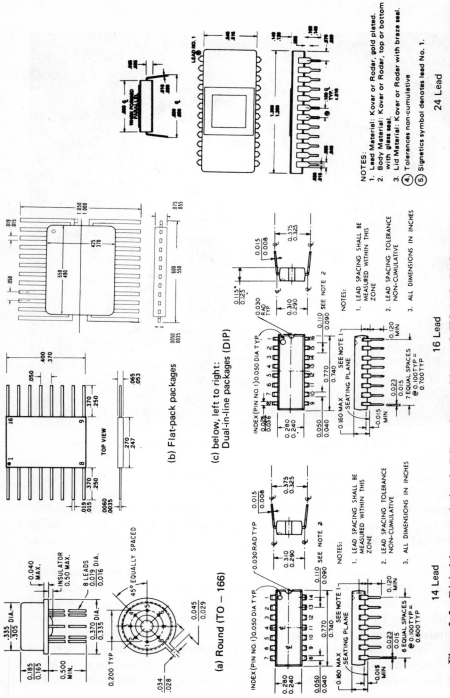

Figure 3–2 Digital integrated circuit (IC) packages; (a) round (TO-166), (b) flat-pack packages, (c) dual-in-line packages (DIP)

50

are typical. The information to be transferred may be applied to one of the inputs of an AND gate and its output may be routed to the MEMORY section. Information should not be transferred, however, until the arithmetic operation is complete and the MEMORY is ready to accept the data. These conditions may be concisely described in the following manner.

> A useful output (information) is made available to MEMORY if and only if the arithmetic operation is complete AND the MEMORY is ready to accept the information AND information (data) is present at the input.

A complete description of computer operation entails thousands of such statements and obviously is quite unwieldy. Furthermore, mathematical manipulation of such statements (a requirement for understanding computer operation) is practically impossible. The mathematical technique of assigning letters as abbreviations for English-language statements is borrowed for digital logic manipulation.

$$X = \text{useful output}$$
$$A = \text{arithmetic operation complete}$$
$$MR = \text{MEMORY ready}$$
$$D = \text{data}$$

and
$$X = A \text{ AND } MR \text{ AND } D \tag{3–1}$$

Thus the complete description of what is required to transfer the results of an arithmetic operation to MEMORY is shown in relatively simple algebraic form. The branch of algebra applicable to manipulation of logic quantities is called Boolean algebra (after George Boole, 1815–1864). Concepts and uses of Boolean algebra are shown in Chapter 4.

Equation 3–1 describes the operation of a specific AND function, but without additional description the full meaning may not be apparent. For example, what are the output conditions when input data is present, the arithmetic operation is complete, but the MEMORY is not ready? Or when input data is present and the MEMORY is ready but the arithmetic operation is not complete? Or any of a number of other possibilities?

Investigation of all possible combinations of a number of conditions may be accomplished in tabular form using *truth tables*, a technique borrowed from formal logic. The *truth value* of English-language phrases and combinations of phrases is investigated with truth tables. Consider the phrase "the arithmetic operation is complete." If the arithmetic operation *is* complete, the phrase is true (T); if the operation is *not complete*, it is false (F). (For the purpose of this discussion, T is defined as useful form and F is defined as not useful form.) No other condition can occur. The arithmetic operation *must* be either true or false; *it cannot be both together nor can it be non-existent.* All other input conditions may be viewed in this same manner.

Each condition, however, must be examined with all possible combinations of every other condition. Since each condition has *two* possible forms, the total number of possible combinations may be expressed by the equation

$$N = 2^m \qquad (3\text{--}2)$$

where $\qquad N = $ total number of possible combinations

$\qquad\qquad m = $ total number of variables

Example 3–1.

How many possible combinations exist with three variables?

Solution:

$$N = 2^m$$
$$N = 2^3$$
$$N = 8$$

Three variables are used in Eq. 3–1. The eight possible combinations of the three variables may be tabularly arranged in a number of different ways, but the most common form is shown in Table 3–1(a). It is now merely necessary to apply the AND gate rule to each of the combinations to determine the outputs. Note that only *one* combination of inputs supplies a useful (T) output, that is, that combination of inputs where *all* inputs are useful (T) at the same time. Note the ease with which this information is derived.

Perhaps by this time the reader has recognized that the means of identifying variable conditions is binary in nature; that is, the conditions

Table 3–1   AND Gate Truth Tables

A	*Inputs* MR	D	*Output* X	*Row*	A	*Inputs* MR	D	*Output* X
F	F	F	F	0	0	0	0	0
F	F	T	F	1	0	0	1	0
F	T	F	F	2	0	1	0	0
F	T	T	F	3	0	1	1	0
T	F	F	F	4	1	0	0	0
T	F	T	F	5	1	0	1	0
T	T	F	F	6	1	1	0	0
T	T	T	T	7	1	1	1	1

| (a) | (b) |

exist in only one of two states. It becomes convenient to use binary notation (1-0) in truth tables rather than the formal logic T-F notation because of the many correlations that exist with numerical operations in the digital computer. One (1) is commonly used to represent true (T) and zero (0) replaces false (F). The truth table of Table 3–1(a) now appears as shown in Table 3–1(b), which is the form used in most applications.

It is now appropriate to ask the question, how can it be assured that *all* possible combinations of variables being investigated are used? It has been shown that eight combinations exist with three variables, and the truth tables of Table 3–1(a) and 3–1(b) have eight combinations. Investigation of the truth tables verifies that each row is different, so all possible combinations must be included. The sequence of rows is unimportant, although the arrangement shown in Table 3–1 is preferred. Random sequencing could be used, but such a method is quite inefficient, especially when a large number of variables are used. The easiest method of arrangement is to assign an identification number to each row and arrange the binary value of each row to correspond to its identification number. The rows are arranged in ascending numerical order, top to bottom.

Correlation of row-identification numbers and the binary value of each row requires the ability to recognize binary equivalents of decimal numbers and vice-versa. Fundamental to this skill is the understanding of the concepts of number systems and conversions between decimal and binary, or vice-versa. Development of these concepts follows.

Numbers and Counting

Any number, in any number system, can be expressed as a summation of products, such as

$$N = \sum_{i=-m}^{i=n} A_i r^i$$

$$N = A_n r^n + A_{n-1} r^{-1} + \cdots + A_1 r^1 + A_{-1} r^{-1} + \cdots + A_{-m} r^{-m} \quad (3\text{–}3)$$

where
$A =$ an admissible mark or symbol*

$r =$ radix (base) of the number system*

$n =$ upper limit

$m =$ lower limit

The concept of positional notation is implicit in Eq. 3–3. This may easily be demonstrated by Example 3–2 and Table 3–2(a).

---

*The decimal number system (radix 10) has ten admissible marks (0, 1, 2, 3, 4, 5, 6, 7, 8, 9). In contrast, the binary number system (radix 2) has only two admissible symbols (0, 1).

Example 3–2.

Express the decimal number 1234.56 in the form of Eq. 3–3.

Solution:

$(n = 3, m = 2)$

$$N = 1 \times 10^3 + 2 \times 10^2 + 3 \times 10^1 + 4 \times 10^0 + 5 \times 10^{-1} + 6 \times 10^{-2}$$

Each position (column) is related to its adjacent columns by a power of ten, such as 10^3, 10^2, 10^1, etc. The value of a digit placed in a specific position is equal to the positional value of the position multiplied by the digit. Thus a 2 placed in the 10^1 position is equal to 20, while a 2 placed in the 10^3 position is equal to 2000. Numerous examples of positional notation for the decimal number system are shown in Table 3–2(a).

Table 3–2(a)   Representation of Decimal Numbers

Decimal number	10^n	Thousands 10^3	Hundreds 10^2	Tens 10^1	Units 10^0	Decimal Point .	Tenths 10^{-1}	Hundredths 10^{-2}	Thousandths 10^{-3}	10^{-m}	Power
	n	3	2	1	0	.	-1	-2	-3	$-m$	Position
		1000	100	10	1	.	.1	.01	.001		Base 10 Equivalent value
1					1	.					
10				1	0	.					
123			1	2	3	.					
1234.56		1	2	3	4	.	5	6			
.789						.	7	8	9		
10.10				1	0	.	1	0			
53				5	3	.					
45.312				4	5	.	3	1	2		
146.64			1	4	6	.	6	4			
2927.975		2	9	2	7	.	9	7	5		

Table 3–2(b)   Representation of Binary Numbers

Decimal number	2^n	*Eights* 2^3	*Fours* 2^2	*Twos* 2^1	*Ones* 2^0	*Binary Point* .	*Halves* 2^{-1}	*Fourths* 2^{-2}	*Eights* 2^{-3}	2^{-m}	Power
	n	3	2	1	0	.	-1	-2	-3	$-m$	Position
		8	4	2	1	.	$\frac{1}{2}$	$\frac{1}{4}$	$\frac{1}{8}$		Base 10 Equivalent value
1					1	.					
2				1	0	.					
5			1	0	1	.					
15		1	1	1	1	.					
10.5		1	0	1	0	.	1	0			
0.875					0	.	1	1	1		
7.125		0	1	1	1	.	0	0	1		
8.625		1	0	0	0	.	1	0	1		
1.25		0	0	0	1	.	0	1	0		
5.375		0	1	0	1	.	0	1	1		

Binary numbers are also formed using positional notation. Example 3–3 and Table 3–2(b) supply samples of binary numbers.

Example 3–3.

Express the binary number 1010.10 in the form of Eq. 3–3.

Solution:

$(n = 3, m = 2)$

$$N = 1 \times 2^3 + 0 \times 2^2 + 1 \times 2^1 + 0 \times 2^0 + 1 \times 2^{-1} + 0 \times 2^{-2}$$

In binary numbers each position (column) is related to its adjacent column by a power of two, such as 2^3, 2^2, 2^1, etc. The value of a digit placed in a specific position is equal to the positional value of the position multiplied by the digit. Thus a 1 placed in the 2^1 position is equal to 2, while a 1 placed in the 2^3 position is equal to 8. Numerous examples of positional notation for the binary number system are shown in Table 3–2(b).

Correlation between the decimal number system and the binary number system (for decimal 0 through decimal 15) can be seen in Table 3–3.

Table 3–3   Decimal-Binary Number Comparison

Decimal	Binary
0	0000
1	0001
2	0010
3	0011
4	0100
5	0101
6	0110
7	0111
8	1000
9	1001
10	1010
11	1011
12	1100
13	1101
14	1110
15	1111

The table may be constructed by converting each decimal number to its binary equivalent using any of the common conversion methods. A step-by-step procedure for the *successive division* method of binary conversion is detailed below, along with some typical conversions.

1. Successively divide the decimal number by 2.
2. Place the quotients directly beneath the dividend.
3. Place the remainders opposite the quotients.
4. The equivalent binary number is the remainders, arranged with the final remainder being the most-significant digit (MSD) and the first remainder being the least-significant digit (LSD).

$$
\begin{array}{ll}
2\lfloor 14 & \\
2\lfloor 7 \quad 0 \ \text{(LSD)} & \\
2\lfloor 3 \quad 1 & \\
2\lfloor 1 \quad 1 & \quad 1110_2 = 14_{10} \\
\ \ 0 \quad 1 \ \text{(MSD)} &
\end{array}
\qquad
\begin{array}{ll}
2\lfloor 6 & \\
2\lfloor 3 \quad 0 \ \text{(LSD)} & \\
2\lfloor 1 \quad 1 & \quad 110_2 = 6_{10} \\
\ \ 0 \quad 1 \ \text{(MSD)} &
\end{array}
$$

More detailed discussions follow in subsequent chapters.

Binary-decimal integer conversion may be approached by a *successive multiplication* method, sometimes referred to as the *double-dabble method.*

This is the inverse of the successive division method used in decimal-binary conversion. Binary-to-decimal conversion of integer numbers can be performed by application of the following steps.

1. Double the highest-order binary digit.
2. Add this doubled value to the next lower-order binary digit and record the sum.
3. Double the sum obtained.
4. Add this doubled value to the next lower-order binary digit and record the new sum.
5. Continue steps 3 and 4 until the last, or lowest-order, binary digit has been added to the previously doubled sum and a final sum has been obtained. The final sum will be the decimal equivalent of the binary number.

Sample conversions are shown below.

$$1110_2 = ?_{10}$$

$$10100_2 = ?_{10}$$

Application of the successive multiplication and successive division methods for number system conversion can result in the construction of truth tables using practically any number of variables.

3–2 SIMPLE GATES AND AMPLIFIERS

OR gates, AND gates, NOT circuits, NOR gates, and NAND gates are logic circuits that fit into the general classification of *combinational* circuits. Each of these circuits performs specific logic operations on its input.

One aid to understanding the new concept of digital logic is to use analogies based on well-known and every-day situations. Also, the use of a physical analogy sometimes helps visualization of such abstract concepts as digital logic. It is convenient, even necessary, to consider each logic operation as a physical entity during early exposure to this new subject. Using this approach, the reader may get the impression that logic operations have a close correlation with the hardware performing the logic operations. This is precisely the impression that should be obtained, since the fundamental operations of logic are commonly made available as integrated circuit packages of hardware such as OR gates, AND gates, etc.

The OR Gate

The conventional mixing-type water faucet (Figure 3–3(a)) found in many kitchens provides an excellent analogy of a logic operation. By observation, if *both* the hot and cold water controls are turned OFF, no water comes from the faucet. If, however, *either* the hot water control or the cold water control, or both together, are turned ON, a flow of water results. A table of all possible combinations of the controls and the resultant flow or lack of flow of water is also shown in Figure 3–3(b). Performing the following substitutions

$A =$ hot water faucet
   True (1) if ON
   False (0) if OFF

$B =$ cold water faucet
   True (1) if ON
   False (0) if OFF

$X =$ output
   True (1) if water flows
   False (0) if no water flows

simplifies the table describing the faucet's operation to that shown in Figure 3–3(c).

This table completely describes the fundamental logic operation called DISJUNCTION. The common name for DISJUNCTION is OR, and the mathematical symbol used to represent the logical OR operation is $(+)$. Mathematically stated, the OR operation is written $A + B$, which is spoken "*A* OR *B*." (Due to its similarity to conventional algebraic addition, this logical operation is sometimes called logical addition.) Thus the logical operation OR has a mathematical name called DISJUNCTION and a symbol $(+)$, just as the familiar algebraic operation "plus" has a mathematical name called addition and a symbol $(+)$. The graphic symbol for a device that performs the OR operation is shown in Figure 3–3(d).

Logic operation explanations also employ the *waveform* method of displaying circuit characteristics. Many different methods of electronically implementing logic functions exist, but actual values of voltage and/or current are not used descriptively when output and input conditions are discussed. Instead, HIGH (H) and LOW (L) notations are used to describe

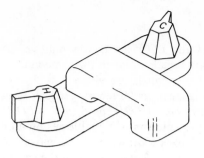

(a) Physical analogy

Hot water control	Cold water control	Faucet output
OFF	OFF	No water (OFF)
OFF	ON	Water (ON)
ON	OFF	Water (ON)
ON	ON	Water (ON)

(b) Combinations table

Row	A	B	X
0	0(L)	0(L)	0(L)
1	0(L)	1(H)	1(H)
2	1(H)	0(L)	1(H)
3	1(H)	1(H)	1(H)

(c) Truth table

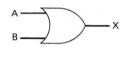

(d) Symbol

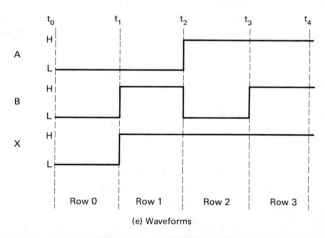

(e) Waveforms

Figure 3–3   The OR gate; (a) analogy, (b) combinations table, (c) truth table, (d) symbol, (e) waveforms

logic signals. HIGH and LOW are merely relative terms, and they describe the condition of logic signals in much the same manner as T and F or 1 and 0. However, when logic signals are viewed on electronic test devices called oscilloscopes, they appear as different vertical levels (Figure 3–3(e)). *A HIGH level is higher than a LOW level, and a LOW level is lower than a HIGH level.* The representation of signal levels on an oscilloscope is called a *waveform.* Figure 3–3(e) is a drawing of the waveforms showing the logical OR operation and should be correlated with the truth table of Figure 3–3(c) so that both methods of explanation can be recognized.

The device that performs the OR operation is called an *OR gate.* It may physically take on many forms. In common practice it may be constructed of discrete components, or it may be in integrated circuit (IC) form. Figure 1–7 and Figure 3–2 show typical examples of physical packaging of OR gates.

The number of inputs are not restricted to 2 as has been implied in earlier discussions. Input limitations are a matter of electronic design, and OR gates are commonly packaged with 2, 3, 4, or 8 inputs in an attempt to standardize production and subsequent use by logic designers. Some manufacturers provide special configurations of OR gates with greater input capability.

The AND Gate

Another logic function, the AND operation, is also seen in practically all homes. In order for a light to be illuminated, both the associated wall switch AND the protective circuit breaker must be ON. If either the switch or the circuit breaker is OFF, the light will not illuminate. A simplified schematic diagram showing this *switch* implementation of the AND operation may be seen, with its associated table of combinations, in Figure 3–4(a) and 3–4(b).

As with the OR gate, the following substitutions simplify the table describing the light's operation to that shown in Figure 3–4(c).

$C =$ Wall switch
　　True (1) if ON
　　False (0) if OFF

$D =$ circuit breaker
　　True (1) if closed
　　False (0) if open

$Y =$ light
　　True (1) if on
　　False (0) if off

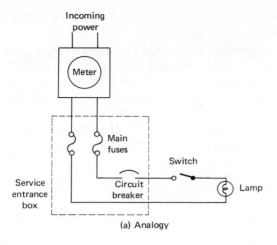

(a) Analogy

Circuit breaker	Switch	Lamp	Row	C	D	Y
OFF	OFF	OFF	0	0(L)	0(L)	0(L)
OFF	ON	OFF	1	0(L)	1(H)	0(L)
ON	OFF	OFF	2	1(H)	0(L)	0(L)
ON	ON	ON	3	1(H)	1(H)	1(H)

(b) Combinations table   (c) Truth table

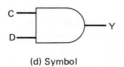

(d) Symbol

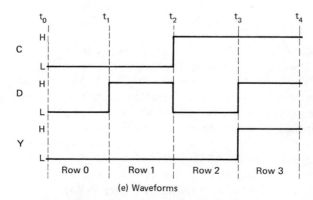

(e) Waveforms

Figure 3–4 The AND gate; (a) analogy, (b) combinations table, (c) truth table, (d) symbol, (e) waveforms

This table completely defines the fundamental logic operation called CONJUNCTION. (Note the similarity of the CONJUNCTION operation and the AND gate described in Section 3–1.) The common name for CONJUNCTION is AND, while the mathematical symbol used to represent the logical AND operation is ($\cdot$). Mathematically stated, the AND operation is written $A \cdot B$, and spoken "A AND B." (Due to its similarity to conventional algebraic multiplication, the logical operation AND is sometimes called logical multiplication.) Thus the logical operation AND has a mathematical name called CONJUNCTION and a symbol ($\cdot$), just as the familiar algebraic operation "times" has a mathematical name called multiplication and a symbol ($\cdot$).

The graphic symbol for a device that performs the AND operation is shown in Figure 3–4(d). Waveform representation is as useful for AND gate explanations as it is for OR gate circuits. (See Figure 3–4(e).)

AND gates physically appear the same as OR gates and have the same limitations on number of inputs.

The NOT Function

The last of the fundamental logic operations, that of NEGATION (the NOT function), is not as easily visualized with physical analogies as the OR and the AND function. Perhaps the engine oil pressure warning indicator system on a modern automobile comes as close to a familiar physical analogy as might be found. If oil pressure is within limits, the warning light is OFF. If oil pressure falls below required values, the warning light is ON. All possible combinations of this system are shown below.

A	B
Oil pressure	Warning light
Normal (1)	Off (0)
Low (0)	On (1)

Oil pressure (A) is the "input" to the logic operation, and the warning light (B) is the "output." When the oil pressure (A) is normal (1), the warning light (B) is OFF (0). Similarly, when $A = 0$, $B = 1$. Thus the output of a logic device that performs the NOT operation is the opposite of the input. The symbol for negation is a bar placed above the variable symbol, $\bar{B}$, and the logical operation shown above is written as $A = \bar{B}$, $\bar{A} = B$. (No *direct* correlation to this operation exists in conventional algebra.) $A = \bar{B}$ is spoken as "A is equal to NOT B." $\bar{A} = B$ is spoken as "NOT A is equal to B." A table showing all possible combinations of the variables A and B under the operation of NEGATION is shown in Figure 3–5(a).

Figure 3–5(b) is the graphic symbol used for the negation operation.

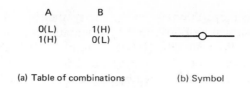

A	B
0(L)	1(H)
1(H)	0(L)

(a) Table of combinations   (b) Symbol

Figure 3–5   The NOT function; (a) table of configurations, (b) symbol

It may not appear by itself; that is, it must be attached to some other logic symbol.

Before continuing the discussion of the NOT operation, it might be appropriate to introduce another "logic" symbol. Within digital logic systems, a need often arises to increase the current or power capabilities of a logic signal. A device called an *amplifier* is provided for this purpose, and its symbol is shown in Figure 3–6(a). The amplifier output signal may have greater current or power capabilities, but *no logical operation* is performed on the signal applied to the amplifier and this symbol.

Depending on design and construction, an amplifier may or may not "invert" the incoming signal. Means are provided within MIL-STD-806B to denote the inverting characteristics of amplifiers used in logic systems. The NOT symbol is commonly attached to the amplifier symbol (Figure 3–6(b) and 3–6(c)) to show the inversion process; and when this combination of symbols is used, it represents a device that performs the NOT operation. Such a device is commonly called an INVERTER. Physically the INVERTER may resemble other logic devices, and identification of the INVERTER is usually made by part number from the manufacturers' specification sheets.

Since the NOT symbol *cannot* appear alone, obviously it must be physically connected to the amplifier symbol. *Where* it connects is extremely important. The NOT symbol is placed adjacent to other logic symbols to indicate that a LOW signal either activates the logic operation on input or is a desired result of the logic operation on output. If the NOT symbol is connected at the output side of the amplifier symbol (Figure 3–6(b)), it means

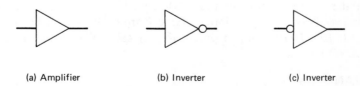

(a) Amplifier   (b) Inverter   (c) Inverter

Figure 3–6   Logic amplifier/inverter; (a) amplifier, (b) inverter, (c) inverter

that when the logic operation shown by the symbol is performed (NEGA-TION), the output will be LOW. LOW has tentatively been correlated with false, or 0, so the input must be HIGH (true, or 1). Had the NOT symbol been attached to the input side of the amplifier (Figure 3–6(c)), then it would have indicated that the desired *input* would have to be LOW to provide the activation of the NEGATION function.

The NOT symbol, then, is a clue indicating what can be expected of the symbol to which it is attached. The placement of the NOT symbol on the amplifier symbol has little meaning as far as construction of the hardware is concerned, but as has been demonstrated, it means much in terms of logic.

3–3 DERIVED GATES

Two specific cases exist where basic circuits are combined into other basic circuits. These cases are the NOR gate and the NAND gate. The rationale behind these gates can be found in economic requirements. Using either the NOR or the NAND gate, a designer can obtain all other basic gate configurations. Although it may require more NOR or NAND gates to implement a particular logic task, modern manufacturing techniques make it possible to realize considerable monetary savings when only one type of logic circuit is used. It will be shown in subsequent discussions that all combinational and sequential operations are easily realized with either of the derived gates. Hence a real cost savings is realized.

The algebraic manipulations required to justify the equivalent expressions for NOR/NAND gates is shown in Chapter 4.

NOR Gates

The NOR gate performs the same function as an OR gate followed by an inverter, or NOT operation. It has been shown that the output of an OR operation is true (1 or HIGH) when any of the inputs are true (1 or HIGH). If an inverter follows the OR gate, then the output will be false (0 or LOW) when any of the inputs to the OR gate are true (1 or HIGH). The only condition that results in a true (1 or HIGH) output is when both inputs are false (0 or LOW). This information is summarized in Figure 3–7.

If the desired output of the NOR gate is to be HIGH, the logical function is fulfilled *only* when inputs A and B are LOW, $\bar{A} \cdot \bar{B}$. Thus a means now exists (the NOR gate) to obtain the logical AND operation for false (0 or LOW) inputs.

NAND Gates

The NAND gate performs the same function as an AND gate followed by an inverter, or NOT operation. It has been shown that the output of an AND operation is true (1 or HIGH) when and only when all inputs

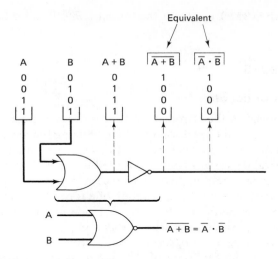

Figure 3–7 The NOR operation

are true (1 or HIGH). If an inverter follows the AND operation, then the output will be false (0 or LOW) when and only when all inputs to the AND gate are true (1 or HIGH). All other input conditions result in a false (0 or LOW) output. This information is summarized in Figure 3–8.

If the desired output of the NAND gate is to be HIGH, the logical function is fulfilled when either A or B is LOW, $\bar{A} + \bar{B}$. Thus a means now

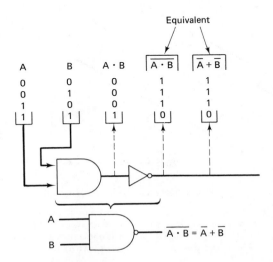

Figure 3–8 The NAND operation

exists (the NAND gate) to obtain the logical OR operation for false (0 or LOW) inputs!

3–4 FLIP-FLOPS

General Concepts

As mentioned in the introduction to this chapter, logic circuits called flip-flops (FFs) are used to perform the storage/timing functions of *sequential* operations. Actual physical analogies of FFs are rather uncommon, so the simple mechanical device of Figure 3–9 is used to explain the basic concepts.

The rocker assembly is pivoted so that it may be positioned against one or the other of the stops by application of a force. Once a force has been applied to one side, additional force to that side will have no effect. The rocker stays in its position even after removal of the force and displays its "state" by uncovering the appropriate indication. For example, when a force is applied to the SET side of the rocker, it moves to the left stop, uncovering the "1" to display its state. When the "1" is shown, the device is said to be in the SET state. Further application of force to the SET side shows no change. However, if force is applied to the RESET side, the rocker moves to the right stop, covering the "1" and uncovering the "0." Just as

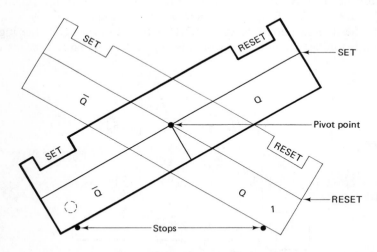

Mechanical flip-flop shown in SET condition

1. Input to SET side	1. Input to RESET side
2. FF depresses to left	2. FF depresses to right
3. Q output is high	3. $\bar{Q}$ output is high
4. 1 is uncovered	4. 0 is uncovered

Figure 3–9 Physical analogy of a flip-flop (FF)

with the SET side, no further application of force will change the display of the RESET condition.

An interesting problem appears when a force is applied to both the SET and RESET sides of the rocker at the same time. With equal forces applied, the displayed output is indeterminate. Due to individual differences in input magnitudes, rocker construction, and so forth, the actual position of the rocker cannot be predicted. *Therefore application of activating forces to both sides at the same time must be avoided.*

The rocker assembly just discussed is quite capable of performing the required storage/timing functions of sequential operations in a digital computer. However, it is slow. If speed of operation is needed, a *bistable* electronic circuit called a flip-flop (FF) may be used instead of the rocker. The bistable FF duplicates the action of the rocker and possesses the same functional characteristics. As with the combinational logic devices, detailed electronic circuitry discussions are not required if the functional characteristics are supplied.

The graphic symbol for a device that performs the same function as the mechanical rocker is shown in Figure 3–10(a). This FF (called the RS FF) has two inputs, R and S, and two outputs, Q and $\bar{Q}$ (NOT Q). The S input is called the SET input, while the R input is called the RESET input.

The reaction of FFs to the original application of power is both unimportant and indeterminate. Most linear or analog devices assume a specific input/output relationship when power is initially applied. A FF, however, is *bistable* and may take on *either* of its two stable states upon application of power. Many different terms are used to describe these states. Some of the more common terms are ON and OFF, SET and RESET, SET and CLEAR, ONE and ZERO, 1 and 0, and Q and $\bar{Q}$. Within the framework of MIL-STD-806B, a means is provided to determine the state of a FF, and it is a part of the basic rules and definitions of FF operation.

> If the flip-flop is in the set state, the Q output is HIGH and the $\bar{Q}$ output is LOW. Conversely, in the reset state, the $\bar{Q}$ output is HIGH and the Q output is LOW.

Application of an *activating** input to the SET input places the RS FF in the SET state, while the application of an activating input to the RESET input results in the RS FF assuming the RESET state. As drawn, the RS FF of Figure 3–10(a) requires a HIGH-going input as an activating signal. HIGH-going is defined as a transition from a LOW logic level to a HIGH logic level, as shown in Figure 3–10(b).

This type of diagram is representative of conventional presentations encountered in instruction handbooks furnished with digital computers.

---

*An activating input is one that causes the logic device to perform its intended or indicated function.

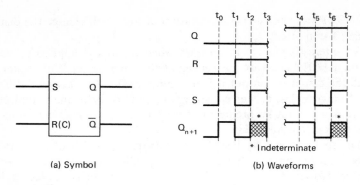

(a) Symbol   (b) Waveforms

$$Q_{n+1} = \overline{R}Q_n + \overline{R}S$$

Input		If Q output			
R	S	Was	It becomes	Was	It becomes
Inactive	Inactive	Inactive → Inactive		Active → Inactive	
Inactive	Active	Inactive → Active		Active → Active	
Active	Inactive	Inactive → Inactive		Active → Inactive	
Active	Active	*		*	

(c) General operating characteristics

R	S	Q_n	Q_{n+1}
0	0	0	0
0	0	1	1
0	1	0	1
0	1	1	1
1	0	0	0
1	0	1	0
1	1	0	*
1	1	1	*

R	S	Q_{n+1}
0	0	Q_n
0	1	1
1	0	0
1	1	*

(d) Detailed state table   (e) Simplified state table

Figure 3–10 *RS* FF summary; (a) symbol, (b) waveforms, (c) general operating characteristics, (d) detailed state table, (e) simplified state table

Such diagrams are *time oriented*, and time is usually considered to *start* at the left side of the page and to progress to the right. Time intervals are represented by subscripted letters, such as t_0, t_1, and so forth. Conventionally, the start of an operation is represented by t_0 as in Figure 3–10. The FF's response to various inputs (keyed to time intervals) is shown in Figure 3–10(b).

Both of the bistable states of the *RS* FF have now been shown, and in both cases the Q and $\bar{Q}$ outputs were opposite to each other. As noted in later chapters, this is equivalent to having available *both* a binary number and its *1's complement*. This availability proves to be very advantageous for performing arithmetic operations in the binary number system.

The indeterminate output with both SET and RESET inputs activated exists in the *RS* FF just as in the mechanical rocker. And, of course, with no activating inputs, no changes take place in the state of the FF. The complete characteristics of the *RS* FF are shown in Figure 3–10(c). This information may be rearranged into the form of Figure 3–10(d) by combining functions and including the time-dependent information that shows the FF's state dependency on its previous state. Further simplifications may be made by removing the redundant entries and the prior state information. Many different names are used to describe these tables, but the term state table (Figure 3–10(e)) is used in this book to describe the tabular representation of sequential logic element characteristics.

Algebraic expressions are also used to define FF operation. Equations describing what is required to establish a specific FF state may be derived directly from the state table. Figure 3–10 shows *RS* FF equations.

Although the *RS* FF is the basis for almost all other FFs, it does not appear in great numbers in modern digital computers. The basic *RS* function is commonly required, but implementing it directly presents a fundamental problem. Any spurious input signals which appear on either the R or the S inputs cause the FF to change state at a time when such a change may not be desired.

To alleviate this problem, the FF is often conditioned (enabled) first with a level and then allowed to make its required transition *after* it receives another input from a different source. By providing gates at the input, as shown in Figure 3–11, the *RS* FF may be controlled by both the SET/RESET inputs and an additional input (commonly called the clock input). The clock input signal (called a clock pulse) is normally of short duration compared with the time between FF state changes, so the SET and RESET inputs may be changed almost any time between clock pulses, and the FF does not change state until arrival of the clock pulse. Operation of the FF is now isolated from spurious changes of the SET and RESET inputs except for the extremely short time that the clock pulses are present.

The clocked *RS* FF responds exactly as the regular *RS* FF except for the function of the clock input. Figure 3–11 shows the clocked *RS* FF symbol, the state table, operating equations, and typical waveforms.

The Master-Slave Principle

Adoption of the clocked *RS* concept alleviates the problem of spurious input signals triggering the FF into operation at unwanted times. However, if the *RS* FF (either basic or clocked) is used in other than simple storage applications, other difficulties arise. In many counting and shift register

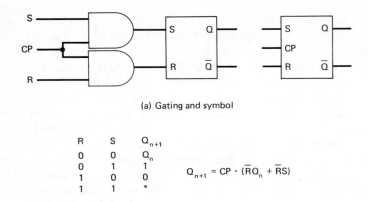

(a) Gating and symbol

R	S	Q_{n+1}
0	0	Q_n
0	1	1
1	0	0
1	1	*

$$Q_{n+1} = CP \cdot (\overline{R}Q_n + \overline{R}S)$$

Clock pulse is assumed present

(b) State table

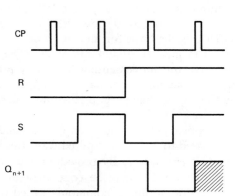

(c)

Figure 3–11   The clocked *RS* FF; (a) gating and symbol, (b) state table, (c) waveforms

applications the Q and $\overline{Q}$ outputs of one FF are connected to the S and R inputs of another FF. The change in state of the first FF tends to cause an immediate and sometimes undesired change in state of the next FF, depending on clock pulse width and internal delays. External gating may be used to prevent such undesired changes, but common practice is to employ the *master-slave* principle.

The basic concepts of the master-slave principle can be seen in Figure 3–12. Information on the S and R inputs is stored in the master FF at the HIGH-going transition of the clock input and transferred to the slave FF at

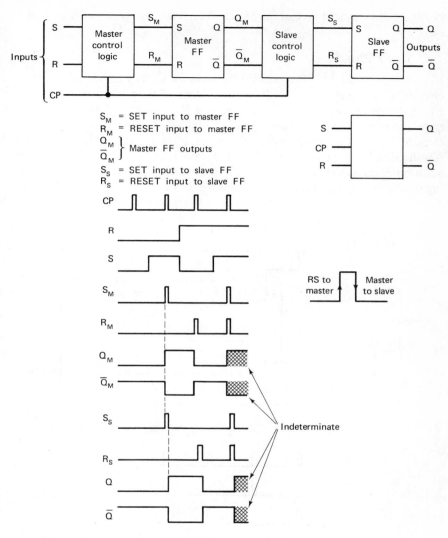

Figure 3–12   The master-slave FF

the LOW-going transition of the clock. The S and R inputs are isolated from the Q and $\bar{Q}$ outputs, since the slave control logic is disabled when the master control logic is enabled, and vice-versa.

Symbology and state tables for the master-slave (sometimes called *dual-rank*) *RS* FF are identical to the conventional clocked *RS* FF. It is necessary, however, to realize that the actual change in the outputs does not occur until the "trailing edge" of the clock pulse. The waveform diagrams in Figure 3–12 should be carefully studied to verify operation of the master-slave FF.

The *T* Flip-Flop

Although the *RS* FF is perhaps the basis for all sequential logic memory circuits, many other forms of FFs exist. Most of these circuits use the *RS* FF as the basic component. For example, a *T*, or *toggle*, FF (which changes state *every* time an activating signal is applied) is often used in counting circuits. Such *T* FF variations are numerous, although the basic logic circuit is quite simple. It is constructed from the simple *RS* binary element, with the addition of gates (or additional inputs to existing gates) to route the incoming signal, or trigger, to the appropriate side of the FF. Figure 3–13 shows the

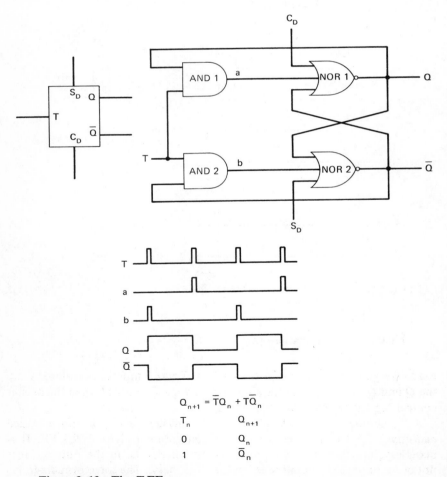

$$Q_{n+1} = \overline{T}Q_n + T\overline{Q}_n$$

T_n	Q_{n+1}
0	Q_n
1	$\overline{Q}_n$

Figure 3–13   The *T* FF

logic symbol used for the T FF, its state table, construction using combinational logic elements, equations, and typical waveforms.

A retractable-point ball point pen acts in a manner similar to a T FF. If the operating button of the pen is pushed while the point is retracted, the point is lowered to the operating position. If already in the operating position when the operating button is pushed, the point retracts. The "output" changes every time the button is operated.

Many applications require the FF in the logic circuit to be in a specific state prior to the start of the circuit function. Direct SET (S_D) and/or direct CLEAR (C_D) are made available in many FFs. These inputs are used to establish the initial state of the circuit. When S_D and C_D are provided, the state table describing that portion of the FF's operation is identical to the RS FF (Figure 3–10). The symbol indicates availability of the direct SET and direct CLEAR as shown in Figure 3–13.

The D Flip-Flop

In all FFs discussed (except the T FF) a major problem has existed. A specific combination of inputs has resulted in an indeterminate output condition, which must be guarded against with external circuitry. One way of insuring that no indeterminate states occur in the circuit operation is to provide only one conditioning input; this can be either HIGH or LOW. This input is called the D, or DATA input. Whatever logic level is present at the D input, prior to and during the clock pulse, appears at the Q output when the clock pulse occurs. Since the Q output does not assume the D input level until *after* the arrival of a clock pulse, this configuration is often called a DELAY FF. Figure 3–14 shows the symbol, state table, equations, logic diagram, and waveforms of the D FF.

The D FF is used most often to delay a change in operation so that the change can occur in synchronization with the clock pulse. For example, the D FF may be used to store the output information from a shift register or counter until readout has taken place. This allows the register or counter to begin its next cycle of operation while readout from the previous cycle is taking place.

The J-K Flip-Flop

The J-K FF is perhaps the closest approach available to a truly universal FF. It was developed primarily to overcome the ambiguity of the RS operation. The characteristics of the RS and T FFs are combined in the J-K FF. New designations for inputs are chosen so that the J-K characteristics will not be confused with the RS characteristics, but the J input may be considered equivalent to the S input and the K input the same as the R input. However, the J-K FF can have both inputs activated at the same time, in contrast to the RS circuit. Activation of the J and K inputs simultaneously causes the FF to change state upon activation by the clock pulse, just as

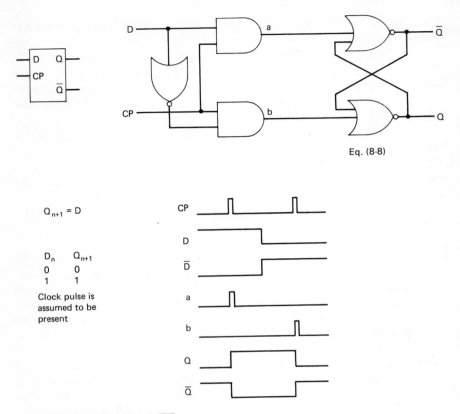

Eq. (8-8)

$Q_{n+1} = D$

D_n	Q_{n+1}
0	0
1	1

Clock pulse is
assumed to be
present

Figure 3–14 The D FF

though the T input of a T binary had been activated. The indeterminate state of RS operation is not present in the J-K FF.

The J-K symbology, state table, equations, logic diagrams, and waveforms appear in Figure 3–15. Note the availability of the direct SET and direct CLEAR operations on the symbol.

Due to the flexibility of the J-K FF, it is found in almost all applications of sequential logic. In fact, many designers use only J-K FFs to take advantage of quantity purchase prices and to reduce spare parts requirements.

3–5 SUMMARY

The characteristics of the combinational logic circuits discussed in this chapter are summarized in Table 3–4. Sequential logic characteristics appear in Table 3–5. Other special functions are used in digital computers and are discussed as they are encountered in later chapters.

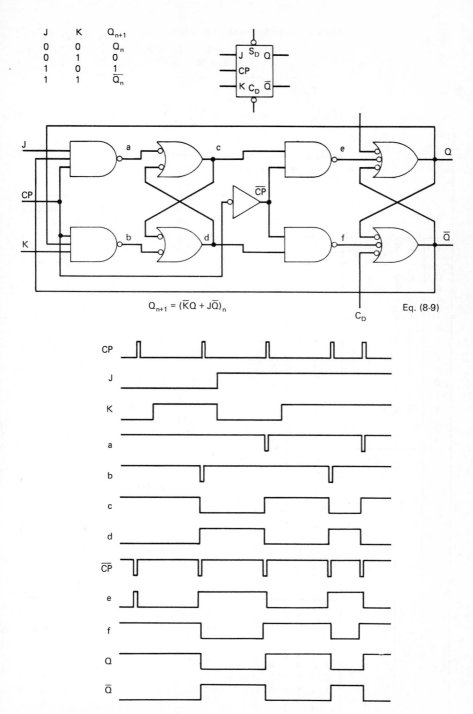

J	K	Q_{n+1}
0	0	Q_n
0	1	0
1	0	1
1	1	$\overline{Q_n}$

$$Q_{n+1} = (\overline{K}Q + J\overline{Q})_n \qquad \text{Eq. (8-9)}$$

Figure 3–15 The *J-K* FF

Table 3–4 Combinational Logic Characteristics

A	B	AND $A \cdot B$	OR $A + B$	NAND $\overline{A \cdot B}$	NOR $\overline{A + B}$
0	0	0	0	1	1
0	1	0	1	1	0
1	0	0	1	1	0
1	1	1	1	0	0

Table 3–5 Sequential Logic Characteristics

			Inputs				$R\text{–}S$ Q_{n+1}	Clocked $R\text{–}S$ Q_{n+1}	T Q_{n+1}	D Q_{n+1}	$J\text{–}K$ Q_{n+1}	Clocked $J\text{–}K$ Q_{n+1}
S	R	T	D	J	K	CP						
0	0						Q_n					
0	1						0					
1	0						1					
1	1						*					
0	0					0		Q_n				
0	0					0		Q_n				
0	1					0		Q_n				
0	1					1		0				
1	0					0		Q_n				
1	0					1		1				
1	1					0		Q_n				
1	1					1		*				
		0							Q_n			
		1							$\bar{Q}_n$			
			0							0		
			1							1		
				0	0						Q_n	
				0	1						0	
				1	0						1	
				1	1						$\bar{Q}_n$	
				0	0	0						Q_n
				0	0	1						Q_n
				0	1	0						Q_n
				0	1	1						0
				1	0	0						Q_n
				1	0	1						1
				1	1	0						Q_n
				1	1	1						$\bar{Q}_n$

*Indeterminate

QUESTIONS

1. Define "combinational" circuits and explain their uses in digital computers.
2. Define "sequential" circuits and explain their uses in digital computers.
3. What is an integrated circuit (IC)?
4. List four methods commonly used to describe logic circuits and discuss the characteristics of each.
5. Discuss the logical operation of DISJUNCTION—that is, what it is, its characteristics, etc.
6. Discuss the logical operation of CONJUNCTION.
7. Discuss the logical operation of NEGATION.
8. What logical function does an amplifier perform?
9. What is a NOR gate? Explain its purpose and how it is derived.
10. What is a NAND gate? Explain its purpose and how it is derived.
11. What is a FF?
12. List the distinguishing characteristics of an *RS* FF, a clocked *RS* FF, and a master-slave *RS* FF.
13. List the distinguishing characteristics of a *T* FF.
14. List the distinguishing characteristics of a *D* FF.
15. List the distinguishing characteristics of a *J-K* FF.

PROBLEMS

Convert the following decimal numbers to exponential form.

1. 7
2. 206
3. 5280
4. 0.6836
5. 914.254

Convert the following exponential numbers to decimal numbers.

6. 5×10^0
7. $1 \times 10^2 + 3 \times 10^1 + 7 \times 10^0$
8. $3 \times 10^3 + 6 \times 10^2 + 4 \times 10^1 + 2 \times 10^0$
9. $1 \times 10^{-1} + 2 \times 10^{-2} + 4 \times 10^{-3} + 3 \times 10^{-4}$
10. $4 \times 10^2 + 7 \times 10^1 + 6 \times 10^0 + 8 \times 10^{-1} + 9 \times 10^{-2} + 3 \times 10^{-3}$

Convert the following binary numbers to exponential form.

11. 1
12. 101
13. 11001
14. 0.1101
15. 1100111.1011

Convert the following exponential numbers to binary numbers.

16. $0 \times 2^1 + 1 \times 2^0$
17. $1 \times 2^2 + 1 \times 2^1 + 0 \times 2^0$
18. $1 \times 2^5 + 1 \times 2^4 + 0 \times 2^3 + 1 \times 2^2 + 0 \times 2^1 + 1 \times 2^0$
19. $0 \times 2^{-1} + 1 \times 2^{-2} + 1 \times 2^{-3} + 0 \times 2^{-4} + 1 \times 2^{-5}$
20. $1 \times 2^3 + 1 \times 2^2 + 0 \times 2^1 + 1 \times 2^0 + 0 \times 2^{-1} + 1 \times 2^{-2}$

Convert the following decimal numbers to their binary equivalents.

21. 3   24. 3.1416
22. 38   25. 0.125
23. 2048   26. 0.42

Convert the following binary numbers to their decimal equivalents.

27. 10111   30. 1.01
28. 101101   31. 1101.0001
29. 111   32. 1.011101

4

Boolean Algebra— The Mathematics of Computers

Algebra, trigonometry, calculus, and other branches of mathematics are commonly used when working with non-digital equipment. These tools are used by engineers and technicians who must be able to apply the basic concepts of the various branches of mathematics. Mathematics is a useful tool also in digital computer analysis. In digital computers, all operations at the logic level depend upon either the existence or absence of a signal, and hence any variable may have only one of two values. Algebra reduces to a two-valued system instead of a multi-valued system, and mathematical operations are greatly simplified. *The mathematics of logic is called Boolean algebra*, and its use greatly simplifies the understanding and analysis of digital computers. The basic postulates, theorems, and laws of Boolean algebra are explained in this chapter and are shown in summary form in Appendix A.

The computer engineer is usually provided with descriptions of the operations of the computer in the form of English-language statements, mathematical definitions, or complex Boolean algebra expressions. If the descriptions are in English-language form, they must be converted to Boolean algebra expressions capable of being implemented with logic hardware. The same is true for mathematical definitions. When all of the computer's operations have been converted to Boolean algebra expressions, one of the primary purposes of the mathematics of logic comes into play. Application of the postulates, theorems, and laws of Boolean algebra to the complex expressions of the computer's operations results in simplified Boolean expressions that may be implemented with considerably less logic hardware. Algebraic simplification of Boolean expressions is discussed in this chapter along with a graphical means of performing the same tasks.

The computer technician also employs Boolean algebra in his work. In digital equipment only one of two values of voltage or current is present, and which value is needed is the result of complex combinations of many different input signals. The actual logic circuits that combine the input signals may be examined and the expected value of the output determined. Logic diagram analysis is one of the tasks of the digital technician, and many logic diagram analyses appear throughout this book.

Often, however, an output signal is defined by a Boolean algebra expression. The technician must then be able to interpret the expression so that the appropriate input signals may be examined. Combinations of logic diagrams and Boolean expressions are perhaps the most commonly encountered method of signal definition within digital computers.

The use of logic diagrams and associated Boolean expressions begins in this chapter and continues throughout the book. As the theorems and rules of Boolean algebra are examined, diagrams showing logic hardware implementation are shown. This technique is especially useful because it is easily seen how many logic packages are saved by performance of simplification.

The computer programmer, especially when working at machine-language level, often requires the use of Boolean algebra. Machine-language programming requires extensive knowledge of the actual hardware of the computer, and Boolean algebra is the most convenient descriptive method.

4–1 THEOREMS AND LAWS OF BOOLEAN ALGEBRA

The Postulates of Boolean Algebra

Some insight into the basic postulates of Boolean algebra may be obtained by examining the AND, OR, and NOT operations tables from Chapter 3. These tables are reproduced in Figure 4–1(a). Reference designators for each row have been added to aid the reader during analysis of Boolean algebra postulates, theorems, and laws. Each of the designated rows is considered to be a basic postulate. All of the theorems and laws of Boolean algebra used in this book can be developed from these basic postulates. Figure 4–1(b) rearranges the Boolean algebra postulates into a more easily remembered format.

The Theorems of Boolean Algebra

A variable is a quantity that can take on the value of any constant in the number system. Thus the variables used in Boolean algebra must be either zero or one, since they are the only constants available in the binary system. The 13 basic theorems of Boolean algebra (as defined in this book) are listed below, with sample proofs.

THEOREM 1. $A \cdot 0 = 0$ (T–1)

Proof:

If A equals 0, Postulate 1 is proof.

$$A = 0, \quad \therefore \quad 0 \cdot 0 = 0 \text{ by P-1.}$$

If A equals 1, Postulate 3 is proof.

$$A = 1, \quad \therefore \quad 1 \cdot 0 = 0 \text{ by P-3.}$$

	AND				OR				NOT	
	A	B	X		A	B	X		A	X
①	0	0	0	⑤	0	0	0	⑨	0	$\bar{1}$
②	0	1	0	⑥	0	1	1	⑩	1	$\bar{0}$
③	1	0	0	⑦	1	0	1			
④	1	1	1	⑧	1	1	1			

(a)

①	$0 \cdot 0 = 0$	(P-1)
②	$0 \cdot 1 = 0$	(P-2)
③	$1 \cdot 0 = 0$	(P-3)
④	$1 \cdot 1 = 1$	(P-4)
⑤	$0 + 0 = 0$	(P-5)
⑥	$0 + 1 = 1$	(P-6)
⑦	$1 + 0 = 1$	(P-7)
⑧	$1 + 1 = 1$	(P-8)
⑨	$0 = \bar{1}$	(P-9)
⑩	$1 = \bar{0}$	(P-10)

(b)

Figure 4–1 Development of Boolean algebra postulates; (a) AND, OR, and NOT operations, (b) postulates of Boolean algebra.

THEOREM 2. $0 \cdot A = 0$ (T–2)

THEOREM 3. $A \cdot 1 = A$ (T–3)

Proof:

If A equals 0, Postulate 2 is proof.

$$A = 0, \quad \therefore \quad 0 \cdot 1 = 0 \text{ by P-2.}$$

If A equals 1, Postulate 4 is proof.

$$A = 1, \quad \therefore \ 1 \cdot 1 = 1 \text{ by P–4.}$$

THEOREM 4. $1 \cdot A = A$ (T–4)

THEOREM 5. $A \cdot A = A$ (T–5)

THEOREM 6. $A \cdot \bar{A} = 0$ (T–6)

Proof:

If A equals 0, $\bar{A}$ equals 1 by Postulate 9.

$$\left.\begin{array}{c} A = 0 \\ \bar{A} = 1 \end{array}\right\} \quad \therefore \ 0 \cdot 1 = 0 \text{ by P–2.}$$

If A equals 1, $\bar{A}$ equals 0 by Postulate 10.

$$\left.\begin{array}{c} A = 1 \\ \bar{A} = 0 \end{array}\right\} \quad \therefore \ 1 \cdot 0 = 0 \text{ by P–3.}$$

THEOREM 7. $A + 0 = A$ (T–7)

THEOREM 8. $0 + A = A$ (T–8)

THEOREM 9. $A + 1 = 1$ (T–9)

THEOREM 10. $1 + A = 1$ (T–10)

THEOREM 11. $A + A = A$ (T–11)

Proof:

If A equals 0, Postulate 5 is proof.

$$A = 0, \quad \therefore \ 0 + 0 = 0 \text{ by P–5.}$$

If A equals 1, Postulate 8 is proof.

$$A = 1, \quad \therefore \ 1 + 1 = 1 \text{ by P–8.}$$

THEOREM 12. $A + \bar{A} = A$ (T–12)

THEOREM 13. $\bar{\bar{A}} = A$ (T–13)

Proof:

If A equals 0, $\bar{A}$ equals 1 by Postulate 9.
If $\bar{A}$ equals 1, another negation operation $(\overline{\bar{A}})$ makes $\bar{\bar{A}}$ equal 0 by Postulate 10.

$$A = 0$$
$$\bar{\bar{A}} = 0 \qquad 0 = 0, \text{ proving } \bar{\bar{A}} = A.$$

In a similar manner, if A equals 1, $\bar{A}$ equals 0 by Postulate 10. If $\bar{A}$ equals 0, then another negation operation $(\overline{\bar{A}})$ makes $\bar{\bar{A}}$ equal 1 by Postulate 9.

$$A = 1$$
$$\bar{\bar{A}} = 1 \qquad 1 = 1, \text{ proving } \bar{\bar{A}} = A.$$

Note in each of the proofs for the basic theorems that all possible values were examined for each variable. The fact that only two values exist for any variable greatly simplifies the task of proving theorems and laws in Boolean algebra.

The theorems of Boolean algebra may also be investigated using actual hardware. (At this time a "true" or "1" is considered as HIGH, and a "false" or "0" is considered as LOW.) For example, Theorem 7 $(A + 0 = A)$ can be viewed as two inputs to an OR gate. By definition, one input is a constant binary 0, or LOW. The other input (A) is a variable and can be either binary 0 or binary 1. If A is binary 0, it is at a LOW level, and the OR truth table (Figure 4–2) shows that when both inputs are LOW, the output is LOW. However, if A is binary 1, then it is at a HIGH level, and

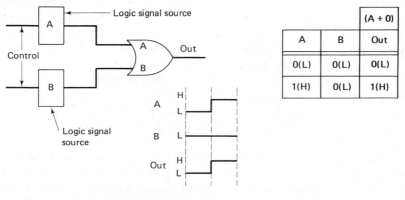

Figure 4–2 Demonstration of Theorem 7, $A + 0 = A$.

the figure shows that these inputs result in a HIGH output. Actual demonstration of this theorem requires a "logic signal source" which has the capability of generating either a HIGH output or a LOW output upon command. Such a device is relatively simple to implement, but at this time is merely represented by a rectangle labeled "logic signal source." Control is provided for each signal source so that the output of the device is either HIGH or LOW, as required. A logic diagram of the hardware required to demonstrate Theorem 7 is shown in Figure 4–2 with the associated waveforms and truth table. The control for each "logic signal source" is set to correspond to the respective values for A and B as required in the truth table. Thus, for the first entry, both "logic signal sources" provide LOW signals to the OR gate. For the second entry, B remains unchanged, and control is exercised to the A "logic signal source" to change its output to HIGH. This technique is used throughout this chapter to prove the various theorems, laws, and identities of Boolean algebra.

A convenient method of visually displaying logic conditions in actual circuits is to use indicator lamps. Since many logic devices do not have the power capability to directly operate indicator lamps, a device called a *lamp driver* (Figure 4–3) is employed. The lamp driver is effectively a switch that is closed when a HIGH input is received and open when a LOW input is received. In logic diagrams power connections are *assumed* to be made and are *not* shown on the diagram. Therefore the lamp driver applies power to the lamp when a HIGH input is present and removes power when a LOW input is present.

Indicator lamps allow easy investigation of logic circuit states when truth table entries are being examined. As each input combination is established (each line on the truth table), the condition of the indicator lamps is noted. If both lamps are in the same condition (*either* off or on), it means that both circuits are reacting in the same manner to the specific input combination. The logic signal source is then set to the next input combination (the next line on the truth table) and the condition of the indicator lamps again is noted. If both lamps are in the same condition (either off or on) for *all* of the possible input combinations, then the two circuits being examined are identical in logic function. Since the condition of the lamps determines whether the output is HIGH or LOW (1 or 0), the truth table may be constructed directly by recording the lamp conditions for each input condition. Figure 4–3 repeats the information of Figure 4–2 with the use of lamp drivers.

One of the most valuable applications of the truth table is to prove Boolean identities. If it can be shown that one column in a truth table (representing a variable) has a one-to-one correspondence with another column in the truth table (representing another variable or the results of a logical operation), then an *identity* exists between the variables/results rep-

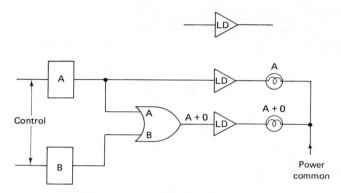

Figure 4–3 The lamp driver and its application.

resented by each column. One-to-one correspondence means that for each entry in a column in the truth table, an identical entry exists on the same row in another column. Thus, in the short truth table used to define $A + 0 = A$, each entry under the A column has a corresponding entry in the OUT column, and identity is established. Regardless of the logical value of A, when it is ORed with binary 0, the result is the logical value of A.

The Laws of Boolean Algebra

As with the other branches of mathematics, laws of Boolean algebra are developed following statement of postulates and proofs of theorems. Table 4–1 lists some of the most common laws of Boolean algebra.

Table 4–1 Laws of Boolean Algebra

(L–1)	Laws of identity	$A = A$	$\bar{A} = \bar{A}$
(L–2)	Commutative laws	$AB = BA$	$A + B = B + A$
(L–3)	Associative laws	$A(BC) = ABC$	$A + (B + C) = A + B + C$
(L–4)	Idempotent laws	$AA = A$	$A + A = A$
(L–5)	Distributive laws	$A(B + C) = AB + AC$	$A + BC = (A + B)(A + C)$
(L–6)	Absorption laws	$A + AB = A$	$A(A + B) = A$
(L–7)	Expansion laws	$AB + A\bar{B} = A$	$(A + B)(A + \bar{B}) = A$
(L–8)	De Morgan's laws	$\overline{AB} = \bar{A} + \bar{B}$	$\overline{A + B} = \bar{A}\bar{B}$

Proving the laws of Boolean algebra is a convenient method of building upon the concepts of truth tables and manipulation of algebraic expressions. Selected proofs are shown in this chapter, and the reader is encouraged to perform the end-of-chapter exercises for the remainder of the proofs.

The Laws of Identity (L–1) are practically self-explanatory. A variable surely must be equal to itself. The Commutative Laws (L–2) may be proven using truth tables and/or actual hardware as shown in Figure 4–4. Thus

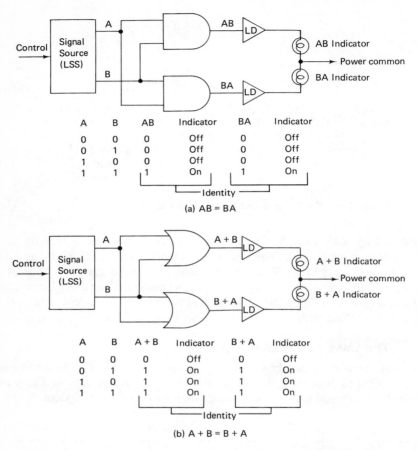

Figure 4–4 Logic diagram and truth table proofs for the commutative laws; (a) $AB = BA$; (b) $A + B = B + A$.

variables may be logically combined in any order without changing the logic value.

The Commutative Law is not limited to two variables. One can see that $W + X + YZ$ and $ZY + X + W$ are the same, even though the order of *both* the ANDed variables and the ORed variables has been changed. The Commutative Laws still apply as proven in Table 4–2. Note that with four variables 2^4 or 16 possible combinations of variables exist and that they are arranged in the truth table in ascending decimal order for ease of inspection.

The expression $(J + L)K$ is *not* the same as $(J + K)L$. The Commutative Law applies *only* to inputs to the *same* logic symbol. Note that the logical values of the output do *not* match, showing that the two expressions

Table 4-2   Commutative Law Truth Table, $W + X + YZ = ZY + X + W$

W	X	Y	Z	YZ	ZY	$(W + X + YZ)$	$(ZY + X + W)$
0	0	0	0	0	0	0	0
0	0	0	1	0	0	0	0
0	0	1	0	0	0	0	0
0	0	1	1	1	1	1	1
0	1	0	0	0	0	1	1
0	1	0	1	0	0	1	1
0	1	1	0	0	0	1	1
0	1	1	1	1	1	1	1
1	0	0	0	0	0	1	1
1	0	0	1	0	0	1	1
1	0	1	0	0	0	1	1
1	0	1	1	1	1	1	1
1	1	0	0	0	0	1	1
1	1	0	1	0	0	1	1
1	1	1	0	0	0	1	1
1	1	1	1	1	1	1	1

└────Identity────┘

are *not* identical. Logic diagram, truth table, and waveform proofs for $(J + L)K \neq (J + K)L$ are shown in Figure 4–5. A composite restatement of the Commutative Law might say that "in a simple AND or OR relationship the positions of the input signals may be interchanged with no change in the output signal."

With the introduction of Boolean algebra expressions containing more than one type of logical operation (both AND and OR), it becomes necessary to decide *how* logic diagrams representing such expressions are constructed. The procedure for developing a logic diagram from simple Boolean algebra expressions consists of the following steps.

1. Identify the general type of circuit.
2. Start with the output expression, drawing the logic symbol which represents the last or final operation.
3. Work toward the input, drawing logic symbols for each operation until all inputs are accounted for.
4. Label inputs and outputs of all gates as required.

As expressions become more complex, it is necessary to expand the procedure. Details are provided as they are needed.

The *order* in which Boolean algebra operations are performed is important. It affects the logical value of an expression, just as the order of arithmetic operations in conventional arithmetic affects the arithmetic value of an expression. Consider the three variables *A*, *B*, and *C*. Combining

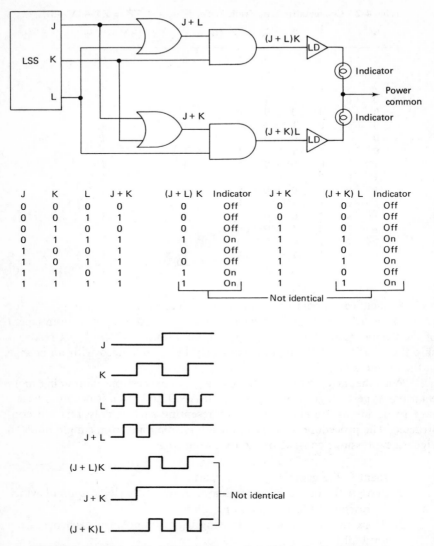

J	K	L	J + K	(J + L) K	Indicator	J + K	(J + K) L	Indicator
0	0	0	0	0	Off	0	0	Off
0	0	1	1	0	Off	0	0	Off
0	1	0	0	0	Off	1	0	Off
0	1	1	1	1	On	1	1	On
1	0	0	1	0	Off	1	0	Off
1	0	1	1	0	Off	1	1	On
1	1	0	1	1	On	1	0	Off
1	1	1	1	1	On	1	1	On

Not identical

Figure 4–5 $(J + L)K \neq (J + K)L$: truth table, logic diagram, and waveforms.

them in the expression $A + B \cdot C$ can result in different logical values, depending on the order in which the operations are performed. Comparison of the effect of performing the OR operation prior to the AND operation $[(A + B) \cdot C]$ with performing the AND operation prior to the OR operation $[(A + (B \cdot C)]$ is shown in Table 4–3.

Table 4–3   Truth Table, $(A + B)C \neq A + (BC)$

A	B	C	$A + B$	$(A + B)C$	BC	$A + (BC)$
L	L	L	L	L	L	L
L	L	H	L	L	L	L
L	H	L	H	L	L	L
L	H	H	H	H	H	H
H	L	L	H	L	L	H
H	L	H	H	H	L	H
H	H	L	H	L	L	H
H	H	H	H	H	H	H

└────Not equal────┘

The assumed order of priority in Boolean algebra is inversion (NOT) first, AND second, and OR last unless otherwise indicated by *grouping* signs such as parentheses, brackets, braces, or the vinculum ($^{-}$). By following these rules, the previously discussed expression $A + B \cdot C$ could *only* have been evaluated as $A + (B \cdot C)$, with the existence of the parentheses implicitly understood. In fact, the expression could have been further simplified and written as $A + BC$. As a matter of convention, the AND operator is usually omitted in Boolean algebra. BC is also considered to be grouped naturally because the letters are written together and are separated from A by the OR operator. Both of the conventions ($B \cdot C$ and BC) will be used, with BC preferred unless it is necessary to show the logical operator for clarity of understanding.

If an expression already contains parentheses, and additional grouping signs are required, brackets [ ] could be used. Additional grouping requirements would result in the use of braces { }. The vinculum ($^{-}$) is also a grouping sign. It groups whatever portion or portions of an expression that are to be or have been inverted. Remember, letters and expressions are also considered grouped when they are written together without a connecting operator. A complex expression containing examples of common grouping practices is

$$\{Y + W\} \cdot \{[W(XZ + YZ)] + [WXYZ + X + Y + WZ]\}$$

Expressions such as this are often encountered in digital computer analysis.

Proof of the Distributive Law identity $[A(B + C) = AB + AC]$ and the associated logic diagram are shown in Figure 4–6(a). This first identity of the Distributive Law is easily proven by application of the familiar rules of logical multiplication (ANDing). When variables inside parentheses are logically multiplied by a variable outside the parentheses, the result will be the logical product of the "outside" variable and each of the "inside" variables, joined by the operator connecting the "inside" variables. Thus both B

A	B	C	B + C	A(B + C)	Indicator	AB	AC	AB + AC	Indicator
0	0	0	0	0	Off	0	0	0	Off
0	0	1	1	0	Off	0	0	0	Off
0	1	0	1	0	Off	0	0	0	Off
0	1	1	1	0	Off	0	0	0	Off
1	0	0	0	0	Off	0	0	0	Off
1	0	1	1	1	On	0	1	1	On
1	1	0	1	1	On	1	0	1	On
1	1	1	1	1	On	1	1	1	On

Identity

A	B	C	BC	A + BC	Indicator	A + B	A + C	(A + B)(A + C)	Indicator
0	0	0	0	0	Off	0	0	0	Off
0	0	1	0	0	Off	0	1	0	Off
0	1	0	0	0	Off	1	0	0	Off
0	1	1	1	1	On	1	1	1	On
1	0	0	0	1	On	1	1	1	On
1	0	1	0	1	On	1	1	1	On
1	1	0	0	1	On	1	1	1	On
1	1	1	1	1	On	1	1	1	On

Identity

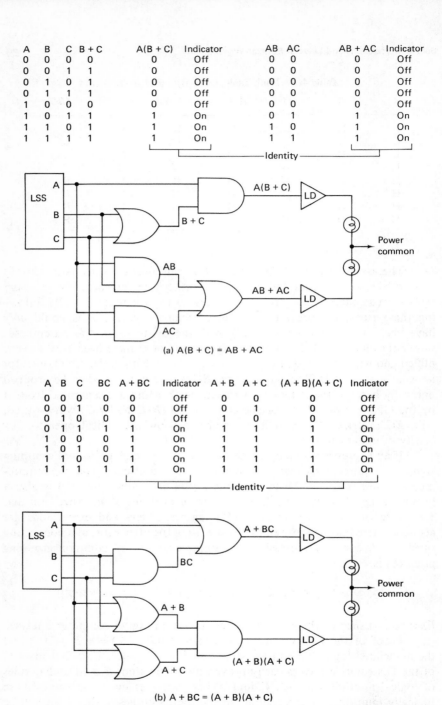

(a) A(B + C) = AB + AC

(b) A + BC = (A + B)(A + C)

Figure 4-6 Distributive Laws: logic diagrams and truth tables; (a) $A(B + C) = AB + AC$; (b) $A + (B + C) = A + B + C$

and C are logically multiplied by A, resulting in the logical products AB and AC. The resultant logical products are then connected by the $(+)$ operator, giving a final answer of $AB + AC$. As in conventional algebra, the steps are listed in sequence on the left and the justification for the steps is listed on the right.

Steps	*Justification*
$A(B + C) = AB + AC$	Logical multiplication

The second identity of the Distributive Law is

$$A + BC = (A + B)(A + C)$$

This identity is valid in Boolean algebra but *not* in ordinary algebra. The logic diagram and truth table that prove the second Distributive Law identity, $A + BC = (A + B)(A + C)$, are shown in Figure 4–6(b).

A proof of this identity of the Distributive Law using the postulates and theorems of Boolean algebra follows.

Steps	*Justification*
$(A + B)(A + C) = AA + AC + AB + BC$	Logical multiplication
$= A + AC + AB + BC$	$AA = A$
$= [A(1 + C)] + AB + BC$	Factoring
$= A + AB + BC$	$1 + A = 1; A \cdot 1 = A$
$= [A(1 + B)] + BC$	Factoring
$= A + BC$	$1 + A = 1; A \cdot 1 = A$
$(A + B)(A + C) = A + BC$	

It should be noted that this is only one of the forms that the Boolean algebra proof can assume. Many other approaches will have the same results, some with fewer steps. The specific algebraic proofs for this and the remaining laws and identities have been selected to demonstrate important aspects and uses of Boolean algebra. The reader is encouraged to investigate other forms of algebraic proofs.

De Morgan's Laws $(\overline{A \cdot B} = \bar{A} + \bar{B}; \overline{A + B} = \bar{A} \cdot \bar{B})$ express a relationship between the OR and the AND operation in Boolean algebra. Stated in simple terms, De Morgan's Laws say that inversion or negation of a Boolean expression or statement may be accomplished by negating each variable/constant, changing each AND to OR, and each OR to AND. Be sure that the difference between the expression $\overline{A + B}$ and the expression $\bar{A} + \bar{B}$ is recognized. In one case A and B are combined in an OR relationship and then the output is inverted. In the other case A and B are each

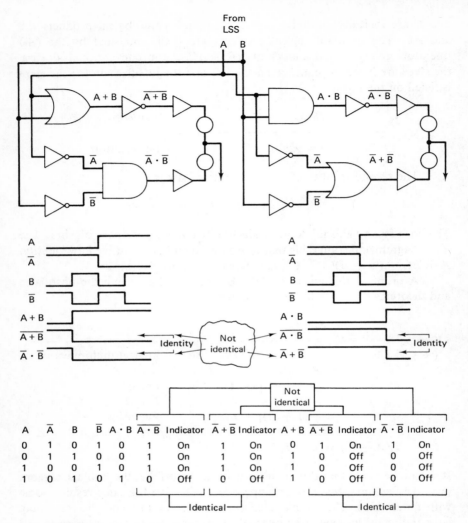

Figure 4–7 De Morgan's Laws; logic diagrams, waveforms, and truth tables.

inverted first and then the inverted variables are combined in the OR relationship. *The two expressions are not equal*, as will be evident from inspection of the truth tables and waveforms in Figure 4–7.

These laws are very powerful tools that can be used to simplify Boolean expressions and statements and to help minimize the number of logic devices necessary to perform a particular function. Consider the expression

$(\bar{A} + \bar{B} + \bar{C}) \cdot D$. Three inverters (to negate A, B, and C), one three-input OR gate (to OR $\bar{A}$, $\bar{B}$, and $\bar{C}$), and one AND gate (to AND $(\bar{A} + \bar{B} + \bar{C})$ with D)—a total of five logic devices—are needed to implement this expression. De Morgan's Laws, however, indicate that $(\bar{A} + \bar{B} + \bar{C}) = \overline{A \cdot B \cdot C}$. The original expression then can be restated as $(\overline{A \cdot B \cdot C}) \cdot D$, which requires one three-input AND gate to AND A, B, and C; one inverter to negate $(A \cdot B \cdot C)$; and a two-input AND gate to AND $(\overline{A \cdot B \cdot C})$ with D, a total of only three logic devices. Another example, even more dramatic, is the simplification of the expression $R + S + (TV) + \overline{RS}$.

Steps	Justification
$R + S + (TV) + \overline{RS} = R + S + (TV) + (\bar{R} + \bar{S})$	De Morgan's Laws
$= (R + \bar{R}) + (S + \bar{S}) + TV$	Commutative/ Associative Laws
$= 1 + 1 + (TV)$	Theorem 12
$= 1 + (TV)$	Postulate 8
$= 1$	Theorem 10

The complete expression then reduces to 1, which can be represented by a direct connection. No logic devices are required.

De Morgan's Laws also mathematically state the equivalence of certain gate forms. Since $\overline{A \cdot B} = \bar{A} + \bar{B}$, the hardware implementation of each side of the equation provides identical results, as demonstrated in Figure 4–7. Thus the negated input OR gate is functionally equivalent to the negated output AND (NAND) gate. Similarly, since $\bar{A} \cdot \bar{B} = \overline{A + B}$, the negated input AND gate is equivalent in function to the negated output OR (NOR) gate.

Many suppliers make available only certain types of gates in the interests of cost and ease of manufacture. For example, one source of hardware may provide only AND, OR, and NOT functions. Another source may furnish only NOR, or perhaps only NAND, functions. Application of De Morgan's Laws and the Distributive Laws shows that all combinational functions that may be implemented by the AND, OR, and NOT method may also be implemented by the NOR method alone or by the NAND method alone. All that should be necessary to verify the above statement is to show that NOR gates alone or NAND gates alone can perform the AND, OR, and NOT functions. NOR gates are examined first (see Figure 4–8).

NAND gates may also be used to perform the AND, OR, and NOT operations (Figure 4–9).

A commonly encountered form of logic diagram which is device oriented rather than logic operation oriented is shown in Figure 4–10(b).

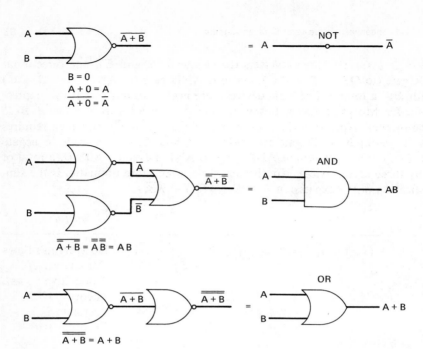

Figure 4–8 NOR to AND-OR-NOT conversions.

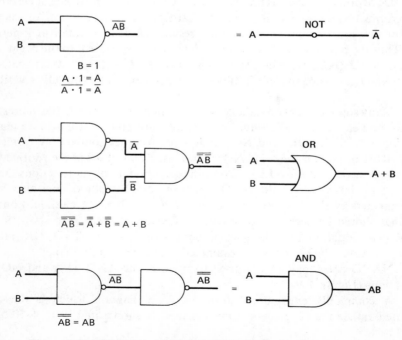

Figure 4–9 NAND to AND-OR-NOT conversions.

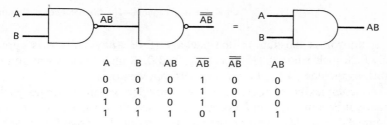

(a) AND operation using NAND gates — Logic diagram and truth table

A	B	AB	$\overline{AB}$	$\overline{\overline{AB}}$	AB
0	0	0	1	0	0
0	1	0	1	0	0
1	0	0	1	0	0
1	1	1	0	1	1

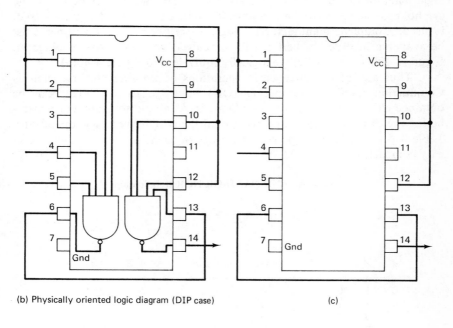

(b) Physically oriented logic diagram (DIP case)   (c)

A	$\overline{A}$	B	$\overline{B}$	$\overline{A} \cdot \overline{B}$	$\overline{\overline{A} \cdot \overline{B}}$	A + B
0	1	0	1	1	0	0
0	1	1	0	0	1	1
1	0	0	1	0	1	1
1	0	1	0	0	1	1

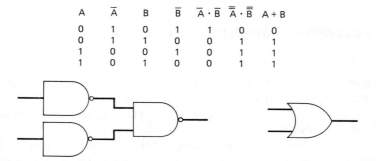

(d) OR operation using NAND gates — Logic diagram and truth table

Figure 4–10 AND and OR operations using NAND gates; logic diagrams and truth tables; (a) AND operation using NAND gates, (b) and (c) physically oriented logic diagram (DIP case).

This is known as the dual-in-line package (DIP). Physically it is approximately 0.28 inch wide, 0.785 inch long, and 0.18 inch thick. Common configurations include 14-pin (shown) and 16-pin versions.

As complexity of logic functions provided within a single package increases, it becomes less and less practical to use the form of diagram shown in Figure 4–10(b). It is common practice to provide the capability to perform complete arithmetic operations such as addition on a single "chip." The logic diagram of this type of operation obviously would not fit inside the symbol provided and still be readable. Therefore the form of Figure 4–10(c) is used. Complete manufacturers' logic descriptions and diagrams must be available in order to perform logic analysis with this type of diagram. Figure 4–10(b) and 4–10(c) are logically equivalent to Figure 4–10(a).

Thus any of the three basic operations of Boolean algebra, such as Conjunction (AND), Disjunction (OR), and Negation (NOT), can be obtained either from NOR or NAND gates. As an aid to using and remembering the three basic logic operations and the two derived logic operations, Table 4–4 provides the logic characteristics of each in a format that allows easy comparison.

Table 4–4   AND-NAND-OR-NOR Relationships

A	$\bar{A}$	B	$\bar{B}$	$A \cdot B$	$\overline{A \cdot B}$	$A + B$	$\overline{A + B}$
0	1	0	1	0	1	0	1
0	1	1	0	0	1	1	0
1	0	0	1	0	1	1	0
1	0	1	0	1	0	1	0

4–2   ALGEBRAIC SIMPLIFICATION

Definitions and Procedures

In general, the word "simplification" implies a reduction in complexity. There are many different ways to describe a logic circuit in terms of AND, OR, NOT, NAND, and NOR, and an arbitrary definition of "simplest circuit" must be determined.

Two definitions of "simplest" form are used. First, after applying the procedures for simplification that are detailed in this section, the algebraic form that results in the *smallest number of logic elements* is considered as the most simple form for the Boolean expression. It may be necessary to examine several different alternatives to determine the final form. Second, the Boolean expression should also be stated in the AND-OR form in such a way that no variables are enclosed in parentheses and no vincula extend over more than one variable. This second form may not necessarily be the form with the smallest number of logic elements but should be recognized in preparation for use in the next section concerning graphical simplification.

Two general methods of logic simplification are in common use today. One method makes use of the postulates, theorems, laws, and identities of Boolean algebra and is the subject of this section. The other method makes use of graphical methods and is detailed in Section 4–3. Each has its advantages and disadvantages. Certain similarities will become obvious as the simplification methods are developed, and mastery of both methods is a big step toward a complete understanding of logic circuits.

Every logic circuit has its own peculiarities and requires its own analysis and simplification procedure. However, enough similarities exist to make it practical to develop a suggested procedure for all logic circuits and then modify the procedure slightly as required for each circuit encountered. The general algebraic simplification procedure is shown in outline form to summarize the important steps.

1. Obtain the Boolean expression for the original circuit.
   a. From the English-language description.
   b. From a truth table.
   c. From a logic diagram.
2. Simplify algebraically.
   a. Apply postulates, theorems, laws, and identities as required.
   b. Factor, substitute, expand, modify, and convert as required.
   c. Try all over again to make sure the simplest form has been obtained.
3. Compare the new expression with the original expression by use of truth tables.
4. Draw the simplified logic diagram.

This procedure has been demonstrated during proof of the Distributive Laws and De Morgan's Laws.

Proving Logic Identities with Boolean Algebra

Some of the common identities used with the postulates, theorems, and laws of Boolean algebra during logic simplification are shown in Table 4–5. Further demonstrations of the procedures of logic simplification are shown as proofs are developed for selected identities.

Table 4–5 Boolean Algebra Identities

(I–1)	$A(\bar{A} + B) = AB$
(I–2)	$A + \bar{A}B = A + B$
(I–3)	$(AB)(A + B) = AB$
(I–4)	$(\overline{AB})(A + B) = A\bar{B} + \bar{A}B$
(I–5)	$A\bar{B} + \bar{A}B = AB + \bar{A}\bar{B}$
(I–6)	$(A + B)(B + C)(A + C) = AB + BC + AC$
(I–7)	$(A + B)(\bar{A} + C) = AC + \bar{A}B$
(I–8)	$AC + AB + B\bar{C} = AC + B\bar{C}$
(I–9)	$(A + B)(B + C)(\bar{A} + C) = (A + B)(\bar{A} + C)$

The identity $A(\bar{A} + B) = AB$ is a simple example of application of the theorems of Boolean algebra.

Steps	*Justification*
$A(\bar{A} + B) = A\bar{A} + AB$	Logical multiplication
$= 0 + AB$	$A\bar{A} = 0$ (Theorem 6)
$= AB$	$0 + A = A$ (Theorem 8)

Figure 4–11 shows the logic diagrams for both the original and simplified circuits. Note the reduced number of logic assemblies needed in the simplified implementation of the logic circuit.

Although only minor simplification in terms of the number of gates saved, the identity $\overline{A\bar{B}} + \overline{\bar{A}B} = AB + \bar{A}\bar{B}$ shows application of many laws and theorems of Boolean algebra.

Steps	*Justification*
$\overline{A\bar{B}} + \overline{\bar{A}B} = (\overline{A\bar{B}})(\overline{\bar{A}B})$	De Morgan's Law
$= (\bar{A} + B)(A + \bar{B})$	De Morgan's Law
$= A\bar{A} + \bar{A}\bar{B} + AB + B\bar{B}$	Multiplication
$= 0 + \bar{A}\bar{B} + AB + 0$	$A\bar{A} = 0$
$= \bar{A}\bar{B} + AB$	$A + 0 = A$
$= AB + \bar{A}\bar{B}$	Commutation

Figure 4–12 is the logic diagram for both implementations.

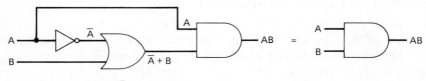

Figure 4–11 $A(\bar{A} + B) = AB$

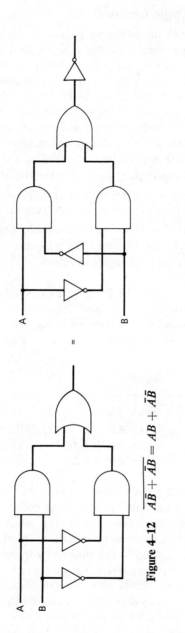

Figure 4-12 $\overline{A\overline{B} + \overline{A}B} = AB + \overline{A}\overline{B}$

Converting Logic Expressions

Often it becomes necessary to convert a logic expression to a form which is readily implemented by the type of logic elements available. For example, a logic circuit may have been originally implemented strictly with NOR elements due to a particular designer's choice or for economic reasons. Assume that the logic diagram given in Figure 4–13(a) must be implemented with AND-OR elements, not NOR elements as shown.

The first step is to determine the logic expression that this diagram represents. Derivation of the logic expression starts with inputs and moves toward the output, one gate or logic element at a time. The output at ① is $\overline{\overline{A} + \overline{B}}$. At ② the output is $\overline{C + \overline{D}}$. Combining these two expressions in the NOR gate results in the expression $\overline{\overline{A} + \overline{B} + \overline{C + \overline{D}}}$ at ③. Inversion of the expression at ③ by the single input NOR gate provides the final output expression $\overline{\overline{\overline{A} + \overline{B} + \overline{C + \overline{D}}}}$ at ④. The double negation may be removed by application of Theorem 13, and the final expression is usually written as $\overline{\overline{A} + \overline{B}} + \overline{C + \overline{D}}$. Truth table representation of this expression is provided in Figure 4–13(b).

Simplification of the NOR form to the AND-OR form is accomplished by the use of De Morgan's Laws and Theorem 13. Each group of terms in the expression is simplified separately in this example, although the experienced logic analyst would probably combine steps to reduce the scope of the overall task.

Steps	*Justification*
$\overline{\overline{A} + \overline{B}} + \overline{C + \overline{D}} = \overline{\overline{A}}\,\overline{\overline{B}} + \overline{C + \overline{D}}$	De Morgan's Laws
$= AB + \overline{C + \overline{D}}$	Theorem 13
$= AB + \overline{C}\,\overline{\overline{D}}$	De Morgan's Laws
$= AB + \overline{C}D$	Theorem 13

Comparison of the truth table for the simplified expression in Figure 4–13(d) demonstrates the equivalence of the NOR form and the AND-OR form in this example. Conversion from the NOR form to the AND-OR form is a commonly encountered situation in digital logic. Other form conversions will be discussed as the chapter progresses. The logic diagram of the AND-OR form in Figure 4–13(c) shows a reduction in gate count from four NOR gates to two AND and one OR gates. Even more important, derivation of logic expressions from logic diagrams and applications of De Morgan's Laws have been demonstrated.

Another example of logic simplification will demonstrate excellent application of Boolean algebra theorems and laws along with a considerable reduction in logic element requirements. The complete simplification process

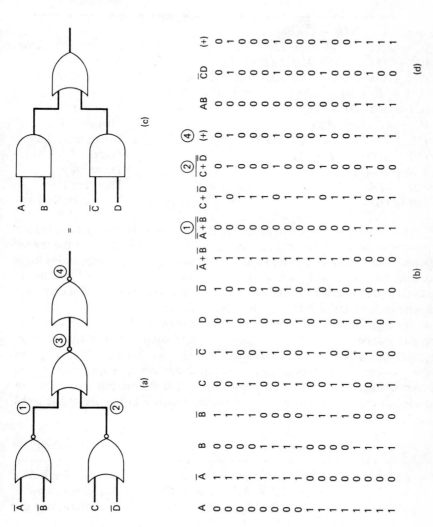

Figure 4–13 Logic conversion, NOR to AND/OR.

for the expression $(A + \bar{C})(A + D)(B + \bar{C})(B + D)$ is detailed in the following proof.

Steps	Justification
$(A + \bar{C})(A + D)(B + \bar{C})(B + D)$	
$= (\bar{C} + A)(D + A)(\bar{C} + B)(D + B)$	Commutative Law
$= [(\bar{C} + A)(\bar{C} + B)][(D + A)(D + B)]$	Associative Law
$= (\bar{C}\bar{C} + \bar{C}B + A\bar{C} + AB)(DD + DB + AD + AB)$	Distributive Law
$= [\bar{C}(1 + B + A) + AB][D(1 + B + A) + AB]$	Factor
$= (\bar{C}1 + AB)(D1 + AB)$	Theorem 9
$= (\bar{C} + AB)(D + AB)$	Theorem 3
$= \bar{C}D + \bar{C}AB + ABD + ABAB$	Distributive Law
$= \bar{C}D + AB(\bar{C} + D + 1)$	Factor
$= \bar{C}D + AB(1)$	Theorem 9
$= \bar{C}D + AB$	Theorem 3
$= AB + \bar{C}D$	Commutative Law

Once again, no major steps are omitted. By now it should be apparent that some steps may be combined, and as exercises are performed the reader may find it advantageous to do so as experience is gained. Comparative logic diagrams are shown in Figure 4–14(a) and 4–14(b), and a truth table showing both expressions is provided in Figure 4–14(c). This example demonstrates conversion from OR-AND form to AND-OR form.

Another three-level logic circuit is shown in Figure 4–15(a). The straightforward derivation of the Boolean expression is shown on the logic diagram. In the algebraic simplification that follows, it should be noted that as the number of variables in an expression increases, more and more of the theorems, laws, and identities come into play. Numerous exercises are provided at the end of this chapter to supply practice in the use of the techniques of logic simplification.

Steps	Justification
$(A + \bar{B})C + (A\bar{B} + C) = (AC + \bar{B}C) + (A\bar{B} + C)$	Distributive Law
$= AC + \bar{B}C + A\bar{B} + C$	Associative Law
$= AC + C + \bar{B}C + \bar{B}A$	Commutative Law
$= C(A + 1) + \bar{B}C + \bar{B}A$	Factor
$= C(1) + \bar{B}C + \bar{B}A$	Theorem 9
$= C + \bar{B}C + \bar{B}A$	Theorem 3
$= C(1 + \bar{B}) + \bar{B}A$	Factor
$= C(1) + \bar{B}A$	Theorem 10
$= C + \bar{B}A$	Theorem 3
$= A\bar{B} + C$	Commutative Law

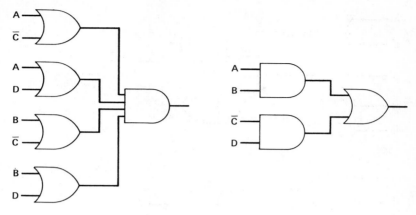

(a) Original implementation   (b) Simplified implementation

A	B	C	$\bar{C}$	D	$A+\bar{C}$	$A+D$	$B+\bar{C}$	$B+D$	X	AB	$\bar{C}D$	Y
0	0	0	1	0	1	0	1	0	0	0	0	0
0	0	0	1	1	1	1	1	1	1	0	1	1
0	0	1	0	0	0	0	0	0	0	0	0	0
0	0	1	0	1	0	1	0	1	0	0	0	0
0	1	0	1	0	1	0	1	1	0	0	0	0
0	1	0	1	1	1	1	1	1	1	0	1	1
0	1	1	0	0	0	0	1	1	0	0	0	0
0	1	1	0	1	0	1	1	1	0	0	0	0
1	0	0	1	0	1	1	1	0	0	0	0	0
1	0	0	1	1	1	1	1	1	1	0	1	1
1	0	1	0	0	1	1	0	0	0	0	0	0
1	0	1	0	1	1	1	0	1	0	0	0	0
1	1	0	1	0	1	1	1	1	1	1	0	1
1	1	0	1	1	1	1	1	1	1	1	1	1
1	1	1	0	0	1	1	1	1	1	1	0	1
1	1	1	0	1	1	1	1	1	1	1	0	1

└— Identical —┘

$X = (A + \bar{C})(A + D)(B + \bar{C})(B + D)$
$Y = AB + \bar{C}D$

(c) Truth table

Figure 4–14 $(A + \bar{C})(A + D)(B + \bar{C})(B + D) = AB + \bar{C}D$; logic diagrams and truth tables.

The simplified logic diagram appears in Figure 4–15(b). Comparison of the original expression and the simplified expression is provided in the truth tables of Figure 4–15(c).

Figure 4–16 represents a logical function that has been implemented strictly with **NAND** gates. For the purpose of discussion, assume that it

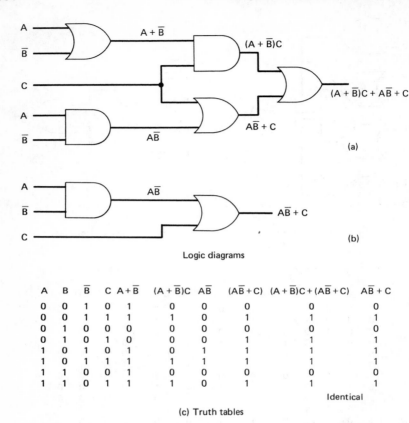

(a)

(b)

Logic diagrams

A	B	B̄	C	A+B̄	(A+B̄)C	AB̄	(AB̄+C)	(A+B̄)C+(AB̄+C)	AB̄+C
0	0	1	0	1	0	0	0	0	0
0	0	1	1	1	1	0	1	1	1
0	1	0	0	0	0	0	0	0	0
0	1	0	1	0	0	0	1	1	1
1	0	1	0	1	0	1	1	1	1
1	0	1	1	1	1	1	1	1	1
1	1	0	0	1	0	0	0	0	0
1	1	0	1	1	1	0	1	1	1

Identical

(c) Truth tables

Figure 4–15 $(A + \bar{B})C + (A\bar{B} + C) = A\bar{B} + C$; logic diagrams and truth tables.

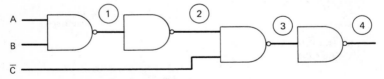

Figure 4–16 $(AB)\bar{C} = AB\bar{C}$; logic diagram.

is necessary to implement this same function with AND-OR-INVERTER type logic elements. The first step is to determine the Boolean expression at each of the numbered outputs. Since the two input variables A and B are present at the input to the first NAND gate, its output ① is $\overline{AB}$. The single input NAND gate serves as an inverter, resulting in $\overline{\overline{AB}}$ at ②. $\overline{\overline{AB}}$ is combined with $\bar{C}$ in the third NAND gate, giving $(\overline{\overline{AB}})\bar{C}$ at ③. Finally, the last single input NAND gate, acting as an inverter, provides $(\overline{\overline{\overline{AB}}})\overline{C}$ at ④, the circuit output.

Simplification of the output expression of this circuit is relatively simple. $(\overline{\overline{\overline{AB}}})\overline{C}$ is reduced to $(\overline{\overline{AB}})\overline{C}$ by Theorem 13. In fact, Theorem 13 can be applied again, resulting in $(AB)\overline{C}$. The Associative Law allows removal of the parentheses, and the initial output expression becomes $AB\overline{C}$. Truth table proof of the equivalence of the original and the simplified circuit is left to the reader as an additional exercise. A simple three-input AND gate will then perform the logical function previously requiring four NAND gates. From the viewpoint of the simplification criteria used in this text, a savings of three gates has been realized.

The reader should be prepared to encounter many NAND or NOR implemented systems. Recognition of the actual logical functions being performed may not be as easy as with AND-OR-INVERTER implemented systems. This situation calls for application of the techniques being discussed in this chapter. Conversion of the logic expressions to straightforward AND-OR-INVERTER form can quite often make an apparently senseless logic circuit become easily understandable.

A Boolean expression which can be simplified by use of one of the common identities of Boolean algebra is $[A\bar{B} + (\bar{A} + B)\bar{C}] + C$. Many of the theorems and laws of Boolean algebra are applied, in addition to the technique of substituting variables for the purpose of clarification of an expression. Simplification follows.

1. $[A\bar{B} + (\bar{A} + B)\bar{C}] + C$
2. $[A\bar{B} + \bar{A}\bar{C} + B\bar{C}] + C$
3. $A\bar{B} + (\bar{A}\bar{C} + B\bar{C}) + C$
4. $A\bar{B} + \bar{C}(\bar{A} + B) + C$
5. $A\bar{B} + [C + \bar{C}(\bar{A} + \bar{B})]$
6. $A\bar{B} + [C + (\bar{A} + \bar{B})]$
7. $\bar{A} + A\bar{B} + B + C$
8. $\bar{A} + \bar{B} + B + C$
9. $\bar{A} + 1 + C$
10. $1 + C$
11. 1

Step 1. This is a reproduction of the original problem statement.

Step 2. The term $(\bar{A} + B)\bar{C}$ inside the brackets is expanded to $\bar{A}\bar{C} + B\bar{C}$ by use of the Distributive Law.

Step 3. Two applications of the Associative Law are used in this step. Brackets are first removed to give $A\bar{B} + \bar{A}\bar{C} + B\bar{C} + C$. Parentheses are then added to form $A\bar{B} + (\bar{A}\bar{C} + B\bar{C}) + C$ in preparation for further processing.

Step 4. Since $\bar{C}$ is common to both terms inside the parentheses, it may be factored to obtain $A\bar{B} + \bar{C}(\bar{A} + B) + C$.

Step 5. Use of the Commutative Law to rearrange the expressions and the Associative Law to add grouping signs (brackets) results in the expression taking on a form which may be simplified using one of the common identities of Boolean algebra.

Step 6. The term within brackets $[C + \bar{C}(\bar{A} + B)]$ should be recognized as equivalent to the form $A + \bar{A}B = A + B$. Application of this identity simplifies the bracketed term to $C + (\bar{A} + B)$.

Step 7. Removal of the grouping signs is accomplished by use of the Associative Law. The Commutative Law is applied to rearrange the expression so that further simplification can be performed.

Step 8. An exercise in logical visualization results from this simplification step. First, the term $\bar{A} + A\bar{B}$ should be considered enclosed in parentheses, as though the Associative Law has been applied. This serves to isolate that portion of the expression so that it can be worked on separately. Although not exactly the same, the term $(\bar{A} + A\bar{B})$ may be recognized as the form $A + \bar{A}B$. Substituting X for $\bar{A}$, $\bar{X}$ for A, and Y for $\bar{B}$ makes the form easier

A	$\bar{A}$	B	$\bar{B}$	C	$\bar{C}$	$A\bar{B}$	$\bar{A}+B$	$\bar{C}(\bar{A}+B)$	$[A\bar{B}+(\bar{A}+B)\bar{C}]$	$[A\bar{B}+(\bar{A}+B)\bar{C}]+C$
0	1	0	1	0	1	0	1	1	1	1
0	1	0	1	1	0	0	1	0	0	1
0	1	1	0	0	1	0	1	1	1	1
0	1	1	0	1	0	0	1	0	0	1
1	0	0	1	0	1	1	0	0	1	1
1	0	0	1	1	0	1	0	0	1	1
1	0	1	0	0	1	0	1	1	1	1
1	0	1	0	1	0	0	1	0	0	1

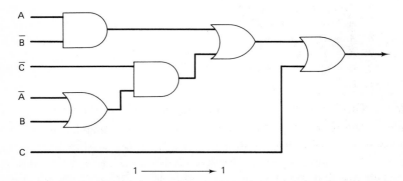

Figure 4–17 $[A\bar{B} + (\bar{A} + B)\bar{C}] + C = 1$; logic diagram and truth tables.

to visualize; that is, $X + \bar{X}Y = X + Y$. Therefore the expression simplifies to $\bar{A} + \bar{B}$.

Step 9. The Associative Law groups $\bar{B} + B$ so that Theorem 12 may be used to obtain $\bar{A} + 1 + C$.

Step 10. Theorem 9 is used following application of the Associative Law to simplify the expression to $1 + C$.

Step 11. $1 + C$ is simplified to 1 by use of Theorem 10, and the task is complete. Two AND and three OR gates are replaced by a direct connection.

There should be no doubt that the simplified expression meets all criteria for the "least complex" implementation of the original expression. Less logic elements are used, the cost of a direct connection is surely less than five logic gates, and no further algebraic simplification is possible. Comparative logic diagrams and truth tables appear in Figure 4–17.

4–3 LOGIC MAPS AND SIMPLICATION

Concepts and Construction

Sections 4–1 and 4–2 have shown that logic expressions may often be simplified using the postulates, theorems, laws, and identities of Boolean algebra. Increased numbers of variables and levels of complexity have made it progressively more difficult to recognize precisely how to perform the simplification operations. It requires considerable ingenuity, judgment, and experience to perform logic simplification consistently and satisfactorily using Boolean algebra. However, just as graphical representation of a conventional algebraic expression makes that expression much easier to visualize, so the graphical portrayal of logic expressions reduces the trauma of logic simplification. A minimized expression, requiring the *fewest possible logic elements* for implementation, is the goal of both graphical and algebraic simplification. It will soon be apparent that in cases where graphical methods are employed, the simplification solution is much more obvious and easier to obtain. But it may also be apparent that graphical solutions by themselves may not work every time. Combinations of algebraic and graphical solutions are often required.

Numerous non-algebraic methods of logic simplification employing charts, graphs, and maps have been and are being used. The graphic method of John Venn, a 19th-century British mathematician, is still used to visually demonstrate simple theorems and laws of Boolean algebra. The staff of the Harvard Computation Laboratory developed a chart method of simplification in the 1950s. In the same general time period, W. V. Quine proposed another chart method. Both the Harvard chart and the Quine method are somewhat cumbersome and time consuming to use. However, the concepts behind the Harvard chart and the Quine method are being put to use in computer-aided logic simplification operations despite the relative difficulty of their use by "paper-and-pencil" methods.

In 1952 E. W. Veitch proposed a diagrammatic means for simplifying logical functions. His method attempted to represent logical functions in a manner that would make algebraic factors more evident. The following year M. Karnaugh suggested a reorganization of the Veitch diagram. Identification of factorable terms was more obvious in Karnaugh's map, and variations and simplifications of this map have seen widespread use. The similarities of the Veitch diagram and the Karnaugh map have generated much confusion. In order not to perpetuate this confusion, only the term "map" is used in this book.

Logic maps use rectangles to represent logical relationships. Each variable in the logic expression is assigned a position within the rectangle, and sufficient positions are provided so that every possible combination of all of the variables in the expression is represented. Thus a logic map is merely another way to display truth table information. It has been shown that for n variables, 2^n combinations exist. A 2-variable truth table must have 2^2 or 4 entries, a 3-variable truth table must have 2^3 or 8 entries, etc. Two-variable maps therefore must have 4 positions, 3-variable maps 8 positions, etc.

Figure 4–18 shows the map forms used in this book for 2, 3, and 4-variable expressions. Each position (usually a square) represents a conjunctive (ANDed) combination of all variables in the expression being evaluated. The actual physical placement of the squares is determined by *one* basic criterion. *Each square must differ from any adjacent square by only one variable.* In this way the map clearly displays the *factorable* terms in a Boolean expression.

Algebraically factoring a simple Boolean expression such as $\bar{A}BC + ABC$ is a good example.

$$\bar{A}BC + ABC = \bar{A} + A(BC)$$
$$= 1(BC)$$
$$= BC$$

A logic map performs the same functions. $\bar{A}BC$ and ABC are identified in Figure 4–19, and marks are placed in each of the identified squares on a blank map to define the fact that those terms are included in the expression being simplified. All of the squares are then investigated; and when marked squares having a difference of only one variable (marked squares adjacent to each other) are recognized, these squares are grouped for future reference.

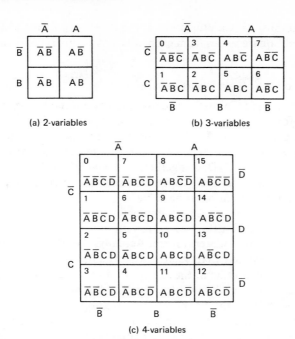

(a) 2-variables   (b) 3-variables

(c) 4-variables

Figure 4–18   Construction of logic maps.

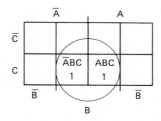

Figure 4–19 $\bar{A}BC + ABC = BC$; logic map.

In this example, the grouped squares represent the term *BC*, since *B* and *C* remain the same for both squares and *A* is zero for one square and one for the other square. When a variable and its complement are both present in an ANDed expression, that variable may be discarded as demonstrated in the algebraic simplification of the expression being used. Thus, in the 3-variable map, when two squares are properly grouped, the new term described by the grouped squares has *one less* variable than the original term or expression.

In actual use, the maps will not have the terms indicated within each square. These are provided initially so that the pattern of square identification can be established. Careful study of the three map forms of Figure 4–18 shows that each square varies from each adjacent square by only one variable, as required.

Forms of Boolean Expressions

In order to use map methods of simplification, the Boolean expression must be in a form that can be represented on the map. Two basic forms of Boolean expressions exist, neglecting negated expressions. The *logical sum of logical products form* contains terms ORed together, each term containing one or more variables ANDed together. The *logical product of logical sums form* contains factors ANDed together, each factor consisting of one or more variables ORed with other variables.

Logical sum of logical products expressions go by many different names. Commonly encountered titles are AND-OR form, sum of products form, standard sum form, and minterm form. Actually, the latter two names require a definition more explicit than merely logical sum of logical products. Not only must the expression be in the logical sum of logical products form, but each term must contain all variables in either the normal or complemented (negated) form. Rather than confuse the situation with numerous different definitions and terms, the name "minterm" is used in this book to define a Boolean expression in which each term contains all of the variables (in either the normal or complemented form) ANDed together and all of the terms ORed together. Minterm comes from a mathematical definition of a particular type of expression called a minimal polynomial.

The *logical product of logical sums* form is also known as the OR-AND form, the product of sums form, the standard product form, and the maxterm form. As above, the standard product form and the maxterm form have more explicit definitions than the product of sums form definition. In the standard product form and the maxterm form all variables (in either the normal or complemented form) are ORed together in each factor, and all of the factors are ANDed. Maxterm is used exclusively in this book.

Conversion of Boolean expressions to minterm form, which is the form required for entry of the expression into the logic map, requires the use of the methods of algebraic simplification. For example, $\overline{A + B}$ is not in minterm form. However, the vinculum may be split, using De Morgan's Laws, and $\overline{A + B}$ becomes $\overline{A} \cdot \overline{B}$. Individual terms also should be simplified, as when a variable appears more than once within the term ($ABCA = ABC$). When a variable and its complement appear within the same ANDed term, simplification should also be accomplished ($ABC\overline{A} = 0$). Where appropriate, the distributive law should be applied to remove parentheses [$AB(C + D) = ABC + ABD$].

Another way to obtain the minterm form for *any* expression is by use of truth tables. A truth table should be constructed for the expression being used. The output column should be examined for combinations of inputs that provide an output equal to one. Each of these terms may then be combined disjunctively to give the minterm form. Thus when a Boolean expression is read from a truth table, it is in the logical sum of logical products, or minterm, form.

Since each term contains all of the variables in either the inverted or non-inverted form when the expression is read from the truth table, it can be directly entered into the simplification map. An expression that is not in minterm form must either be subjected to truth table manipulations or it must be converted to the proper form. The Boolean expression $X\bar{Y}Z + XY + \bar{X}Y\bar{Z}$ is not in minterm form because it does not contain all of the variables in the second term. Expansion to minterm form by both truth table and algebraic methods is shown in Table 4–6.

Table 4–6 Expansion of an Expression to Standard Sum Form Using (a) the Truth Table, (b) Algebraic Expansion

X	$\bar{X}$	Y	$\bar{Y}$	Z	$\bar{Z}$	$X\bar{Y}Z$	XY	$\bar{X}Y\bar{Z}$	$X\bar{Y}Z + XY + \bar{X}Y\bar{Z}$	
0	1	0	1	0	1	0	0	0	0	
0	1	0	1	1	0	0	0	0	0	
0	1	1	0	0	1	0	0	1	1	$\bar{X}Y\bar{Z}$
0	1	1	0	1	0	0	0	0	0	
1	0	0	1	0	1	0	0	0	0	
1	0	0	1	1	0	1	0	0	1	$X\bar{Y}Z$
1	0	1	0	0	1	0	1	0	1	$XY\bar{Z}$
1	0	1	0	1	0	0	1	0	1	XYZ

As shown in the truth table, $X\bar{Y}Z + XY + \bar{X}Y\bar{Z} = \bar{X}Y\bar{Z} + X\bar{Y}Z + XY\bar{Z} + XYZ$

(a)

$$X\bar{Y}Z + XY + \bar{X}Y\bar{Z} = X\bar{Y}Z + XY(1) + \bar{X}Y\bar{Z} \qquad XY(1) = XY$$
$$= X\bar{Y}Z + XY(Z + \bar{Z}) + \bar{X}Y\bar{Z} \qquad Z + \bar{Z} = 1$$
$$= X\bar{Y}Z + XYZ + XY\bar{Z} + \bar{X}Y\bar{Z} \qquad \text{Distributive Laws}$$

(b)

Maxterms are less commonly used than minterms. The maxterm form of a given expression can be obtained by (a) writing the inverse of the desired expression in minterm form and (b) inverting the expression obtained in the first step. As an example, derive the maxterm for the expression described by the truth table in Table 4–7.

The minterm form is read directly from the truth table as

$$D = \bar{A}\bar{B}\bar{C} + \bar{A}\bar{B}C + \bar{A}B\bar{C} + A\bar{B}\bar{C} + A\bar{B}C$$

Table 4-7   Truth Table, $D = \bar{A}\bar{B}\bar{C} + \bar{A}\bar{B}C + \bar{A}B\bar{C} + A\bar{B}\bar{C} + A\bar{B}C$

A	B	C	D	$\bar{D}$
0	0	0	1	0
0	0	1	1	0
0	1	0	1	0
0	1	1	0	1
1	0	0	1	0
1	0	1	1	0
1	1	0	0	1
1	1	1	0	1

Writing the inverse of D in minterm form from the truth table yields

$$\bar{D} = \bar{A}BC + AB\bar{C} + ABC$$

Inverting $\bar{D}$ provides the required maxterm form

$$D = (A + \bar{B} + \bar{C})(\bar{A} + \bar{B} + C)(\bar{A} + \bar{B} + \bar{C})$$

The use of maxterm forms in map simplification will be demonstrated in future paragraphs.

Entering Information on Maps

As previously stated, each square on a map represents only one unique combination of the variables in the expression being entered. The expression must be converted or expanded, as necessary, to the form required for entry. Each term of the expression is examined, and a one is placed in the square representing the true condition for that term. Zeros *may* be inserted in all of the remaining squares to represent the false terms, but common practice dictates omitting the zeros for clarity of reading. Entry of information into 2-variable through 4-variable maps is shown as each type of map is encountered.

Logic Map Applications

An easy way to get started with map methods of simplification is to compare map simplification of a simple 2-variable expression with algebraic simplification of the same expression. The many advantages of map simplification may not be immediately obvious with simple 2-variable expressions, but the use of maps can be demonstrated without too much difficulty. Consider one form of the Laws of Expansion (L–7), $AB + A\bar{B}$.

$$AB + A\bar{B} = A(B + \bar{B})$$
$$= A(1)$$
$$= A$$

The original expression is in the required minterm form, and all that remains is to insert ones into the appropriate map squares corresponding to each of the minterms. The completely filled-in map appears in Figure 4–20. The next step is to learn how to use the map. Since the physical layout of the map is such that each square varies from each adjacent square by only one variable, examination of adjacent squares can yield valuable information. For example, the ones in Figure 4–20 are adjacent. While each one occupies a square which is equivalent to the variable A, one of the squares shares A with B and the other square shares A with $\bar{B}$. It should be evident that the map is displaying graphically the same thing as the algebraic factoring $A(B + \bar{B})$. Theorem 12 showed that when a variable and its complement are ORed, the result is logical one. It is also known that a variable ANDed with one is equivalent to that variable (Theorem 3). Thus the map performs factoring in much the same manner as algebraic factoring.

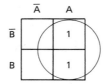

Figure 4–20 $AB + A\bar{B} = A$; logic map.

Identification of patterns of filled squares is usually made by *circling* groups of squares. When using the 2-variable map, the following patterns are allowed, shown in order of preference.

1. All four squares filled represents a constant value of logical one for the expression entered.
2. Any two adjacent squares filled represents a single-variable term.
3. A single square filled represents a 2-variable term.

In the example being simplified, only the two adjacent squares shown in Figure 4–20 can be grouped. By the given rule, this must represent a single-variable term. When the grouping operation encompasses both a variable and its complement, that variable and its complement are canceled. Only the variable that is included in the grouping operation by itself (with no complement) is left. In this case, $B + \bar{B}$ cancels, leaving only A.

The 3-variable logic map can be demonstrated by proving the Distributive Law identity $(A + B)(A + C) = A + BC$. $(A + B)(A + C)$ is not in the correct form to be entered in the map and must be expanded to minterm form either by algebraic expansion or truth table methods. Figure 4–21(a) is the truth table expansion of $(A + B)(A + C)$ to its equivalent form

A	B	C	A + B	A + C	(A + B) (A + C)	
0	0	0	0	0	0	
0	0	1	0	1	0	
0	1	0	1	0	0	
0	1	1	1	1	1	$\bar{A}BC$
1	0	0	1	1	1	$A\bar{B}\bar{C}$
1	0	1	1	1	1	$A\bar{B}C$
1	1	0	1	1	1	$AB\bar{C}$
1	1	1	1	1	1	ABC

(a) Truth table expansion

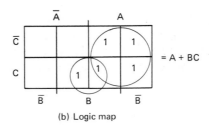

(b) Logic map

Figure 4–21 $(A + B)(A + C) = A + BC$; truth table expansion and logic map.

$\bar{A}BC + A\bar{B}\bar{C} + A\bar{B}C + AB\bar{C} + ABC$. Each term is entered in the map by placing a one in the square corresponding to the term (Figure 4–21(b)).

Rules for simplifying the expression by use of the map are similar to the 2-variable map rules. Certain expansions are necessary, though, to compensate for the additional squares. The following patterns of ones are allowed, once again shown in order of preference.

1. All eight squares filled represents a constant value of logical one for the expression entered.
2. Any four adjacent squares filled represents a single-variable term. Squares at opposite ends of rows are adjacent, as though the map were inscribed on the surface of a cylinder.
3. Any two adjacent squares filled represents a 2-variable term.
4. A single square filled represents a 3-variable term.

The preference in all cases is to detect patterns having the maximum number of ones, as long as the number of ones is a power of 2—for example, 1, 2, 4, 8, 16, etc. In the 3-variable map, the first order of preference is to have all eight squares filled. This would represent a logical value of one for the complete expression, and all of the gates required to implement the expression could be replaced with a direct connection.

The four squares on the right may be grouped (A), as may the two squares in the center of the lower row (BC), giving a final result of $A + BC$.

Note that the four grouped squares actually represent $A\bar{B}\bar{C}$, $A\bar{B}C$, $AB\bar{C}$, and ABC. Since both B and $\bar{B}$, along with C and $\bar{C}$, appear in the grouped squares, those variables cancel to leave only A. Similarly, A and $\bar{A}$ cancel in the two-square group, leaving BC.

A relationship exists between the number of variables in a term and the number of squares occupied by that term on the map. In a 3-variable map, for example, a term containing all three variables will occupy only one square. That one square is completely defined by the intersection of the rows and columns on the map used to describe each of the variables. When the number of variables in the term of a 3-variable map drops to only two, then two squares must be used to describe that term. This occurs because the 2-variable term may occupy the square which it shares with the missing variable and also the square which it shares with the complement of the missing variable. Reduction of the number of variables in a term to one results in four squares being required to describe that term. Now the variable in the term must share squares with the normal and complemented forms of *both* of the missing variables. The implied relationship between number of variables in a term and the size of the map can be expressed in the following manner.

1-variable term	$\frac{1}{2}$ of the squares
2-variable term	$\frac{1}{4}$ of the squares
3-variable term	$\frac{1}{8}$ of the squares
4-variable term	$\frac{1}{16}$ of the squares
5-variable term	$\frac{1}{32}$ of the squares

Note that as the number of variables in the term increases, the number of squares occupied decreases by a power of two. In the 3-variable map, a 1-variable term occupies half, or four, of the squares. A 2-variable term occupies one-fourth, or two, of the squares. Note the reduction by a power of 2. A 3-variable term occupies one-eighth, or one, of the squares. Again note the reduction by a power of 2. Thus an n-variable term occupies $1/2^n$ squares. This relationship holds for all maps to be discussed in this chapter.

Simplification of the 4-variable expression $(A + \bar{C})(A + D)(B + \bar{C})$ $(B + D)$ is shown in Figure 4–22. The expression is converted to minterm form by the truth table in Figure 4–22(a) and the result entered in the map of Figure 4–22(b). Grouping of squares follows the general guidelines already discussed,* and since all 16 squares or even any eight adjacent squares are not filled, groups of four adjacent squares are circled. The vertical grouping represents AB, while the horizontal group may be identified as $\bar{C}D$. Therefore $(A + \bar{C})(A + D)(B + \bar{C})(B + D) = AB + \bar{C}D$.

---

*By visualizing the 4-variable map as being inscribed on the surface of a sphere, additional adjacencies may be identified; that is, the top and bottom rows are adjacent, as are the left and right columns and the four corner squares.

A	$\overline{A}$	B	$\overline{B}$	C	$\overline{C}$	D	$\overline{D}$	$(A+\overline{C})$	$(A+D)$	$(B+\overline{C})$	$(B+D)$	X	
0	1	0	1	0	1	0	1	1	0	1	0	0	
0	1	0	1	0	1	1	0	1	1	1	1	1	$\overline{A}\,\overline{B}\,\overline{C}\,D$
0	1	0	1	1	0	0	1	0	0	0	0	0	
0	1	0	1	1	0	1	0	0	1	0	1	0	
0	1	1	0	0	1	0	1	1	0	1	1	0	
0	1	1	0	0	1	1	0	1	1	1	1	1	$\overline{A}\,B\,\overline{C}\,D$
0	1	1	0	1	0	0	1	0	0	1	1	0	
0	1	1	0	1	0	1	0	0	1	1	1	0	
1	0	0	1	0	1	0	1	1	1	1	0	0	
1	0	0	1	0	1	1	0	1	1	1	1	1	$A\,\overline{B}\,\overline{C}\,D$
1	0	0	1	1	0	0	1	1	1	0	0	0	
1	0	0	1	1	0	1	0	1	1	0	1	0	
1	0	1	0	0	1	0	1	1	1	1	1	1	$A\,B\,\overline{C}\,\overline{D}$
1	0	1	0	0	1	1	0	1	1	1	1	1	$A\,B\,\overline{C}\,D$
1	0	1	0	1	0	0	1	1	1	1	1	1	$A\,B\,C\,\overline{D}$
1	0	1	0	1	0	1	0	1	1	1	1	1	$A\,B\,C\,D$

$$X = (A + \overline{C})(A + D)(B + \overline{C})(B + D)$$

(a) Truth table expansion

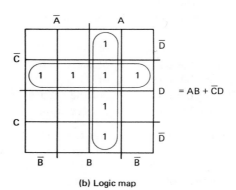

(b) Logic map

Figure 4-22 $(A + \overline{C})(A + D)(B + \overline{C})(B + D) = AB + \overline{C}D$; truth table expansion and logic map.

Comparison of Simplification Methods

The reader has undoubtedly noted that much of the work in both map and algebraic simplification has common effort. Most expressions requiring simplification will not be in the logical sum of logical products form needed for map simplification. Algebraic methods are used to obtain the proper form. Until considerable experience is gained, it is good practice to convert all expressions to be simplified to the logical sum of logical products form before making the decision as to which simplification method is to be employed. If the logical sum of logical products form of the expression contains more than four terms and two variables, the map method will usually yield a faster answer. It should also be mentioned that the map method may yield more than one simplified answer. At this point, ingenuity and insight must be relied upon to determine which of the multiple answers, if any, is the one which will simplify best in accordance with definitions being used for the system being analyzed.

If more than five variables are contained in the expression, both the map method and the algebraic method become exceedingly complex. The expression should be separated into two or more smaller individual expressions, each of these expressions simplified, and the simplified expressions combined either algebraically or with maps to yield an overall simplification.

The computer engineer/technician should also be on the alert for expressions that do not have to be converted to logical sum of logical products form in order to provide the simplified expression. This type of expression will most commonly be encountered when working with multiple applications of De Morgan's Laws.

Devising a fixed set of rules to cover all logic analysis cases is out of the question. The general guidelines and examples shown merely prepare the reader for the more complex work to follow. No attempt has been made to insist upon any specific method. Sufficient information has been provided to this point to practice each method.

Summary

Figure 4–18 showed how to construct 2-, 3-, and 4-variable logic maps.

ENTERING INFORMATION ON LOGIC MAPS

1. Convert the Boolean algebra expression to AND-OR (logical sum of logical products) or minterm form.
2. Plot one term at a time, according to the following rules.
   a. Determine the column(s) according to the column headings.
   b. Determine the row(s) according to the row headings.
   c. Place ones in all squares covered by the intersection of the selected row(s) and column(s). When more than one term generates a one in the same square, a single one is sufficient. This is equivalent to the logical operation $1 + 1 = 1$ (Postulate 8).
3. The number of squares to be marked for any term is determined by the relationship $X = 1/2^n$, where X is the number of squares to be marked and n is the number of variables in the term. For example,

1-variable term	$\frac{1}{2}$ of the squares
2-variable term	$\frac{1}{4}$ of the squares
3-variable term	$\frac{1}{8}$ of the squares
etc	

EXTRACTING INFORMATION FROM LOGIC MAPS

1. Look for groups of squares that are "adjacent" to each other.
   a. An adjacent square is one which differs from another square by only one variable.
   b. Squares may be considered adjacent if the following occurs.
      1. They are physically next to each other in the same row or column.
      2. They are at opposite ends of rows or columns.
      3. They occupy identical positions in adjacent maps.
2. Adjacent squares may be grouped together in integral powers of 2, such as, 1, 2, 4, 8, etc. Groups should generally have as many squares included together as possible, as long as they are in integral powers of 2. Circles or loops are usually drawn around the group for identification purposes.
3. The number of variables in each term can be determined by the relationship shown in the rules for entering information on logic maps.
4. A marked square may be used in as many loops as needed.
5. Combine all of the extracted terms disjunctively (logical OR) to form the simplified expression.
6. When unmarked squares consist of only one term, those squares may be grouped and considered as the complement of the expression.
7. Logic maps can be used to simplify multi-output logic expressions where more than one output is developed from common inputs. The maps for each of the output expressions are compared. If the same squares are marked, the terms are common and can be used by all output expressions.

QUESTIONS

1. What is Boolean algebra?
2. Why is the use of Boolean algebra necessary when dealing with digital computers?
3. What is the source of the postulates of Boolean algebra as defined in this text?
4. Show how the Boolean expression $A \cdot 1 = A$ can be proven using logic diagrams of actual hardware.
5. Describe the basic function of a lamp driver.
6. Show how a Boolean algebra identity can be proven using truth tables.
7. List two examples of each of the following laws of Boolean algebra:
   a. Commutative laws
   b. Distributive laws
   c. De Morgan's Laws.

8. Explain the procedure for developing a logic diagram from a Boolean expression. Show an example.
9. What is the order of priority in Boolean algebra operations? Show an example.
10. Describe the application of De Morgan's Laws to simplification of Boolean algebra expressions.
11. What is the difference between:
   a. NAND and AND gates?
   b. NAND and OR gates?
   c. NAND and NOR gates?
   d. NOR and NAND gates?
   e. NOR and AND gates?
   f. NOR and OR gates?
12. Give a procedure that can be used to algebraically simplify Boolean algebra expressions. Show an example.
13. What is a logic map?
14. Explain the concept of Boolean algebra expression simplification using logic maps.
15. What are the characteristics of an expression in the logical sum of logical products form?
16. What are the characteristics of an expression in the logical product of logical sums form?
17. Give a procedure that can be used to graphically simplify Boolean algebra expressions. Show an example.
18. What is the relationship that exists between the number of variables in a term and the number of squares occupied by that term on a logic map?

PROBLEMS

Algebraically simplify the following expressions.
1. $A + AB$
2. $A + \bar{A}B$
3. $(AB)(A + B)$
4. $(\overline{AB})(A + B)$
5. $(A + B)(B + C)(A + C)$
6. $(A + B)(\bar{A} + C)$
7. $AC + AB + BC$
8. $\bar{A}\bar{B} + (A\bar{B} + \bar{A}B)$
9. $B\bar{C} + ABC$
10. $ABC + \bar{A}BC + \bar{B}C$
11–20. Simplify problems 1–10 using logic maps.

Implementing
Computer Operations

Review of basic computer operation discussed in Chapter 2 reveals that three general types of functions must be provided by the computer's hardware. *Timing circuits* must be provided to assure that all of the internal operations of the computer occur at the proper times and without interference from each other. *Decision-making* circuits are needed to perform decoding and comparison functions. Finally, *information handling* circuits are necessary to store instructions and data temporarily and to move data from one place in the computer to another. Each type of circuit is discussed in detail in this chapter, using first the basic circuits of Chapter 3 and Boolean algebra of Chapter 4, followed by modern integrated circuit (IC) examples.

5-1 COUNTING AND TIMING CIRCUITS

Concepts and Definitions

Timing circuits are used to develop the various timing signals needed throughout the computer and to count such things as bits in a computer word, the number of times a program loop has been performed, etc. Although not immediately apparent, counting and timing signals development are closely related. Counting circuits are discussed first so that they may be used to explain timing signals and their use.

A *counter* is a device, composed of properly connected sequential (and sometimes combinational) elements, which performs the function of counting. Counters are binary in nature but may be modified to count in other than the natural binary sequence—for example, base 8, base 10, etc.

One factor that should be taken into consideration when investigating the implementation of computer functions is the type of hardware that is used. When integrated circuit packages containing only basic logic functions are used, it becomes necessary to examine the operation of each of the gates, flip-flops, etc to obtain circuit characteristics. When, however, integrated circuit packages that contain a number of interconnected basic logic functions are used, the input/output relationships may be shown *without* the intervening descriptions. In fact, it may be entirely unimportant *how* the function is accomplished internally, as long as its inputs and outputs are compatible with the rest of the equipment. A case in point is that of the common 4-stage binary counter. It may be constructed of four separate flip-flops, using *any* of the basic flip-flops described in Chapter 3. It also may be a single integrated circuit package, with only the input and outputs available for examination. And within the integrated circuit package, it may be possible to accomplish the counting function in numerous different ways. Besides using equivalents of the basic flip-flops in various combinations, the counter may also be one of a number of different counting configurations. The internal connections may result in an *asynchronous counter*, where the counted inputs "ripple" the whole length of the counter. Perhaps the counter is *synchronous*, where each flip-flop is dependent on the condition of all of the rest of the flip-flops. Both the asynchronous and the synchronous counter provide the same outputs but operate in an entirely different manner, each possessing its own advantages and disadvantages. The important consideration, however, is that the counting function is performed and that the operation may be described without tedious examination of all of the internal workings of the package.

UP Counters

Figure 5–1 is a typical example of an asynchronous binary UP counter. The name adequately describes the principle of the counter's operation. It starts counting from some predetermined point (often all FFs CLEARed) and counts in ascending order. The count is accumulated in the binary system, which may be converted to decimal numbers with very little difficulty. Note that the output of each FF represents one binary digit. The first stage, to which the inputs to be counted are applied, represents the number 2^0, or 1. The following stage has a positional value of 2^1, or 2; the next stage a value of 2^2, or 4; and the final stage represents 2^3, or 8. By adding the values of all stages that are in the SET (1) condition, the total count is obtained. Thus n FFs can store any binary number from 0 to $2^n - 1$. The counter of Figure 5–1 stores the binary equivalents of all decimal numbers from 0 to 15 in the familiar manner shown in Table 3–3.

Flip-flops used to implement the binary UP counter are not restricted to the T type. D, R-S, and J-K FFs are all easily worked into ripple counters and merely require input connections that allow them to perform as a T FF. The waveforms should be closely observed so that the relationship between the input pulses and the outputs of each stage can be seen. The first-stage

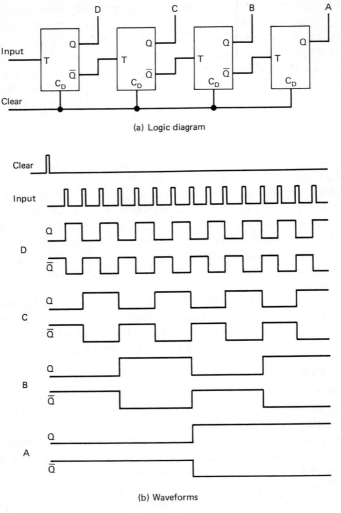

(a) Logic diagram

(b) Waveforms

Figure 5-1   Asynchronous binary UP counter.

output, for example, goes through a complete cycle (from LOW to HIGH and back to LOW again) one time for each two input pulses. Thus it effectively has an output frequency that is half the frequency of the incoming signals. The second stage has a frequency that is half the frequency of the first stage, or one-fourth the incoming frequency. *Counters are sometimes called frequency dividers* for this reason and find extensive use in applications requiring sub-multiples of input frequencies.

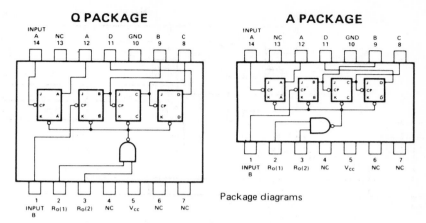

Figure 5–2 Four-bit IC counter (asynchronous).

A common 4-bit binary counter (Figure 5–2) serves as an IC example. Note that the IC contains four *J-K* FFs, with the *A* and *B* FF inputs available externally, in addition to the outputs of all four FFs. This arrangement allows external connections for other than straight binary counting, but by connecting the *A* output to the *B* input, the exact counting sequence encountered in Figure 5–1 is obtained. Thus it is shown that the internal configuration of a circuit may be entirely different, even containing different types of FFs, yet the outputs are identical. The straight binary counter, formerly containing four individual FFs, may thus be replaced with a single integrated circuit package.

Furthermore, the same counting sequence may be obtained with a *synchronous* counter such as shown in Figure 5–3. All FFs are clocked or triggered at the same time in the synchronous (parallel) counter. Combinational logic elements (gates) are used to control FF state changes so that the stored count progresses only one unit each time a clock pulse is received. Because the count does not have to "ripple" the complete length of the counter each time a change occurs, the synchronous counter is far better suited to high-speed operation than is the asynchronous counter.

Although the waveforms of Figure 5–3 are almost self-explanatory, the operation of the synchronous binary UP counter is partially discussed to develop an understanding of the use of waveforms with synchronous circuits. Counter operation is based on the already familiar characteristics of the *J-K* FF. Specifically, the *J-K* FF changes state with every clock pulse if both the *J* and the *K* inputs are HIGH at the same time. This fact is used to allow the FFs to perform the required toggling operation. This is seen in the following analysis of circuit performance.

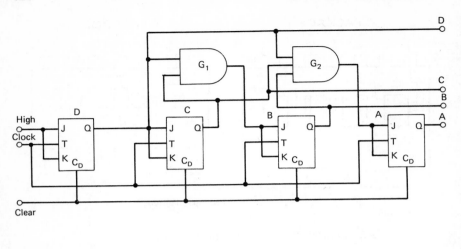

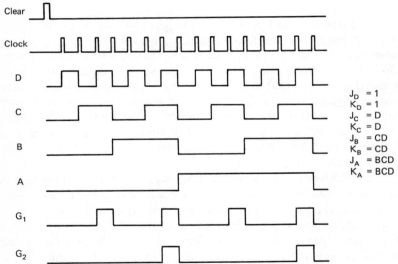

Figure 5–3 The synchronous binary UP counter.

Following the initial CLEAR operation, all FFs are in the CLEAR state and all Q outputs are LOW. The Q output of FF D disables FF C (when both J and K are LOW, no change occurs in FF state upon arrival of a clock pulse). B is similarly disabled due to the LOW output of G_1, and A is disabled by G_2. The only FF that can change state with the next clock pulse is D, because its J and K inputs are permanently HIGH. Therefore the first clock pulse changes D from the CLEAR to the SET condition, and Q_D goes HIGH. C is enabled by Q_D, and the next clock pulse not only changes the state of C but also that of D. Investigation of the remainder of the waveforms shows that B can change state only at the time both D and C are SET (G_1), and A can change state only at the time D, C, and B are SET (G_2).

It may be seen that the waveforms for the synchronous binary UP counter are identical to the waveforms for the asynchronous binary UP counter. Thus the circuits of Figures 5–2 and 5–3 are functionally equivalent. However, it should be recognized that certain limitations exist for each type of circuit, and the asynchronous counter may not be able to replace the synchronous counter in all cases. When speed and power parameters are met, either of the circuits may be used to perform simple binary counting.

UP counters are used throughout digital computers. As an example, it may be recalled that the CONTROL section automatically sequenced the selection of instructions from memory, based on initial loading of the instructions in the order in which they were to be used. Assuming that the first instruction is stored in location zero in memory, it is merely necessary to initially clear the counter to select the first instruction. Upon selection of the first instruction the UP counter is incremented by one count to select the second instruction. This process continues, following the sequence of selection of instruction, obtaining the data, executing the instruction, and selection of the next instruction, until the counter is stopped by selection of the appropriate instruction. It should be noted also that more than four stages are required if more than 16 storage locations are used. The interconnections shown are merely repeated for each FF or IC counter used.

DOWN Counters

In some cases, however, the initial instruction in a program is loaded into the *highest* memory location, with subsequent instructions appearing in the next lower positions. A DOWN counter is then required to select each instruction in sequence.

In contrast to the UP counter, the DOWN counter *decreases* its stored count every time an input pulse is received. One of the easiest ways to obtain the descending count operation is to use the complement outputs of the FFs in the UP counter. Since the Q outputs were used to obtain the ascending count in the counter of Figure 5–1, it is merely necessary to complement the Q outputs, or use the $\bar{Q}$ outputs, to obtain the descending count. The waveforms of Figure 5–1 show that all of the $\bar{Q}$ outputs are HIGH following the initial CLEAR operation, and the count represented at that time (using the $\bar{Q}$ outputs) is 1111. Following the first input pulse, the $\bar{Q}$ output of FF D goes LOW while the other FFs' Q outputs remain HIGH. The number represented is now 1110, or 14_{10}. The first pulse, then, has decreased the stored count by one. Additional pulses should be examined by the reader to verify the functioning of Figure 5–1 as a DOWN counter using the $\bar{Q}$ outputs in place of the Q outputs.

Another method of obtaining a binary DOWN counter is to use the Q outputs of each FF to activate the following FF rather than the $\bar{Q}$ outputs as used with the UP counter. Waveforms, the state table, the state flow diagram, and a simple logic diagram of a DOWN counter are shown in Figure 5–4.

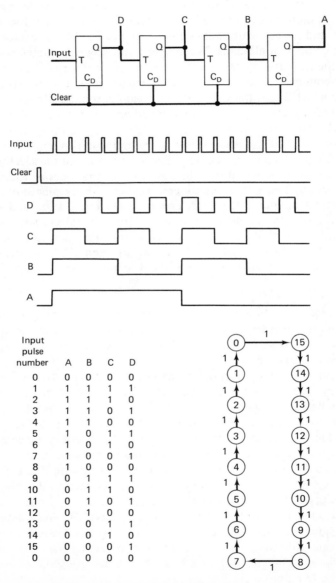

Figure 5–4   An asynchronous binary DOWN counter.

As with the asynchronous UP counter, the only requirement to convert from UP to DOWN operation is to use the opposite outputs to feed the following stages. The UP counter of Figure 5–2 becomes a DOWN counter by merely connecting the $\bar{Q}$ outputs to the following gates and/or FFs. Actual counter outputs continue to be identified with the Q output terminals. Explanatory information in the form of equations and waveform diagrams appears in Figure 5–5.

The $\bar{Q}$ outputs of the UP counter may also be used as DOWN counter outputs in the same manner as the asynchronous counter.

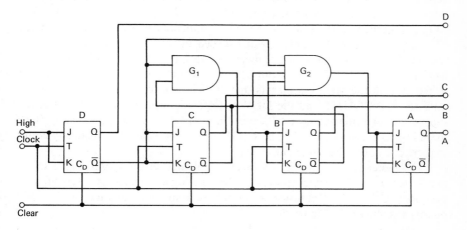

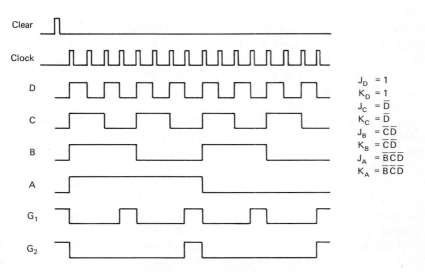

$$J_D = 1$$
$$K_D = 1$$
$$J_C = \bar{D}$$
$$K_C = \bar{D}$$
$$J_B = \bar{C}\bar{D}$$
$$K_B = \bar{C}\bar{D}$$
$$J_A = \bar{B}\bar{C}\bar{D}$$
$$K_A = \bar{B}\bar{C}\bar{D}$$

Figure 5–5 The synchronous binary DOWN counter.

Bi-Directional Counters

The characteristics of both the UP and the DOWN counter may be combined into a single UP-DOWN counter. From a practical viewpoint, all that is necessary to obtain the bi-directional feature is to decide whether the input to each FF in the series string comes from the Q or the $\bar{Q}$ output. The logic diagram of a simple device which performs the UP-DOWN counting operation is shown in Figure 5–6.

The sequence of operation is similar to the other binary counters described in this section. Following an initial CLEAR signal to establish a starting point, input pulses are applied to the T input of FF D. If the UP COUNT input is HIGH, all of the gates connected to the $\bar{Q}$ outputs of the FFs are enabled, and counting will proceed in the UP direction, just as in the UP counter in Figure 5–1. Lowering the UP COUNT input and establishing the DOWN COUNT input in the HIGH condition cause the counter to perform in the same manner as the DOWN counter of Figure 5–4. While both the UP COUNT and the DOWN COUNT inputs may be LOW at the same time (this prevents any FF other than FF D from changing state), both these inputs are *not* allowed to be HIGH simultaneously. The resulting count sequence is somewhat unusual.

Bi-directional counting may be accomplished in the synchronous mode just as it was in the asynchronous mode. The logic diagram of a typical synchronous UP-DOWN counter contained in a single integrated circuit (IC) package is shown in Figure 5–7.

Because of the complexity of the logic diagram, the package form is often used in system diagrams. Figure 5–7(a) is the 14-pin DIP form that is commonly seen in such diagrams. It should be apparent that it is necessary to have either a complete description of the counter operation or the logic diagram available to analyze system diagrams using this form of representation.

The counter of Figure 5–7 provides the output sequence 0 through 15 in the natural binary code (8–4–2–1) when counting in the UP direction or 15 through 0 when counting in the DOWN direction. SET and RESET inputs allow a count of either 15 or 0 to be placed in the counter so that a convenient starting point may be established. When these inputs are present, they disable the counting process. LOW-going signals are required to perform the SET and RESET operations.

Input to the counter is via the CARRY IN and the COUNT ENABLE lines. Both must be present (and SET and RESET *not* present) in order for the counter to operate in either the UP or the DOWN configuration. A LOW level at the UP/$\overline{\text{DOWN}}$ input results in a DOWN count, while a HIGH level results in an UP count. All four Q outputs are available, as is the $\bar{Q}$ output of the final FF. Another output, called CARRY OUT, is provided to indicate that a complete count has occurred.

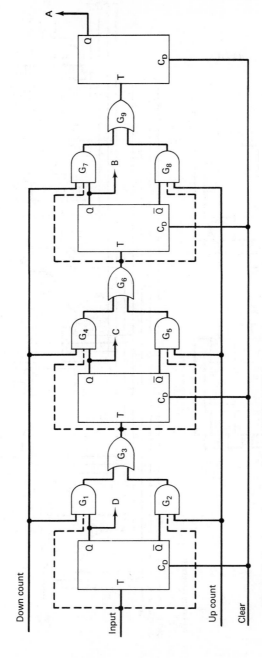

Figure 5-6 Asynchronous binary UP-DOWN counter.

130

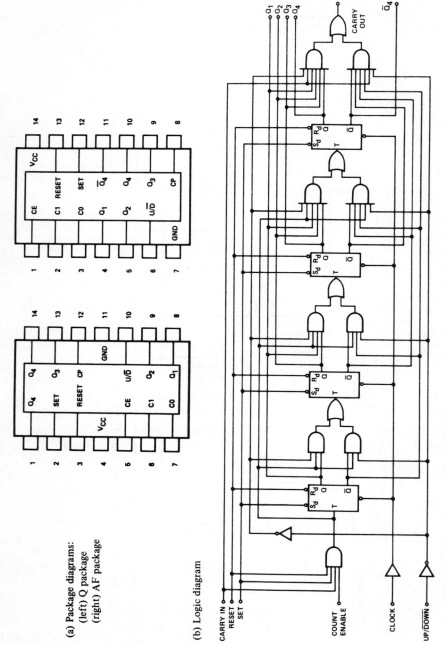

(a) Package diagrams:
(left) Q package
(right) AF package

(b) Logic diagram

Figure 5–7 The synchronous binary UP-DOWN counter, Type 8284 (courtesy of Signetics, Sunnyvale, CA).

The T input of each FF is gate controlled, so that all previous stages must be in the one state (for UP counting) or in the zero state (for DOWN counting) before the following FF is allowed to change state on the next clock pulse. Note the increasing complexity in gating structure as count value increases.

One more point is worthy of note on the logic diagram of the UP/ DOWN counter. The CLOCK and the UP/$\overline{\text{DOWN}}$ inputs have inverting amplifiers inserted prior to use of the signal. These amplifiers are required not only to obtain the correct logic level for circuit operation but also to provide power amplification. The power amplifiers provide sufficient power to operate all of the required circuits and also isolate the complete circuit from causing interference with preceding and following circuits. Such isolation is commonly necessary in complex digital systems.

Divide-by-*N* Counters

All of the counters discussed so far have been based directly or indirectly on the binary system, or *modulus* 2. *Modulus* is a term which is used to describe *the maximum number of counts that a counter can achieve*. When using natural binary counting, the modulus of a counter may be determined by the equation

$$\text{modulus} = 2^n \quad \text{where } n \text{ equals the number of FFs} \qquad (5\text{--}1)$$

Thus a single-stage counter is modulus 2, a 2-stage counter is modulus 4, a 3-stage counter is modulus 8, etc.

However, the "real" world is not necessarily base 2 oriented. Time of day uses counts of six, ten, and twelve; distance is measured in inches, feet, and yards (or millimeters, centimeters, and meters); and quantity is measured in multiples of twelve (dozen or gross). A need, then, exists to be able to count in other than modulus 2 or multiples of modulus 2.

This section investigates methods of counting in numerous bases, using both asynchronous and synchronous circuits.

A typical counter package consists of four *J-K* FFs and a 2-input NAND gate. Internal connections provide a divide-by-2 and a divide-by-8 capability. External connections allow shortening of the basic count cycle and development of various counters with moduli from 2 through 16. The basic logic diagram showing the divide-by-2 (*A* FF) and the divide-by-8 (*B*, *C*, and *D* FF) connections is seen in Figure 5–8. Natural binary counting to base 16 is provided by externally connecting A_{out} (pin 12) to B_{in} (pin 1). At this time the counter performs exactly as the asynchronous binary UP counter of Figure 5–1, with the exception of the LOW-going trigger requirement.

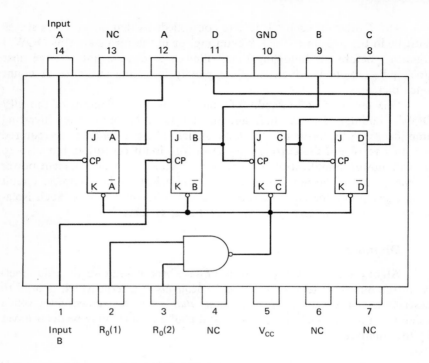

Figure 5–8   Divide-by-N IC counter.

The NAND gate is used to RESET or CLEAR all stages of the counter, either for an initial starting count or to return all stages to the reference count following completion of the count cycle.

In order to operate the J-K FFs in the counter as T FFs, both the J and the K inputs must be enabled. The method of design in the FFs in this counter allows both J and K inputs to be left *unterminated* to accomplish such enabling.

In all count applications, the frequency of the incoming triggers is divided by two in the first FF. The natural binary equivalent of the required modulus is decoded by the reset gate and any additional gating necessary, and the complete counter is reset to 0000. A divide-by-12 connection that could be used to count inches of measurement or hours of the day (Figure 5–9) is an excellent example of this technique. The logic diagram and waveforms of Figure 5–9 should be self-explanatory.

The count progresses in natural binary sequence from 0_{10} through 11_{10}. When count 12_{10} occurs, the reset gate is enabled and all FFs are returned to the 0 state. The actual count of 12 exists only for as long as it takes to reset all FFs, so the counter can be considered to be counting from 0 to 11, or modulus 12.

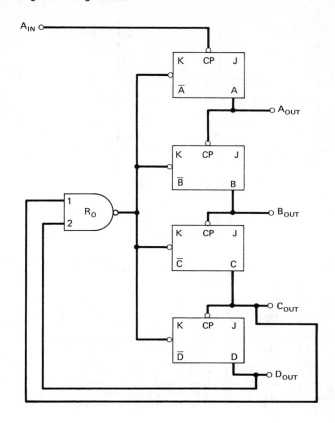

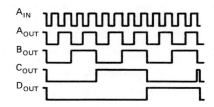

Figure 5–9 Binary divide-by-12 ripple counter.

Another divide-by-12 counter is the IC shown in Figure 5–10. A divide-by-2 and a divide-by-6 connection is made internally. Divide-by-12 operation is accomplished by externally connecting output A to the clock 2 input.

The circuit of Figure 5–10 has *strobed parallel data entry*, which allows the counter to be preset to any desired output state. Consider a one as HIGH and a zero as LOW. A one or a zero at any data (D) input is transferred to the associated output (stored in that FF) when the STROBE input goes

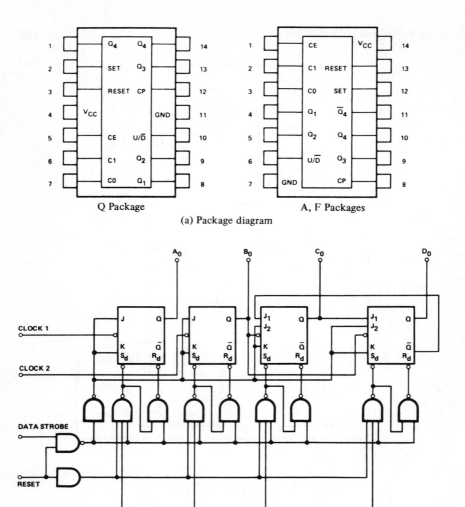

(a) Package diagram

(b) Logic diagram

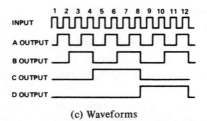

(c) Waveforms

Figure 5–10 Divide-by-12 counter, Type 8288 (courtesy of Signetics, Sunnyvale, CA).

LOW. The usual COMMON RESET is also available to place zeros in all four FFs. Both the STROBE and RESET inputs are asynchronous with respect to the CLOCK input.

FF output waveforms for the divide-by-12 portion of the circuit are included in Figure 5–10 (the reader may find it enlightening to develop the intermediate waveforms). Strobed parallel data entry is also analyzed for one of the four FFs (Figure 5–11) to demonstrate this common technique. Due to the relative timing of the STROBE, RESET, and DATA inputs, a truth table analysis of circuit operation is shown instead of the usual waveforms. One important point must be emphasized in this analysis. Both the S_D and R_D inputs require LOW-going activating signals, as indicated by the FF symbols. Therefore the outputs of G_3 and G_4 that are important are the zero outputs, not the one outputs. With this point in mind, it can be seen that S_D is activated *only* when $Z = 1$, $Y = 1$, and the strobe pulse is LOW.

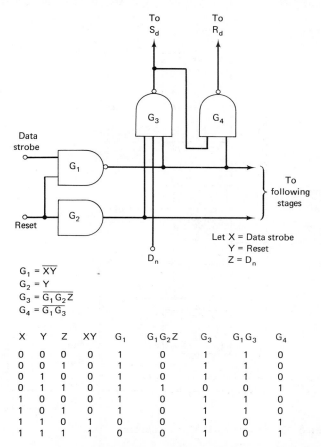

$G_1 = \overline{XY}$
$G_2 = \overline{Y}$
$G_3 = \overline{G_1 G_2 Z}$
$G_4 = \overline{G_1 G_3}$

X	Y	Z	XY	G_1	$G_1 G_2 Z$	G_3	$G_1 G_3$	G_4
0	0	0	0	1	0	1	1	0
0	0	1	0	1	0	1	1	0
0	1	0	0	1	0	1	1	0
0	1	1	0	1	1	0	0	1
1	0	0	0	1	0	1	1	0
1	0	1	0	1	0	1	1	0
1	1	0	1	0	0	1	0	1
1	1	1	1	0	0	1	0	1

Figure 5–11 Strobed parallel data entry for the Type 8288 counter.

Even if the strobe pulse is LOW and $Z = 1$, Y must also be 1 in order to SET the FF. If $Y = 0$, RESET takes place, since the RESET input overrides any attempt to preset the counter. The reset functions are as anticipated by the description of the circuit operation.

Binary-Coded-Decimal (BCD) Counters

By far the most common of the divide-by-N counters is the modulus-10 circuit. Most measurements, physical and electrical, plus much of the mathematics in the world today, use base 10 numbers. So it is no wonder that many IC packages contain binary-coded-decimal counters in one form or another.

Just as with the divide-by-12 and divide-by-6 circuits, the count representative of the counter modulus is decoded and used to reset all FFs. Figure 5–12 shows the FF interconnections and the associated waveforms of the commonly used 8–4–2–1 BCD (Binary Coded Decimal) counter. Other possible arrangements of FF states are used and have valid applications in

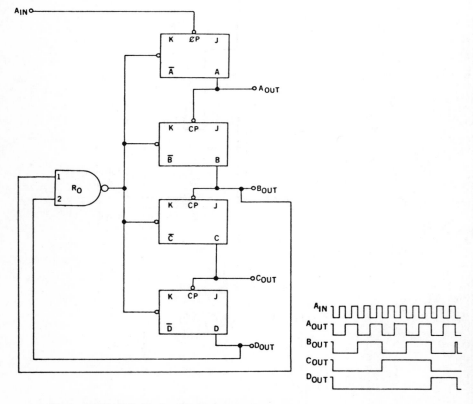

Figure 5–12   Divide-by-10 ripple counter.

special circuits, but the 8–4–2–1 weights provide simple decoding and excellent correlation with the already discussed natural binary counter. The IC of Figure 5–13 is a presettable decade IC counter which may be connected in the standard BCD counting mode or in a divide-by-5/divide-by-2 Bi-Quinary mode. The logic rules concerning STROBE, RESET, COUNT or CLOCK, and DATA inputs are identical with the previously discussed divide-by-12 package. Figure 5–13 shows the logic diagram, along with state tables and waveforms, for both standard BCD and Bi-Quinary counting. Standard BCD counting is achieved by using CLOCK 1 as the circuit input and connecting A_{out} to CLOCK 2. Connection of D_{out} to CLOCK 1, using CLOCK 2 as circuit input and A_{out} as circuit output, results in the Bi-Quinary mode of operation.

Miscellaneous Timing/Counting Circuits

Shift counters are a specialized type of clocked counter that uses *shift registers* (Section 5–3) to perform the counting operation. This type of counter generally results in outputs which are easily decoded. No gating is usually required between stages. A 1 is loaded into the first stage and is shifted one stage to the right upon arrival of each clock pulse. By providing a feedback from the last stage to the first stage in the shift counter (Figure 5–14), count recycling is provided. A 10-stage decimal counter could then count from 0 through 9 and start the count at 0 again automatically. Ten stages are needed (*A* through *M*). A 1 is preset into the first stage of the register and shifted through one stage per count until the final stage is reached. Note that the Q output of the final stage feeds the J input of the first stage, and the $\bar{Q}$ output feeds the K input. As long as the final stage is in the CLEARed state, the $\bar{Q}$ output is HIGH and the K input to the first stage is HIGH. Each time a clock pulse is received, the first stage is returned to or left in the CLEARed state. When the propagating 1 reaches the final stage, the J input of the first stage is enabled, and the 1 transfers from the final stage of the register to the first stage. Ten counts are required for the propagating 1 to recycle, and the circuit of Figure 5–14 functions as a *decimal counter*. Since the propagating 1 effectively travels in a circle, the counter of Figure 5–14 is sometimes also known as a *ring counter*. A count sequence table showing the state of each stage is used in place of waveforms.

Another timing circuit used in many computers is known as a *one-shot*. It accepts a LOW to HIGH or HIGH to LOW transition as an input and supplies a pulse of predetermined duration at the output (see Figure 5–15). External components set the output pulse duration, which appears within the symbol. One-shots are used in many applications where circuits must be enabled for only very short periods of time. Examples of one-shot operation and applications are shown in subsequent chapters.

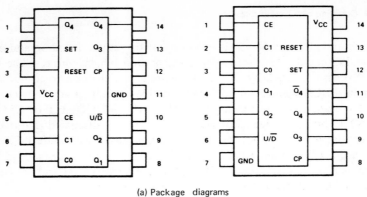

(a) Package diagrams

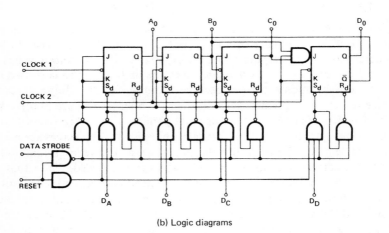

(b) Logic diagrams

Bi-Quinary (5-2)				
Input	A_0	B_0	C_0	D_0
0	0	0	0	0
1	1	0	0	0
2	0	1	0	0
3	1	1	0	0
4	0	0	1	0
5	0	0	0	1
6	1	0	0	1
7	0	1	0	1
8	1	1	0	1
9	0	0	1	1

Decade (BCD)				
Input	A_0	B_0	C_0	D_0
0	0	0	0	0
1	1	0	0	0
2	0	1	0	0
3	1	1	0	0
4	0	0	1	0
5	1	0	1	0
6	0	1	1	0
7	1	1	1	0
8	0	0	0	1
9	1	0	0	1

(c) State tables

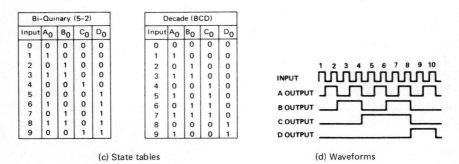

(d) Waveforms

Figure 5–13 Type 8290 decade counter (courtesy of Signetics, Sunnyvale, CA).

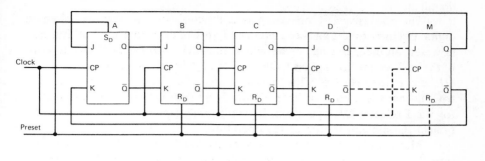

	A	B	C	D	E	F	G	H	L	M
0	1	0	0	0	0	0	0	0	0	0
1	0	1	0	0	0	0	0	0	0	0
2	0	0	1	0	0	0	0	0	0	0
3	0	0	0	1	0	0	0	0	0	0
4	0	0	0	0	1	0	0	0	0	0
5	0	0	0	0	0	1	0	0	0	0
6	0	0	0	0	0	0	1	0	0	0
7	0	0	0	0	0	0	0	1	0	0
8	0	0	0	0	0	0	0	0	1	0
9	0	0	0	0	0	0	0	0	0	1

Count sequence

Figure 5–14   Ring counter.

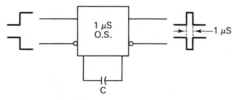

Figure 5–15   One-Shot symbol.

5–2   DECISION-MAKING CIRCUITS

Decision-making circuits range from simple 2-input gates that detect the simultaneous occurrence of two events to complex multi-gate combinations that decode computer words and compose system control signals. These circuits generally consist of combinational logic elements (gates, inverters, etc), interconnected to perform the required functions.

Comparison Circuits

One general group of decision-making circuits *compares* inputs and supplies an output based on the relationship of those inputs. For example, it is a common requirement in digital computers to decide whether two binary numbers are equal or not equal. In simple form, the *Exclusive-OR* circuit (Figure 5–16(a)) can perform this function.

The Exclusive-OR operation is a function that appears so often in digital circuitry that it has been assigned a special operating symbol. It is not, however, an independent operation and thus may also be expressed in terms of the basic connectives (AND, OR, and NOT). The expression *A Exclusively-OR B* is written $A \oplus B$. This function is true ($A \oplus B = 1$) when *A* or *B* is true but *not* when both are true. Figure 5–16(a) shows the standard symbol for the Exclusive-OR operation, its truth table, algebraic expression, and a typical IC implementation of the operation.

Many useful logic functions are derived from the Exclusive-OR operation. The expression for the Exclusive-OR circuit ($A\bar{B} + \bar{A}B$) shows that the

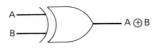

8241   Quad Exclusive-OR

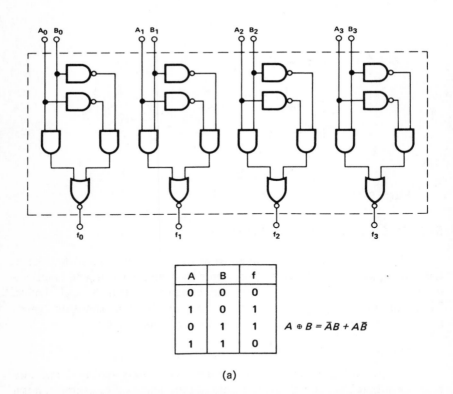

A	B	f
0	0	0
1	0	1
0	1	1
1	1	0

$A \oplus B = \bar{A}B + A\bar{B}$

(a)

Figure 5–16   EXCLUSIVE-OR Circuits; (a) Exclusive-OR operation, (b) Exclusive-NOR (Equality) operation, (c) Single-order comparator (courtesy of Signetics, Sunnyvale, CA).

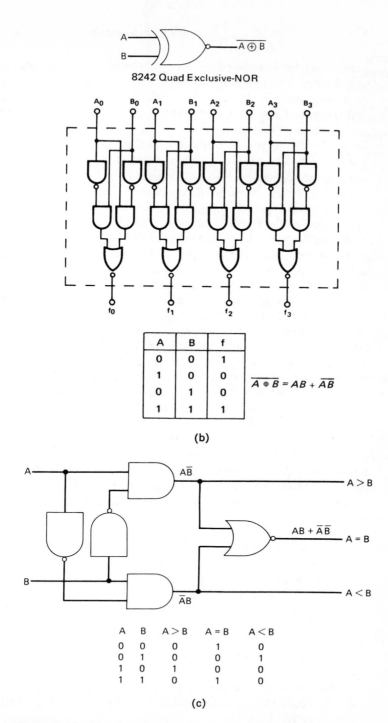

8242 Quad Exclusive-NOR

A	B	f
0	0	1
1	0	0
0	1	0
1	1	1

$$\overline{A \oplus B} = AB + \overline{A}\overline{B}$$

(b)

A	B	A > B	A = B	A < B
0	0	0	1	0
0	1	0	0	1
1	0	1	0	0
1	1	0	1	0

(c)

Figure 5–16 (Continued)

non-equal cases may be determined by noting the logic level at the output. The output is 1 when $A = 1$ or $B = 1$ but not when both are 1 at the same time or when both are 0 at the same time. The mere addition of a logic inversion following the Exclusive-OR results in a circuit which can determine if the inputs are equal or unequal.

Negating the Exclusive-OR expression and simplifying the resulting expression $\overline{A\overline{B} + \overline{A}B}$ yield $AB + \overline{A}\overline{B}$. When A and B are both 1 or both 0, the logic value of the negated Exclusive-OR operation is 1. This is sometimes called the *Equality*, or *Exclusive-NOR*, operation. Details of the Equality operation are shown in Figure 5–16(b).

An application of the Equality circuit is found in the digital computer. The values of variables are quite often compared and the results used to determine future computer action. For example, if A is less than B, the computer is instructed to do a specific program step. If A is greater than B, it must do a different step. When $A = B$, yet another "branching instruction" is required. So far, logic circuitry to determine $A = B$ or $A \neq B$ has been discussed. Determination of the relative magnitude ($A < B$ or $A > B$) is left to logic circuitry that is called a *comparator*.

Actually, the Exclusive-NOR circuit is capable of furnishing all three of the comparisons mentioned above, provided it is implemented as in the logic circuit of Figure 5–16(c). As shown in the accompanying table, $A > B$ is 1 only when $A = 1$ and $B = 0$, $A = B$ is 1 when A and B are both either 0 or 1, and $A < B$ is 1 only when $A = 0$ and $B = 1$. This is a relatively simple circuit, as it compares only two single-digit numbers.

When comparators are used in computers, they must be capable of comparing multi-digit numbers, and the logic circuitry becomes quite complex. A comparator that determines the relative magnitude of two 3-bit binary numbers is shown in Figure 5–17. The accompanying table lists circuit outputs for the magnitude relationships between A and B. The function of each gate is listed below.

G_1 Determines equality of the most-significant digits in A and B. A HIGH output indicates $A_2 = B_2$.

G_2 Same as G_1 except A_1 and B_1.

G_3 Same as G_1 except A_0 and B_0.

G_4 Determines if $A_2 > B_2$ ($A_2 = 1$ and $B_2 = 0$). A HIGH output means $A_2 > B_2$.

G_5 Determines if $A_1 > B_1$ ($A_1 = 1$ and $B_1 = 0$) and $A_2 = B_2$. A HIGH output results if the gate is activated by the above conditions.

G_6 Determines if $A_0 > B_0$ ($A_0 = 1$ and $B_0 = 0$), $A_2 = B_2$, and $A_1 = B_1$. A HIGH output means the gate has been activated by all of the above conditions.

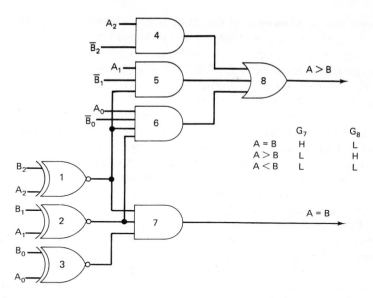

	G_7	G_8
A = B	H	L
A > B	L	H
A < B	L	L

Figure 5–17 3-Bit comparator.

G_7 ANDs the outputs of all three Equality gates to furnish an overall HIGH indication that $A = B$. A LOW output signifies $A \neq B$.

G_8 ORs the output of comparison gates G_4, G_5, and G_6, so that a HIGH output results if an $A_n B_n$ combination of $A = 1$ and $B = 0$ is present. A LOW output is interpreted as $A < B$.

Circuit operation of the 3-bit comparator is summarized as follows.

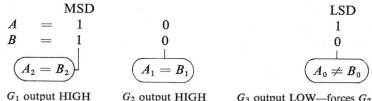

	MSD		LSD
A =	1	0	1
B =	1	0	0

$\left(A_2 = B_2 \right)$ $\left(A_1 = B_1 \right)$ $\left(A_0 \neq B_0 \right)$

G_1 output HIGH G_2 output HIGH G_3 output LOW—forces G_7 output LOW
G_4 output LOW G_5 output LOW G_6 output HIGH—allows G_8 output to be HIGH; $A > B$ due to $A_0 > B_0$

Parity

The constant movement of digital data both within digital machines and from machine to machine requires very close to 100% accuracy. If the 15-bit computer word 000001000000000 is used to represent the amount of $512 to be written as a payroll check, any error in transmission can dramatically affect the actual face value of the check. Just a single 0 changed to a 1 by noise during movement of the data, as in 000001100000000, results in a value of $768. Increasing reliability of solid-state logic devices is helping to attain high accuracy, but external influences in the transmission path commonly cause errors to develop. Duplication of the system, using a different transmission path and then comparing both sets of data, is another, though expensive, way of increasing accuracy.

One of the common and relatively inexpensive methods of insuring data movement accuracy is the addition of a standardizing, or *parity*, bit at the end of each word. It is arbitrarily determined that all data words will contain either an even or an odd number of ones. If the standard, or parity, is an *even number of ones*, it is said that *even parity* is being used. If an *odd number of ones* is required to meet the standard, *odd parity* is the name applied to the standardizing system.

Prior to movement of a data word, the number of ones in the word is determined. For an odd parity system, if the number of ones is even, a one is placed in the final or 16th position. Thus a 16-bit word is formed so that the data is moved with an odd number of ones present. When received, the number of ones is again determined. If an odd number of ones is present, it is assumed that the data word has been moved correctly. If an even number of ones is detected, a warning is provided that the transferred data is *not* correct.

It should be noted that this type of parity system is only effective in detecting an odd number of zeros which have changed to ones—that is, 1, 3, 5, etc. A simple 4-bit parity detector/generator, along with its algebraic expression and truth table, is shown in Figure 5–18. Each Exclusive-OR gate is effectively an even parity generator for the two inputs. Parity generation for a 4-bit word thus requires one Exclusive-OR gate for each pair of inputs plus a third Exclusive-OR gate to compare the outputs of the first two gates.

The four bits of the binary word to be transmitted are applied to A, B, C, and D, respectively. Parity is checked, and if an odd number of ones is detected (as it will be if the input is $A\bar{B} + \bar{A}B$), the output of the parity generator becomes one. A one is then attached as a fifth bit to the transmitted word. If an even number of ones is detected ($AB + \bar{A}\bar{B}$), a zero is attached. The circuit that adds the parity bit is not shown.

Parity systems capable of detecting and even correcting multiple errors in transmitted data are presently in use. They are beyond the scope of this text and are not discussed.

Recognition Circuits

Another broad group of decision-making circuits concern themselves with *recognition* of a prescribed set of conditions. For example, G_2 in Figure 5–3 *recognizes* the fact that FFs D, C, and B are in the SET state and allows the clock pulse to SET FF A. Furthermore, the *reset gate* in the IC package

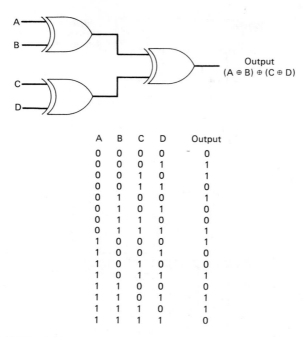

A	B	C	D	Output
0	0	0	0	0
0	0	0	1	1
0	0	1	0	1
0	0	1	1	0
0	1	0	0	1
0	1	0	1	0
0	1	1	0	0
0	1	1	1	1
1	0	0	0	1
1	0	0	1	0
1	0	1	0	0
1	0	1	1	1
1	1	0	0	0
1	1	0	1	1
1	1	1	0	1
1	1	1	1	0

Figure 5–18   4-Bit parity detector/generator.

of Figure 5–8 *recognizes* the binary equivalent of the counter modulus to reset the counter. These circuits are usually constructed either integral to the IC or by using separate IC gate packages.

In the CONTROL section of the computer it becomes necessary to inspect computer words and determine what information is present. The *instruction decoder*, which examines the OP-CODE portion of the computer word, uses decision-making circuits to determine what coded indication is present in the word. Since each instruction consists of a unique combination of ones and zeros, it is necessary to use a separate combination of gates to recognize each instruction. As an example, consider the *simplified* instruction decoder in Figure 5–19(a). A 4-bit instruction is stored in the instruction register, and the decoder is connected to each of the register stages. The decoder examines the four inputs and activates the 1-of-16 outputs that correspond to the input combination present. Figure 5–19(b) is a logic diagram of a typical 1-of-16 decoder in IC form.

The IC decodes four binary coded inputs to 1-of-16 mutually exclusive outputs when enabled by G_1 and G_2. Each of the 16 output gates requires HIGH inputs for activation, and since they are NAND gates, the activated output is LOW. The accompanying truth table explains the decoder's operation.

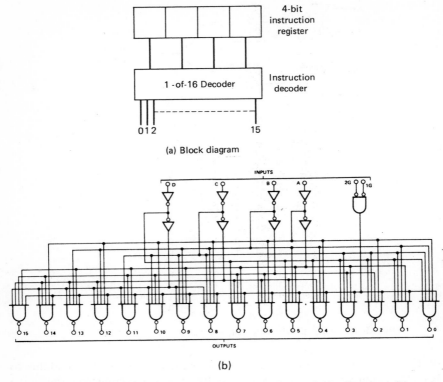

(a) Block diagram

(b)

Figure 5–19 Simplified instruction decoder; (a) block diagram, (b) logic diagram, 1-of-16 decoder (courtesy of Signetics, Sunnyvale, CA).

If the computer word contains more than four bits in the instruction, it is necessary to furnish greater decoding capability to realize the complete available capability.

Similar decoding requirements exist in the OUTPUT section, where the internal binary information must be changed to a form that the human user can apply. A common approach to simple information display uses either a 7-segment or a 16-segment synthesis of letters, numbers, and symbols. Figure 5–20(a) shows, for example, how numbers may be formed from seven separate lighted segments.

Activation of the 7-segment display depends on converting the binary information into the proper combination of lighted segments. A logic diagram of a BCD-to-7 segment decoder is shown in Figure 5–20(b). The decoder also incorporates a blanking circuit to suppress chip operation and a lamp test control to turn on all segments. A truth table (Figure 5–20(c)) completely explains the decoder's operation. Each line on the table should be investigated to insure that the proper segments are illuminated to form the desired number.

Conversion Circuits

The BCD-to-7 segment decoder of Figure 5–20 more properly belongs to a class of decision-making circuits called *converters*. For the purpose of this book, *converters change information from one form to another.* Converters are required at numerous places throughout the computer, especially at the INPUT and OUTPUT sections. The BCD-to-7 segment decoder

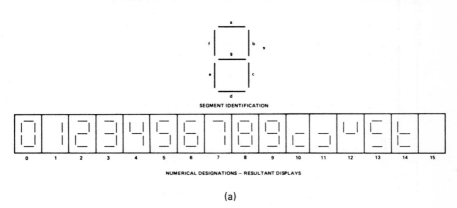

(a)

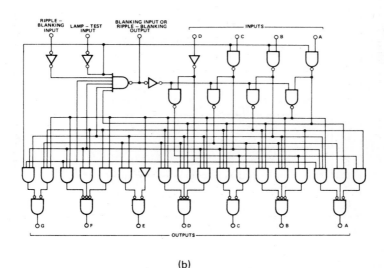

(b)

Figure 5–20 BCD-to-7 Segment Decoder; (a) segment identification, (b) logic diagram (courtesy of Signetics, Sunnyvale, CA).

FUNCTION	LT	RBI	D	C	B	A	BI/RBO	a	b	c	d	e	f	g
0	1	1	0	0	0	0	1	1	1	1	1	1	1	0
1	1	x	0	0	0	1	1	0	1	1	0	0	0	0
2	1	x	0	0	1	0	1	1	1	0	1	1	0	1
3	1	x	0	0	1	1	1	1	1	1	1	0	0	1
4	1	x	0	1	0	0	1	0	1	1	0	0	1	1
5	1	x	0	1	0	1	1	1	0	1	1	0	1	1
6	1	x	0	1	1	0	1	0	0	1	1	1	1	1
7	1	x	0	1	1	1	1	1	1	1	0	0	0	0
8	1	x	1	0	0	0	1	1	1	1	1	1	1	1
9	1	x	1	0	0	1	1	1	1	1	0	0	1	1
10	1	x	1	0	1	0	1	0	0	0	1	1	0	1
11	1	x	1	0	1	1	1	0	0	1	1	0	0	1
12	1	x	1	1	0	0	1	0	1	0	0	0	1	1
13	1	x	1	1	0	1	1	1	0	0	1	0	1	1
14	1	x	1	1	1	0	1	0	0	0	1	1	1	1
15	1	x	1	1	1	1	1	0	0	0	0	0	0	0
BI	x	x	x	x	x	x	0	0	0	0	0	0	0	0
RBI	1	0	0	0	0	0	0	0	0	0	0	0	0	0
LT	0	x	x	x	x	x	1	1	1	1	1	1	1	1

INPUTS — OUTPUTS

(c)

Figure 5–20 (c) truth table (Continued)

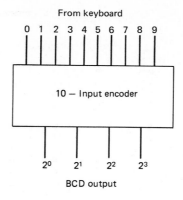

(a) Input converter — decimal-to-BCD

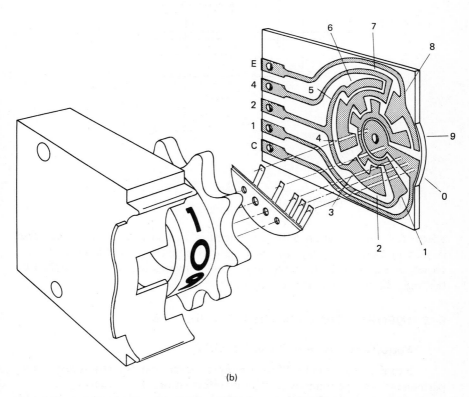

(b)

Figure 5–21 Input conversion; (a) input converter, decimal-to-BCD, (b) decimal-to-BCD switch (courtesy of the Digitran Company, Pasadena, CA), (c) decimal-to-binary conversion logic diagram.

Decimal	Binary			
	2^3	2^2	2^1	2^0
0	0	0	0	0
1	0	0	0	1
2	0	0	1	0
3	0	0	1	1
4	0	1	0	0
5	0	1	0	1
6	0	1	1	0
7	0	1	1	1
8	1	0	0	0
9	1	0	0	1

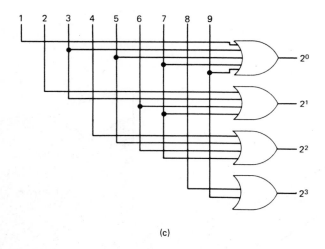

(c)

Figure 5-21   (Continued)

adequately represents an output application. A converter used at the input
is seen in Figure 5-21(a). *Decimal input* is converted mechanically by the
switch of Figure 5-21(b), while logic level conversions are accomplished by
the logic diagram of Figure 5-21(c).

5-3 INFORMATION-HANDLING CIRCUITS

Requirements and Classification

Requirements exist within the digital computer for temporary, semi-
permanent, and permanent storage of information. The stored information
must also be manipulated internal to the computer during most computer
operations. These functions may be accomplished by computer logic circuits
called *registers*, although semi-permanent and permanent storage are usually
accomplished by *memory* devices (Chapter 8).

A *register* is a group of logic circuits, usually flip-flops (FFs), arranged in a manner that allows storage and processing of information in binary form. The number of FFs in a register is determined by the requirements of the specific application. For example, a register in a small digital computer might have 16 stages, since a word (which is the unit of information handled by many "minicomputers") contains 16 bits.

A *storage register retains information*, while a *shift register processes information*. Registers may be further classified in terms of the input-output methods used. Information is entered into and taken from most registers sequentially bit-by-bit (*serial form*) or all bits at once (*parallel form*). If information is entered and removed in serial form, the device is categorized as *serial-serial*. If entered and removed in parallel form, the classification is *parallel-parallel*. The *serial-parallel* and *parallel-serial* designations (similarly defined) are commonly encountered.

The Storage Register

Each FF in a register can store one piece of binary information (one bit). When storage registers must store more than one bit at a time, additional FFs are used. The interconnections between FFs determine the functional and input/output characteristics of the register. Storage registers are used in applications where *temporary storage* of information is needed, as in digital computers where data from the computer's memory is transferred temporarily to a storage register before it is distributed to other functional parts of the computer.

In equipment requiring storage register functions, prepackaged IC registers are very common. A typical IC buffer register (Figure 5–22(a)) is an array of ten clocked *D* FFs which may be used in any parallel input-parallel output application. *Buffer register* is a term often used to describe a register which serves as a temporary store in transferring information between two units which are asynchronous, operating at different speeds, or performing independent tasks. The logic diagram of Figure 5–22(b) shows that two groups of five *D* FFs with separated clock inputs are provided to add to the versatility of the package.

A practical, though ficticious, computer application of the typical buffer register is shown in Figure 5–22(c). All of the instructions for solution of a problem and the data required for the problem are placed in the computer memory prior to actually performing the steps of the problem. The computer works in an automatic sequential manner (unless told to change the sequence), selecting one step after the other and performing the operations required, working toward the problem solution. Information required to perform the operations is contained in the computer word. One type of computer word consists of 16 bits, divided so the first six bits define what action is to be taken (the operation), and the other ten bits define the address of the data that is to be operated on (the operand). Each word is removed

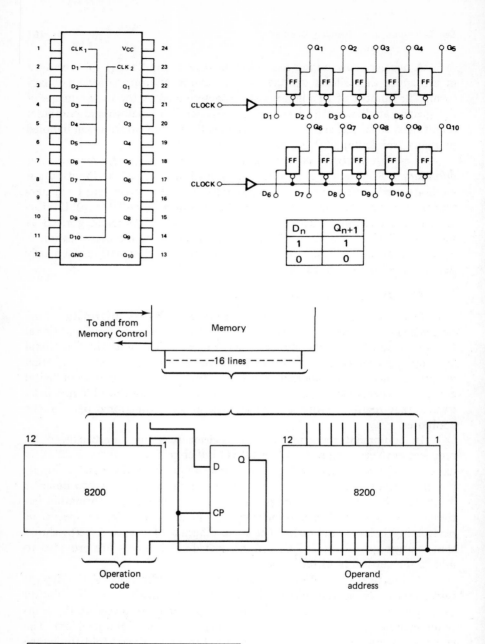

Figure 5–22 Type 8200 buffer register; (a) package diagram, (b) logic diagram, (c) Memory Buffer Register (courtesy of Signetics, Sunnyvale, CA).

from memory and placed in a storage register until it is needed. This allows the memory to go on with its other business without being limited by waiting for computer operations to be performed.

Since the typical buffer register is available only in a 5-bit configuration, an extra D FF is used as shown in Figure 5–22(c) to provide storage for the 16th bit of information. When the 16 bits of a computer word are to be loaded into the storage register (sometimes called the Memory Buffer Register), the memory supplies the logic levels to the 16 lines feeding the D input of each of the register stages. A clock pulse is generated by the memory (or memory control) to tell the register to accept the data, and the complete word is "dropped" in parallel into the Memory Buffer Register. The outputs of the register may now be fed elsewhere in the computer to perform various functions, and the memory may proceed with its next step. The Memory Buffer Register has provided the *parallel in-parallel out* storage register function.

The Shift Register

The *shift register* also fits into the overall class of registers, since it may be constructed of FFs and is used to operate on binary data. *Shift registers move data*, usually from one stage of the register to an adjacent stage. The movement, or shift, of data may be from left to right, right to left, or in both directions. Hence both *unidirectional* and *bidirectional* shift registers exist.

Shift registers differ from storage registers in that adjacent stages are connected to allow movement of data from stage to stage, whereas the storage register can only operate on data in one stage at a time. The shift register also may serve as a storage register when proper controls exist. Data may be loaded into the shift register in parallel, and read out of the register in parallel, just as in the storage register. However, the same shift register can also accept data one bit at a time (serial), move it from stage to stage until all data is in the register, and then store the data until ready for readout. The data may be read out one bit at a time (serial) or all bits at once (parallel). Properly designed, then, the shift register can perform all four input/output operations: serial-serial, serial-parallel, parallel-parallel, and parallel-serial.

A common application of the shift register is seen in the block diagram of Figure 5–23. An information display device such as the keyboard control of a digital computer (similar to an electric typewriter in form and operation) uses a multi-bit representation of each character to be displayed or entered. One particular representation often used for remote computer control employs an 8-bit code. This specific code is discussed in detail in Chapter 6. Each alphabetic, numeric, or control character is represented by a group of eight bits, all of which must be present at the same time (parallel). Transfer of data from one location to another requires eight separate lines, one for each bit. When sending and receiving locations are physically separated by great distances, the cost of multi-line transmission becomes prohibitive.

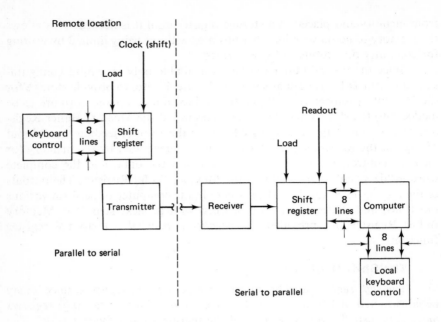

Figure 5–23   A shift register application to data transmission.

Shift registers allow transmission of the complete 8-bit character with only a single line. The eight bits resulting from actuating a key on the keyboard are stored in a shift register (eight stages) using parallel loading. As soon as loading is completed, the register is commanded to shift the data. One bit at a time is shifted from the register and converted for transmission. After the eighth bit is shifted out and converted, the register is ready to accept (in parallel) the next character.

At the receiving end, the 8-bit character is converted to logic levels and placed, one bit at a time, into another shift register. When all eight bits are received, the information is "read out" to the receiving device and displayed. Thus, at the sacrifice of speed of transmission, the requirement for eight transmission lines has been reduced to one, and cost of system implementation has been cut drastically.

Perhaps the simplest of shift registers is the *serial in-serial out* circuit shown in Figure 5–24. (The AND gate and READ OUT input should be disregarded at this time.) It consists of D FFs and requires only a logic level that represents the data to be moved into the register and a shift input. The CLEAR input is assumed to be activated just prior to arrival of the first shift input so that all stages begin operation in the CLEAR condition.

The output of a D FF is the same as its input *after* the occurrence of the CLOCK or SHIFT input. Thus when the D input to a FF is HIGH, the

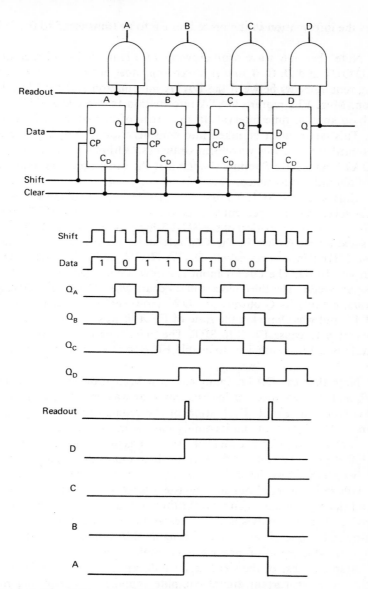

Figure 5–24 Shift register logic diagram and waveforms.

Q output is HIGH following the next clock pulse. The same is true of the LOW output. Note that the Q output of the A FF is the D input of the B FF. Whatever logic level is present at the Q output of the A FF appears at the Q output of the B FF upon occurrence of the shift pulse. Thus every shift pulse causes the information in the preceding FF to be transferred to the following FF.

Note that the waveform drawing of Figure 5–24 (disregarding the READ OUT and D, C, B, and A waveforms) does not really show the precise timing requirements between the DATA information and the SHIFT information. Most FFs require DATA information to precede SHIFT information by a specific time interval (in the order of nanoseconds in high-speed FFs). This factor must be taken into consideration during logic design but is assumed when using waveform drawings. Although the drawing shows the DATA and SHIFT inputs changing at the same time, the required finite time differential is assumed.

Thus when the SHIFT input goes HIGH to activate the FF, it uses the DATA level that was present just before the change in SHIFT input. The first HIGH-going transition of the SHIFT input occurs when DATA is LOW, and since all stages are in the CLEAR state, no change takes place. The second SHIFT input occurs with DATA HIGH, and FF A SETs, making its Q output HIGH. The DATA input has now been transferred to FF A from the input circuit. The third clock pulse occurs when DATA is LOW, and FF A clears, making its Q output go LOW. However, at the same time that the SHIFT input was changing the state of FF A, it was also using the HIGH Q output of A to cause FF B to SET. The finite time that it takes to change the state of a FF is sufficient to enable FF B to change before FF A changes state.

Note that the DATA input has now been transferred from FF A to FF B, and the new piece of information that was present on the input line is now stored in FF A. Evaluation of the remainder of the operations in Figure 5–24 shows that the incoming data is moved to the right one stage every time a shift pulse is provided. As soon as all of the data is loaded into the shift register, one bit at a time, it is shifted out of the "right-most" FF and may disappear unless the shift pulses are stopped. The usual mode of operation with serial in-serial out shift registers is to provide enough shift pulses to load the register and then stop shifting until a time when the output data is needed. The shift pulses are then restarted, and the data feeds from the right-most FF one bit at a time as long as shift pulses are present. Used in this manner, the register functions as a combination shift and storage register.

A special case of the serial-serial shift register is the *circulating register* which is used in certain digital computer applications requiring repetitive use of the same information. In the serial-serial shift register the information is shifted out the last stage and lost, while in the circulating register the last stage supplies its information back to the first stage so that it may be recirculated. The information being recirculated is also available at the output of the register for use in the rest of the circuit.

Conventional serial-serial shift registers may be used as circulating registers by providing input gating similar to that shown in Figure 5–25.

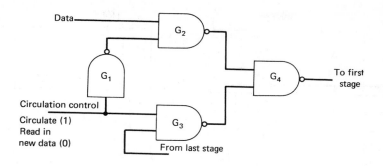

Figure 5–25 Circulating register input gating.

Input to the first stage of the register may be either original data or the data from the last stage of the register, as selected by the circulation control input. If HIGH, the circulation control input enables G_3 and allows data from the last stage to be fed through G_4 to the first stage of the register. G_2 is disabled by the LOW output of G_1. Changing the circulation control input to a LOW level disables G_3 and is inverted by G_1 to enable G_2 and allow the original data to be read in.

Serial in-parallel out register operation also may be implemented using the gates connected to each of the FFs' Q outputs. Data is shifted in until all desired information is stored. The readout operation is enabled prior to the next clock pulse and the information in each FF appears at the output of its respective output gate. No information is lost, and the register can continue its shifting operation as though nothing had happened. This operation is shown on the waveform diagram of Figure 5–24. It is representative of the type of register that would be used to convert the received serial data in the example of Figure 5-23 to the required parallel data for machine operation.

Parallel in-parallel out shift registers are somewhat uncommon and more properly fit into the storage register catagory. Coverage of this configuration was provided earlier.

J-K FFs are used to demonstrate the *parallel in-serial out* shift register in Figure 5–26. This type of circuit may also be used in the remote computer control unit of Figure 5–23 to convert the parallel keyboard data to serial form for transmission. The data to be entered is provided at the *A, B, C,* and *D* inputs. When the "enter" pulse arrives, whichever of the two control gates becomes enabled for each FF allows a pulse to be developed, and each FF will be placed in the state represented by the inputs. The FFs do not have to be CLEARed prior to entering information, since both the CLEAR and SET inputs are capable of being activated by the input levels. Following entry of the data, clock pulses may be applied to cause the shifting of the data toward the output. If a one has been entered in a FF, its Q output is

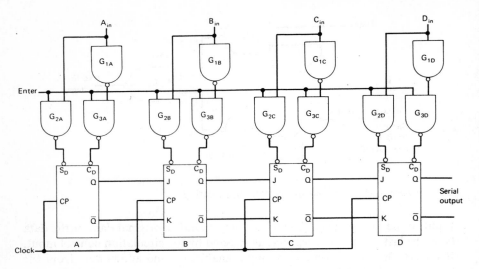

Figure 5–26   Parallel-serial shift register.

HIGH, enabling the following FF's J input. In a like manner, if a zero has been entered, the following FF will have its K input enabled. Due to the interconnections, both the J and K inputs cannot both be either zero or one, and the FF will respond to the next clock pulse by reproducing the state that was in the previous FF.

The wide use of registers in computers makes it feasible to provide packages usable in more than one of the operating modes. Figure 5–27(a) shows a 4-bit shift register with *both serial and parallel data entry* capability. Operation of the serial/parallel shift register is indicated by the logic diagram of Figure 5–27(b). The element is composed of four clocked master-slave FFs with D inputs. The D input of every stage can be switched between two logical sources by the Parallel Enable (PE) input. When the PE input is LOW, the D inputs of the four stages are connected to the parallel inputs P_0, P_1, P_2, and P_3. When the PE input is HIGH, the D inputs of the second, third, and fourth stages are connected to the outputs of the first, second, and third stages, respectively, thus forming a 4-bit shift register. The D input to the first stage (with PE HIGH) is obtained from the J and $\bar{K}$ inputs via gating elements to produce the action of the first stage as shown in Figure 5–27(b). All stages are set to zero when the master reset (MR) input is LOW, overriding the effects of any other input.

One additional important note: the $J\bar{K}$ input is the same as the more common JK input except that the LOW level activates the $\bar{K}$ input (as indicated by the circle at the $\bar{K}$ input shown in Figure 5–27(a)). The HIGH level activates the J input so that connecting the J and $\bar{K}$ inputs together results in a D-type input.

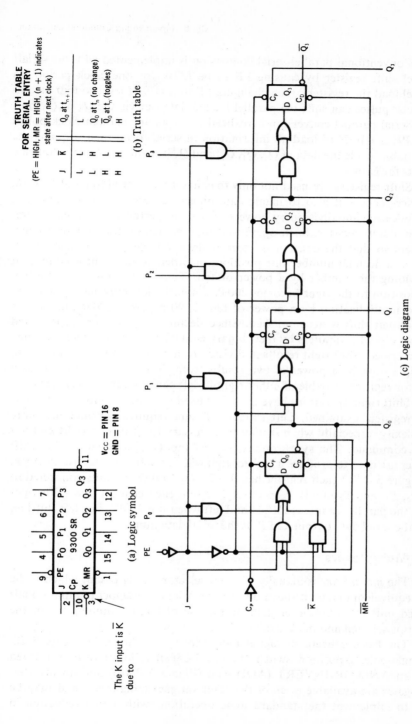

Figure 5-27 Type 9300 IC shift register; (a) logic symbol, (b) logic (courtesy of Fairchild Camera and Instrument Corp.).

159

Conventional parallel-serial conversion is implemented with the serial/parallel shift register by causing PE to be LOW for one clock period (to parallel load the register), then changing PE to a HIGH level so that incoming clock pulses can shift the parallel-loaded data out via the Q_3 or $\bar{Q}_3$ outputs. Serial-parallel conversion is realized by supplying enough clock pulses while PE is HIGH to load all information in serial form, then stopping the clock pulses while the data at Q_0, Q_1, Q_2, and Q_3 is made available to outside circuits for gating.

Shift registers are used not only to convert from serial to parallel form, and vice-versa, but also to manipulate binary representations of numbers. Multiplication and division by powers of two are performed on binary numbers in a shift register. Such operations may be demonstrated with decimal numbers so that the concept is more understandable. A movement of all digits in a decimal number one position, or order, to the right is equivalent to dividing the number by a power of ten. Thus 2000 moved, or shifted, one position to the right becomes 200.0. Similarly, left movement is equivalent to multiplication by a power of ten. 20.00 becomes 200.0 when a one position left shift is accomplished. Since decimal numbers are represented in most digital computers by their binary equivalent, similar operations may be performed. Shift right results in division by a power of two instead of ten. Multiplication by a power of two results from shift left operations. Thus a need for registers capable of either right or left shifting can be visualized.

Shift right operations have been discussed in detail in all of the previous shift registers examined. Left shifting of data requires considerably more complexity, especially when it may be necessary to shift *both* right and left upon command. The synchronous parallel inputs of a serial/parallel shift register are used to produce a register that will shift left or right on each clock. In Figure 5–27(c) each register has the Q_1, Q_2, and Q_3 outputs connected to the P_0, P_1, and P_2 inputs, respectively, so that each element now shifts right when the parallel enable is HIGH and left when it is LOW. For left shifting, Q_0 is the serial data output and P_3 is the serial data input.

Multiplexers

The *multiplexer* is actually a signal selector gating circuit which is the logic equivalent of a multi-position selector switch. A number of input signals are fed into the multiplexer, and by the use of control inputs, one of the signals is selected and made available at the output.

The basic concept of digital data selection is shown in Figure 5–28. A single-pole, 2-position switch (Figure 5–28(a)) is logically implemented with an AND-OR-INVERT (AOI) gate (Figure 5–28(b)) and an inverter. AOI gates are available in all of the common packaging forms and may be used to implement the standard logic operations with actual reduction in

(a) Single-pole, 2-position swtich

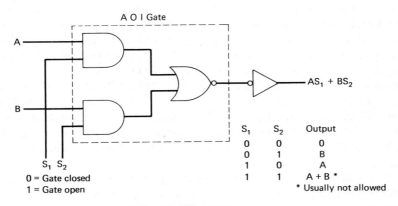

S_1	S_2	Output
0	0	0
0	1	B
1	0	A
1	1	A + B *

* Usually not allowed

S_1 S_2
0 = Gate closed
1 = Gate open

(b) Logic implementation

Figure 5–28   Multiplexer switching concept.

cost and package count in some cases. The accompanying truth table defines the operation of the *2-input multiplexer*. As is shown, the output of the multiplexer is either *A* or *B*, depending on the logic level at the control inputs S_1 and S_2. When both controls are HIGH at the same time, the conventional OR operation is performed, and this is usually not considered a multiplexer operation.

As it becomes necessary to accommodate more inputs, the requirements for control signals can become restrictive. For example, if eight inputs must be switched by a multiplexer, eight control signals are necessary, and the number of connections for inputs and outputs exceed the capability of a standard 16-pin IC package. This problem is solved by using different combinations of control inputs to perform selection. Eight different control signals may be derived from only three control inputs by using all possible combinations of one and zero that exist with three variables.

The IC multiplexer in Figure 5–28(c) uses this concept. Selection of I_2, for example, is made by an address of $A_2 = 0$, $A_1 = 1$, and $A_0 = 1$. G_2 is then enabled so that the information on input line I_2 is fed to the output NOR gate G_8. Both true and complemented outputs are provided and may be inhibited to provide a constant zero at both outputs. The truth table accompanying Figure 5–28(c) defines the operation of the 8-input digital multiplexer.

5–4 SUMMARY

The circuits discussed in Chapter 5 appear throughout the computer. Counting and timing circuits establish basic computer cycle times in the CONTROL section, control information input and output rates, help perform arithmetic operations, and govern MEMORY functions. Decision-making circuits determine information validity at key transfer points in all computer sections, decode instructions in the CONTROL section, determine numerical and logical relationships in the ARITHMETIC/LOGIC section, and perform information conversions in both INPUT and OUTPUT sections. Information-handling circuits temporarily store information in all sections of the computer, perform arithmetic/logic operations in the ARITH-METIC/LOGIC section, and route information from section to section internal to the computer.

Two general types of circuits are conspicuous by their absence. First, logic circuits that perform arithmetic operations have been purposely left out. These circuits are used only in the ARITHMETIC/LOGIC section and are more appropriately discussed there. Second, memory circuits that store information in more than one-word quantities or that may be classed as semi-permanent or permanent storage are discussed in Chapter 8. A tendency is developing in modern computers to scatter memory assemblies throughout the functional sections, but greater continuity is established by restricting detailed memory discussions to one chapter.

QUESTIONS

1. What is a counter? Discuss its composition, construction, and functions.
2. Identify the difference between synchronous and asynchronous counters.
3. Draw a logic diagram of a 4-stage asynchronous UP counter using $R\text{-}S$ flip-flops.
4. Draw a logic diagram of a 4-stage synchronous DOWN counter using $J\text{-}K$ flip-flops.
5. How is bi-directional counting accomplished?
6. Define "modulus."
7. Using the diagram of Figure 5-8, draw a diagram of a divide-by-6 and a divide-by-3 counter.
8. What is a BCD counter? List three possible applications.
9. Discuss the operation of a ring counter.
10. Draw the symbol for a *one-shot* and explain its operation.

11. Where are Exclusive-OR circuits used? Exclusive-NOR circuits?
12. Explain the use of *parity* in digital computers and show a logic diagram of a simple parity detector.
13. What is a decoder? Where would it be used?
14. Define "register."
15. List the differences between storage and shift registers; the similarities.
16. Show an application of a storage register.
17. Show an application of a shift register.
18. Define "multiplexer."
19. Show an application of a multiplexer.

6

Communicating with the Computer

6–1 BASIC CONCEPTS

Before discussing detailed operation of digital computers, it is necessary to understand how information is presented to the computer and how the computer makes information available to the user. The starting point must be, of course, at the level that the computer can work with, the binary symbols 1 and 0. Although a digital computer may use binary representation throughout, when it becomes necessary for man to intervene, the information representation must be in a form that is easily interpreted. That is, the input of information to the device and the output of information from the device must be in other than conventional binary form.

A way of satisfying this requirement is to assign a unique combination of ones and zeros to each number, letter, or symbol that must be represented. Such representations are called *codes*. Many digital devices employ one form of code on input, other forms internally, and possibly still a different form for output. Despite the numerous codes used in digital computers it should be recognized that all operations within the heart of the computer are of a binary nature. *The only purpose of the external codes is convenience for the user.* The most efficient use of the computer's capabilities and hardware is at the binary level. Each of the storage cells in memory can be used, and maximum advantage taken of control capabilities. Binary-level computer operations, however, require that the user be intimately familiar with Boolean algebra, binary mathematics, computer logic, computer organization, etc. Such requirements greatly restrict the use of digital computers. By using binary coded representations of common characters and supplying conversion devices to change the *user-oriented* codes to binary codes, it is possible to extend digital computer applications to every user. Of course, much more hardware, both at the input/output and memory level, is needed. Modern digital computers, using advanced integrated circuit (IC) techniques, possess the capability to use English-language-oriented codes and programs at maximum effectiveness.

Even when troubleshooting, which must be at the binary level, modern techniques are allowing the use of English-language-oriented codes. Effective troubleshooting requires isolation of defective components to the smallest replaceable device, which is usually a plug-in module in modern digital computers. (More detailed isolation of defective components may be accomplished at a repair facility with assembly/disassembly capability.) Most plug-in modules contain many complex ICs, and each of the ICs must be exercised to determine if it properly responds to input signals. Binary inputs, of course, are required. If, however, conversion devices in the form of dedicated hardware or portions of memory storing troubleshooting programs are employed, once again English-language-oriented codes may be used to locate defective components. In some cases, an output device may print the location of the defective module when located by troubleshooting efforts. Some mammoth multi-million dollar computers are even designed with spare modules included. When a malfunction occurs, the spare module is automatically switched into action, and the defective module identified.

First we will discuss codes that are used to represent numbers and then

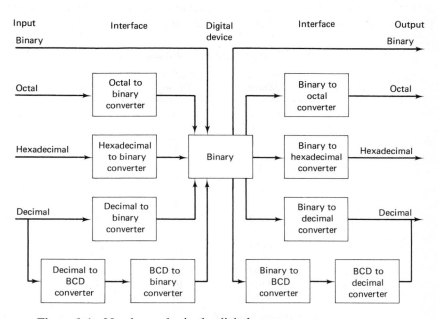

Figure 6–1   Number codes in the digital computer.

proceed to more complex codes which represent letters and symbols in addition to the decimal digits. Since it was shown in Chapter 3 that decimal numbers may easily be represented in binary form, it should be recognized that, with adequate converters, decimal numbers may be presented at the input of the computer and end up in binary form internal to the computer. Actually, many different internal-external code combinations are possible. Figure 6–1 shows some of the various forms of number codes possible in a digital computer.

The need for number representation in digital computers is almost obvious, since the digital computer was initially designed to perform mathematical operations. Extension of mathematical and logic techniques, combined with the concepts of programming, allows alphabetical, punctuation, and special characters to be manipulated with ease in the modern digital computer. Common computer codes are shown in this chapter.

6–2 REPRESENTING NUMBERS WITH BINARY-RELATED RADIX CODES

Three related number systems (binary, octal, and hexadecimal) may be used to represent numbers in digital equipment. Table 6–1 shows the relationship between these systems. Positional notation, binary-to-decimal conversion, and decimal-to-binary conversion should be reviewed in preparation for discussion of other number systems.

Table 6–1 Binary and Related Radix Codes

Decimal	Radix 2 Binary	Radix 8 Octal	Radix 16 Hexadecimal
0	0	0	0
1	1	1	1
2	10	2	2
3	11	3	3
4	100	4	4
5	101	5	5
6	110	6	6
7	111	7	7
8	1000	10	8
9	1001	11	9
10	1010	12	A
11	1011	13	B
12	1100	14	C
13	1101	15	D
14	1110	16	E
15	1111	17	F
16	10000	20	10

The Octal System

Numbers are stored within a computer in binary form, but the input/output devices and the storage areas may be arranged in such a manner that the number can be represented in another number system quite easily. The *octal* (base 8) number system, for example, is closely related to the binary system. Representation of the basic digits of the octal system (0 through 7) is easily accomplished with three binary digits. In fact, if any binary number is separated into groups of three digits, the octal number is immediately obtained. Limiting each group to three binary digits provides equivalent octal digits from 0 to 7, which is the range of the octal system. *Note the use of positional notation* in Example 6–1.

Example 6–1.

What is the octal equivalent of 101_2?

Solution:

$$101 = 1 \times 2^2 + 0 \times 2^1 + 1 \times 2^0 = 4 + 1 = 5_8.$$

Example 6–2.

What is the octal equivalent of 110101_2?

Solution:

$$\begin{array}{cc} 110 & 101 \\ 6 & 5 \end{array} = 65_8$$

Conversion from *octal* to *binary* is the reverse process. The three binary digits representing each octal digit are written, starting with the least-significant digit first.

Example 6–3.

What is the binary equivalent of 65_8?

Solution:

$$\begin{array}{cc} 6 & 5 \\ 110 & 101 \end{array} = 110101_2$$

The relationship between the binary and octal number systems is diagramed in Figure 6–2.

The octal number system is used for digital data processing input and output devices. Ease of encoding and decoding numbers makes the octal system the ideal choice for "minimum hardware" input and output applications. However, recent advances in semiconductor technology and IC availability are moving away from octal operations. Converting binary

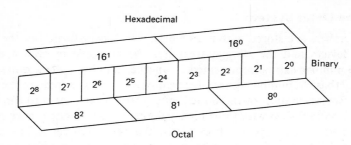

Figure 6-2   Binary, octal, and hexadecimal number system relationships.

to decimal and vice-versa no longer requires extensive hardware and excessive storage space. As existing digital equipment is updated, it is anticipated that octal operations will gradually disappear in favor of the more easily manipulated decimal input and output devices.

The Hexadecimal Code

Some digital computers handle numbers in groups of four binary digits. One code used to represent the sets of four digits is the *hexadecimal* (base 16) number system. Sixteen numbers are representable in the hexadecimal system, and additional symbols are required to designate digits greater than nine. Table 6-1 shows a commonly employed set of symbols for the hexadecimal number system.

Conversion from binary to hexadecimal is conveniently performed by grouping the binary number into sets of four digits and determining the equivalent value using Table 6-1.

Example 6-4.

What is the hexadecimal equivalent of 1010_2?

Solution:

$$1010 = 1 \times 2^3 + 0 \times 2^2 + 1 \times 2^1 + 0 \times 2^0$$
$$= 8 + 0 + 2 + 0$$
$$= A_{16}$$

Example 6-5.

What is the hexadecimal equivalent of 10011010_2?

Solution:

$$\begin{array}{cc} 1001 & 1010 \\ 9 & A \end{array} = 9A_{16}$$

The process is reversed when converting from hexadecimal to binary. The four binary digits representing each hexadecimal number are written starting with the least-significant digit first.

Example 6–6.

What is the binary equivalent of $9A_{16}$?

Solution:

$$
\begin{array}{cc}
9 & A \\
1001 & 1010 = 10011010_2
\end{array}
$$

The relationship between the binary, octal, and hexadecimal number systems is diagramed in Figure 6–2.

The hexadecimal system will continue to find widespread use in the so-called character-organized digital computers. Engineers, technicians, and programmers who work closely with computers find no difficulty using this non-decimal number system. Conversion hardware is reduced in these cases without loss of utility. However, when information must be displayed for the non-computer-oriented user, the decimal system is employed.

6–3 REPRESENTING NUMBERS WITH BCD CODES

Introduction to BCD

One of the major problems facing the engineer, technician, programmer, and user of digital computers is the conversion of a code readily handled by man to a code readily handled by equipment. Most people can work with a decimal code, while digital machines work most effectively with binary codes.

A solution to the problem is found in the use of binary-coded-decimal (BCD) codes. The fact that ten unique symbols are used to represent the decimal number system dictates a requirement for means to represent these symbols in terms of only two unique symbols (the binary number system). In other words, ten unique combinations of two symbols must be found. Previous discussion has shown that the possible combinations of the two symbols of the binary number system are an integer power of 2—that is, 2^0, 2^1, 2^2, etc. Thus some integer power of 2 must be used that will allow at least ten combinations of binary digits (bits) to exist. Ten is greater than 2^3 but less than 2^4, so four bits must be employed to obtain the ten combinations. This results in 16 combinations, six of which are not used. Any ten of the combinations may be used, and the specific combination used results in a particular type of BCD code. Each decimal digit, then, is represented by a combination of four binary digits. The decimal number 345 may be represented in BCD by 0011 0100 0101. In binary, 345_{10} is represented as

101011001. Note that only nine bits are required for the binary representation, while 12 bits are required for the BCD form. However, it is easier to recognize the BCD form. The extra three bits is the price paid for ease of representation.

BCD codes may be classified as either *weighted* or *unweighted* codes. The weighted codes follow a positional notation structure. Positional values do not necessarily have to be ascending powers of 2; they may be arbitrarily assigned. In unweighted codes the digit positions do not indicate the relative value of the represented number.

8-4-2-1 Weighted BCD Code

The most common weighted BCD code is the natural 8-4-2-1 code. The most-significant digit possesses a weight of 8, the next most-significant digit a weight of 4, etc. Correlation between decimal digits and the 8-4-2-1 BCD representation is shown in Table 6–2. All that is required to convert an 8-4-2-1 BCD number to a decimal number or vice-versa is a slight familiarity with the binary number system. Remember, each decimal digit is represented by four binary digits, weighted in an 8-4-2-1 order.

Example 6–7.

Convert 1001 0101 (BCD 8-4-2-1) to a decimal number.

Solution:

$$1001 \quad 0101$$
$$9 \qquad 5 \quad = 95_{10}$$

Example 6–8.

Convert 95_{10} to a BCD (8-4-2-1) number.

Solution:

$$9 \qquad 5$$
$$1001 \quad 0101 = 1001 \ 0101$$

Table 6–2   BCD Codes

Decimal	Natural 8421	2421	Excess 3 (XS3)	Gray	2-out-of-5
0	0000	0000	0011	0000	00011
1	0001	0001	0100	0001	00101
2	0010	0010	0101	0011	00110
3	0011	0011	0110	0010	01001
4	0100	0100	0111	0110	01010
5	0101	1011	1000	0111	01100
6	0110	1100	1001	0101	10001
7	0111	1101	1010	0100	10010
8	1000	1110	1011	1100	10100
9	1001	1111	1100	1101	11000

Some digital computers actually operate in a BCD mode, and it can be shown that arithmetic operations may be performed directly in BCD without conversion to binary equivalents.

2-4-2-1 Weighted BCD Code

Another weighted BCD code that sees wide use in computers is the 2-4-2-1 code (Table 6–2). In this case the most-significant digit of the 4-bit representation of a decimal number has a weight of 2 rather than 8, as in the 8-4-2-1 code. The major advantage of the 2-4-2-1 code is that it is *self-complementing*. Any two numbers which add up to their radix minus 1 *complement* each other—that is, *are opposite*. Thus the 2-4-2-1 representation of 1 (0001) is the opposite of 8 (1110) and 0 (0000) is the opposite of 9 (1111). All BCD numbers represented in the 2-4-2-1 code have this property, and therefore the code is called self-complementing. Since one method of subtraction in a digital computer uses the minuend *added to* the complement of the subtrahend, the self-complementing feature is quite valuable.

Gray Code

Unweighted BCD codes find use in digital computers, measurement, data processing, and data transmission applications. When it becomes necessary to convert a physical paramater such as a shaft position on a motor, conventional codes become difficult to use. Mechanical construction methods place overly restrictive requirements on the encoding device. For example, if the conventional 8-4-2-1 BCD code is used, the encoding device *could* show a change in as many as four bit positions simultaneously (0111 to 1000). The *Gray code* has been devised to alleviate this problem. When transitioning from one number representation to the next, only one bit position changes. Table 6–2 shows the Gray code representation of the ten decimal digits, while Figure 6–3 shows a typical mechanical encoder using both 8-4-2-1 and Gray code methods. It should be apparent from these comparisons that Gray code implementation of BCD is preferable when minimum possibility of generating improper representation of numbers due to bit change is required. Also, since fewer bits must change for each advance, binary counters implemented with a Gray code tend to have less operating delay. The conversion complexity of the Gray code has limited its applications generally to the areas mentioned at the beginning of this section.

Excess 3 (XS3) Code

Another unweighted BCD code that is often encountered in digital computer applications is the XS3 code. It is characterized by being equivalent to the natural (8-4-2-1) BCD representation *plus* 3. Table 6–2 equates the XS3 code with decimal digits. Conversion from decimal to XS3 code may be accomplished by first converting to binary, then adding 3, or by adding 3 to the decimal number and then converting.

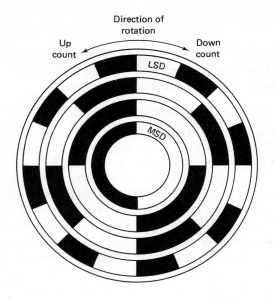

Dark areas represent conductive material and light areas insulative material.
Electrical connection to the disc is via wire brushes. A complete circuit (logic 1)
exists when a dark area is contacted; an open circuit (logic 0) exists when a light
area is contacted.

(a) 8-4-2-1 BCD encoder

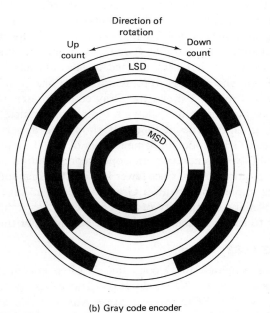

(b) Gray code encoder

Figure 6–3   Encoding binary codes; (a) 8-4-2-1 BCD encoder, (b) Gray
code encoder.

Example 6–9.

Convert 9_{10} to an XS3 coded number.

Solution:

$$9_{10} = \begin{array}{r} 1001 \\ +11 \\ \hline 1100 \end{array} \text{(XS3)} \qquad \text{or } 9 + 3 = 12 = 1100 \text{ (XS3)}$$

Example 6–10.

Convert 12_{10} to an XS3 number.

Solution:

1	2	decimal		1	2	decimal
				+3	+3	add 3
				4	5	
0001	0010	binary				
+11	+11	add 3				
0100	0101	XS3		0100	0101	XS3

Note that each decimal digit is converted separately. XS3-to-decimal conversion is essentially the reverse process. Each digit is converted to its decimal equivalent, and 3 is subtracted as shown in Example 6–11. The subtraction may also be performed at the binary level.

Example 6–11.

Convert 0100 0101 (XS3) to a decimal number.

Solution:

0100	0101	XS3		0100	0101	XS3
4	5			−11	−11	−3
−3	−3	−3		0001	0010	binary
1	2	decimal		1	2	decimal
	12_{10}				12_{10}	

The XS3 code is self-complementing, just as the 2-4-2-1 BCD code mentioned previously. In addition, the proper carry is *always* generated as though the XS3 number were in decimal form. Both of these characteristics make the XS3 code an excellent choice for arithmetic operations in digital computers. Since many digital measuring instruments are designed to interface directly with computers, the XS3 code may be encountered in this area of digital applications also.

2-out-of-5 Code

All of the BCD codes mentioned so far may be used in applications where number representations must be transmitted from one location to another, either within the digital device or to a remote location. Each of the codes may be implemented with one or more extra bits to establish a parity check, as discussed in Chapter 5. Another way of assuring correct transmission is to use an *exact count code*, where the total number of ones in each number representation is the same. The *2-out-of-5* code (Table 6–2) is an example. A pseudo-weighted BCD method (7-4-2-1) represents the ten decimal digits in the first four bit positions, while the final bit position is reserved for an exact count digit. The added digit in position five is selected so that each word has exactly two ones and three zeros. When decimal numbers are transmitted in this form, all single errors are detected. Any character received with less than or more than two ones is regarded as in error.

Conversion to and from the 2-out-of-5 code is relatively straightforward due to the pseudo-weighted format. However, it should be noted that the decimal digit 0 is represented in a non-weighted manner.

6–4 ALPHAMERIC CODES

Introduction

Codes discussed to this point have been used to represent only numerical data. When communicating information from one point to another, other data such as alphabetical characters and symbols is also commonly used. The concept of total numbers of possible combinations of binary digits is used to obtain representation of numbers, special symbols, and alphabetical characters (called alphameric representation).

As may have been noted in earlier sections of this chapter, a direct correlation *may not* exist between a number and its representation in binary digits. The Gray code, for example, adequately represents the decimal digits, but the position of the binary digits in the representation is unweighted. Code design was such that the important consideration was a single digit change from one representation to the next, *not* a consistent value for each bit position. Alphameric codes usually fall into the unweighted category, although in some codes a design pattern is noticeable.

5-Level Code

Four binary digits (bits) allow only 16 different combinations, which are insufficient for alphameric representations. Up to 32 different characters may be represented by five bits, which allows at least the 26 letters of the alphabet to be represented. If two of the 32 bits are reserved for the purpose of selecting one of two separate "sets" of information, then a total of 62 available combinations are obtained.

A 5-level code, developed by Jean Baudot (a French engineer) in the late 19th century, has been employed in data communication applications using a typewriter-like device called a Teletypewriter. The 26 letters of the alphabet are represented on the "lower case" set of information, while numbers, punctuation marks, and special symbols are represented by the "upper case" set.

The teletypewriter mechanism contains a group of switches which may be opened and closed by the depression of any key on the keyboard. Switch conditions may be translated into binary representation, such as 0 = open switch and 1 = closed switch. Actuation of each key then results in a specific combination of ones and zeros which is representative of the selected alphameric character. The switches operate in sequence, following a beginning synchronizing indication and followed by a "stop" indication. Of interest here are the switch conditions, not the start and stop methods.

The Baudot code is shown in Figure 6–4, correlated with a drawing of the perforated tape used with this and many other alphameric code devices. A black mark represents a hole in the tape (1), while an unmarked circle represent solid tape (0). Information to be transmitted from one location to another is usually prepared by "punching" a tape and transmitting large amounts of data at a time without interruption. Devices which read the tape sense a hole or a lack of a hole at each of the five hole locations and generate the appropriate binary digit to represent the selected character.

A 5-level code, then, is adequate for representing all alphabetical and numerical characters, in addition to a number of punctuation marks and special symbols. However, no means to determine the accuracy of the binary representation is possible with the 5-level code; that is, no *parity* is used. Of course, the code could be expanded to six bits to provide parity, but it is often necessary to communicate more than the minimal number of characters possible with five bits.

6-Level Code

A 6-level code, capable of 64 different combinations, easily supplies sufficient variety without the necessity of "upper case" and "lower case" control. One possible arrangement of a 6-level code is shown in Figure 6–5. Representation of letters and numbers in this code is of a BCD nature. The two most-significant bits (b_6 and b_5) are used to indicate that the next four bits that follow represent either numbers ($b_6 = 0$ and $b_5 = 0$), the *first* third of the alphabet ($b_6 = 1$ and $b_5 = 1$), the *second* third of the alphabet ($b_6 = 1$ and $b_5 = 0$), or the *final* third of the alphabet ($b_6 = 0$ and $b_5 = 1$). Each group is arranged in ascending BCD order (0 through 9) to match either

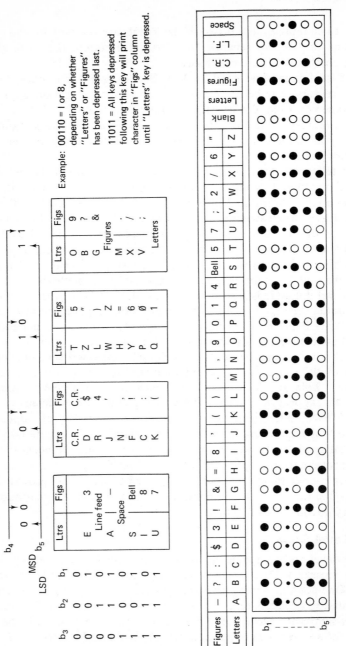

Figure 6-4 Baudot code.

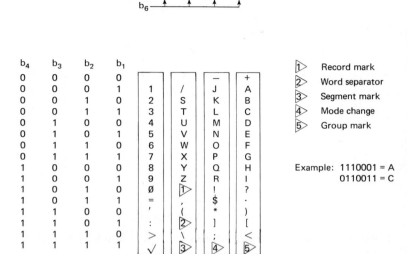

Figure 6–5 6- and 7-level Codes (6-level without parity; 7-level with Parity).

increasing numerical value or letters of the alphabet progressing from the first toward the last. Codes arranged in a sequential manner lend themselves well to computing applications. In fact, the 6-level code of Figure 6–5 is commonly used within computers and, when expanded to seven bits with a parity position, finds application in both magnetic tape and paper tape data systems. It should be noted at this time that codes are described by the number of bit positions, *whether or not* all of the bit positions are used to represent information. Thus, although the data representations are the same in both codes described in Figure 6–5, the addition of the parity bit resulted in reclassifying the code as a 7-level rather than a 6-level code.

7-Level Code

The use of seven data positions results in a total of 128 possible combinations. A code commonly used in digital control of industrial machines is shown in Figure 6–6. It is compatible with the standard code to be discussed shortly, which means that machine operation may be easily integrated with digital computers. Many blank areas appear where no characters are used, but this is a result of the compatibility requirement. This code is also expandable to eight bits for the purpose of parity-type error recognition.

b4	b3	b2	b1	b7 b6 b5 0 0 0	b7 b6 b5 0 0 1	b7 b6 b5 0 1 0	b7 b6 b5 0 1 1	b7 b6 b5 1 0 0	b7 b6 b5 1 0 1	b7 b6 b5 1 1 0	b7 b6 b5 1 1 1
0	0	0	0			Space	0		P		
0	0	0	1				1	A	Q		
0	0	1	0				2	B	R		
0	0	1	1				3	C	S		
0	1	0	0				4	D	T		
0	1	0	1			%	5	E	U		
0	1	1	0				6	F	V		
0	1	1	1				7	G	W		
1	0	0	0	BS		(	8	H	X		
1	0	0	1	HT		)	9	I	Y		
1	0	1	0	LF			:	J	Z		
1	0	1	1			+		K			
1	1	0	0					L			
1	1	0	1	CR		—		M			
1	1	1	0					N			
1	1	1	1			/		O			

* Expandable to 8-level if parity bit is used

Figure 6–6 7-level numerical control code (expandable to 8-level if parity bit is used).

The most commonly encountered 7-level (expandable to 8-level) code is called the United States of America Standard Code for Information Interchange (ASCII for short), and appears in Figure 6–7. It is sometimes called the ANSI (American National Standards Institute) code or the Data Interchange code. Any of the 128 locations may be described by a unique combination of high-order (b_7, b_6, and b_5) bit locations and low order (b_1, b_2, b_3, and b_4) locations. The ASCII code is quite versatile and is organized along logical lines. Note, for example, that the device using this code does not have to go beyond the two most-significant bits to determine whether the represented information is a control (both zeros) or a character (not both zeros).

Numerous variations of the ASCII code are in use, but most are compatible. The differences lie specifically in the area of names of the control functions and the actual symbol represented when neither letters, numbers, nor control functions are being used. Note that all 128 locations are used.

Expansion to eight bits allows either the use of parity checks or doubling of the number of characters that may be represented. Both uses of the eighth bit may be encountered.

8-Level Code

One final example of alphameric codes is the Extended Binary-Coded-Decimal Interchange Code (EBCDIC). It is a full 8-level code (see Figure

b4	b3	b2	b1	000	001	010	011	100	101	110	111
0	0	0	0	NUL	DLE	SP	0	@	P	`	p
0	0	0	1	SOH	DC1	!	1	A	Q	a,	q
0	0	1	0	STX	DC2	"	2	B	R	b	r
0	0	1	1	ETX	DC3	#	3	C	S	c	s
0	1	0	0	EOT	DC4	$	4	D	T	d	t
0	1	0	1	ENQ	NAK	%	5	E	U	e	u
0	1	1	0	ACK	SYN	&	6	F	V	f	v
0	1	1	1	BEL	ETB	'	7	G	W	g	w
1	0	0	0	BS	CAN	(	8	H	X	h	x
1	0	0	1	HT	EM	)	9	I	Y	i	y
1	0	1	0	LF	SUB	*	:	J	Z	j	z
1	0	1	1	VT	ESC	+	;	K	[	k	{
1	1	0	0	FF	FS	,	<	L	\	l	|
1	1	0	1	CR	GS	–	=	M	]	m	}
1	1	1	0	SO	RS	.	>	N	^	n	~
1	1	1	1	SI	US	/	?	O	_	o	DEL

(a) Basic 7-level ASCII code
b₁ . . . . . . b₂ Parity

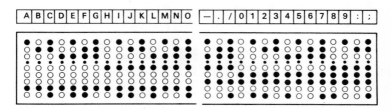

| A | B | C | D | E | F | G | H | I | J | K | L | M | N | O | — | . | / | 0 | 1 | 2 | 3 | 4 | 5 | 6 | 7 | 8 | 9 | : | ; |

(b) Tape sample showing 7-level code
expanded to 8 level by Parity position

Figure 6–7 ASCII code.

6–8), since each letter, number, symbol, or control function is represented by two BCD numbers, the equivalent of eight binary digits. A number of similarities are noted when comparing the EBCDIC with other codes discussed in this chapter. The BCD aspects of the letters and numbers are as explained in the 6-level code. Identification of control functions is easily made by checking the two most-significant digits as with the ASCII code. As an advantage over other codes, it can be seen that identification of symbols is also easy by investigating the two most-significant digits.

The EBCDIC is used when the data transmission and reception devices must interface with a computer that operates predominantly in the BCD

Figure 6-8 Extended Binary-Coded-Decimal Interchange Code (EBCDIC).

Column bit assignments: b0 b1 b2 b3 (columns 0–15). Row bit assignments: b4 b5 b6 b7 (rows 0–15).

Column → Row ↓	0 (0000)	1 (0001)	2 (0010)	3 (0011)	4 (0100)	5 (0101)	6 (0110)	7 (0111)	8 (1000)	9 (1001)	10 (1010)	11 (1011)	12 (1100)	13 (1101)	14 (1110)	15 (1111)
0 (0000)	NUL	DLE	DS		SP	&	-						{	}	\	0
1 (0001)	SOH	DC1	SOS				/		a	j	~		A	J		1
2 (0010)	STX	DC2	FS						b	k	s		B	K	S	2
3 (0011)	ETX	DC3							c	l	t		C	L	T	3
4 (0100)	PF	RES	BYP	PN					d	m	u		D	M	U	4
5 (0101)	HT	NL	LF	RS					e	n	v		E	N	V	5
6 (0110)	LC	BS	EOB	UC					f	o	w		F	O	W	6
7 (0111)	DEL	IDL	PRE	EOT					g	p	x		G	P	X	7
8 (1000)		CAN							h	q	y		H	Q	Y	8
9 (1001)	RLF	EM						`	i	r	z		I	R	Z	9
10 (1010)	SMM	CC	SM		¢	!	¦	:								
11 (1011)	VT	CU1	CU2	CU3	.	$	,	#								
12 (1100)	FF	IFS	DC4		<	*	%	@					⌐		⌐	
13 (1101)	CR	IGS	ENQ	NAK	(	)	_	'								
14 (1110)	SO	IRS	ACK		+	;	>	=					⌐			
15 (1111)	SI	IUS	BEL	SUB	|	¬	?	"								LVM

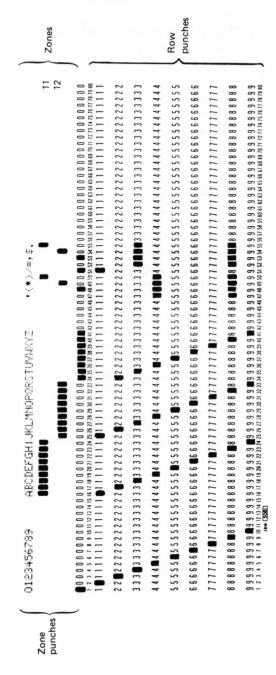

Figure 6–9 Hollerith-coded punched card.

mode. Parity is not provided in EBCDIC, and the code must be expanded to nine levels in order to obtain this function.

Hollerith Code

The punched card should not be overlooked when discussing data representation codes. Letters, numbers, and some symbols are represented by certain combinations of holes punched in a special card. The most widely used code in punched cards in the *Hollerith* code, which is shown in Figure 6–9. Each of the 80 columns carries one digit, letter, or symbol.

Punch positions are arranged horizontally in 12 rows—the bottom ten rows for the digits 0 through 9 plus two rows numbered 11 and 12 along the top of the card for *zone* punching. Referring to Figure 6–9, it can be seen that the digits 0 through 9 each are coded with a single punch. Alphabetical characters require a single row punch *plus* a zone punch. Special characters use multiple combinations of row and zone punches.

When a punched card is read, each row in each column is investigated separately. Thus the Hollerith-coded punch card may be viewed as representing data with a 12-level code. Due to the large number of digits, the Hollerith code is not usually considered in its binary form but rather by listing the rows and/or zones that are punched for each character. Figure 6–10 shows a typical listing of the Hollerith code, which should be correlated with the punched card shown in Figure 6–9.

It may be enlightening to compare Hollerith coding with the 6-level code of Figure 6–5. The similarity of the codes may be seen by considering the 01 column as the 11 punch and the 11 column as the 12 punch. Thus conversion from Hollerith to the 6-level BCD code is easily performed and is a good reason for using BCD coding in digital devices which may employ punched card input.

Number	Punch	Letter	Punch	Letter	Punch	Letter	Punch	Char	Punch
0	0								
1	1	A	12,1	J	11,1			#	3,8
2	2	B	12,2	K	11,2	S	0,2	,	0,3,8
3	3	C	12,3	L	11,3	T	0,3	$	11,3,8
4	4	D	12,4	M	11,4	U	0,4	.	12,3,8
5	5	E	12,5	N	11,5	V	0,5	&	12
6	6	F	12,6	O	11,6	W	0,6	@	4,8
7	7	G	12,7	P	11,7	X	0,7	%	0,4,8
8	8	H	12,8	Q	11,8	Y	0,8	*	11,4,8
9	9	I	12,9	R	11,9	Z	0,9	¤	12,4,8

Figure 6–10   Hollerith code listing.

6–5 SUMMARY

Some of the common binary codes used to represent letters, numbers, and symbols have been discussed in this chapter. More important, however, has been the discovery that information may be represented in binary form. With this knowledge, it is apparent that *intelligence* may be encoded, transmitted, decoded, and manipulated with logic circuits. Such capability has provided the impetus for the revolution in machine aids to improvement of the intellectual processes that is so apparent today.

Many of the more complex codes used in digital computers have not been covered in this text. Parity checking methods may be extended to more than one bit per character and even extended to checking complete blocks of information (many groups of characters). "Exotic" error detection and correction schemes are in use, but this information is left to the many excellent texts devoted to principles and practices of data handling and transmission.

In the majority of the cases the digital computer engineer/technician will encounter, the codes used will be listed in the technical information furnished with the computer. If such information is not available, the principles discussed in this chapter will enable the reader to systematically approach the equipment and determine the important characteristics of the codes before proceeding with any analysis or troubleshooting activities.

QUESTIONS

1. Why are external codes necessary when using digital computers?
2. Discuss the characteristics of the octal number system.
3. Discuss the characteristics of the hexadecimal number system.
4. Show the relationships between the binary, octal, and hexadecimal number systems.
5. What is a BCD code?
6. Compare the characteristics of weighted vs unweighted BCD codes.
7. Discuss the characteristics of the 8-4-2-1 code.
8. Discuss the characteristics of the 2-4-2-1 code.
9. Discuss the characteristics of the Gray code.
10. Discuss the characteristics of the XS3 code.
11. Discuss the characteristics of the Baudot code; list typical applications.
12. Discuss the characteristics of a 6-level code; list typical applications.
13. Discuss the characteristics of the ASCII (ANSI) code; list typical applications.
14. Discuss the characteristics of the EBCDIC code; list typical applications.
15. Discuss the characteristics of the Hollerith code; list typical applications.

PROBLEMS

1. Convert 5_{10} to binary form, octal form, hexadecimal form, 8-4-2-1 BCD form, 2-4-2-1 BCD form, and XS3 form.
2. Convert 76_{10} to binary form, octal form, hexadecimal form, 8-4-2-1 BCD form, 2-4-2-1 BCD form, and XS3 form.
3. Convert 348_{10} to binary form, octal form, hexadecimal form, 8-4-2-1 BCD form, 2-4-2-1 BCD form, and XS3 form.
4. Show how the words "6-level alphameric code" would appear in the Baudot code, 6-level BCD code without parity, 6-level BCD code with parity, 7-level ANSI code, and EBCDIC code.

7

The Control Section

Any discussion of computer operation must of necessity be a compromise. As each of the functional sections of the computer is approached in this and subsequent chapters, concepts of operation rather than specific computer details are stressed. State-of-the-art examples are used throughout, however, so that the reader will be adequately prepared to use and analyze modern computers. Chapter 13 combines the information from each of the chapters concerned with separate functional sections and provides a detailed discussion of the complete computer. Thus the broad approach of Chapter 2 will be expanded in Chapters 7 through 11 and updated to modern computer technology in the "revisited" computer of Chapter 13.

7–1 INTRODUCTION

The overall function of the CONTROL section is implicit in its name. It *controls* the computer. Control is implemented by (a) timing and (b) knowing what to do next. Timing is supplied by electronic circuits. Knowing what to do next is a function of the basic design of the computer and the instructions supplied by the programmer. Design of the computer dictates how the computer responds to each of its instructions. Therefore, to understand the operation of the CONTROL section, basic computer timing, computer instructions, and responses to those instructions must be investigated. Reference to the CONTROL section functional block diagram of Figure 2–6 is used throughout this chapter. Correlation of this chapter, the referenced figure, and Section 2–2 will aid the reader as the details of the CONTROL section and its operation are developed.

7–2 COMPUTER TIMING

Concepts

All digital computer operations are *cyclic* in nature and require some means of synchronizing and timing computer operations. The CONTROL section supplies these functions, which may be only nanoseconds in duration, second or minutes in duration, or any time in between. Obviously very versatile timing circuits are needed.

Figure 7–1 depicts the broad spectrum of computer timing requirements. The basic timing for the computer consists of a continuous train of electronic pulses with a period in the nanosecond-to-microsecond range (depending on the computer). It is from this basic timing that all other computer timing operations are derived. For example, it may be recalled from Chapter 2 that a sequential series of operations are required every time the storage medium of the computer is accessed for information. The *memory cycle* timing is made up of a number of basic timing periods. Also, information must be moved between locations in the various sections of the computer, arithmetic and logic operations performed, and input/output devices operated. Each of these operations requires timing derived from the basic timing period.

During operation a digital computer is always in one of two states (perhaps more than two in more complex computers than the simple example used here), identified by the functions being performed at the time. During the *fetch* state, information is obtained from MEMORY, the operation is decoded, and the Program Counter (see Figure 7–7) is readied to obtain the next program instruction. The actual operation is performed during the *execute* state. (Choice of the terms "fetch" and "execute" are purely arbitrary, although they often appear in computer manuals and texts.)

A fetch and an execute state (sometimes called fetch and execute phases) combine together to become a *computer cycle*. During the *fetch phase*, a computer word is obtained from MEMORY and stored in the CONTROL section. The fetch phase is generally completed in a fixed period of time (nanoseconds to microseconds), since it is determined primarily by the time it takes to obtain information from the storage medium. *Execute phase* timing is variable, depending on the complexity of the operation(s). Data required to perform the operation(s) identified in the information retrieved from MEMORY during the fetch phase is obtained from MEMORY during the first portion of the execute phase and the actual operation(s) performed in the latter portion of the execute phase. Thus computer cycle time is of variable length (usually a number of microsecond), determined by the complexity of the operation(s) being performed. Another fetch and execute phase

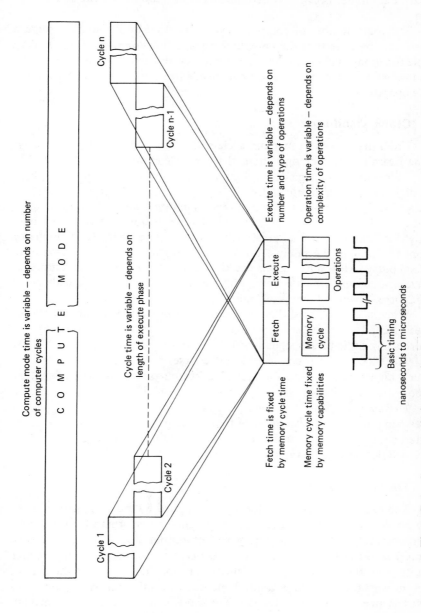

Figure 7-1 Computer timing requirements.

(the next computer cycle) follows immediately if required by the stored program.

The total number of computer cycles required by the stored program determines the time that the computer remains in the *compute mode*. Very simple functions may require that the computer remain active for only microseconds, while complex functions can result in many minutes of compute mode operation.

Clock Oscillator

From the very short memory cycle which occurs during the fetch phase to the overall computer operation, the timing circuits are in control. The basic source of timing signals for digital computers is usually provided by a non-digital electronic circuit called an *oscillator*. An oscillator is an electronic circuit which provides a signal whose repetition rate is determined by a highly accurate and stable controlling element. The repetition rate is chosen high enough so that the time interval between successive changes in oscillator output is less than the minimum time required for the fastest operation in the computer. All timing signals are then derived from the basic output of the *clock oscillator*, which is commonly identified as "clock" and is depicted in the form shown at the top of Figure 7–2.

When it is considered that some computer operations occur in a matter of nanoseconds, it can be seen that the clock oscillator may have to be capable of furnishing basic timing signals with a repetition rate as high as 10,000,000 to 100,000,000 changes per second. Of course, not all computers operate at such high rates. In fact, the actual repetition rate used for explanatory purposes is unimportant, since it is the *relationships between timing signals that determine computer sequences*. The *actual* repetition rate merely determines computer speed. Examples of timing are provided to indicate present "state of the art" computer operation, and it should be recognized that all times will decrease as technology advances.

Timing Generator

The *timing generator* uses the signal supplied by the clock oscillator to develop the basic timing waveforms required for performance of all computer operations. Typical timing generator output waveforms are seen in Figure 7–2. Such waveforms can be generated by most conventional counter circuits, even though the counting function is not the purpose of the circuit. Only the waveforms are important. A modulus-10 shift counter (Figure 5–14) is used as an example in this chapter. The waveforms identified as T_0 through T_9 in Figure 7–2 represent the outputs of the shift counter stages A through M, respectively, and are the output signals of the timing generator. All waveforms may not be required for a specific operation, so the *control generator*

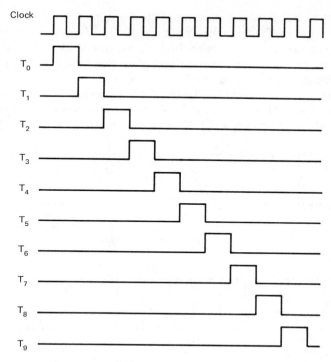

Figure 7–2 Timing generator waveforms.

selects the appropriate timing as determined by the operation to be performed. (The control generator is discussed shortly.)

7–3 THE COMPUTER WORD

As stated in Section 2–1, the computer is given information in groups of binary symbols called *computer words*. If the information is data to be processed, such as letters, numbers, symbols, etc, the package of information is called a *data word*. If the computer is being told what to do, then the package of information is called an *instruction word*. Both are discussed in this section.

Data Words

Data is represented within the computer in computer words which have the same number of bits as computer words that provide instructions. The computer differentiates data words from instruction words *only* by being told that data words are stored in specific memory locations, which is a function of the computer program. When a data word is retrieved from memory for use within the computer, it must be in a format that is consistent with all other data words and with the designed capabilities of the computer. (Data words for one manufacturer's computer quite likely will not be compatible with another manufacturer's computer.)

As previously explained, all data in the computer is binary in nature, no matter what that data represents. When *numbers* are being represented, two general arrangements exist. One form, shown in Figure 7–3(a) and

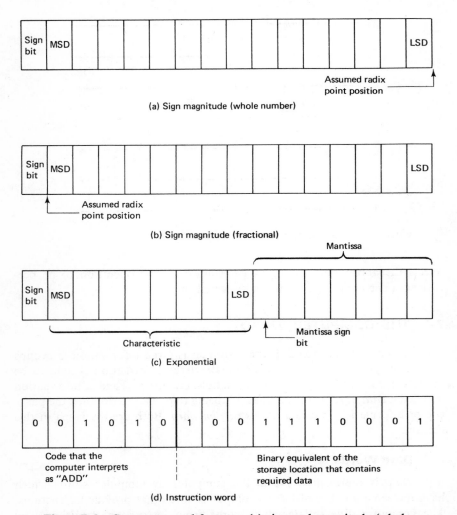

(a) Sign magnitude (whole number)

(b) Sign magnitude (fractional)

(c) Exponential

(d) Instruction word

Figure 7–3 Computer word formats; (a) sign and magnitude (whole number), (b) sign and magnitude (fractional), (c) exponential, (d) instruction word.

7–3(b), presents *sign* and *magnitude* information. The first bit position represents the algebraic sign (0 = plus and 1 = minus in most computers) of the data, while the remaining bits present the actual value. Two sign and magnitude conventions exist. In one case the radix point is considered to be to the *right of the least-significant digit* (*whole number*), while in the other case it is considered to be to the *left of the most-significant digit* (*fractional*). It makes no difference which convention is used, as long as the *same* convention is consistently applied. The programmer *scales* the data (see Chapter 9) so that the ARITHMETIC section can perform its functions properly. Sign plus magnitude representation of data is often called *fixed-point* operation.

Floating-point operation is accomplished by using an *exponentially* arranged data word. The concepts of exponential notation discussed in Chapter 3 made it apparent that a number could be written in sum of products form with each term as a digit times some power of the base of the number system in use. In the decimal number system this technique is used to represent numbers in scientific notation—that is, as a number between one and ten times some power of ten. For example, $12345 = 1.2345 \times 10^4$. This technique allows automatic *scaling* of the numbers in use and simplifies arithmetic operations.

Binary numbers may also be represented in exponential form. A binary number such as $+101010100000000$ may be shown as 10101010×2^7. The data word is arranged as shown in Figure 7–3(c). Within the ARITHMETIC section, parts of the word are acted upon separately, in accordance with the rules of exponential arithmetic (see Chapter 9). Fixed-point and floating-point operations are both in common use in modern computers.

Instruction Words

The simplest of instruction words contain two major parts: the operation code (*op-code*) and the address of the operand (often abbreviated merely *operand*). See Figure 7–3(d). Op-codes vary among computers and depend on the design and implementation of computer functions. Since 16-bit computer words have generally been discussed in this book, op-codes compatible with 16-bit words are used as examples. Relatively simple examples are used so that the logic circuits associated with carrying out computer instructions can be examined. Once these examples are understood, the reader will find it easy to expand his thinking to more complex instructions. Table 7–1 lists a number of these simple op-codes that could be used to implement computer operations.

Each of the op-codes, when recognized, causes a pre-determined sequence of operations to be performed. The operation code 1010, for example, adds the contents of the memory address in the associated computer word to the contents of the *A* register (accumulator) and places the sum in the *A* register. The code 0010, however, loads the contents of the memory address in the associated computer word into the *B* register, and so forth. The re-

Table 7-1   Typical Computer OP-Codes

Binary	Description	Mnemonic
000000	Halt	HLT
000001	Load *A* Register	LDA
000010	Load *B* Register	LDB
000011	Load *X* Register	LDX
000100	Increment Memory and Replace	INR
000101	Store *A* Register	STA
000110	Store *B* Register	STB
000111	Store *X* Register	STX
001000	(Not used)	
001001	OR Memory and *A* Register	ORA
001010	Add Memory to *A* Register	ADD
001011	EX-OR Memory and *A* Register	ERA
001100	Subtract Memory from *A* Register	SUB
001101	AND Memory and *A* Register	ANA
001110	Multiply	MUL
001111	Divide	DIV

mainder of this chapter investigates typical processing of instructions and development of the control signals which operate other sections of the computer.

7-4   COMPUTER CONTROL

Processing Instructions

The *instruction decoder*, in combination with the *instruction register*, supplies the control inputs to the *control generator*. An *instruction register* is provided in most computer CONTROL sections to store the op-code portion of the instruction word. This allows the MEMORY circuits to proceed to other tasks while the *instruction decoder* is determining what operation is to be performed. The operation of the instruction decoder/instruction register can be explained by the partial logic diagram of Figure 7-4.

The actual number of bits assigned to the op-code portion of an instruction word is a design decision, depending on the total number of instructions which must be accomplished. For the purpose of explanation, a 6-bit op-code is used in Figure 7-4. The op-code is transferred from the MEMORY section to the previously cleared instruction register at the end of a *fetch* cycle, using the LOAD input. In the arrangement shown in Figure 7-4 a separate gate is used to recognize each op-code. Therefore the ADD gate is activated *only* when the op-code representing the ADD operation is in the instruction register, the ORA gate is activated *only* when the op-code representing the ORA operation is in the instruction register, etc. The selected operation output line remains active as long as the proper op-code is in the instruction register.

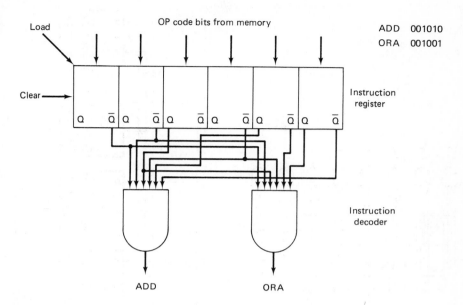

Figure 7–4 Instruction register/instruction decoder.

If a large number of operations are to be decoded, op-codes are often grouped to reduce total gate requirements. Sixty-four possible combinations exist with a 6-bit op-code, requiring 64 separate 6-input AND gates for total decoding. Modern technology seldom implements this type of operation with discrete AND gate circuits. Trends toward smaller and less expensive computers dictate the use of complex integrated circuit assemblies. One possible approach is seen in Figure 7–5(a). A conventional IC package which performs the binary-to-octal conversion is the basis for this 1-of-64 decoder. Each of the ICs decodes the equivalent of the binary numbers 0 through 7 which are applied to the input pins (C, B, A). The fourth (D) input provides gating of the input. When D is HIGH, decoding is inhibited; when D is LOW, decoding occurs (see Figure 7–5(b)). Note that HIGH inputs on C, B, and A are activating inputs, while a LOW input on D provides the activating operation. All outputs are LOW when activated.

A binary number representing a specific op-code is made available to the decoder of Figure 7–5 directly from the instruction register. For the sake of drawing clarity, the op-code is reversed on this diagram, with the least-significant digit on the left and the most-significant digit on the right. F_{in} thus is the most-significant digit, while A_{in} is the least-significant. IC_1 controls the other eight ICs by their D inputs. Thus IC_2 is enabled at its D input *only* when the three most-significant bits of the op-code are $F_{in} = 0$, $E_{in} = 0$, and $D_{in} = 0$. Under these circumstances IC_2 will decode the equivalents of binary numbers 000000 through 000111, or 0 through 7. When the inputs

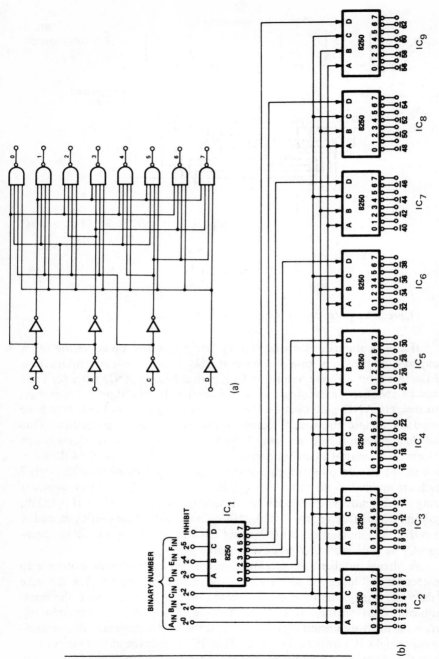

Figure 7–5 64-instruction decoder; (a) 8250 binary-octal decoder, (b) 1-of-64 decoder.

to IC_1 change to $F_{in} = 0$, $E_{in} = 0$, and $D_{in} = 1$, IC_2 is inhibited by its D input and IC_3 is enabled to decode 001000 through 001111, or 8 through 15. Similar actions occur in the remaining ICs, resulting in only 1-of-64 active outputs occurring at any one time. Thus any of 64 different op-codes may be represented and decoded using common IC packages.

Control Generator

The *control generator* supplies sequenced control signals to all sections of the computer. This function is performed by combining *timing generator* timing signals with operation-controlling signals from the *instruction decoder*. Each operation-controlling signal (there may be dozens of them) enables gates in the *timing generator* so that the appropriate timing signals are allowed to pass through to other computer sections.

A typical computer cycle requires numerous timed control signals to obtain an instruction from memory, decode the operation, obtain the data to be operated upon, and perform the operation. For the sake of simplicity, only a very small portion of one of the steps is shown. Figure 7–6 shows the simplified logic diagram and waveforms that depict generation of the first three and the last sequential control signals which might be used to perform an addition operation (ADD).

It is assumed that a computer word has been retrieved from MEMORY and that the operation (ADD) has been decoded. Decoding the ADD operation causes G_1, G_2, G_3, and G_4 to be enabled. At T_1, G_1 activates to transfer the data word address to MEMORY. No further action occurs until T_2, when G_2 activates to initiate a MEMORY read/write (restore) cycle. The data word is obtained, transferred to the *Memory Buffer Register* in the MEMORY, and the word is rewritten into MEMORY. At T_3, G_3 activates to transfer the data word to the ARITHMETIC section. Numerous other actions occur before G_4 and G_5 supply the "Initiate Next Fetch" signal, but the operation of G_1, G_2, and G_3 adequately describes the concepts of *control generator* operation. The complete sequence of control signals required to perform a typical operation is shown in Chapter 13.

In addition to the timing signals furnished directly from the individual stages of the shift counter, it may also be necessary to have control signals of more than one count-period duration. Such signals may be obtained by ORing adjacent counts, as shown in the memory cycle OR gate (G_6) of Figure 7–6(a).

Program Counter

Addresses used by the MEMORY to obtain computer words are supplied by the *program counter* in the CONTROL section. (Note: Other sources of addresses are available and are discussed later.) The program counter functions to make available, at the right time, the address of the *next* step in the computer program being executed. Since, in simple programs, the steps

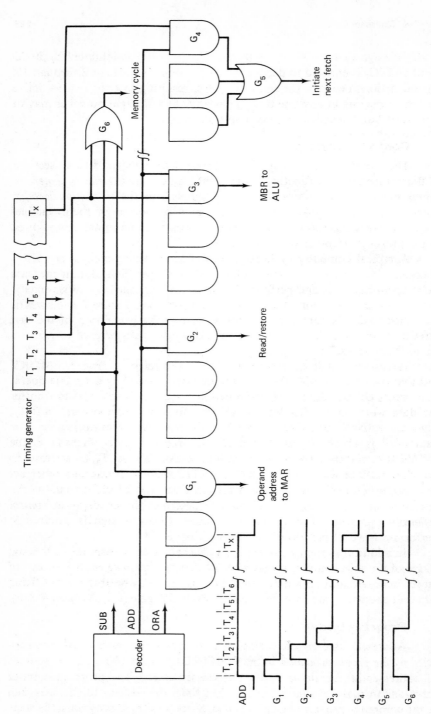

Figure 7-6 Control signals generation; (a) logic diagram, (b) timing.

are sequentially stored, it is only necessary that the *program counter* change its value by one count each time a new step is to be obtained. Any simple counter performs this function.

However, other requirements exist. The starting address of a stored program is hardly ever something simple like zero. The program counter must be pre-loaded to the required address so that the first program step can be retrieved before starting its counting sequence. Most computer programs also contain decisions that can alter the simple step-by-step counting of the program counter. For example, the results of a simple arithmetic operation may generate a negative answer which requires a difference sequence of events than a positive answer would require. Thus the program may have to "jump" to another location.

An integrated circuit assembly that could be used in constructing a program counter is shown in Figure 7–7(a). It is a synchronous 4-bit binary UP/DOWN counter with preset inputs. It contains four FFs and associated gating circuits to accomplish these functions. All four stages of the counter are fully programmable. The outputs may be preset to any state by entering the desired data at the data inputs while the load input is LOW. The output

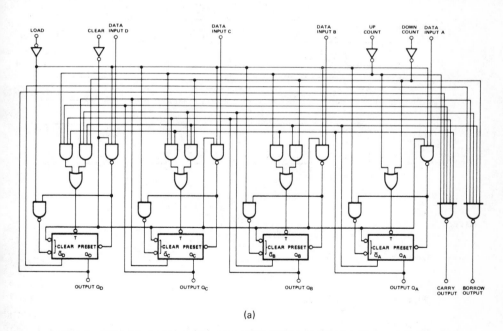

(a)

Figure 7–7 Program counter basic assembly; (a) logic diagram, 4-bit synchronous counter assembly, type 74193, (b) typical clear, load, and count sequences (courtesy of Signetics, Sunnyvale, CA).

Illustrated below is the following sequence:
1. Clear outputs to zero.
2. Load (preset) to BCD seven.
3. Count up to eight, nine, carry, zero, one, and two.
4. Count down to one, zero, borrow, nine, eight, and seven.

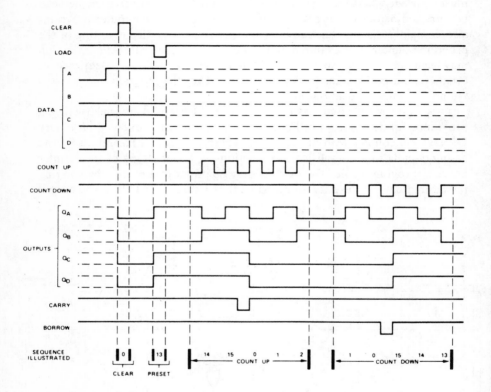

NOTES:
A. Clear overrides load, data, and count inputs.
B. When counting up, count-down input must be high;
   when counting down, count-up input must be high.

(b)

Figure 7–7 (Continued)

will change to agree with the data inputs independently of the count pulses. Once preset, the direction of counting is determined by which count input is pulsed while the other count input is HIGH. A typical CLEAR, LOAD, and COUNT sequence is shown in Figure 7–7(b).

When employed as a program counter, enough assemblies are cascaded so that the overall counter is able to count to a binary number representing the largest address ever expected in memory. The counter may be preset to zero by use of the *CLEAR* input or to any preset number by supplying the required binary number to the *data* inputs and activating the *LOAD* input. Data input to the counter is either from the panel controls or from MEM-ORY. As soon as loading is completed, either UP or DOWN counting may be accomplished. Control circuits external to the counter determine which of the count inputs is to be clocked and which is to remain HIGH. Figure 7–8 is a simplified logic diagram of a program counter that will address up to 4096 locations in MEMORY.

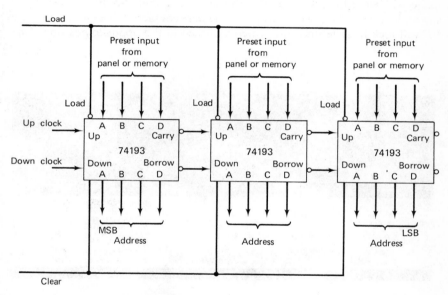

Figure 7–8   16-bit program counter.

Control Panel

The *control panel* of the computer contains many functions, some of which are directly associated with the CONTROL section. Most computers provide a switch for each bit of a computer word so that single words of information may be placed in MEMORY from the control panel. Op-codes, addresses, and/or data may be placed in MEMORY simply by setting the bit switches to their appropriate values (1 or 0) and transferring that information to the required register. A typical sequence of actions that would place a data word in MEMORY follows.

1. Set appropriate bit switches to address where data is to be stored.
2. Transfer the address to the program counter.
3. Set bit switches to represent data.
4. Transfer data to Memory Buffer Register.
5. Load data.

Figure 7–9 is a typical small computer control panel.

The bit switches on the control panel seldom feed directly to the program counter or any of the memory interfaces. Switches tend to make and/or break more than once during each activation, thus generating false information. An intermediate group of flip-flops, called a switch register, is often used to store the switch information. Any FF that actuates on the *first* contact made will serve this purpose. For example, a simple *R-S* FF connected as shown in Figure 7–10 will activate at the *first* contact of the switch, and the FF will lock in state until the switch is placed in the opposite position. One

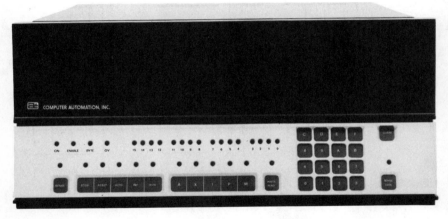

Figure 7–9 Small computer control panel (courtesy Computer Automation, Inc; Irvine, CA. 92664.).

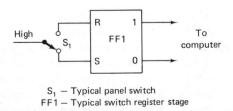

S_1 — Typical panel switch
FF1 — Typical switch register stage

Figure 7–10 Switch-register stage (typical).

FF is provided for each switch, and the combination of all FFs is called the *switch register*.

7–5 SUMMARY

This chapter has shown the complete dependence of the computer on the CONTROL section. From the initial retrieval of information from the MEMORY section to the arithmetic operation on data in the ARITH-METIC section, the CONTROL section supplies timing and control functions. Each of the functional blocks in Figure 2–6 was expanded to show a means of implementation with logic circuits, and the combination of timing and control signals to initiate operation of computer functions was explained. As each of the functional sections of the computer is discussed in subsequent chapters, it will be seen that the timing and control signals from the CONTROL section play a major part in each section's operation. The general concepts of computer timing should be kept in mind and Figure 7–1 referred to as necessary for understanding of discussions to follow. These concepts are expanded as other functional sections are discussed so that the reader may understand *complete* computer timing from input to output upon completion of this book.

It should be further recognized that computer operation is entirely dependent on the instructions supplied by the programmer. Whether it be such a basic operation as movement of data from the storage medium or as complicated as printing the results of a complex calculation, the computer must be told what to do and how to do it by the operator. Chapter 12 supplies a broad overview of computer programming.

One of the limiting factors of the conventional CONTROL section organization discussed in this chapter is that often a number of excursions must be made to MEMORY in order to complete a computer operation. Each time MEMORY is accessed, much time is consumed. The addition of a high-speed *control memory* containing the complete control sequences for each instruction materially speeds up the system's operation. This technique is called *microprogramming* and is discussed partially in Chapter 8 and more fully in Chapter 13.

QUESTIONS

1. What is the primary function of the CONTROL section?
2. Explain what is meant by the statement "all digital computer operations are cyclic in nature."
3. Name the two major states encountered during computer operation and describe what happens during each state.
4. Describe the functions of the clock oscillator.

5. Describe the functions of the timing generator.
6. The type of computer word that contains information to be processed is called a _____ word.
7. The type of computer word that tells the computer what to do is called a/an _____ word.
8. Explain "fixed-point" computer operation and, using this technique, show some examples of computer words.
9. Explain "floating-point" computer operation and, using this technique, show some examples of computer words.
10. What are the two major parts of an instruction word? Describe the function of each.
11. Describe the relationship between the instruction register and the instruction decoder.
12. How many different computer operations can be described using an op-code consisting of 4 bits; 6 bits; 8 bits?
13. Describe the relationship between the control generator, timing generator, and instruction decoder.
14. List the major functions of the program counter.
15. Show a simplified logic diagram of a program counter that is capable of addressing up to 2048 memory locations.
16. What would you expect to see on the control panel of a small-scale digital computer?
17. Discuss the subject of microprogramming.

PROBLEMS

Show the representation of the following numbers in fixed-point whole number, fixed-point fractional, and floating point. Assume a 16-bit computer word.

1. $+16_{10}$
2. -32_{10}
3. $+2048_{10}$
4. $+5000_{10}$
5. -1000_{10}
6. -7777_8
7. $+11610_8$

Explain how the computer would react to the following instruction words. Use Table 7-1 as a reference. Assume the computer word format of Figure 7-3.

8. 0010101001110001
9. 0000101001110001
10. 0001011111111111
11. 0000000000000000
12. 0011011010101010

8

The Memory Function

8–1 INTRODUCTION TO INFORMATION STORAGE

Classification by Location

Defining "memory" in terms of actual hardware is difficult, since "memory" implies storage of information, and storage functions exist throughout, and external to, the computer. Actually, memory (storage) exists in all of the functional sections of the computer. Memory is used in the *functional* diagram to designate the so-called "main memory" of the computer where information that is *immediately* needed to operate the computer is stored. The capacity of this portion of computer storage depends on the computer under study and can vary from as little as 1K (1024) 8-bit words in a minicomputer to as great as 1048K 36-bit words in some of the giants. This type of *internal* storage is characterized by access times* on the order of 500 nanoseconds to 2 microseconds, with the 500 nanosecond time being steadily reduced as technology advances. Semiconductor storage cells, magnetic cores, and magnetic films are used in internal storage.

Even faster storage elements exist in other functional sections of the computer. A typical example is the semiconductor-implemented Instruction Register in the CONTROL section, where the op-code from a portion of the instruction word is temporarily stored. Information is available at the output of the Instruction Register within a few nanoseconds of the time it is initially stored. This type of fast, temporary, extra-small capacity storage (one word or less) is characterized by access times on the order of 10 to 100 nanoseconds. Examples of register storage are seen throughout the INPUT/ OUTPUT, ARITHMETIC/LOGIC, and CONTROL sections.

---

*Access time is the time interval between information request and information availability.

As computers grow larger and more powerful, the need for storage capacity grows. Since the rate at which a computer can use information is generally limited by the rate at which instructions can be processed (and only one instruction can be processed at a time in most computers), the need for massive amounts of short access time storage is not great. As long as sufficient storage is available to keep the computer from having to *wait* to get information from memory, then storage methods with longer access time may be employed. A computer may have to be capable of operation with a number of programming languages, but only *one* language at a time. The "translator" for the language being used can be placed in the fast access memory where it is immediately available, while the other languages can be stored in the slower storage device. The slower memory devices are characterized by capacities on the order of many millions of bits and access times from microseconds to seconds. The number of words stored per cubic foot of space is much greater, and cost per bit drops dramatically as slow access times are allowed. Magnetic discs and drums are the most common *auxiliary* storage devices. It should be noted, however, that technological advances are providing cost and size reductions in the short access memory devices, and the cost dividing line between medium-capacity and small-capacity memories is less well defined than in the past.

Needs exist in some large-scale computers for storage of extremely large amounts of information. A bank, for example, stores all of its savings, checking, and investment account information along with day-to-day operating requirements. Much of this information may be needed at monthly intervals, and there is no need to have it available within microseconds, or even milliseconds. Access within seconds, even minutes, is quite adequate. Large-capacity, slow-access-time storage devices, such as magnetic tape, result in considerable economy in both price and space.

Thus there exists within, and adjunct to, the modern digital computer information storage capabilities ranging from capacities of one word or less to many millions of words. Access times range from ten nanoseconds to minutes, generally determined by the capacity of the storage device. Figure 8–1 pictorially depicts the hierarchy of storage devices in a digital computer.

Classification by Access Methods

Storage devices are often classified in terms of the manner in which information is made available from or to the memory. Two methods of accessing storage devices are commonly employed: random access and sequential access.

Random-access methods allow *any* of the storage locations to be accessed at will without cycling through other locations. *Fixed* access time is an identifying characteristic of a random-access storage device. A "jukebox" uses random-access methods. The desired record is selected by identify-

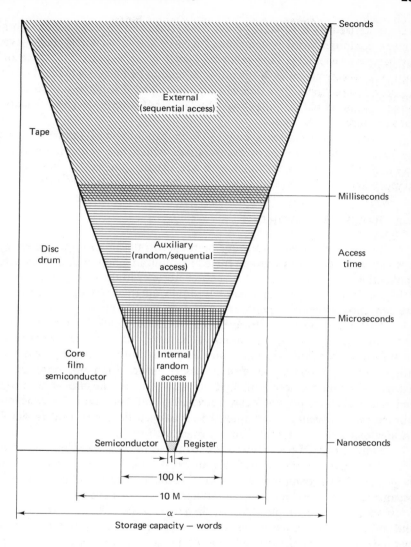

Figure 8–1 Computer storage device hierarchy.

ing its storage location and the retrieval mechanism goes from its resting place directly to the selected record. The conceptual memory discussed in Chapter 2 is an example of a random-access memory. Internal memories are generally random-access devices.

Sequential-access methods require cycling through all previous storage locations before arriving at the desired information. This type of access is characterized by a *variable* access time, since the time it takes to obtain a given computer word is determined by its location in the storage device. An inexpensive casette tape recorder/player is an excellent example of a sequential-access machine. If the music desired to be played is the first recording on the tape, the access time is very short; yet, if it is the last recording, the access time could be quite long. Most external storage devices are sequential in nature.

Some memory devices employ both random- and sequential-access methods. Such devices have access times which fall between sequential-access and random-access limits and are usually classed in the auxiliary memory area. Figure 8–1 includes access classification information.

8–2 INTERNAL STORAGE

The use of *registers* for very high speed internal storage presents no new concepts. Registers were discussed in detail in Chapter 5, and an actual application was shown as the Instruction Register in the CONTROL section (Chapter 7). Review of these areas will supply adequate background to apply the concepts of register operation to storage applications.

The main computer storage area, commonly called internal storage, constitutes the "working" memory. It is here, as discussed earlier, that all information (program steps and data) that must be *rapidly* obtained is stored. The requirement for fast access to information not only dictates the use of a random-access method but also requires the use of techniques and materials that do not delay retrieval of information. The concept of storage cells presented in Chapter 2 is employed in this section to develop various methods of internal memory organization.

Storage cells in the memory are arranged in a manner that allows easy recovery of their information. Since information is handled in the computer in groups of bits (computer words or portions of such), the memory is also organized in the same manner. Computer words are stored as a single entity consisting of, for example, 16 bits. Sixteen storage cells thus are required, and all cells must be activated when a word is to be used. Two common methods of selecting the desired location in storage are used: *linear selection* and *coincident selection.*

Linear Selection

Linear selection of data in memory is accomplished by using a separate address line for each storage location. This concept was developed in Chapter 2 and should be reviewed at this time to reestablish the principles of linear selection operation. More detailed information appears later in this section, where a linear selection, magnetic core memory organization is discussed.

Coincident Selection

As the size of memory requirements grows, the number of individual address signals used in a linear selection method becomes restrictive. The *matrix addressing (coincident selection) system* of Figure 8–2(a) is commonly used in such cases. Each cell is defined as the intersection (*coincidence*) of

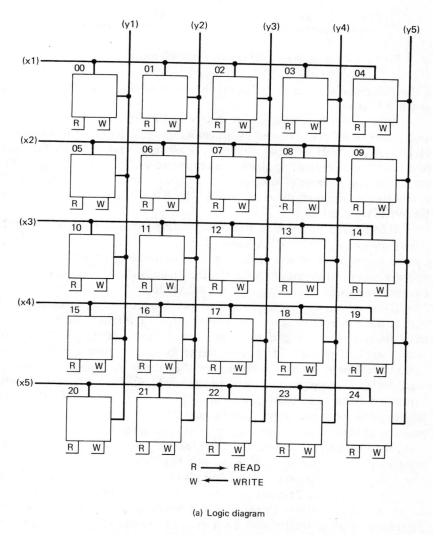

(a) Logic diagram

Figure 8–2 Coincident-selection concepts; (a) logic diagram

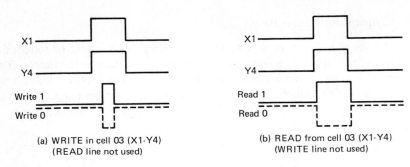

Figure 8–2   (Continued) (b) typical single-bit memory waveforms.

a row (X) and a column (Y). Cell number 03 is addressed as $X1$-$Y4$; cell 22 as $X5$-$Y3$; etc.

Information is written into a specific cell by enabling the required X and Y selection lines, followed by an enabling signal on the WRITE input. Note that the WRITE input connects to *all* cells. Only the cell that has *both* an X and a Y enabling signal present, however, will accept the WRITE input. For the purpose of simplification, it is assumed that a "0" and a "1" are written by opposite direction pulses. The READ line is not used during the WRITE operation.

Information in a cell is read by enabling the appropriate X and Y inputs and examining the READ line. During the time that the cell is enabled by the appropriate X and Y inputs, the information present in the cell appears as shown in Figure 8–2(b). Once again, only the cell that is fully enabled will produce an output on the READ line.

The operation of a single-bit memory has now been described, and with it the concepts of storage functions required within a computer. The only difficulty remaining is that very few single-bit computer words are encountered. Expansion of these concepts to include more common computer situations is not too difficult. For the sake of simplicity, however, a small-scale, 25-word memory will be retained, although the word length is now expanded to 16 bits. Expansion of the memory size to more than one bit per word does not really complicate matters. Instead of representing a package of information with only one bit, that information is represented with, in our example, 16 bits. Therefore, at each location, or address, there must be provision for storage of not one but 16 bits. Instead of enabling one storage cell when the computer word is desired, 16 cells must be enabled.

The single-bit, 25-word memory previously discussed is sometimes called a *memory plane*. Properly interconnecting a number of memory planes can result in multiple-bit memory. The number of planes used determines the number of bits per word, while the number of cells per plane determines the capacity (number of words) of the memory. By using 25 cells per

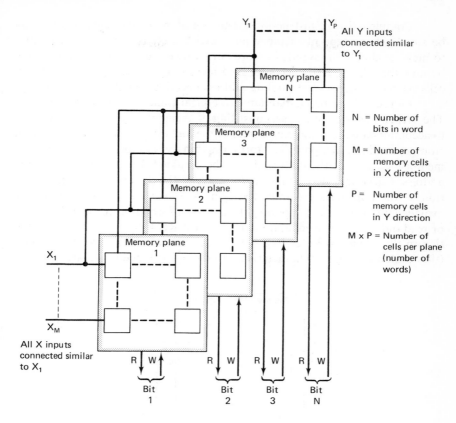

Note: each memory plane constructed like figure 8.2

Figure 8–3 Concept of memory planes.

plane, interconnecting 16 planes will result in a 25-word, 16-bit memory device. This concept is shown in Figure 8–3.

When the computer word at a specific location is desired, it is necessary to enable the appropriate X and Y inputs for *all* 16 planes. This is accomplished by connecting $X1$ of plane 1 to $X1$ of plane 2 to $X1$ of plane 3, etc, to include all 16 planes. Similarly, all of the remaining X lines are connected together, as are all of the Y lines. Therefore, when an X line is selected, it enables that X line on all 16 planes. The same actions exist for the selection of a Y line. Since 16 bits instead of 1 bit are now made available to the READ/WRITE operation, 16 bits are either written or read. In the practical 16-bit memory, then, each time an address is selected, a complete 16-bit computer word is either written or read. Thus information is handled in groups of bits, rather than the much slower single bit at a time approach.

Complete lists of instructions, made up of many computer words, may be stored in the type of memory just described. It is necessary, of course, to make available thousands of words of storage, but it should be apparent by now that this is easily accomplished merely by increasing the number of cells on each plane and expanding address decoding capability.

Figure 8–4 is a block diagram of a typical coincident selection memory. The *Memory Address Register*, consisting of as many stages as are necessary to accommodate the complete address of the highest-numbered address in the storage medium, temporarily stores the binary number representing the memory location of the information to be obtained. Decoding of the binary address is accomplished by the *X decoder* and the *Y decoder*, causing selection of the appropriate storage location. A *Memory Buffer Register* is also provided and is used as temporary storage for information to be written into or read out of the selected address. During a WRITE operation the information in the Memory Buffer Register is transferred through driver amplifiers (they match the register characteristics to the storage medium characteristics)

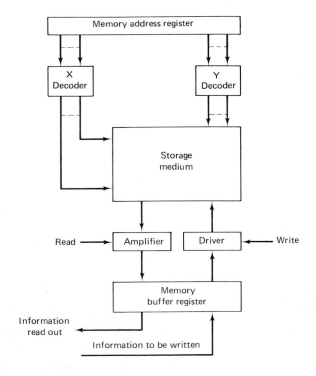

Figure 8–4   Typical coincident memory organization.

to the storage location. Readout of information is accomplished by enabling "sense amplifiers" that are connected to the storage medium and storing the resulting information in the Memory Buffer Register. All coincident-selection memories, regardless of the storage medium, operate in this manner. More detailed information appears as specific examples are discussed later in this chapter.

Semiconductor Memories

Memories constructed with semiconductor devices generally fit into two categories: *static* and *dynamic*. Static memories use storage cells that resemble the flip-flop circuit, storing information in one of two stable states. The actual circuitry of a static memory cell is not important from a *functional* viewpoint; only knowledge of the actions and reactions of the FF (discussed in Chapter 5) is required. Static memory cells are *non-destructive* during information readout. *The stored information remains in the cell even though it is transferred to other parts of the computer.* In addition, as long as power remains "on," the memory retains its information. Unfortunately, the static semiconductor cell is *volatile* in nature, *losing its information when power is removed.* (Some storage media are non-volatile.)

A *dynamic* memory cell stores information, using the absence or presence of an electric charge on a capacitor.* The charge on a capacitor tends to deteriorate with time and must be refreshed periodically. Typically the refresh operation must be performed about every 2 milliseconds and requires less than 1% of the memory's available time.

Although single-transistor storage cells are used in some dynamic memories, the most common dynamic storage cell consists of three semiconductor devices (transistors) (see Figure 8–5). The storage mechanism consists basically of the storage of electric charge in a capacitor (C_S), which is actually the gate input capacitance of the storage transistor (Q_2). A second transistor (Q_1) in the cell is used as a switch through which the charge passes to the gate of the storage transistor during a WRITE or REFRESH cycle. The third device (Q_3) is connected to the output of Q_2. During the READ cycle Q_3 is turned on. Since Q_2 and Q_3 are effectively in series, the charge condition at the gate of Q_2 determines the reaction of the cell. If a charge is present, Q_2 is also turned on, and the charge is (in simplified terms) "transferred" to the sense line.

---

*A capacitor is a device that stores electric energy (charge) based on the physical parameters of the capacitor, the amount of energy available, and the amount of time the source of energy is applied to the capacitor. In the dynamic storage cell, the physical parameters are determined by the construction of the cell. The source of energy is the power supplied from the computer to the memory. Timing originating in the CONTROL section determines the amount of time the energy is applied to the capacitor.

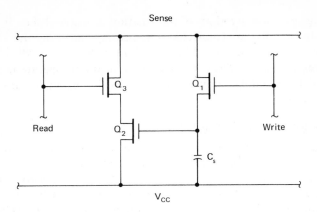

Figure 8–5 Dynamic memory cell.

Dynamic cells are non-destructive during information readout as long as refresh operations occur as required. As with static cells, dynamic cells are volatile.

STATIC MEMORY

The basic building block of the static memory discussed in this section is a 16-pin integrated circuit (IC) assembly (chip). Each IC stores 1024 (1K) one-bit words, and is organized into a 32×32 array (see Figure 8–6). Ten address inputs from an external source are decoded into 32 rows and 32 columns to coincidentally select one of the *static* memory cells. Address lines A_0 through A_4 are decoded to select 1-of-32 rows (word lines). Each word line feeds 32 storage cells, connecting them to 32 bit lines. Addresses A_5 through A_9 are decoded to select 1-of-32 columns (bit lines). Thus the ten address lines select one cell out of 1024 for reading or writing.

A CHIP SELECT input enables and disables the write amplifiers and SENSE outputs. It also is used to select a specific chip when memories of more than 1024 words are used. The operating mode of the chip is determined by the READ/$\overline{\text{WRITE}}$ (R/$\overline{\text{W}}$) input. As long as the READ/$\overline{\text{WRITE}}$ input is HIGH, a READ operation is performed. Any time it is LOW, however, when the chip is selected, *something* will be written.

The READ cycle for this type of memory chip is very easy to execute (see the timing diagram in Figure 8–6(b)). With the chip selected and in the READ state, it is only necessary to input an address. The data will then be valid at the output after the access time has elapsed.

The WRITE cycle is also measured by the required stable address time. Since the Chip Select signal gates the write circuitry, it must arrive earlier than in a READ cycle so that the write pulse can propagate properly into the cell array. Details are shown in the timing diagram of Figure 8–6(b).

A practical memory can be assembled by using a number of IC chips. For example, if the computer in use employs 16-bit words, then it is only necessary to provide 16 chips, such as those shown in Figure 8–6, to obtain 1K of 16-bit storage. All similar address inputs and chip select inputs are connected together, of course, so that all 16 chips will be enabled at the same address to obtain the information stored. *Each* chip will have its own D_{in} and D_{out} lines, however, since each chip stores one bit of the computer word, and each bit must be recovered separately. Expansion to greater than 1K capacity merely requires repetition of the 1K block requirements. Figure 8–7 provides the concepts of memory expansion just discussed.

DYNAMIC MEMORY

The basic building block of the *dynamic* memory is also an integrated circuit (IC) chip housed in a standard 22-pin ceramic or epoxy package.

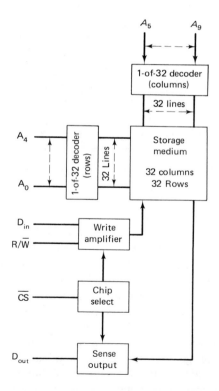

(a) 1 K memory chip organization

Figure 8–6 1K static memory chip; (a) 1K memory chip organization.

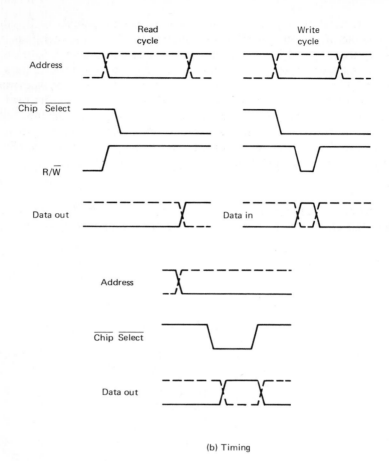

(b) Timing

Figure 8–6 (Continued) (b) timing.

Each of the ICs stores 2048 (2K) 1-bit words and is organized into four 512 × 1 arrays (see Figure 8–8(a)). Eleven address inputs, which are stored *on the IC*, are decoded into 64 rows and 32 columns to provide for coincident selection of one out of 2048 of the dynamic cells of Figure 8–5. Actually, the columns are decoded into two groups of 16 columns and two groups of 32 rows so that advantage may be taken of the 512 × 1 organization. An extra row of 32 storage cells is also provided to store the polarity status of each column of storage cells for refresh and data writing functions. The remainder of the logic on the IC uses the column inversion memory to determine the appropriate data states for input and output.

All operations on the chip are controlled by the three clock signals shown in Figure 8–8(b). General timing and operation follow.

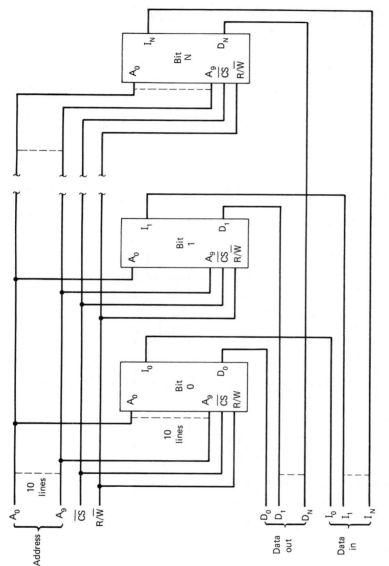

Figure 8-7 1K static memory expansion.

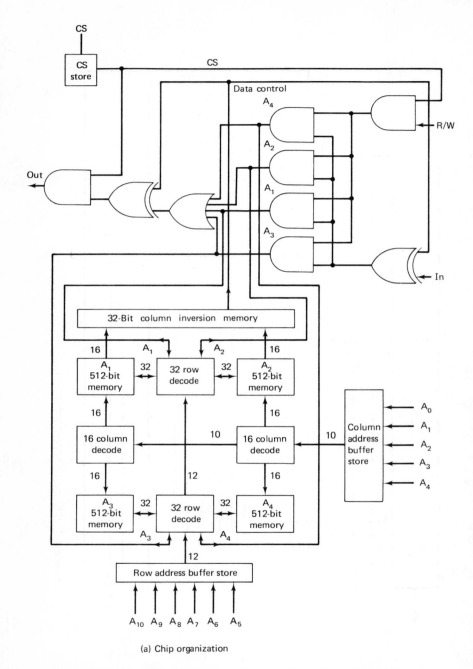

(a) Chip organization

Figure 8–8 2K dynamic memory chip; (a) chip organization, (b) chip timing, (c) chip operating cycles.

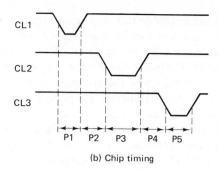

(b) Chip timing

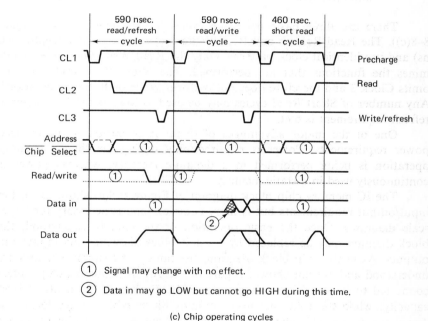

① Signal may change with no effect.

② Data in may go LOW but cannot go HIGH during this time.

(c) Chip operating cycles

Figure 8–8 (Continued)

Period 1 (P1): Internal circuits store power to be used during the remainder of the operating cycle. At the end of *P1* the rising edge of Clock 1 (CL1) transfers input address and CHIP SELECT (CS) information into the internal buffer stores.

P2: Row and column decoders select the desired bit.

P3: The information in the bit is Exclusive-ORed with the selected information contained in the column inversion memory. The result is made available to the output terminal of the chip. Output information reaches a stable value near the end of P3.

P4: Write enable circuitry is activated. The internal data-in level is determined by Exclusive-ORing the *actual* input with the selected information contained in the column inversion memory.

P5: If a "write" is desired during this period, data is written into the selected bit. Information stored in all other bits sharing the *same* addressed column is inverted and refreshed. The appropriate bit of the column inversion memory is also inverted and refreshed. If a "refresh" only is desired during this period, the information stored in *all* bits sharing the same addressed column is inverted and refreshed.

There are three basic operating cycles for the memory (see Figure 8–8(c)). The Read/Refresh and Read/Write cycles are the same length (590 ns) and use identical clock patterns. Only the Read/Write input level determines the functions that are performed. The Short Read cycle (460 ns) omits Clock 3 and therefore does not perform Write or Refresh operations. Any number of Short Read cycles may be used as long as the 2 ms column refresh requirement is met.

One of the major advantages of dynamic operation is the reduced power requirements. Power is required only during the time a memory operation is being performed in a dynamic memory, whereas power is continuously used in a static memory.

The IC memory chip block diagram of Figure 8–8(a) shows all of the input/output requirements but is more complex than is necessary for large-scale diagrams. Once the basic operation of the chip is understood, the block diagram may be replaced by a single block showing only inputs and outputs. As in the chip block diagram, the timing and supply voltages are understood and are not shown. Figure 8–9 shows a number of chips interconnected to form a large memory assembly. Each chip has a 2K × 1-bit capacity, while the total assembly contains 8K × n-bit storage locations. The memory assembly diagram is general in nature. If a 16-bit computer word is to be used, then $n = 16$, and the memory contains 8K × 16-bit storage locations.

Each chip must be supplied with address information, data in and data out capability, a Read/Write control, and a means of enabling (CS). Expanded storage capacity (from 2K to 8K) is accomplished by merely adding increments of 2K (adding more chips in the "vertical" direction). Assuming a single-bit word again, it can be seen that the four chips in the first column furnish 8K of single-bit storage, in increments of 2K. Row address inputs A_5 through A_{10} connect to *each* of the four chips, as do the column addresses A_0 through A_4 (see Fig. 8–8). Therefore, upon selecting a particular storage

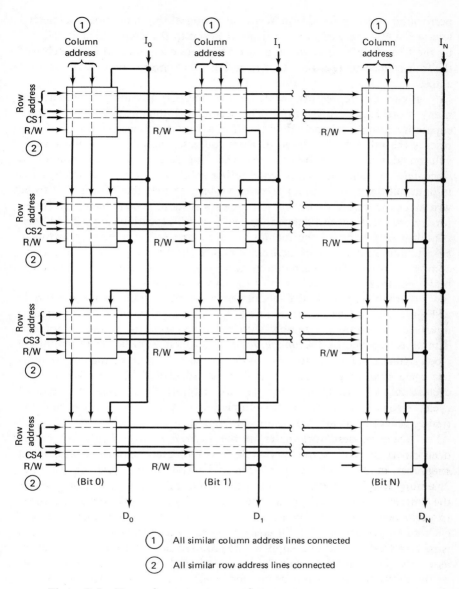

Figure 8–9 Dynamic memory expansion.

location by the row and column addresses, that location is selected on all four chips. The data inputs to each chip are also connected together, as are the data outputs. (The R/W input controls the data in/data out function, and all R/W inputs are also connected together.) All four chips will then be performing either a Read or a Write operation at the same time at a selected location. Only the data coming from or going to the chip which is selected by the Chip Select input will appear on the data out/data in line. One chip of the four is selected at a time, thus selecting a location in only one of the four chips.

Figure 8–9 represents an 8K by n-bit memory assembly, however, and many more chips are required. The second column provides a 2-bit word capability, a third column would result in a 3-bit word, and column "n" represents the nth bit in each word. Row addresses connect to all chips, as do column addresses and R/W controls. The Chip Select inputs are common to *rows only*, so that each chip representing a bit in a word is enabled. Data in/data out lines are common to *columns only*, so that the information to be written or the retrieved information appears at its respective location. Therefore, word locations are defined vertically and bit locations are defined horizontally. Any word in the memory can be accessed merely by selecting a chip to obtain a *group* of addresses and a specific chip row and column combination to select the required address. Actually, the chip select combinations are included as a part of the overall address.

A complete MEMORY section using the 8K by n-bit memory assembly of Figure 8–9 may be seen in Figure 8–10. Additional circuits are required to interface the memory assembly with the other sections of the computer.* Timing is supplied by the *timing generator*, which furnishes the three phase clock signals shown in Figure 8–8. A "cycle request" begins a memory operating cycle consisting of $\emptyset 1$, $\emptyset 2$, and $\emptyset 3$ in Read/Refresh and Read/Write cycles; only $\emptyset 1$ and $\emptyset 2$ are generated for a Short Read cycle. An "end of cycle" signal is generated upon completion of the memory cycle, and the timing generator awaits the next cycle request.

"Cycle request" originates in the *Refresh Control Logic*, where the decision as to type of memory cycle is made. The memory request input originates in the CONTROL section and results in a "cycle request" and "memory busy" outputs. "End of cycle" from the timing generator removes the "memory busy" indication. The *Refresh Control Logic* includes a timer to periodically interrupt the normal memory operation and cause a refresh cycle to be performed. A 5-bit *address counter* keeps track of which column is to be refreshed next and supplies the required information to the memory assembly via the *address multiplexer*. Selection of either the address counter or the memory address bus as column selection address source is provided by the address multiplexer. Refresh Control Logic furnishes the control signal (Refresh/System cycle) to the address multiplexer.

Bits A_{11} and A_{12} of the memory address are the source of Chip Select inputs. A 1-of-4 decoder converts the four combinations of A_{11} and A_{12} to

---

*The additional circuits will add 50 ns to 100 ns to the overall memory access time.

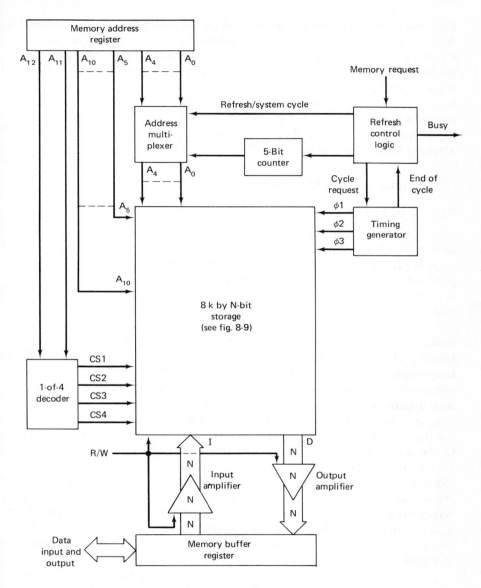

Figure 8–10 Complete dynamic memory.

the four outputs CS_1, CS_2, CS_3, and CS_4. The remaining interface requirements of data input and output are a function of the *Memory Buffer Register*, *Input Amplifiers*, and *Sense Amplifiers*. Input and/or output data are supplied to and/or from other sections of the computer to the Memory Buffer Register.

Data to be stored in memory, for example, is supplied to the Memory Buffer Register shortly before the storage operation is to take place. The storage address is selected and a "memory request" is initiated, starting the timing generator. The R/W control takes on the Write configuration, each of the Input Amplifiers is enabled (n amplifiers, one for each bit of the word to be stored), and upon completion of the Read/Write cycle all of the information in the word is stored at the selected location. Similar actions take place during retrieval of information, with the selected word appearing in the Memory Buffer Register upon completion of the memory cycle.

Magnetic Core Memories

THE MAGNETIC CORE AS A STORAGE CELL

A common device used for the storage of binary information is a tiny toroid (doughnut-shaped piece) of ferromagnetic material commonly called a *core*. It can be magnetized very easily and will retain its magnetism unless purposely changed. Operation of the magnetic core as a storage cell can best be understood by examining the characteristics of ferromagnetic materials.

The ferrite memory core toroid is pressed or stamped from an iron oxide-compounded material containing a binder to hold the shape. The toroid is effectively a ceramic material and requires firing in a kiln at high temperatures to achieve the necessary chemical, physical, and magnetic properties. Cores are available in many different sizes, but a relatively common dimension encountered is an 18 mil outside diameter.

Any magnetic material may be studied by means of a graph showing the flux density* (B) that results from the magnetizing force (H) applied to the material. The graph is commonly called a *B-H* curve, and Figure 8–11(a) shows the reaction of a typical ferrite memory core material to changes in magnetizing force. A magnetizing force can be generated by causing electrical current to flow through a wire, since a magnetic field surrounds a wire in which current is flowing. The strength of the magnetic field is a function of the amount of current flow, while the direction of the magnetic field is a function of the direction of flow of current. This is depicted in Figure 8–11(b).

If a wire carrying electrical current is threaded through the center of a magnetic core toroid, then the magnetic field surrounding the wire will transfer to the core in the manner shown in the *B-H* diagram of Figure 8–11(c). Assume that in some way a magnetic core has been manufactured entirely devoid of any magnetic flux and that a wire carrying zero current

---

*Flux density is a measure of the concentration of a magnetic field; hence it is concerned with magnetic field strength.

is threaded through the core. If current is caused to increase in the direction equivalent to $+H$, then the magnetic flux of the core will increase as shown from X in an increasing $+B$ direction. Magnetic flux will only increase so far and then a point of "saturation" is reached where increase in current in the wire will cause very little or practically zero increase in magnetic flux. This point is labeled a on the B-H curve.

Now a strange thing happens. As the magnetizing force is returned to zero (b and c), the magnetic flux does not return to zero. In fact, the change in magnetic flux from the saturating magnetizing force back to zero magnetizing force is barely perceptible. In other words, the core has "remembered" the direction of current in the wire, despite the fact that the current has returned to zero. If the current in the wire is now increased in the opposite direction (d to e), no change in magnetic flux in the core occurs until sufficient magnetizing force (e) is applied to cause the core to "switch" to the opposite direction of magnetic flux f. Returning the current in the wire to zero (g to h) now leaves the core magnetized in the opposite direction to that previously held, and the core once again "remembers," but this time it remembers something different than before.

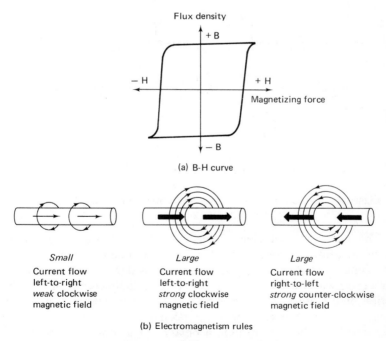

(a) B-H curve

(b) Electromagnetism rules

Figure 8–11 Properties of magnetic cores; (a) B-H curve, (b) electromagnetism rules

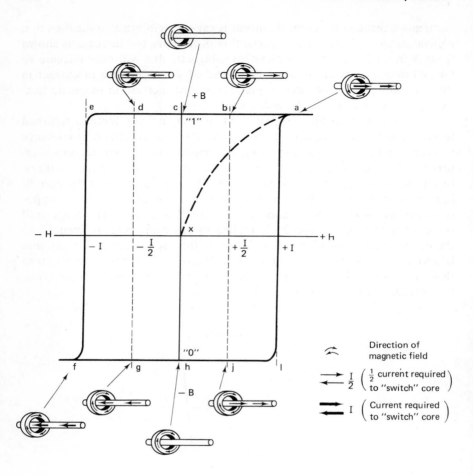

(c) Magnetic cores and the B.H. core

Figure 8–11 (Continued) (c) magnetic cores and the *B-H* curve.

Thus the core is capable of storing the fact that the current in a wire through the center of the core has been in either one direction or the other, by retaining a direction of magnetic flux that is dependent on the direction of the center wire current. And, since the current direction can be only one direction or the other, the core stores *binary* information. For discussion purposes, when the core is at the $+B$ portion of its curve, storage of a binary 1 is assumed. At the $-B$ portion, a binary 0 is assumed to be stored. The important aspects of the *B-H* curve and storage of binary information are synopsized in Figure 8–11(c).

Now that binary information has been stored in a magnetic core, how can it be retrieved? Another fundamental property of electromagnetic circuits is applied. When a magnetic field collapses, or changes direction, any wires in the vicinity will have a current induced in them. Actually, a flow of current cannot exist without an attendant magnetic field, and vice-versa (a changing magnetic field cannot exist without causing a flow of current in adjacent wires). Another wire, in addition to the wire placing information into the core, is threaded through the core. The second wire is used to sense any change that might occur in the magnetic field of the core. A commonly employed method to determine the contents of a magnetic core is to write a zero into the core using the input wire. If a zero is *already* in the core, very little change in magnetic flux occurs, and the sense wire detects very little induced current. However, if a one was in the core, the core switches direction of magnetic flux when the zero is written. The sudden change in flux direction causes a large current to be induced into the sense wire, and it is then known that a one had been written in the core.

Unfortunately, this method of reading information in a magnetic core destroys that information. In modern core memories, the information that was in the core is temporarily stored in a register and written back into the core via the input wire. This approach is discussed in more detail as the complete core memory is developed.

READING AND WRITING INFORMATION

The most common selection technique employed in computer core memory systems is the *coincident-current* method. The *B-H* characteristics of the magnetic core (Figure 8–11(c)) are used to select a given core. As previously discussed, the magnetic core is magnetized in one of two directions, depending on the direction of current flow causing the magnetizing force. Furthermore, the magnitude of current must exceed a value determined by the material used in the core before the core can be "switched." Any current less than this critical value will have negligible effect on the magnetic field of the core. In other words, if, for example, a wire threaded through the center of a magnetic core carries only $+\frac{1}{2}I$, it will not cause the core to change state. If another wire, also carrying $+\frac{1}{2}I$, is threaded through the core, then the combination of the two currents will result in $+I$, and the core can switch. This is the concept of *coincident-current* core selection. Figure 8–12(a) shows a simple *matrix* consisting of 16 cores, with two wires threaded through each core. Each wire is given a conventional matrix coordinate designation, X_1, X_2, X_3, X_4, Y_1, Y_2, Y_3, and Y_4. In addition, each intersection where a core is located is assigned a numerical designation, or address. Note that with 16 cores, addresses 0 through 15 are used.

A $+\frac{1}{2}I$ is applied to X_2, causing a magnetic field to be applied to all cores threaded on X_2. However, it is only $\frac{1}{2}I$ and is not of sufficient magni-

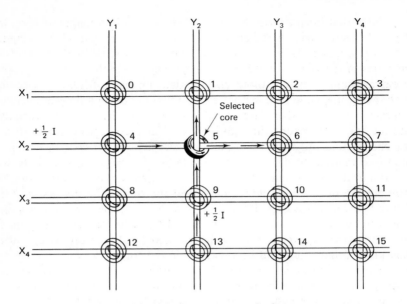

(a) Coincident-current core selection

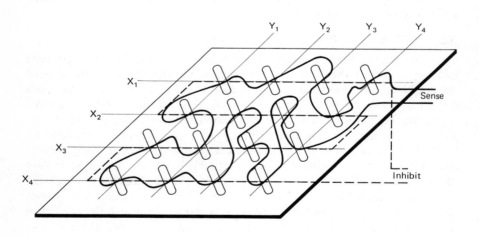

(b) Core threading pattern

Figure 8–12 Magnetic core matrix; (a) coincident core selection, (b) core threading pattern.

tude to cause any of the cores to assume the state dictated by the direction of the current. Y_2 also carries $+\frac{1}{2}I$ and all of the cores threaded thereon have a weak magnetic field applied. The core labeled 5 is at the junction of X_2 and Y_2 and is subjected to a $+\frac{1}{2}I$ from both wires. Therefore, enough current exists at this junction to develop a magnetic field of sufficient magnitude to cause core 5 to assume the state dictated by the current direction. In other words, the currents are *coincident* at this point. Upon removal of the half-currents, core 5 retains its information. The only way to destroy the information now stored at core 5 location is to supply sufficient current in the proper direction on the X_2 and Y_2 lines so that the *opposite* binary bit is stored. According to previous information, the counterclockwise field represents a binary 1 and has been the result of $+$ currents. Reversing the currents will cause a binary 0 to be stored in the same location.

In fact, in our example, this is the method used to retrieve information from a magnetic core. Negative half-currents are applied to the appropriate X and Y lines (X_2 and Y_2 in this case) and the reaction of the core is sampled. If the core did not switch, the stored information was already a binary 0. However, if the core did switch, the information *was* a binary 1. Two problems now arise: (a) how can a core switching be detected, and (b) what about destroying the information when it is read?

In the coincident-current selection method, core switching is detected by threading another wire through all of the cores in the matrix. This *sense* wire is then connected to a sensitive amplifier that detects the induced current resulting from the magnetic field of the core collapsing and rebuilding in the opposite direction. Figure 8–12(b) shows the threading plan of the sense wire in a typical matrix of memory cores. (Disregard the *fourth* wire for the moment.) One might assume that, with the sense wire threaded through all of the cores on the matrix, any core that changes state would cause the sense line to be activated. Such is true, but consider that only *one* core can switch at a time, because only one X and one Y line are carrying current at any one time. Therefore, knowing the "address" of the core, if a core switching is detected, it is known that only that core could have furnished the information.

At this point it might be informative to view the memory core matrix as a 1-bit memory and develop the interfacing devices that allow this memory to function with the rest of the computer. A *Memory Address Register* (MAR) is used to store the address of the information desired. In our simple matrix, four bits of address are adequate, and they are arranged with the decoding devices in the manner shown in Figure 8–13(a). The two most-significant digits of the address are supplied to the X decoder, and the two least-significant digits are supplied to the Y decoder. Only one line of each decoder output is active at any one time, and in the case of Fig. 8-12 it is the 01 (X_2) line from the X decoder and the 01 (Y_2) line from the Y decoder. The MAR and associated decoders operate in the same manner as the Instruction Register and its decoder shown in the CONTROL section. Each of these lines enables a circuit called a *driver amplifier*, which is capable of passing the high current required to switch the cores. The drivers receive the necessary magnitude and direction of current from the *Read/Write Control*.

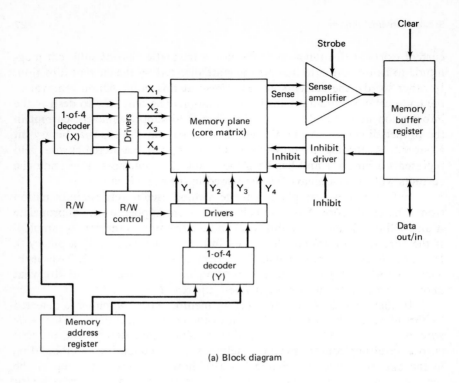

(a) Block diagram

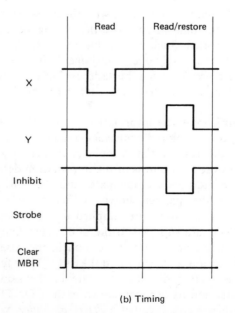

(b) Timing

Figure 8–13   Single-bit, 16-word magnetic core memory; (a) block diagram, (b) timing.

As commanded from the CONTROL section, the Read/Write Control determines the direction of current required to either insert information into the memory or to obtain information from the memory.

The *sense amplifier* functions in conjunction with the sense line threaded through the cores to detect the information stored. Recalling that reading of information from a core results in no appreciable output on the sense line if a zero is stored and an easily detectable output if a one is stored, it can be seen that the sense amplifier operates to amplify the information to a value that can be used by the Memory Buffer Register (MBR). The function of the *strobe* input to the sense amplifier is to improve the signal-to-noise capabilities of the memory system. Since the sense line is threaded through all cores in our single-bit memory, *any* change, no matter how slight, in any core will induce some current into the sense line. Even though the $\frac{1}{2}$ currents in the X and Y drive lines are not by themselves sufficient to switch a core, they do slightly disturb the cores through which they are threaded. (Note that the horizontal portions of the *B-H* curve are not completely flat—that is, from a to e on Figure 8–11(c))—and small changes in magnetic flux do occur. These changes induce unwanted currents into the sense line and may result in misinterpretation of the information stored in the core. The *strobe* input to the sense amplifier causes the amplifier to act somewhat like an AND gate and turns it on only at the specific time that the current change will be most rapid in a switching core. Thus the "noise" is effectively blocked out and only the desired information is passed through the sense amplifier.

The *Memory Buffer Register* stores the information recovered from the selected core. In this case it is a single flip-flop (FF) that assumes a state, depending on the core information. The FF is cleared at the beginning of each READ cycle. If the recovered information is a binary 1, the FF is SET; if it is a binary 0, it remains CLEAR, or RESET. The output of the MBR then is made available to the remainder of the computer and also is fed to the *inhibit driver*. The *inhibit driver* is connected to a wire which, like the sense wire, threads through all cores in the matrix.

Four wires now are threaded through each core, and all but the *inhibit* line have been discussed. As part of the READ/RESTORE cycle, the information destroyed when the core was read is placed back in the core. This is accomplished by performing a WRITE operation that places a binary 1 back into the selected core. A $+\frac{1}{2}I$ is placed on each of the appropriate X and Y driver lines as a WRITE command, and at the same time an INHIBIT $-\frac{1}{2}I$ is supplied to the *inhibit driver*. However, the inhibit driver is activated *only* if the MBR is storing the fact that the information recovered from the core is a binary 0. If the recovered information in the MBR is a binary 1, the INHIBIT current is not allowed through the inhibit driver, and consequently there is no current supplied to the inhibit line. The two $+\frac{1}{2}Is$ on the X and Y driver lines thus write a one back into the core during the RESTORE portion of the READ/RESTORE cycle.

If, however, a zero had been stored in the selected core, the inhibit driver is enabled. Upon generation of the WRITE and INHIBIT commands, two $+\frac{1}{2}I$s and one $-\frac{1}{2}I$ are in coincidence at the selected core. The $-\frac{1}{2}I$ cancels one of the $+\frac{1}{2}I$s, and only a $+\frac{1}{2}I$ is effective at the selected core. Insufficient magnetic force is available to change the core from zero state, and it remains storing its original information.

Another type of cycle is used to write original information into the core. It is very similar to the just-described cycle and is discussed only briefly. During the CLEAR/WRITE cycle, a zero is written into the selected core so that a starting point may be established. The information to be written into the core is placed into the MBR, and another regular WRITE cycle is initiated. WRITE and INHIBIT are generated, and the same sequence is performed as occurred during the WRITE portion of the READ/ RESTORE cycle. Figure 8–13(b) shows the gross timing of the READ/ RESTORE cycle.

Complete operation of a core matrix capable of storing 16 single-bit words has now been discussed. However, single-bit words are not especially useful, and some additional concepts must be developed to apply the coincident-current selection method to a practical situation. For simplicity's sake, the core matrix is first expanded to 2-bit words and then to a more practical n-bit scheme.

A separate matrix assembly is provided for each *bit* of the computer word, as shown in Figure 8–14. The X_1 line threads through the X_1 row cores on *all* matrix assemblies (often called bit planes). Likewise, all X_2, X_3, and X_4 cores on all planes have common drive lines. Therefore, when an X line is selected, $\frac{1}{2}I$s will flow through that line and all cores on all bit planes will be partially energized. Similarly, the Y lines are threaded through all of their respective cores on each bit plane. Thus, when an X and a Y line are selected, two $\frac{1}{2}I$s combine at the intersection of the X and Y line on *all* bit planes, and all cores at the selected address are energized. Whether there are two, three, four, or N planes, selection of a specific address energizes all cores at that address.

When recovering information from the memory, however, it is important to keep each bit of the word separate. Therefore a separate sense line is used in each plane. Each sense line supplies information to a separate stage of the MBR. The actual threading of the sense line follows special design techniques so that minimum interference from "disturbed" cores results. The pattern used in Figure 8–12 is not necessarily representative of actual threading patterns but is used for the sake of clarity.

The final line on each plane is the inhibit line, and as discussed previously, it allows proper restoring of information in the addressed core on each bit plane. The inhibit line is threaded through all of the cores on each plane, supplying an inhibiting $\frac{1}{2}I$ to all cores. Inhibiting only occurs at the

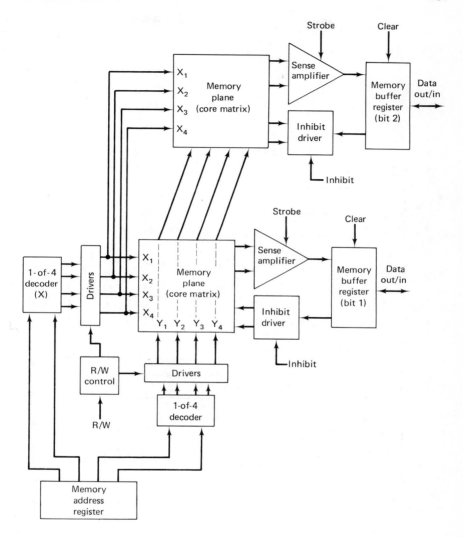

Fig. 8–14 2-bit magnetic core memory.

addressed core, however. A separate inhibit driver is provided for each bit plane.

The important characteristics of a coincident-current memory can be seen in Figure 8–15. This type of memory consists of N separate planes (N is the number of bits in the computer word), each plane containing M cores (M is the number of storage locations in the memory). Each core has four wires threaded through its center. Two of the wires (X and Y) are

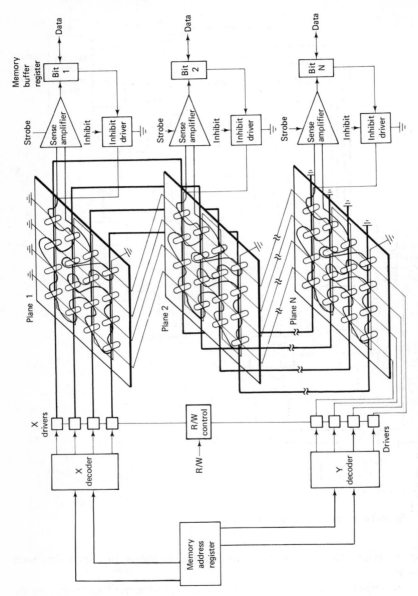

Figure 8-15 Detailed block diagram, coincident current memory organization.

used to select a desired location for reading from or writing into the memory. The selected location energizes the core at that location in each of the bit planes when sufficient magnitude of current is present. It requires current in the same direction in both the X and Y line to energize a core. A sense line, which is threaded through all cores on each bit plane, and its associated sense amplifier (one for each bit plane) detect the presence of information in the selected core and store that information in the MBR stage for the appropriate bit plane. Since obtaining information from a core destroys the information therein, a restore operation is required. During the restore period, a one is written into all cores at the selected address. If a zero had previously been stored, the inhibit drivers prevent writing a one into that plane. The inhibit drivers do not function if a one is to be written. Information at the selected address is now stored in the MBR and ready for use by the rest of the computer. It is also restored in the core and available for recall at some later time if required.

One of the difficulties encountered in manufacturing high-speed core memories is that of threading a large number of wires through the very small cores required to obtain high-speed operation. The 3D-4 wire organization just discussed can be improved by using a 3D-3 wire method and reducing the number of wires needed. In the 3D-3 wire organization the sense and inhibit functions are shared by one wire. The timing diagram of Figure 8–13(b) shows that these functions occur at different times and that there is no reason why the functions should not be shared by a single wire. An increase in circuitry complexity results, of course, since electronic switching must be provided so that the functions do not interfere with each other.

Another common selection technique employed in computer core memory systems is the 2D word organized or *linear selection* method. The concept of linear selection is shown in Figure 8–16, a 4-word, 4-bit memory. Information is stored by coincidence of two partial-write currents, one provided along the selected word wire, the other on the bit wire.

The read operation is performed by supplying a full read current on the selected word wire, driving all cores to the zero state. Those cores which were in the one state are fully switched, generating a large one voltage on the bit line. This voltage is sensed by a sense amplifier. The zero state cores do not switch further, and the sense amplifier does not detect any change.

The 2D-2 wire organization of Figure 8–16 shares the read and write functions in a single word line, while the bit line provides both write and sense functions. Due to the relative timing of these functions and the complexity of the R/W control circuits, it is possible to perform the complete Read/Write operations with only these two wires. 2D-3 wire and 2D-4 wire organizations also exist.

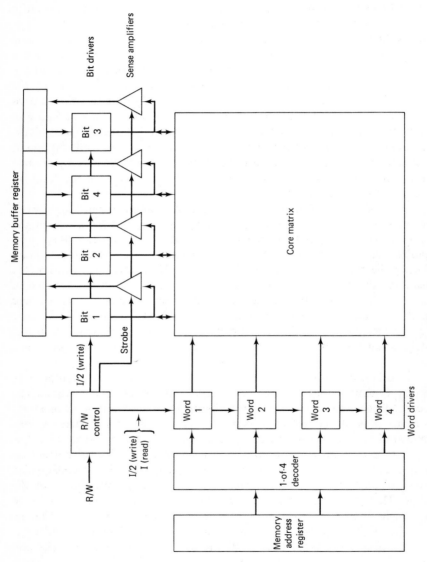

Figure 8–16 Linear-select memory organization (4-word, 4-bit).

234

Plated Wire Memories

Another form of information storage in a magnetic field uses a thin magnetic film (about 0.0004 inch thick) that is electroplated on a small copper wire (about 0.005 inch diameter). The thin magnetic film is anisotropic (magnetized easier in one direction than the other). The closed magnetic path *around* the plated wire (called the easy axis of magnetization) can either be clockwise or counterclockwise. If the magnetization is clockwise, a "0" is stored; and if it is counterclockwise, a "1" is stored (see Figure 8–17(a)).

A plated wire memory consists of a number of digit/sense lines crossed by a number of word lines. Although the magnetic coating on a digit/sense line is continuous, only the area of the magnetic material adjacent to the intersection of the word and digit/sense lines contains memory due to the anisotropic characteristic of the magnetic material. Thus a single plated wire is divided into many memory elements.

Operation of a plated wire memory can be shown by considering first a read operation at a single-bit location. Assume that at time t_1 (Figure 8–17(c)) a "0" is stored. Hence, the direction of magnetization will be clockwise as viewed in Figure 8–17(a). The *B-H* curve will be in position 1 as indicated in Figure 8–17(b). At time t_2 a current pulse in the word line generates a magnetic field that reduces the magnetic field of the memory element. This corresponds to moving to position 2 on the *B-H* curve. The change in flux density from position 1 to 2 induces a voltage on the digit/ sense line which is sensed as a "0" output. At time t_4 the word current is removed and the magnetic material returns to its "0" state. It is noted in Figure 8–17(b) that the word current is insufficient to completely switch the magnetization direction. This insures that when the read current is removed, the magnetization of the film will return to its previous state. This type of memory can be interrogated over and over again without destroying the stored information. This nondestructive readout (NDRO) characteristic greatly increases the effective speed of the memory, since data readout of the memory does not have to be written back into the memory if the data is to be retained.

If a "1" is stored in the memory element at time t_1, then the magnetization direction will be counterclockwise in Figure 8–17(a) and the *B-H* curve will be in position 5. At time t_2 the magnetic field generated from the read current in the word line will again rotate the magnetic field. The change in flux from position 5 to position 6 will induce a voltage on the plated wire opposite in polarity to that generated for a "0." Hence output signals of opposite polarities are generated for a stored "1" and a stored "0." The magnetic material rapidly returns to the "1" state with the removal of the read current. This corresponds to movement from position 3 to position 4 in Figure 8–17(b).

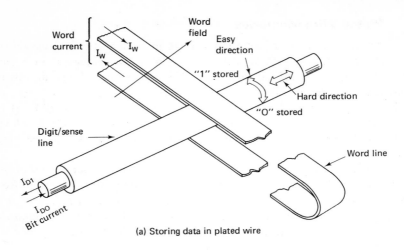

(a) Storing data in plated wire

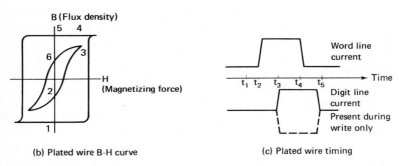

(b) Plated wire B-H curve   (c) Plated wire timing

Figure 8–17   Plated wire memory concepts; (a) storing data in plated wire, (b) plated wire *B-H* curve, (c) plated wire timing (courtesy Motorola Semiconductor Products, Inc. Phoenix, AZ)

For a write operation, assume that at time t_1 a "0" is stored (the magnetization direction is clockwise) and a "1" is desired. The word current is applied as explained earlier for the reading operation. However, now a current pulse (see Figure 8–17(c)) is passed at time t_3 through the plated wire that is labeled the digit/sense line. The magnetic field generated by this current tips the magnetization direction from position 2 to position 3. At time t_4, word current is removed. This corresponds to point 3 moving to point 4 on the *B-H* curve. At time t_5 the digit current is removed and the field is returned to zero. Consequently, the magnetic field is in the remanent "1" state corresponding to position 5 on the *B-H* curve. The same procedure is followed to write a "0" with the exception that the digit current is opposite in polarity to that as indicated in Figure 8–17(c).

Both linear-select and coincident-select organizations are used in NDRO plated wire memories. A *linear-select* organization is preferred for high-speed memories with long word lengths and small to medium word capacity. In this memory organization, the number of plated wires (digit/sense lines) is equal to the number of bits per word, and the number of word lines is equal to the number of words in the system as indicated in Figure 8–18. During a write cycle all of the digit/sense lines are selected, and data is stored at the intersection of the word line current and the digit/sense line current. Whether a "1" or a "0" is stored depends on the polarity of the digit current as explained previously. During a read cycle, current is pulsed down a selected word line, and the stored data at the intersection of word line and digit/sense lines is read out and sensed.

The *coincident-select* organization is preferred for medium- to high-speed memories with small word lengths and medium to large word capacity. Figure 8–19 shows a block diagram of a typical coincident-select memory. It might be noted that coincident-select organization used in plated wire is not the same as in core memories. For this application the plated wire memory has almost a square matrix. That is, the number of plated wires (digit/sense lines) is almost equal to the number of word lines. Accordingly, a single word line can be partitioned into several words of shorter bit lengths. As an example, consider a memory that has 256 word lines and 144 digit/sense lines as illustrated in Figure 8–19. Each word line could be partitioned into 16 words of nine bits each. Overall the memory would have 4096 words of nine bits each rather than 256 words of 144 bits each. The example just given would require nine digit drivers and nine sense amplifiers in conjunction with a selection matrix to route the nine digit drivers and nine sense amplifiers to one of the 16 words on a single word line.

During a read cycle, data is read out on all 144 digit/sense lines, but only nine bits of a selected word line are sensed. On the next read cycle a different word of nine bits can be sensed. To perform a write operation, the selection matrix connects the nine digit drivers to the desired digit/sense lines, and only at those bits of the word line which have coincident word current and digit current is data stored. The data in the remaining 135 bits is left unchanged.

Read-Only Memory (ROM)

A *Read-Only Memory* is a system for storing information in a permanent form. In applications requiring fixed data, the Read-Only Memory offers advantages where speed, cost, and reliability are factors. In gross block diagram form (Figure 8–20(a)), the basic ROM has two types of inputs and one type of output. Operationally, the address of a word is placed on the address lines, and the Enable input is activated. The contents of the addressed

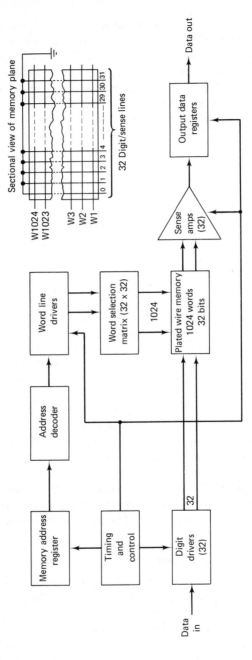

Figure 8–18 Linear-select plated wire memory system, 1024 words/32 bits (courtesy Motorola Semiconductor Products, Inc. Phoenix, AZ).

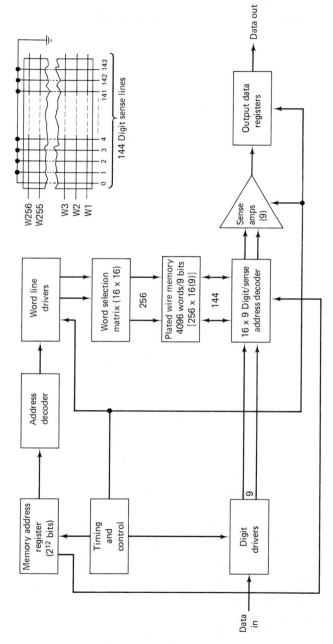

Figure 8-19 Coincident-select plated wire memory system, 4096 words/9 bits (courtesy Motorola Semiconductor Products, Inc., Phoenix, AZ).

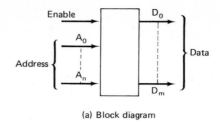

(a) Block diagram

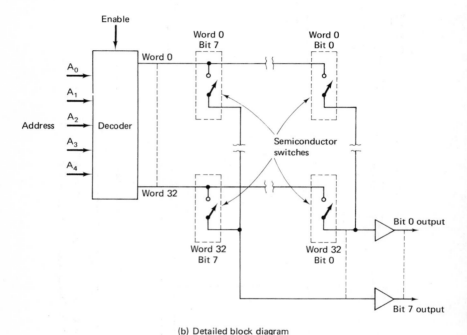

(b) Detailed block diagram

Figure 8–20   Read-Only Memory (ROM) concept; (a) block diagram, (b) detailed block diagram (courtesy of Motorola Semiconductor Products, Inc., Phoenix, AZ).

location then appear at the output. Most ROMs are not capable of being changed once data has been stored. This means, of course, that loss of power to the equipment or error in operations cannot destroy the contents. However, it does also mean that if new data is required, another ROM package must be used. Alterable ROMs are becoming common, and the future promises increasing use of this type of memory package.

The storage mode in ROMs is somewhat different than the random-access memories discussed earlier. Whereas some type of semiconductor FF is usually the storage media in semiconductor random-access memories, a simple semiconductor switch is sufficient for the ROM. An "open" switch may be either a logic 0 or a logic 1, depending on the technique used in design and manufacture of the memory. The type 8223 ROM shown in the detailed block diagram of Figure 8–20(b) uses an "open" switch as a logic 1 and a closed switch as a logic 0. Linear selection techniques are used to enable one of 32 8-bit words in the ROM. The configuration of the switch at each bit position in the selected word is determined and applied to individual buffer amplifiers for each bit of the output word. The 8223 ROM may be obtained with any desired storage pattern, or it may be programmed by the user. Remember, however, that once the device has a program stored, it may not be changed. Mistakes are costly with ROMs.

Word selection techniques are not limited to linear methods. Coincident selection is also commonly used, usually in ROMs with larger storage capacity. Up to 2048 12-bit words are available in some of the larger units, and the top limit is not yet in sight.

One of the most recent applications of a ROM is in the so-called "microprogrammed" digital computer. As explained in earlier chapters, the computer is controlled in its actions by a sequence of program steps stored in memory. Each program step can require a large number of logic operations, which are usually defined in the computer by direct connections. The operations are then carried out in the necessary timing order by logic elements such as flip-flops, gates, etc. In the microprogrammed digital computer the sequences are stored in ROMs, which then operate general-purpose logic elements rather than dedicated elements. The instructions stored in the ROM are called *microinstructions*. Since a specific main program step (instruction), such as ADD, always requires the same sequence of operations (microinstructions), a ROM can store this sequence and make it available when required. The ADD instruction, then, can act as an input address, causing all of the microinstructions to be made available at the ROM output.

ROM applications are almost endless. Tables of mathematical data may be stored for use in digital computers, calculators, and computing counters. Digital display devices, such as those used with digital test equipment and computers, must generate individual characters (letters, numbers, symbols, etc). ROMs are used to store the form of each of the characters, so that it may be addressed and put to use without having to form it each time it is required. A code used to develop a digital data message may have to be changed to a different form for transmission. ROMs once again tend to be the most efficient method of translation. The reader is sure to encounter numerous other example of ROM applications as familiarity is gained with the digital computer.

Modern ROMs exist with capabilities from as small as 128 bits to as large as many thousands of bits. Word and bit expansion are accomplished in the same manner as other semiconductor memory assemblies.

8–3   EXTERNAL STORAGE

Principles of Mass Storage Devices

As the requirements for information storage grow, internal storage becomes not only unnecessary but actually may not be cost-effective. The low capacity and high speed of core and semiconductor memories can give way to lower speed storage methods with much greater capacity. The computer programmer then assigns the appropriate type of memory, internal or external, to be used for various applications.

Large-scale storage devices may be approached as a separate system, even though they may be directly linked with a digital computer. The link is most often software (programming), rather than hardware, since the organization of the storage devices tends to differ radically from that of the computer. Most of the devices that store large masses of information have many principles in common and can be viewed as shown in Figure 8–21. The *storage media*, most often a magnetizable surface, retains the information presented to it by the *write heads*. Conversion of the electrical representation of computer information to a form that will activate the storage media

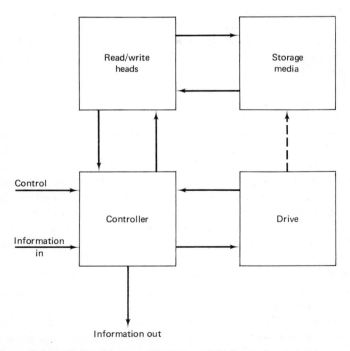

Figure 8–21   General large-scale memory device.

is the function of the write heads. The *read heads* convert the stored information back to electrical form. A *drive* provides the motive force to physically move the storage media. The *controller* is a multi-function device, formatting and converting data from one form to another, checking for errors, maintaining constant drive speed, etc.

Although some large-scale memory devices use other than magnetic techniques, by far the majority depend on some aspect of magnetism. Ferromagnetic cores have already been discussed, but, as noted, large-scale storage capability is too expensive using this method. At the expense of access time, less expensive magnetic techniques may be used. Practically all of the large-scale magnetic storage devices use a common recording/reproducing technique.

A magnetic material that has not previously been magnetized may be considered as made up of millions of tiny magnets randomly scattered throughout the material (Figure 8–22(a)). The random arrangement results in the magnetic fields canceling each other. If, however, an external magnetic field is applied to the material, the tiny magnets align themselves with the field, and the material becomes "magnetized." The direction of magnetization (Figure 8–22(b) and 8-22(c)) depends on the direction of the external field, which is physically designed to be in one direction or another; that is, it is binary in nature. Information may then be recorded by controlling the direction of the external magnetic field.

Using a technique similar to the magnetic core memory allows generation of the required external magnetic field. Section 8–2 showed that a toroidal ferromagnetic core stored information in the direction of its closed magnetic field. If the *magnetic* path is opened by cutting a gap in the core, the field is not maintained when the electrical current causing the field is removed. However, the presence of a magnetic material near the gap completes the *magnetic* path and the magnetic material becomes magnetized at the spot immediately adjacent to the core gap. Removal of the electrical current stops the magnetic field in the core, but the magnetic material is now magnetized and information is stored (see Figure 8–22(d)).

The physical configuration of the core (more commonly called a "head") varies greatly. Typical recording heads are seen in Figure 8–23.

Magnetically recorded information is retrieved by moving the magnetic surface and a "reproducing" head in respect to each other. The reproducing head is constructed in a manner similar to the recording head, so that the recorded magnetic surface moves across a gap in the head. When the magnetized spot is directly under the gap, a complete magnetic path exists and magnetic lines of force flow through the head. A property of magnetism states that when there is relative motion between magnetic lines of force and an electrical conductor, a current will flow in the electrical conductor. Thus, when the magnetic path is closed by the magnetized spot, the sudden flow of

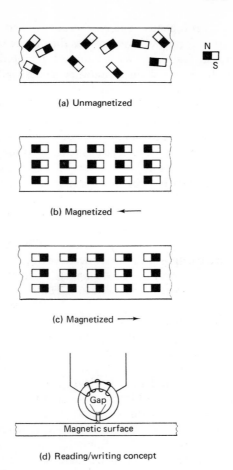

(a) Unmagnetized

(b) Magnetized ⟵

(c) Magnetized ⟶

(d) Reading/writing concept

Figure 8–22   Magnetic recording principles; (a) unmagnetized, (b) magnetized ⟵, (c) magnetized ⟶, (d) Read/Write concept.

magnetic lines of force causes an electrical indication in the wires of the head. The direction of magnetization determines the direction of magnetic lines of force and subsequently the direction of current flow in the winding. Binary information is therefore retrieved from the magnetic surface.

Magnetic recording surfaces are deposited on a non-magnetic surface and physically moved in respect to the recording/reproducing head(s). During the recording (WRITE) operation the recording head is energized by control circuits to record either a one or a zero each time the head is energized. The magnetic surface is continuously moved so that the information is recorded one bit at a time in *serial* fashion. (Note: The use of more than one head at a

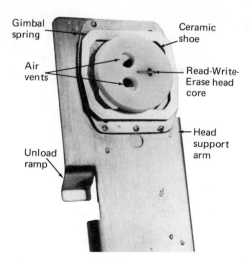

Figure 8–23 Typical recording head (courtesy of Hewlett-Packard, Palo Alto, CA.)

time allows recording a number of bits at the same time; a typical example might be a complete character.) Numerous factors enter into recording density (bits per inch) and speed of operation. These factors are discussed as specific types of devices are encountered.

One factor in common with all of the large-scale magnetic storage devices is *sequential access* to the stored information. In the previous memory devices information was obtained by proceeding *directly* to the storage location (*random access*). Sequential-access methods require proceeding through all intervening storage locations to reach the required information. Obviously such means of obtaining information are much slower than random-access methods.

Data Recording Methods

In all magnetic storage devices information is stored by changing some characteristic of the storage medium and is retrieved by sensing that change. Many techniques exist, and only the most common methods will be discussed. NRZ (Non-Return-to-Zero) and PE(Phase Encoded) are the most popular techniques used in magnetic data recording devices.

As discussed earlier, passing current pulses through wires wound on the cores of recording heads causes the recording medium to become magnetized in a direction determined by the direction of the current. Figure 8–24(a) shows a typical bit sequence and the resultant WRITE head current in a technique called RZ (Return-to-Zero). RZ techniques are explained only

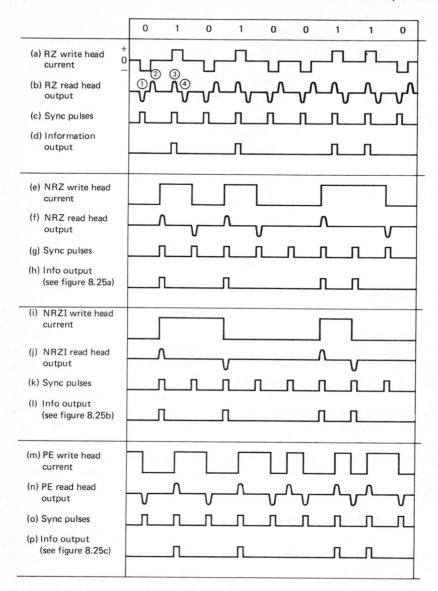

Figure 8–24 Data recording methods.

so that a groundwork may be provided for the more common methods of data recording and reproduction. Note that current directions are opposite ("+" for a binary 1 and "−" for a binary 0) and that no current flows between pulses. Thus the surface is magnetized in a small area for each bit, and a non-magnetized area exists between bits. Since the current causes an area to be magnetized, the current waveforms also represent directions of magnetization for each recorded bit.

A principle of electromagnetism states that the current which is induced in the winding of the READ head is proportional to the *rate of change* of the magnetic field. Furthermore, the polarity depends on the direction of the magnetic field and whether it is increasing or decreasing. As a magnetized area on the surface of the recording medium moves under the READ head, a pulse of current is induced in the winding (see Figure 8–24(a)). The polarity of the pulse is determined by the magnetic field direction (1), and once the magnetic field is no longer changing, the pulses ceases. No output is present from the READ head until the magnetized area moves away from the head (1 to 2). Since the field is now *decreasing*, a pulse of the opposite polarity appears at the READ head (2). Between points 2 and 3 there is no change in magnetic field, and the READ head output is zero. The recorded magnetic pattern between 3 and 4 is opposite to that at 1 and 2, and the READ head output is an opposite pulse. Note that *both* a positive-going and a negative-going pulse appear for *each* stored bit. It is necessary to supply some form of synchronizing pulse, perhaps from a timing track, that assures sampling of the READ output at the time the bit location starts moving under the READ head. Figures 8–24(b), 8–24(c), and 8–24(d) complete the waveform drawings for RZ recording/reproducing techniques.

RZ methods have given way to the aforementioned NRZ and PE techniques, both of which have many variations. The basic characteristic of all NRZ techniques is that the recording medium is *always* saturated in one direction or the other. Each variation is based on the interpretation of the *change* in magnetic field (flux transition). In normal NRZ recording a flux transition indicates a change in bit significance—that is, 1 to 0 or 0 to 1. Groups of ones or groups of zeros do not cause a flux transition within the group (see Figures 8–24(e) through 8–24(h)). A circuit to supply an output pulse for each one bit is shown in Figure 8–25(a).

NRZI (Inverted) uses a flux transition to indicate a one; a lack of flux transition indicates a zero. The waveforms of Figure 8–24(i) through 8–24(l) portray NRZI operation, while Figure 8–25(b) shows a circuit that supplies NRZI drive using sync pulses (Figure 8–24(k)) and input pulses similar to the information output (Figure 8–24(l)). NRZI recording is one of the most popular forms of data storage on a magnetic medium because the bit density is greater. Since bit density is directly proportional to flux changes per inch, NRZI is superior in this category.

As opposed to NRZI recording in which a one is represented by a magnetic flux transition and zeros are the absence of transitions, in phase encoding (PE) the *direction* of transition carries the information. Thus a negative transition may represent a zero and a positive transition represent

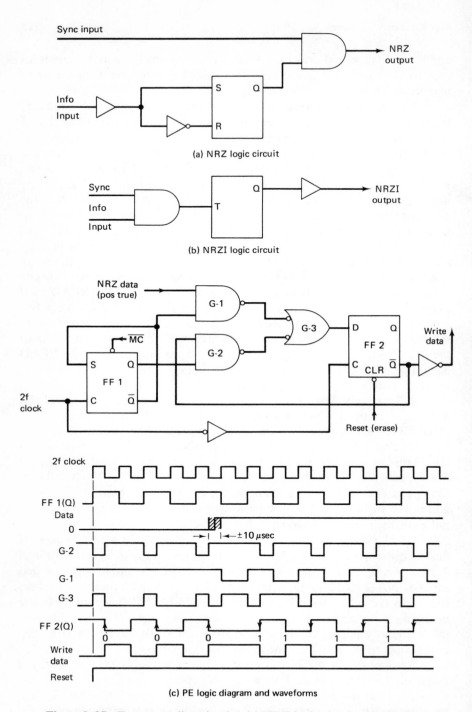

(a) NRZ logic circuit

(b) NRZI logic circuit

(c) PE logic diagram and waveforms

Figure 8–25 Data recording circuits, (a) NRZ logic circuit, (b) NRZI logic circuit, (c) PE logic diagram and waveforms.

a one, as in Figures 8–24(m) through 8–24(p). A logic diagram of a circuit that will generate the required head current for writing PE information is shown in Figure 8–25(c). The accompanying timing diagram shows phase relationships for this circuit.

Disc Memories

INTRODUCTION

Disc memories store information in concentric tracks on rotating disc(s) coated with a magnetizable surface. The disc(s) may be coated on one or both sides, rotating in either the horizontal or vertical plane, and be permanently mounted or removable. Information is recorded/reproduced by a single head per track or by movable heads which select the appropriate tracks. State-of-the-art disc memories provide bit densities greater than 4000 bits per inch, average access times as low as 2.5 milliseconds, rotational speeds up to 6000 rpm, with each surface capable of storing well over 10 million bits. Figure 8–26(a) is representative of a modern small disc memory unit.

THE STORAGE MEDIUM AND DRIVE

Magnetic recording techniques are used in disc memories. A disc of metal or plastic, not unlike a long-playing phonograph record, is coated with a magnetic material. High-density, high-speed disc units require a

Figure 8–26 Typical disc memory (courtesy Diablo Systems, Inc., Hayward, CA.).

metal "platter," usually aluminum, with a very flat shape and high dimensional stability. One form of recording disc has a ferromagnetic iron oxide suspended in an organic binder bonded to both surfaces. This type of coating can be identified by its brown color and relatively soft surface. A more durable magnetic surface can be obtained by electrolytically plating the metal disc with a nickle-cobalt compound which is silver in color.

The flexible plastic disc usually has an iron oxide coating. "Floppy" discs tend to straighten out when they reach rotational speed and, with proper read/record head design, are a convenient and inexpensive means of data storage.

Disc rotation is accomplished by physically mounting the disc(s) to a spindle. The spindle is driven either by a belt and pulley arrangement or directly from a drive motor.

Each recording surface of the disc memory is divided into a number of concentric *tracks*. Every track is divided into a number of *sectors* where information is stored in a predetermined format. Thus information location is identified by recording surface, track, and sector as shown in Figure 8–27(a).

The arrangement of information within each sector varies among disc memory manufacturers but generally consists of a *preamble,* the actual *information*, and a *postamble.* Controller electronic circuits are initialized

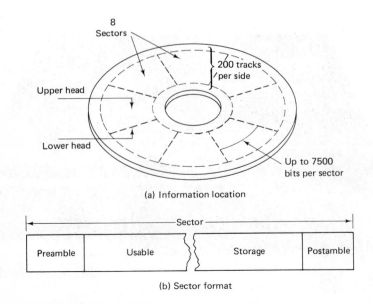

(a) Information location

(b) Sector format

Figure 8–27 Information arrangement on magnetic disc.

by the preamble and a synchronizing pattern is included, if required. Information in the sector consists of computer words and/or portions of words (such as bytes). A number of bytes or computer words is stored in each sector. The postamble checks sector parity and turns off the controller electronics. See Figure 8–27(b) for a typical arrangement of information in a disc sector.

HEADS

Modern disc drives use small ferrite core recording/reproducing heads that "fly" on an extremely thin (50 to 100 microinch) layer of air above the rotating disc surface. Since there is no direct head-to-disc contact, disc and head wear is almost non-existent. Furthermore, drive motor power requirements are significantly reduced due to lack of head-to-disc friction.

Moving-head disc drives use a single read/write head for *each* recording surface, and a mechanical system positions the head over the desired track. The mechanical positioning system allows a track density on the order of 100 to 200 tracks per inch, but access time is relatively slow due to head-positioning time delays. Reliability is also somewhat reduced due to the high degree of accuracy required to place the head *exactly* over the selected track.

Fixed-head disc drives employ a separate head per track. Since moving parts are all but eliminated, data access times are sharply reduced (five or more times faster). In addition, reliability is generally higher than moving-head systems. Track density is reduced with a consequent reduction in overall capacity, however.

CONTROLLER

The disc drive controller contains the electronic circuits that interface the serially recorded information on the disc to the parallel-organized computer. Figure 8–28 is a block diagram of a typical disc drive controller. Data into the controller, if in parallel form, is converted to the required serial form by a *parallel-serial register* before it is made available to the recording head(s) by the *read/write control*. Based on address information from the computer, the *selection logic* enables the correct head(s), causes the *head position control* to move the head(s) to the correct track, and selects the correct sector on the track by using the *sector transducer's* output as a reference. It is then merely necessary to supply the WRITE input to the read/write control, and data is recorded.

Similar head selection and positioning actions occur during the read operation. Timing is separated from the recorded data in the *data/timing separator*. Data is submitted to an *error check* while being reformatted into parallel form by the *serial-parallel register*. If no errors are detected, the *output control* passes the parallel data, along with timing, to the computer. The logic circuits associated with these operations are quite complex, but

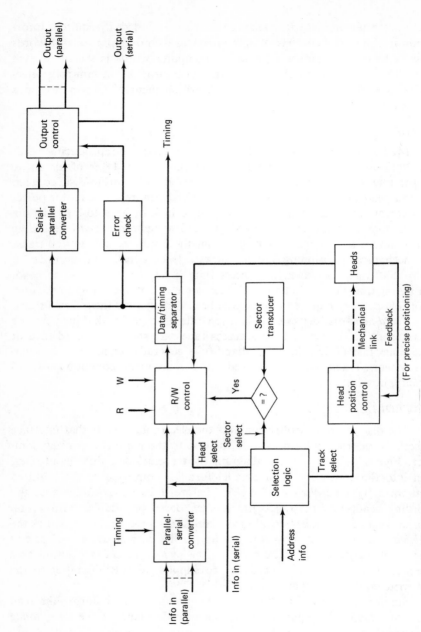

Figure 8–28 Typical disc drive controller.

the basic functions are explained by the block diagram. Reference to the instruction and maintenance manuals for specific units is recommended if more detailed coverage is desired.

Drum Memories

INTRODUCTION

Drum memories store information in parallel tracks on rotating metal cylinders coated with a magnetizable surface. The drum may rotate in either a horizontal or vertical plane and is usually permanently mounted. Information is generally recorded/reproduced by a single head per track. State-of-the-art drum memories provide bit densities similar to disc units, access times somewhat longer than discs, and rotational speeds up to 6000 rpm. Physically the drum may be from four inches to five feet long and six inches to four feet in diameter. A typical drum memory (Figure 8-29) used to augment internal storage of a minicomputer has 16 tracks, each track capable of storing 4096 16-bit words *plus* parity. It rotates at 1800 rpm, transferring information at the rate of 2,180,000 bits per second.

Figure 8-29 Typical drum memory (courtesy DATUM, Inc., Anaheim, CA.)

THE STORAGE MEDIUM AND DRIVE

Magnetic recording techniques are also used in drum memories. The drum is manufactured from a dimensionally stable material and coated with either nickle-cobalt or iron oxide as with magnetic discs. In magnetic drum devices, drive from a motor is applied to the drum via an axle which passes through its axis. Record/reproduce heads record and reproduce data as the drum surface passes adjacent to them. Thus, when accessing particular data, there may be a rotational delay (called *latency time*) of as much as one complete revolution.

One possible organization of information on a memory drum is shown in Figure 8–30. Storage drums may be operated either in parallel or serial mode. The parallel mode of operation stores one bit per track per word, and as many tracks as there are bits in a word are written into or read from at one time. At least one head per track is required for this type of operation. Words stored in parallel on a drum are located using a prerecorded timing track. The desired location is stored in a register in binary form. Timing track signals are counted beginning at a zero location, and when the timing track counter agrees with the desired location, the information that is present at the read heads is recovered, or data is written into the drum.

In the serial mode, words are stored one bit at a time, one after the other, on a single track. When a track is filled, the information is automatically switched to the next track. The prerecorded timing track is also used in serial mode for information location.

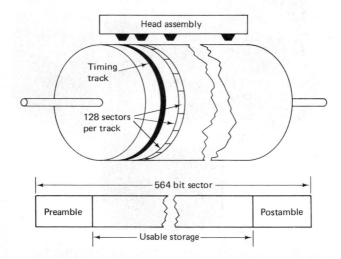

Figure 8–30 Information arrangement on magnetic drum.

HEADS

As with disc memories, in most drums the heads are maintained a given distance from the surface. (Constant head-surface contact with the recording medium results in undesirable wear of the surface as in disc drives.) Early drums had permanently mounted heads, but it was difficult to maintain the required head-surface dimension with changing environment and use. Exacting dimensional tolerances were also required. These difficulties combined to result in a relatively large spacing, with consequent low bit density.* More recent record/reproduce heads are mounted in a pad which "flies" above the surface of the rotating drum, just as in disc drives. The flow of air over a rotating body actually lifts the head away from the surface, yet maintains an optimum spacing of 50 to 150 microinches. Some high-performance systems fly their heads at only 10 to 15 microinches to gain greater bit density. Obviously great care must be taken to keep dust particles away from the surfaces to prevent "head crashes." Flying heads can provide bit densities up to 4000 bits per inch.

CONTROLLER

Typical drum electronics are shown in block diagram form in Figure 8–31. The *clock circuits*, responding to the prerecorded clock signals detected by the *clock heads*, develop (a) an index marker to identify the beginning of each revolution of the drum, (b) timing signals to identify each bit position, (c) a *sector marker*, and (d) a *write clock* to be used during the write operation.

In the *control logic* the correct data heads are selected and either the write or read operation enabled. Address information from external equipment is decoded to select the appropriate track and trunk. *Write control* inputs from the encoder/decoder are used in the control logic to determine the polarity of drum magnetization, while *read control* outputs to the track and trunk selection circuits cause the drum to be in the read mode whenever it is not writing.

Encoder/decoder circuits are the most complex, as many functions must be performed. A *sector counter* keeps a record of what portion of each track is being used. In order to control the initial condition of the encoder during a write condition and to prevent transient conditions from affecting new data being recorded, a *preamble* is added at the beginning of each sector. A *preamble counter* performs this function. *Encoder logic* mechanizes the

---

*Usable bit density depends on head-surface spacing. As the head is moved away from the surface, magnetic fields from adjacent bits tend to overlap, and a maximum spacing exists for a specified bit density. Fixed-position heads usually limit bit densities to the region of 200 bits per inch.

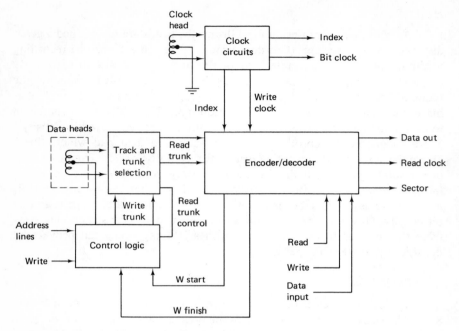

Figure 8–31 Typical drum controller.

function of converting binary data to flux reversals of the magnetic drum surface. *Read amplifiers*, *detectors*, and *decoder/counter* circuits retrieve the magnetic information from the drum and convert it to digital form for use by external circuits.

Therefore, under control of the inputs from external circuits, the drum memory can store and recover large amounts of information at rates somewhat slower than internal memory but faster than magnetic tape systems.

Magnetic Tape Storage

INTRODUCTION

Magnetic tape devices are probably the best known and most widely publicized mass storage devices. The communications media (television, newspapers, etc) never pass up an opportunity to publicize the computer by showing magnetic tape units "whirring away" at their work. Since many of the principles of magnetic tape storage are similar to other principles already discussed, only major differences are covered in this section. A typical magnetic tape transport was seen in Figure 2–15.

THE STORAGE MEDIUM AND DRIVE

This storage medium uses magnetic tape which resembles in appearance and recording/playback techniques the tape used for audio recording/playback. It consists of a flexible base (such as plastic) covered with a ferro-magnetic material such as iron oxide. Widths vary from 0.150 inch up to 2 inches; lengths from 50 to 3600 feet; and thickness from 0.0005 inch to the vicinity of 0.002 inch. A common configuration is 0.5-inch wide, 0.002-inch thick, and 2400-feet-long computer-grade tape.* Many other configurations are used, but the principles of operation are adequately covered using this example.

The tape is physically moved with a precision mechanism that assures rapid start-stop capability, constant speed drive during the time the tape is in movement, and protection against tape breakage. Figure 2–15 is one of the many approaches to solving these problems. The transport is basically a mechanical device, using non-digital controls, and is not discussed in this text.

HEADS AND DATA ORGANIZATION

As explained in earlier discussions, the magnetic characteristic of a region of the tape is changed by an electrical current passed through a winding on a recording head. The tape then moves to the next location for recording another bit of information. The number of bits that can be stored is related to the surface area available and the bit density (number of bits per inch). Total storage capability is increased by using more than one head per tape and recording information in tracks. A typical head assembly used with 0.5-inch tape has seven or nine recording/reproducing heads, as may be seen in Figure 8–32. (One of the heads is often used for error detection.)

The use of multiple heads not only allows an increase in bit density but also results in storage of information in individual characters rather than separate bit form. A 9-head read/write assembly then has a capability to directly record 8-bit codes such as ANSI (ASCII), leaving a separate position for error detection. Information is generally stored in groups of characters called *records*, and records are separated by *inter-record gaps*. The inter-record gaps (typically 0.75 inch) are used to provide sufficient startup and stop time for tape movement. A group of records is called a *file*, and a gap of approximately 3.7 inches separates files. Figure 8–33 shows the general concepts of data storage on magnetic tape. Ranges of packing densities are from 200 to 4000 bits per inch. Tape speeds vary from 1.875 inches per second (tape casettes) up to 200 inches per second.

---

*Although computer tape resembles regular audio tape, it must be a better grade, more precisely manufactured product.

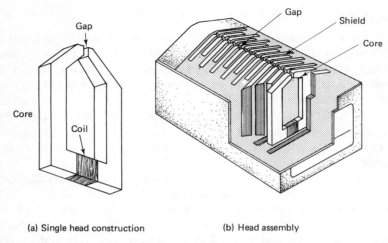

(a) Single head construction   (b) Head assembly

Figure 8–32 Magnetic tape recording head; (a) single head construction, (b) head assembly.

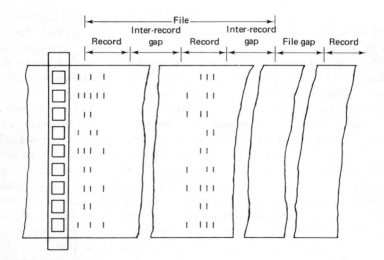

Figure 8–33 Magnetic tape data organization.

CONTROLLER

The controller for a magnetic tape data storage system contains the electronics required to perform the basic functions of transport control, timing, and data reformatting. Design approaches are somewhat varied.

The reader should refer to instruction and maintenance manuals of specific tape units for details.

8–4 THE FUTURE

The reader may well see some of the memory concepts now under development as the major storage medium in the near future.

Magnetic bubble memories have advanced from the research and development stage to prototype production. Under the influence of a properly maintained external magnetic field, single crystal layers of certain ferromagnetic materials can be persuaded to form "bubbles" of magnetized material. The "bubbles" may be thought of as vertical bar magnets and may be manipulated by application of a rotating magnetic field. Data is entered into a bubble memory by electrical impulses that form bubbles and read out by conventional magneto-electrical conversion. Bubble memories presently have a data density of about 2.5 million bits/square inch, an average access time near 2.5 milliseconds, and a price that promises to reach the cost/bit ratio of magnetic tape. The most promising applications are in the area of disc and drum replacement.

Another promising storage medium is the charge-coupled device (CCD). It is organized much like a shift register, except that the storage of information is in the capacitance of each of the stages of the device. Each capacitor is equivalent to a flip-flop stage in a shift register, and information is represented by the existence of a charge or the lack of a charge on each capacitor. The CCD is serial in organization and dynamic in operation. Information must travel the complete length of the "register" before it is available, and it must be recirculated continuously in order to keep the charge from "leaking" off. Integrated circuit chips capable of storing 16K bits are currently in use, and larger capacities are in the near future. CCD storage appears at the present time to be most promising in the magnetic disc, magnetic drum replacement field. Access time of CCDs is much faster than drums and discs; they weigh less, take up less space, and use less power. The lack of any moving parts also improves reliability, and it is anticipated that CCDs will soon take their rightful place in the hierarchy of memory devices.

A relatively recent entry on the external memory scene is the digital casette system (Figure 8–34). Magnetic tape casettes, similar to the common home entertainment recording casettes, are used to store digital data. Most of the tape transports operate bidirectionally and with a 2-speed capability in both read and write mode. Usual recording format is serial on either one or two tracks, and in many cases both the clock and the data are recorded on the same track.

Figure 8–34   Magnetic tape casette storage (courtesy Cipher Data Products Inc. San Diego, CA.).

The common casette contains 300 feet of 0.5-mil, 0.150-inch magnetic tape. With a bit packing density of 800 bits per inch, approximately 360,000 8-bit characters may be stored on each track. Thus it can be seen that the digital casette system is an ideal paper tape replacement, not only faster, but generally more reliable and less costly.

Memory technology is advancing rapidly. Magnetic cores are getting smaller, bit density is increasing, cost per bit is decreasing, and access times are in the sub-microsecond range. Disc density is improving. New and innovative changes are appearing in tape storage systems. More than any other area of interest, computer memory systems are advancing in leaps and bounds. Table 8–1 compares various memory devices.

Table 8–1   Memory Device Comparisons

Memory Type	Capacity* (Bits)	Cycle* Time	Access Method	Volatile?
Semiconductor	Space available	< 100 ns–750 ns	Random	Yes
Core	Space available	300 ns to > 1 ms	Random	Yes
Plated wire	Space available	100 ns–1 ms	Random	Yes
Disc (hard)	25 K–50 M	10 ms–35 ms	Sequential	No
Disc (floppy)	1 M–3.2 M	35 ms–85 ms	Sequential	No
Drum	300 K–2.6 M	8 ms–20 ms	Sequential	No
Tape (reel-to-reel)	200–1600 bpi	Variable	Sequential	No
Casette/Cartridge	750–1600 bpi	Variable	Sequential	No

*Values shown are nominal.
bpi = bits per inch.

QUESTIONS

1. Where in the computer can memory be found?
2. What are the general characteristics of *internal* storage?
3. What are the general characteristics of *external* (*auxiliary*) storage?
4. Explain the concepts of *random access* to stored information.
5. Explain the concepts of *sequential access* to stored information.
6. What kind of memory device possesses the shortest access time?
7. Explain the operation of a coincident-selection memory system.
8. What is a memory plane?
9. Describe the function of (a) Memory Buffer Registers, (b) X decoders, (c) Y decoders, and (d) Memory Address Registers.
10. Contrast and compare static and dynamic semiconductor memories.
11. Explain how a magnetic core can store binary information.
12. How is stored information retrieved from a magnetic core?
13. In a coincident-current selection magnetic core memory, what is the function of (a) X drive line, (b) Y drive line, (c) sense line, and (d) inhibit line?
14. Explain the operation of a linear-selection memory system.
15. How does information storage in a plated wire memory differ from magnetic core storage?
16. What is a Read-Only-Memory? List some typical applications.
17. List the four major functional sections of mass storage devices and explain their basic purposes.
18. Discuss the storage of binary information on magnetic surfaces.
19. Compare the attributes of NRZI vs PE recording methods.
20. Discuss the organization of information on a magnetic disc.
21. Discuss the organization of information on a magnetic drum.
22. Discuss the organization of information on magnetic tape.
23. Make your own predictions concerning computer memory systems of the future.

9

The ARITHMETIC/LOGIC Function

The ARITHMETIC/LOGIC section is that part of the computer that performs basic arithmetic and logic operations upon command of the CONTROL section. It contains circuits to perform addition; complementing devices to use with the adders for subtraction; registers for multiplication, division, and temporary storage; and gate circuits for logic operations such as AND, OR, EXCLUSIVE OR, etc.

Digital computers perform arithmetic and logic operations in some form of binary operations. The only real hindrance to the use of binary operations is the apparent difficulty that many experience when binary-based arithmetic is performed. If one realizes that binary-based arithmetic operates with a set of rules which parallel arithmetic in the decimal (or other) number systems, then part of the mystery disappears. The need for using binary elements in digital computers has been adequately discussed in earlier chapters, and all that remains now is to show the rules for binary-based arithmetic and demonstrate that they supply valid answers to arithmetic problems. Logic elements can then be investigated as they perform arithmetic operations and the complete ARITHMETIC/LOGIC section can be demonstrated.

9–1 BINARY ADDITION AND SUBTRACTION

Concepts

Binary addition operates with the same rules as decimal addition, except that it is simpler. The binary addition rules shown below completely define the operations to be performed.

			A		*B*		*S*	*C*
			Addend		Augend		Sum	Carry
			0	plus	0	=	0	0
			0	plus	1	=	1	0
			1	plus	0	=	1	0
			1	plus	1	=	0	1

Examples of binary addition are shown in Examples 9–1, 9–2, and 9–3.

Example 9–1.

Decimal	Binary
5	101
+ 2	+10
7	111

Example 9–2.

Decimal	Binary
10	1010
+ 9	+1001
19	10011

Example 9–3.

Decimal	Binary
27	11011
+15	+ 1111
42	101010

Circuits

THE HALF-ADDER CIRCUIT

Logic circuits may be used to implement the binary addition operation shown above. By equating numeric 0 with binary 0 and numeric 1 with binary 1, the techniques of Boolean algebra are used to determine the interconnection of logic circuits required to perform binary addition. According to the rules of binary addition, the addition of an addend digit A and an augend digit B results in a sum digit and, perhaps, also a carry digit. Examining the sum requirements first, it can be seen that a sum of 1 exists when A is 0 and B is 1 or when A is 1 and B is 0—that is, $\bar{A}B + A\bar{B}$. A carry of 1 appears only when both A is 1 and B is 1 (AB). Thus a logic circuit is required that will accept two inputs, A and B, and provide two outputs, $S = \bar{A}B + A\bar{B}$ and $C = AB$.

C is easily obtained from a simple 2-input AND gate. The S output occurs from any EXCLUSIVE OR circuit (see Figure 9–1). An assembly that supplies both S and C outputs for the two inputs A and B is called a *half-adder*. The half-adder may be used to add *two* binary digits but is limited in application due to the possibility of a carry occurring in a less-significant position. Examples 9–1 and 9–2 show *specific* cases where half-adders could be used, since no carries result from addition operations except in the most-significant position.

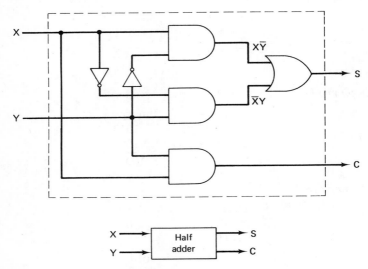

Figure 9–1   EXCLUSIVE-OR circuit (half-adder)

THE FULL-ADDER CIRCUIT

In Example 9–3, however, each addition operation results in a carry which must be added to the next-most-significant addition (except in the least-significant position). A *full-adder*, capable of accepting the addend, augend, and a carry input and furnishing a sum and carry output, satisfies these requirements. Figure 9–2(a) shows a table of all possible combinations of the addend, augend, and carry input with resultant sum and carry outputs. The table is developed using the basic rules of binary addition and supplies sufficient information to develop the logic equations describing the full-adder. Numerous methods of implementing the logic equations exist, one of which is shown in Figure 9–2(b). Multi-unit full-adders exist in integrated circuit form (Figure 9–2(c)) and are also included as part of large-scale and medium-scale integrated circuit computer assemblies.

Serial vs Parallel

Addition may be accomplished in a computer either in a serial manner (one pair of digits at a time) or in parallel (all digits at the same time). Serial addition, although it requires only one full-adder and supporting logic circuitry, is seldom seen in modern digital computer ARITHMETIC/LOGIC sections. Excessive time is required to perform serial addition. Modern

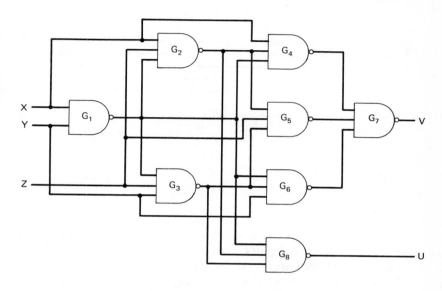

$$\text{Sum} = \overline{A} \cdot \overline{B} \cdot C + \overline{A} \cdot B \cdot \overline{C} + A \cdot \overline{B} \cdot \overline{C} + A \cdot B \cdot C$$

$$\text{Carry out} = \overline{A} \cdot B \cdot C + A \cdot \overline{B} \cdot C + A \cdot B \cdot \overline{C} + A \cdot B \cdot C = A \cdot C + A \cdot B + B \cdot C$$

(a)

A	B	C_i	S	C_o
0	0	0	0	0
0	0	1	1	0
0	1	0	1	0
0	1	1	0	1
1	0	0	1	0
1	0	1	0	1
1	1	0	0	1
1	1	1	1	1

(b)

Figure 9–2 Full-adder; (a) truth table, (b) logic diagram, (c) type 7483 4-bit full-adder.

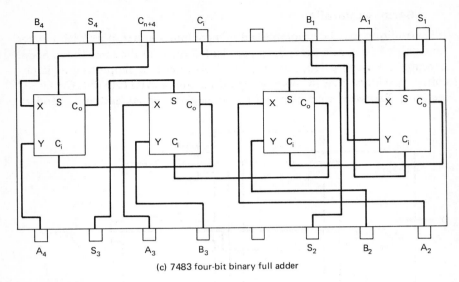

(c) 7483 four-bit binary full adder

Figure 9–2   (Continued)

technology has cut cost and space requirements to the point where the advantages of the high speed of parallel operation can be realized. A full-adder is used for each bit in the computer word, and addition occurs in a fraction of the time taken by serial operation. In simplified form, then, the adder in a typical ARITHMETIC/LOGIC section consists merely of x full-adders, where x equals the number of bits in the computer word.

Block Diagram Operation

If, for example, 5-digit numbers must be added, five full-adders are required. The addend is stored temporarily in the A register and the augend in the B register (Figure 9–3). Note that more detailed investigation of the ARITHMETIC/LOGIC section, as in Figure 9–3, reveals additional circuitry that often does not appear in *functional* diagrams such as Figure 2–9. Stored information is sent to the adders through the block labeled *arithmetic control*, which is a complex network of gates. Thus, if 01000 (addend) is to be added to 00100 (augend), the following simplified sequence is initiated.

1. The addend is retrieved from memory and placed in the A register. The A register now contains 01000 and the B register contains 00000.
2. The augend is retrieved from memory and placed in the B register. The A register now contains 01000 and the B register contains 00100.

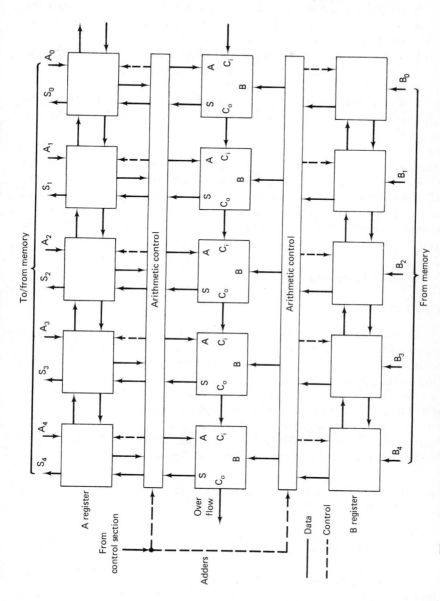

Figure 9-3 Arithmetic section detailed block diagram.

3. Arithmetic control is enabled to ADD and the adders generate the sum of the addend and augend. The A register and B register contents do not change.
4. The sum is routed through the arithmetic control to the A register, and the sum replaces the addend. The A register now contains 01100 and the B register contains 00100.
5. The sum is routed to the memory if this is the last addition to be performed. If additional use of the sum is planned, it remains in the A register.

It should be stressed that 5-bit information (four bits of numeric value and one sign bit) is used only to simplify explanation. Modern computers work with 16-bit, 24-bit, and even greater numbers of bits as packages of information. Explanations with such large numbers of bits become unwieldy, although such operations are mere extensions of the methods used with the shorter examples.

Signed Numbers

CONCEPTS

Perhaps it has been noted that addition examples shown so far have considered only unsigned numbers. In actual practice, numbers in the digital computer are used with an algebraic sign attached, and arithmetic operations using both positive and negative numbers are constantly encountered. Computer words usually contain a sign bit adjacent to the most-significant digit. The most common convention assigns a binary 0 as a positive sign and a binary 1 as a negative sign. For example, $+10_{10}$ exists as the 4-bit binary word (*plus* sign bit) 01010, thereby requiring five bits. However, *negative* numbers may be stored in a number of different forms as shown below.

Decimal	Sign-true magnitude form		One's complement form		Two's complement form	
-10_{10}	1	1010	1	0101	1	0110
	sign	magnitude	sign	magnitude	sign	magnitude

The sign-true magnitude form defines a negative number by the one bit adjacent to the most-significant digit. Number *magnitude* remains in the same form as the equivalent positive number.

Complemented numbers are used most often in the subtraction and mixed sign addition processes, and it will be shown that a machine can be made to both add and subtract using only addition circuits. Every number system has two types of complements: *radix-minus-one* and *true*. The *radix-minus-one complement* is formed by subtracting each digit of a number from the radix of the number system, minus one. Consider the familiar decimal number system (radix ten). The radix-minus-one complement of 7 is 2 ($9 - 7 = 2$), while the radix-minus-one complement of 66 is 33 ($99 - 66 = 33$). The radix-minus-one complement in the decimal system is more commonly called the *nine's complement*. In the binary number system (radix 2), the radix-minus-one complement is formed by changing each one in a number to zero and each zero to one. Thus the radix-minus-one complement of 1 is 0, and the radix-minus-one complement of 10101 is 01010. The radix-minus-one complement in the binary system is called the *one's complement*.

 True complements are obtained by subtracting each digit of a number from the radix of the number system.* The true (ten's) complement of 7 is 3 ($10 - 7 = 3$), while the ten's complement of 66 is 34 ($100 - 66 = 34$). Binary *true (two's) complements* are also easily formed. One merely determines the one's complement and adds one to the result. For example, the two's complement of 10101 is obtained by one's complementing (01010) and adding one (01011).

 Arithmetic section design determines the method of negative number representation for each computer. Advantages of the three negative number methods are discussed as examples of their use are shown. The method selected is usually maintained throughout the computer as numbers are manipulated.

ADDITION OF SIGNED NUMBERS

 Addition of signed binary numbers follows the same rules used for addition of signed decimal numbers.

 Rule 1
 If both the addend and augend have the same signs, the sum is the total of both numbers with the sign retained.

Addition of two signed positive numbers presents no problem as long as the sum is no greater than the absolute value storable in the computer's registers and memory. The circuits shown in Figure 9–3, when used with signed numbers, can accommodate values between 0 (00000) and $+15$ (01111). A sum greater than $+15$, therefore, must provide some indication of "overflow." Example 9–4 shows an addition that falls within the repre-

---

 True complements may also be obtained by subtracting each digit of a number from the radix-minus-one of the number system and then adding one to the least-significant digit of the resulting numbers. For example, $[(9 - 7) + 1 = 3]$; and $[(99 - 66) + 1 = 34]$.

sentable range of the circuit of Figure 9–3, while Example 9–5 shows an example of an overflow condition.

Example 9–4.

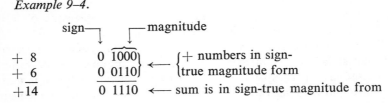

Example 9–5.

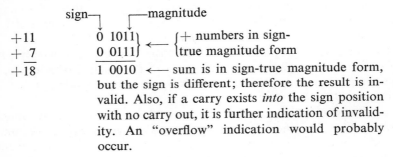

but the sign is different; therefore the result is invalid. Also, if a carry exists *into* the sign position with no carry out, it is further indication of invalidity. An "overflow" indication would probably occur.

Furthermore, if two negative numbers are summed, it is also apparent that difficulties exist (see Example 9–6).

Example 9–6.

$$
\begin{array}{rl}
-\ 5 & \quad 1\ 0101 \\
(+)-\ 9 & \quad 1\ 1001 \\
\hline
-\overline{14} & \quad \boxed{1}\ 0\ 1110 \ \longleftarrow \text{magnitude correct} \\
& \qquad\ \ \text{sign bit incorrect}
\end{array}
$$

Because of the sign bit discrepancy (and other problems soon to be discovered), negative numbers are seldom manipulated in sign-true magnitude form within the ARITHMETIC/LOGIC section. If stored in memory in sign-true magnitude form, conversion to a form compatible with the ARITHMETIC/LOGIC section's operation must be performed *before* and *after* arithmetic manipulation. The use of *complementary addition* solves many of the problems encountered when negative numbers must be used.

Both one's and two's complement operation are used in modern computers. The one's complement is easily formed in binary but requires some increase in complexity in the adder circuits. Two's complements use adder circuits directly but require additional circuitry for conversion. Due to the preponderance of two's-complement-equipped computers, only this system will be discussed.

As described earlier, two's complements are formed by obtaining the one's complement and adding one. The problem of Example 9–6 is developed using both ten's and two's complements in Example 9–7.

Example 9–7.

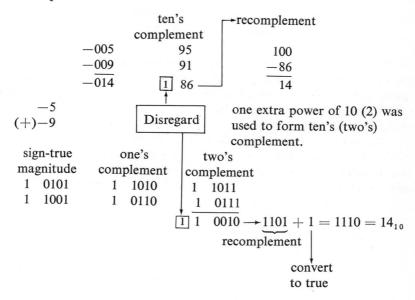

The two's complement result is correct. The sign bit represents a negative number, the result of adding two negative numbers. Furthermore, although an overflow occurs, it is a valid operation since a carry propagating *out* of the sign bit position was accompanied by a carry *into* the sign bit position. Magnitude representation is in the two's complement form and, when converted to true form as shown, reveals the proper value. It should be remembered, however, that conversion probably does not occur until it is necessary to make this information available to the human user. The computer is wired to always recognize a number prefixed with a one as a negative number and responds accordingly. Each of the examples used to demonstrate the rules of signed binary addition should be correlated with the circuit of Figure 9–3.

Rule 2

If the addend and augend have unlike signs, *subtract* the smaller from the larger. The sum is the *difference* in absolute value of the two quantities with the sign of the larger attached.

This rule requires *subtraction*, and such a capability has not yet been discussed. However, an alternate compatible with designs using *only* adders is available and in common use. Verification of the *complementary addition* equivalence of subtraction is shown by demonstration of the above rule. Consider first the addition shown in Example 9–8(a).

Example 9-8.

(a)	$+8$	(b)	$+8$	(c)	0	1000
$(+)-6$			$+4$		1	1010 ← true complement
$+2$		$+\boxed{1}\,2$		$\boxed{1}$ 0	0010

The same result is obtained by true complementing the negative number and adding (Example 9–8(b)). The carry is disregarded for the same reason shown in Example 9–7. Note that the result appears in the sign-true magnitude form. Reversing the position of the numbers, that is, $-6 + (+8)$, shows no difference as long as the negative number is complemented.

If, however, the problem is that of adding a negative number to a smaller positive number as shown in Example 9–9, the technique used with two negative numbers must be used. The negative number is two's complemented, addition performed, and the result recomplemented since the answer is in two's complement form.

Example 9–9.

$$
\begin{array}{ccl}
+6 & +6 & \\
(+)-8 & +2 & \\
\hline
-2 & 8 & \text{complement} \\
& & \text{to } -2
\end{array}
\qquad
\begin{array}{l}
\text{form two's} \\
\overbrace{\text{complement}} \\
1 \quad 1000 \\
\downarrow \\
01\dot{1}1 \\
\underline{+1} \\
1000
\end{array}
\qquad
\begin{array}{l}
0 \quad 0110 \\
1 \quad 1000 \\
\hline
1 \quad 1110 \ \text{two's} \\
\downarrow \quad \text{complement} \\
00\dot{0}1 \\
\underline{+1} \\
0010 \ \text{true magnitude}
\end{array}
$$

The hardware required to perform complementary addition (subtraction) is contained within the control portion of the ARITHMETIC/LOGIC section. From a conceptual viewpoint, it is merely necessary to select the digit to be supplied to the adder for addition or its complement if subtraction is to be performed. Figure 9–4 demonstrates a simple gating network that routes the necessary logic signals for one bit of the complete word from a register to an adder input.

Table 9–1 shows a number of examples which summarize addition of signed binary numbers in a typical ARITHMETIC/LOGIC section.

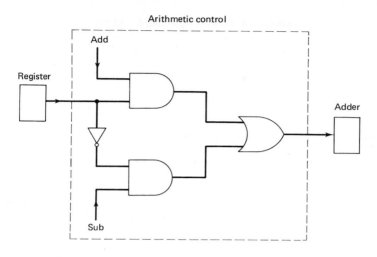

Figure 9–4 Concept of gating.

Table 9–1   Addition and Subtraction of Signed Binary Numbers

	sign	magnitude	
+8	0	1 0 0 0	
(+)+6	0	0 1 1 0	+ numbers in sign-true magnitude form
+14	0	1 1 1 0	

$$-5 \qquad\qquad 1 \quad 1\ 0\ 1\ 1$$
$$(+)-9 \qquad\quad 1 \quad 0\ 1\ 1\ 1 \Big\} - \text{numbers in two's complement form}$$
$$-14 \qquad \boxtimes 1 \quad 0\ 0\ 1\ 0$$

discard⌐
sign⌐   complement → {1 1 0 1 + 1 = 1 1 1 0 = 1 4$_{10}$

convert to true }⌐↑ true magnitude
magnitude form}   form

+8	0	1 0 0 0}	+ numbers in sign-true magnitude form
(+)−6	1	1 1 0 1 0}	− number in two's complement form
+2	⊠ 0	0 0 1 0	sign-true magnitude form

discard⌐
sign⌐

−6	1	1 1 0 1 0}	− number in two's complement form
(+)+8	0	1 0 0 0}	+ number in sign-true magnitude form
+2	⊠ 0	0 0 1 0	sign-true magnitude form

discard⌐
sign⌐

Table 9–1   (Continued)

$$
\begin{array}{r}
-9 \\
(+)\underline{+5} \\
-4
\end{array}
$$

1 0 1 1 1 — number in two's complement form
0 0 1 0 1
1 1 1 0 0

sign $\longrightarrow$ complement $\longrightarrow$ {0 0 1 1 $\underline{+\ 1}$ = $\underline{0\ 1\ 0\ 0}$ = -4_{10}

convert to true ⎫ ↑   true magnitude
magnitude form ⎭   form

$$
\begin{array}{r}
+5 \\
(+)\underline{-9} \\
-4
\end{array}
\qquad \text{same as above}
$$

$+8$	$+8$	-8	-8
$(-)\underline{+6}=(+)\underline{-6}$		$(-)\underline{+6}=(+)\underline{-6}$	
$+2$	$+2$	-14	-14

$+8$	$+8$	-8	-8
$(-)\underline{-6}=(+)\underline{+6}$		$(-)\underline{-6}=(+)\underline{+6}$	
$+14$	$+14$	-2	-2

$+6$	$+6$	-6	-6
$(-)\underline{+8}=(+)\underline{-8}$		$(-)\underline{+8}=(+)\underline{-8}$	
-2	-2	-14	-14

$+6$	$+6$	-6	-6
$(-)\underline{-8}=(+)\underline{+8}$		$(-)\underline{-8}=(+)\underline{+8}$	
$+14$	$+14$	$+2$	$+2$

Subtraction: change sign of subtrahend, complement and add

Rules

Assuming that the arithmetic section of the computer performs arithmetic by the two's complement method, the following rules describe its operation.

1. $+$ numbers are in sign-true magnitude form.
2. $-$ numbers are in two's complement form.
3. The sign is correct as it appears in the sign position of the result.
4. The result is invalid if a *carry propagates into the sign position but not out*, or if there is *no carry into the sign position with a carry out*.
5. Subtraction is performed by changing the sign of the subtrahend and adding the subtrahend to the minuend using the rules for addition of signed numbers.

Table 9–1 shows that each subtraction is actually an addition. Thus subtraction in the ARITHMETIC/LOGIC section uses existing adders, and the inputs are modified by the arithmetic control when subtraction is required.

Flow Chart Representation

Computer people often communicate by means of *flow charts* rather than words. *Flow charts* show the *actions and decisions necessary to accomplish procedures.* For example, the flow chart* in Figure 9–5 describes in general terms the complete addition and subtraction process just discussed.

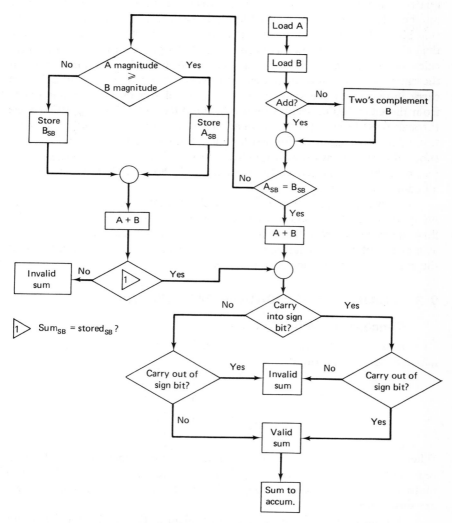

Figure 9–5 Flow chart, add and subtract.

*Diamond-shaped symbols denote a decision, while rectangular symbols are action or information blocks.

Note the ground rules and assumptions as a typical example is followed through the flow chart. Consider the addition $+8$ $(+)$ -6 as shown in Table 9–1. The addend $(+8)$ is loaded into the A register (1) and the augend (-6) is placed in the B register. Remember, negative numbers are in two's complement form. The first decision is add or not add. Since an addtition is indicated, the sign bits are compared. They are not the same, so the relative magnitudes of A and B are determined. The sign of the larger number is stored and the addition is performed. Comparison of the sign bit of the sum and the sign bit of the larger number is made to assure that a valid sum sign bit has occurred. If the signs are the same, the carry rules are evaluated. As noted, a valid sum has been obtained only if the carry into the sign bit matches the carry out of the sign bit or if no carry in or out of the sign bit occurs. Control signals and timing pulses from the CONTROL section sequence the ARITHMETIC/LOGIC section through these events every time an addition operation is performed. Evaluation of the operations performed for the addition $+8$ $(+)$ -6 in Table 9–1 shows direct correlation with the flow chart of Figure 9–5. The other examples of Table 9–1 should be followed through the flow chart to assure that all combinations are considered.

It can be seen that the use of flow charts reducès the requirements for many words and diagrams. Other computer operations are explained with flow charts elsewhere in this text. The wide acceptance and use of flow charts as a means of communication in the computer field make it imperative that the reader become proficient in their use.

9–2 BINARY MULTIPLICATION AND DIVISION

Concepts of Multiplication

Binary multiplication is a very simple process which is performed in accordance with the rules*

$$0 \times 0 = 0$$
$$0 \times 1 = 0$$
$$1 \times 0 = 0$$
$$1 \times 1 = 1.$$

When implemented in the digital computer, however, binary multiplication requires a number of data manipulations. Since both binary and decimal multiplication use similar concepts, the more familiar decimal procedures are shown first.

A typical decimal multiplication problem is 123×32. One viewpoint on multiplication is that the multiplier (32) tells how many times the multiplicand (123) is to be added to itself. Thus 123 is written 32 times and the

---

*Note that these rules are the same as the logical AND rules.

result obtained by *successive addition*. The concept of *partial products* is also useful. Since 32 may also be written as 30 + 2, the multiplication problem becomes 123 × (30 + 2). One partical product is obtained (123 × 2 = 246), and the second partial product (123 × 30 = 3690) is summed with it (246 + 3690 = 3936) to form the final answer.

In examining the "paper and pencil" method of performing multiplication, an interesting point comes to light as shown in Example 9–10.

Example 9–10.

$$
\begin{array}{r}
123 \\
\times\,32 \\
\hline
246 \quad \text{first partial product} \\
369 \quad \text{second partial product} \\
\hline
3936 \\
\end{array}
$$

The second partial product was shifted *one* position to the left to compensate for the fact that the actual multiplication was by 30, *not* 3. The zero in the least-significant position of the second partial product is conveniently left off and the second partial product is shifted left so that its least-significant digit starts in the ten's column. This is actually equivalent to multiplying by 3 × 10.

Sample Problem

Binary multiplication is accomplished in the same manner as decimal multiplication, but since the "multiplication table" is less complex, the actual multiplication operation is much simpler. Both successive addition and partial product methods are used. The popularity of the "shift and add" partial product method has made it a natural choice for discussion in this text.

The rules of binary multiplication may be simplified as follows.

1. Copy the multiplicand to obtain the partial product if the multiplier digit is a 1.
2. The partial product is 0 if the multiplier digit is a 0.

A sample binary multiplication problem using partial products is shown in Example 9–11.

Example 9–11.

$$
\begin{array}{ll}
\quad\,1010 & \text{multiplicand} \\
\quad\;\,101 & \text{multiplier} \\
\hline
\quad\,1010 & \\
\quad\,0000 & \text{partial products} \\
\,1010 & \\
\hline
110010 & \text{final product} \\
\end{array}
$$

The actual operations performed during the multiplication of Example 9-11 follow exactly the simplified binary multiplication rules. The least-significant bit of the multiplier is examined, and since it is a 1, the multiplicand is copied directly. Examination of the next multiplier bit shows that it is 0, so the second partial product becomes all zero. Since this bit is in the

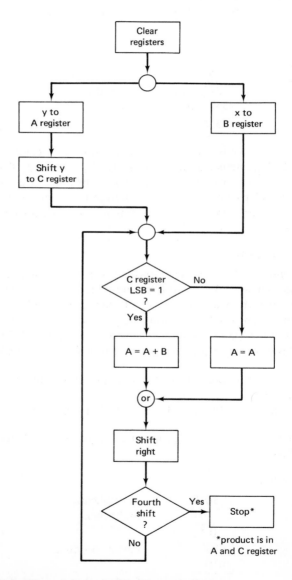

Figure 9–6   Flow chart and table, Example 9-11.

X = 1   0   1   0
Y = 0   1   0   1

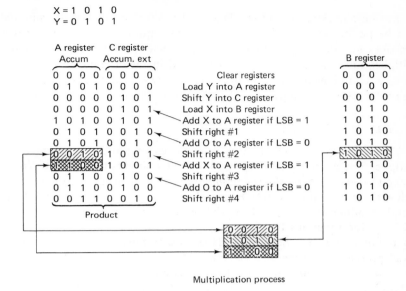

Multiplication process

Figure 9–6   (Continued)

2^1 position, it is necessary to displace either the first partial product one position to the right or the second partial product one place to the left as performed in decimal multiplication.* Most ARITHMETIC/LOGIC sections possess the capability to add only two numbers at a time, so the first two partial products must be summed and stored before proceeding. The next multiplier bit (1) results in a direct copy of the multiplicand, with the usual displacement of the partial product. Addition is once again performed and the result stored. This final partial product is summed with the stored partial products, supplying the completed product. The process of examining the multiplier digit, forming the partial product, shifting, and adding is a common method of performing multiplication in digital computers. Figure 9–6 shows the sequential steps of the shift and add multiplication process.

Determination of the sign of the product presents no problem. When two quantities to be multiplied have the same sign, the product sign is positive. If their signs are different, the sign of the product is negative.

Other Methods of Multiplication

It should be noted that the shift and add method of multiplication uses existing adders and registers in the ARITHMETIC/LOGIC section and

---

*Remember, this operation is equivalent to multiplying by a power of two (binary) or a power of ten (decimal).

requires no additional hardware. Due to the fact that many shifts and adds must be performed, however, multiplication requires a longer time period than does addition or subtraction. Unless separate hardware is provided, multiplication is a process that is performed in the computer by means of software (computer programs) rather than hardware. In other words, a separate routine (series of steps) is used each time a multiplication is required.

DIGITAL MULIPLIERS

Some computers resolve this problem by employing separate digital multipliers. Such multipliers use combinational circuits that accept two factors and generate the product with *only* the delay associated with the gates. Each gate array multiplies (ANDs) each bit of factor A with each bit of factor B, and an adder array adds all partial products by binary weight. A 4 × 4 multiplication generates 16 partial products for an 8-bit sum, and the addition is fairly involved. Several levels of adders must be used, since many partial products have identical weights. Multiplication using digital multipliers can be performed in under 100 nanoseconds, while the shift and add method can require many microseconds. As usual, though, speed costs money, and the digital multiplier method is quite costly.

MICROPROGRAMMING

Another approach to multiplication is gaining favor in modern digital computers. Routines which are used frequently are permanently stored in a ROM, often called a *control memory*. The control memory operates at speeds many times faster than the main memory of the computer. Thus when, for example, a multiplication is to be performed, the routine stored in the control memory is called into operation instead of requiring many trips to the main computer memory to obtain the same steps. The routine stored in the control memory is called a *microprogram* and not only is much faster but also frees the main memory for other operations.

Concepts of Division

Division is a more complex operation than multiplication. A sequence of shift and conditional add operations is usually performed in multiplication, where the multiplier bits determine whether the multiplicand should or should not be added to already calculated partial products. Conversely, division is usually performed by a sequence of shift and conditional *subtract* operations. The decision concerning subtracting the divisor from the dividend is based on whether or not this subtraction yields a valid result. Table 9–2 shows the concepts associated with the "*restoring division*" method. Reference to Example 9–12 provides some insight into the techniques employed by

Table 9–2   "Restoring Division" Concepts

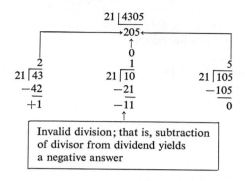

(a) Decimal Division

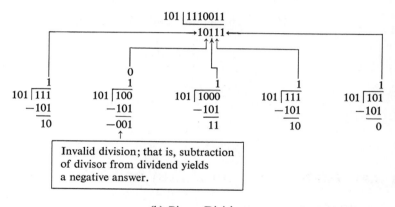

(b) Binary Division

the computer to implement restoring division. The subtraction operation is often performed by the adders in the ARITHMETIC/LOGIC section using two's complement notation. Remember, however, that division, like multiplication, is often software controlled and quite time consuming. When shorter operating times are required, the methods discussed during explanation of the multiplication process may be used.

Rules for Performing Restoring Division

The procedures used in Table 9–2 and Example 9–12 may be summarized.

1. Make a trial subtraction of the divisor from the partial dividend.
2. If the divisor can be subtracted from the partial dividend without

a negative difference, perform the subtraction and enter a 1 in the quotient and continue with division process if possible.

3. If the subtraction cannot be made, enter a 0 in the quotient and do not alter the partial dividend. Shift the divisor one bit right and start again at step 1.

4. If the signs of the divisor and the dividend are the same, the quotient is positive.

5. If the signs of the divisor and the dividend are different, the quotient is negative.

Example 9–12.

```
              10111
        101 | 1110011
              101
             ─────
              100
              000        trial divisor quotient negative
             ─────
             1000
              101        shift divisor right
             ─────
              111
              101
             ─────
              101
              101
             ─────
              000
```

9–3 ARITHMETIC LOGIC UNIT (ALU) OPERATION

Arithmetic Function

The trend in modern computers is away from separate adders, comparators, gates, etc, toward assemblies that contain greater capabilities. One approach uses an integrated circuit assembly called an ARITHMETIC LOGIC UNIT (ALU). Depending on design parameters, an ALU can perform not only addition and subtraction but also several logic functions. A common IC package such as that shown in Figure 9–7(a) accepts two 4-bit binary words and, depending on control signals, performs arithmetic or logic operations on the two words. The operation of the ALU shown in the logic diagram of Figure 9–7(b) is described in detail by Table 9–3. Note that with the Mode Control (M) HIGH, logic functions are selected, while with M LOW, arithmetic operations result. The C_n input further controls the actual arithmetic operations that are performed.*

───────────

*Many exercises in logic diagram analysis may be performed by verifying the entries in Table 9–3.

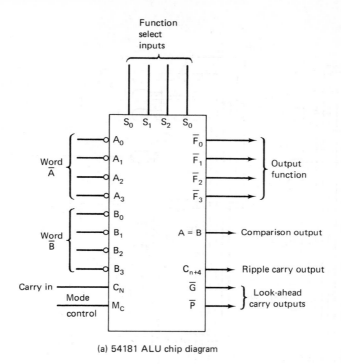

(a) 54181 ALU chip diagram

Figure 9–7   ALU chip, type 54181; (a) chip diagram (courtesy of Signetics, Sunnyvale, CA.)

An $A = B$ output is also provided so that comparator operations may be performed. Furthermore, by use of the C_{n+4} output, relative magnitude indications also may be obtained. The ALU is placed in the subtract mode for these comparator operations, and the comparison results are determined by use of the information in Table 9–3.

The capabilities provided by an ALU therefore replace the adders, comparators, logic operators, and arithmetic control portions of the ARITHMETIC/LOGIC section. It merely remains to furnish registers to manipulate the data into and out of the ARITHMETIC/LOGIC section, and the modern computer performs its required operations much more efficiently than its predecessors. When the computer is revisited in Chapter 13, an example of this type of ARITHMETIC/LOGIC section will be seen.

Logical Functions

Logical operations are performed in the ARITHMETIC/LOGIC section by use of combinational logic elements such as gates and inverters

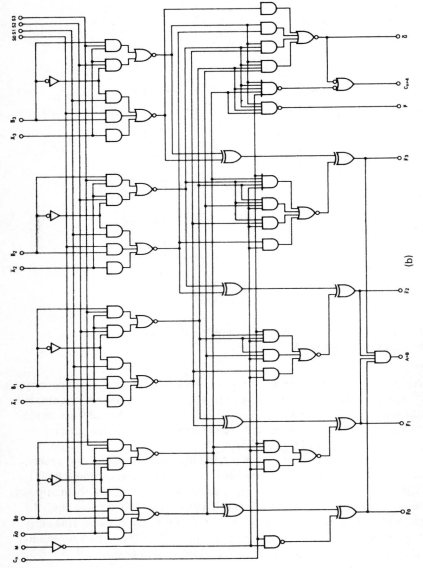

Figure 9-7 ALU chip (Continued); (b) logic diagram (courtesy of Signetics, Sunnyvale, CA.).

Table 9–3   ALU Truth Table

Function Select				Inputs/Outputs Active Low		Inputs/Outputs Active High	
				Logic Function	Arithmetic* Function	Logic Function	Arithmetic* Function
$S3$	$S2$	$S1$	$S0$	$(MC = H)$	$(MC = L, C_n = L)$	$(MC = H)$	$(MC = L, \bar{C}_n = H)$
L	L	L	L	$\bar{A}$	A minus 1	$\bar{A}$	A
L	L	L	H	$\overline{AB}$	AB minus 1	$\overline{A + B}$	$A + B$
L	L	H	L	$\bar{A} + B$	$A\bar{B}$ minus 1	$\bar{A}B$	$A + \bar{B}$
L	L	H	H	Logic "1"	minus 1	Logic "0"	minus 1
L	H	L	L	$\overline{A + B}$	A plus $(A + \bar{B})$	$\overline{AB}$	A plus $A\bar{B}$
L	H	L	H	$\bar{B}$	AB plus $(A + \bar{B})$	$\bar{B}$	$(A + B)$ plus $A\bar{B}$
L	H	H	L	$\overline{A \oplus B}$	A minus B minus 1	$A \oplus B$	A minus B minus 1
L	H	H	H	$A + \bar{B}$	$A + \bar{B}$	$A\bar{B}$	$A\bar{B}$ minus 1
H	L	L	L	$\bar{A}B$	A plus $(A + B)$	$\bar{A} + B$	A plus AB
H	L	L	H	$A \oplus B$	A plus B	$\overline{A \oplus B}$	A plus B
H	L	H	L	B	$A\bar{B}$ plus $(A + B)$	B	$(A + \bar{B})$ plus AB
H	L	H	H	$A + B$	$A + B$	AB	AB minus 1
H	H	L	L	Logic "0"	A plus A	Logic "1"	A plus A
H	H	L	H	$A\bar{B}$	AB plus A	$A + \bar{B}$	$(A + B)$ plus A
H	H	H	L	AB	$A\bar{B}$ plus A	$A + B$	$(A + \bar{B})$ plus A
H	H	H	H	A	A	A	A minus 1

*Expressed as two's complement

or by a device such as the ALU just discussed. AND, OR, and NOT elements were discussed in Chapter 3, while comparator circuits were discussed in Chapter 5. No further amplification is required here. Logical operations by means of an ALU may be verified by analysis of the logic diagram of Figure 9–7 and the information in Table 9–3.

9–4   BINARY-CODED-DECIMAL (BCD) ARITHMETIC

Concepts of BCD Arithmetic

Many of today's electronic calculators, plus some of the smaller computers, use BCD arithmetic methods. (See Chapter 6 for an explanation of some of the common BCD codes.) The usual criterion for use of BCD in favor of direct binary codes is that of predominantly manual input, such as in calculators. Input and output are relatively simple in BCD, and minimum conversion hardware is required.

BCD addition and subtraction are discussed here only as an introduction to BCD operations. Other arithmetic operations can be derived from addition and subtraction as in binary operation and are left to texts specifically directed to BCD arithmetic.

As pointed out in Chapter 6, a decimal digit is represented in four bits. Sixteen possible combinations of four bits exist, yet only ten are required for decimal representation, The remaining six combinations are not used in BCD, although they do occur and must be compensated for in arithmetic operations.

A Typical Problem in 8-2-4-1 BCD

Table 9–4, Part I, shows the 8-4-2-1 BCD codes used to represent the decimal numbers 0 through 15. Note that the only *valid* representations are 0 through 9. No corrections are required. Since four binary digits are used to represent each decimal digit, a correction must be applied when any decimal number greater than ten is required. Consider the BCD form of 12_{10}, which is 0001 0010. However, the 8-4-2-1 representation of 12_{10} is 1100, which is invalid in BCD without correction. Since the difference between the maximum

Table 9–4   BCD Codes—Addition and Carry Concepts

Decimal sum $(A + B)$	Uncorrected sum S_u 8-4-2-1		Corrected sum S	Correction	XS-3 repre- sentation	Uncorrected sum $(A + B + 6)$ S_u	Corrected sum $A + B$ $+ 6 \pm 3$ S	Correction
0	0000		0000		0011	0110	0011	(-3)
1	0001		0001		0100	0111	0100	(-3)
2	0010		0010		0101	1000	0101	(-3)
3	0011		0011		0110	1001	0110	(-3)
4	0100		0100		0111	1010	0111	(-3)
5	0101	Valid	0101		1000	1011	1000	(-3)
6	0110		0110		1001	1100	1001	(-3)
7	0111		0111		1010	1101	1010	(-3)
8	1000		1000		1011	1110	1011	(-3)
9	1001		1001		1100	1111	1100	(-3)
10	1010		0001 0000	$(+6)$	1101	1 0000	1 0011	$(+3)$
11	1011		0001 0001	$(+6)$	1110	1 0001	1 0100	$(+3)$
12	1100	Add 6	0001 0010	$(+6)$	1111	1 0010	1 0101	$(+3)$
13	1101		0001 0011	$(+6)$	1 0000	1 0011	1 0110	$(+3)$
14	1110		0001 0100	$(+6)$	1 0001	1 0100	1 0111	$(+3)$
15	1110		0001 0101	$(+6)$	1 0010	1 0101	1 1000	$(+3)$

Rules:
1. No correction when $S_u \leq 1001$
2. $S = S_u + 0110$ when $S_u > 1001$

Rules:
1. $S = S_u - 0011$ when $S_u \leq 1111$— that is, when no carry results
2. $S = S_u + 0011$ when $S_u > 1111$— that is, when carry results

Part I   Part II

decimal number that can be shown with a 4-bit BCD representation (9) and a 4-bit 8-4-2-1 representation (15) is 6, the binary equivalent of 6 (0110) must be added to any *invalid* 4-bit 8-4-2-1 representation.

Thus, $1110 + 0110 = 1\ 0010$. The carry that results exceeds the four-digit BCD limit and must be applied to the next-most-significant BCD position. Leading zeros are added to complete the BCD ten's position, and the BCD representation of 12_{10} becomes 0001 0010.

An example of the principles of BCD 8-4-2-1 addition shown in Part I of Table 9–4 is detailed in Table 9–5, Part I. Note the applications of Rule 1 in the ten's position and Rule 2 in the unit's position.

Table 9–5   BCD Addition, Examples

	Decimal	8-4-2-1		*XS*3	
	58	0101	1000	1000	1011
	29	0011	1001	0101	1111
Uncorrected sum (S_u)	7 (17)	0111	0001	1101	1010
Correction			+0110	−0011	
carry	10	+0001			+0011
Corrected sum (S)	87	1000	0111	1011	1101
		8	7	8	7

Part I   Part II

Using the XS3 BCD Code

The XS3 BCD code is also frequently used in computing devices for reasons soon to be seen. As noted in Chapter 6, the XS3 code represents decimal digits by adding three to the 8-4-2-1 representation. Since each decimal digit represented in XS3 code is greater by three than the actual 8-4-2-1 representation, the sum of two XS3 coded decimal digits will be greater by six than its actual 8-4-2-1 representation. For example, $2 + 2 = 4$ in decimal, $0010 + 0010 = 0100$ in 8-4-2-1 BCD, and $0101 + 0101 = 1010$ in XS3 BCD. Note that the XS3 sum, when converted to either 8-4-2-1 BCD or decimal, is six greater than the 8-4-2-1 BCD sum.

A close perusal of the Uncorrected XS3 Sum column of Part II of Table 9–4 shows one of the major advantages of using the XS3 code. It is immediately apparent what amount of and when correction must be applied to the uncorrected XS3 sum because the transition from 9_{10} to 10_{10} results in a carry. If a carry does not result it, is merely necessary to subtract 0011 (3) from the uncorrected sum. Conversely, if a carry does result, 0011 (3) is added. More complete examples of XS3 addition are shown in Table 9–5, Part II.

Note the application of Rule 1 in the ten's position and Rule 2 in the unit's position.

Not only does use of the XS3 code simplify addition, but it also allows subtraction to be performed with a minimum of additional hardware. Recall that subtraction is commonly accomplished in the digital computer by complementing and adding. Furthermore, negative numbers are handled by the computer in complement form. XS3 coding results in simpler computation

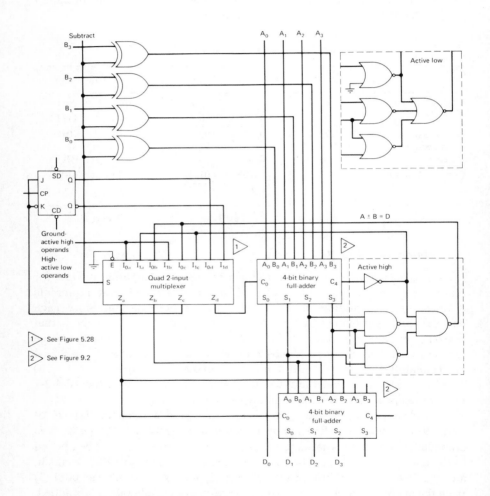

Figure 9–8 BCD adder.

circuits because decimal number pairs that are nine's (radix-minus-one) complements are also complements in the XS3 system. Reference to the XS3 representation verifies that, for example, 1_{10} and 8_{10}, 2_{10} and 7_{10}, etc are nine's complements, and the XS3 equivalents of these pairs are binary complements (0100 and 1011, 0101 and 1010, etc).

It is only necessary, then, to provide circuits capable of BCD addition and complementing, and the computer can operate as though it were performing directly in binary. Figure 9–8 is a BCD adder/subtractor.

BCD Adder Operation

The circuit of Figure 9–8 performs BCD-corrected addition and subtraction on four bits (one BCD digit). For addition, the control input (SUBTRACT) is LOW, the first 4-bit adder adds the B_{0-3} inputs to the A_{0-3} inputs, the binary sum is generated on outputs S_{0-3}, and the binary carry appears on output C_4. Whenever the binary sum exceeds nine, that is, when S_3 AND (S_2 OR S_1) OR C_4 is a true expression, a decimal carry is generated by the gating structure shown. The carry flip-flop is set and a binary 6 is forced onto the B inputs of the second 4-bit adder by the quad multiplexer. The outputs D_{0-3} represent the BCD corrected sum $D = A$ plus B.

For subtraction, the control input (SUBTRACT) is HIGH, inverting B_{0-3} inputs to the first adder. The quad multiplexer feeds the $\bar{Q}$ output of the carry flip-flop into the Carry In of the first adder which performs $\overline{\text{Carry}}$ plus A plus $\bar{B}$, one of the binary subtraction algorithms. The Carry out (C_4) signal is inverted before it is routed through the quad multiplexer into the JK input of the Carry-Borrow flip-flop. Whenever this flip-flop is being set, the binary result at S_{0-3} requires correction by subtracting 6 or adding 10. This is performed in the second 4-bit adder by routing the $\bar{C}_4$ signal into the C_0 (weight 2) and the B_2 (weight 8) inputs. The outputs D_{0-3} represent the BCD corrected result $D = A - B$.

9–5 SUMMARY

In this chapter it has been shown that the common arithmetic and logical operation can be performed using simple logic circuits. Although the methods employed in the digital computer may seem both tedious and foreign to us, the high speed of the computer makes such methods practical and efficient. Examples shown have been limited to four magnitude bits and a sign bit for the purpose of clarity. Expansion to more common 16-, 24-, and 32-bit words merely increases the number of logic circuits required. Complexity is increased by adding more of the same kind of circuits, not because of the addition of any new circuits.

More complex operations, such as square roots, trigonometric operations, etc, use the basic adder or ALU circuits and merely use program steps to repetitively apply basic operations to perform the complex operations. The programming approach to complex operations is shown in later chapters.

QUESTIONS

1. List the rules of binary addition.
2. Draw a logic diagram of a device that will perform addition of two binary digits. Assume no carry input is required.
3. Draw a logic diagram of a device that will perform addition of two binary digits. Assume a carry input is required.
4. Discuss the advantages and disadvantages of parallel arithmetic operations vs serial arithmetic operations.
5. How is the radix-minus-one complement of a number formed?
6. How is the true complement of a number formed?
7. Write the following numbers in sign-true magnitude form, one's complement form, and two's complement form.
   - a. $+10$ e. -30
   - b. -7 f. $+33$
   - c. $+9$ g. -8
   - d. -15 h. -6
8. Give the rule for addition of two positive numbers and show an example.
9. Give the rule for addition of two negative numbers and show an example.
10. Give the rule for addition of two numbers of unlike signs and show an example.
11. Give the rule for subtraction of binary numbers and show an example.
12. What is a flow chart? How are flow charts used?
13. Give the rules for binary multiplication and show an example.
14. Give the rules for binary division and show an example.
15. Explain how a *control memory* can simplify computer arithmetic operations.
16. What arithmetic operations can be performed by the ALU of Figure 9-7?
17. What logic operations can be performed by the ALU of Figure 9-7?
18. Why would XS3 BCD representation be used in digital equipment in place of 8-4-2-1 BCD?
19. Why would BCD representation be used in digital equipment in place of direct binary representation?
20. Explain the operation of the BCD adder of Figure 9-8.

PROBLEMS

Perform the following arithmetic operations, using complementary arithmetic where appropriate.

1. $1101101 + 1011010$
2. $11011 + 1010$
3. $100111 + 1011101$
4. $1110 + 1110$
5. $110110 - 10111$
6. $1001001 - 101110$

7. 110101 − 1011
8. 1110101 − 111111
9. 1011 × 101

10. 1000010 × 111
11. 101001 ÷ 101
12. 101101 ÷ 110

Perform the following arithmetic operations, using *both* 8-4-2-1 BCD and XS3 BCD

13. 14 + 14
14. 27 + 10

15. 66 + 36
16. 109 + 90

10

The INPUT Function

The INPUT section is the interface between the external world and the computer. The external world is one of decimal numbers, letters, and symbols, while the computer's world is one of strictly binary digits. It has often been implied that the INPUT section converts external world language to computer language. This is an oversimplified viewpoint. Although the INPUT section does convert decimal numbers, letters, and symbols to a binary code, more often than not the resulting code is not the same as the machine language of the computer. Chapter 6 showed the many codes used to represent information in the computer, and it may have been noted that those codes do not necessarily lend themselves to the binary representation of information within the limitations of computer word lengths. The INPUT section often merely formats the inputted information so that it can temporarily be placed in memory. A computer program called an *assembler*** then translates the symbolic information to machine language and places the machine language version of the symbolic information back in memory.

For the purpose of this chapter it is assumed that the INPUT section takes the coded information from the input device and formats it for most efficient storage. Conversion of the inputted information to machine language code will be assumed to be performed by the assembler program unless otherwise noted.

10–1 FUNCTIONAL REQUIREMENTS

Concepts

Computer input may be viewed as a three-part operation. First, some means of representing the information to be input must be provided. It may be as simple as a handwritten list or as complex as changing fields on mag-

---

*Assemblers are discussed in Chapter 12.

netic tape. Second, a mechanism is required to convert the input information into electrical signals that the computer can use. Finally, control circuitry is needed to change the input information into computer word format, time the input operations, etc. Complete computer input requirements and typical solutions are summarized in Table 10–1.

Table 10–1   Input Information Conversion Requirements

| Input Information Representation | Converter Mechanism | Controller | |
		Input from Converter	Output to Computer
Written form (ones and zeros)	Switches	One computer word at a time	Parallel
Holes in paper tape (binary format)	Paper tape reader	Part of a computer word	Parallel
Holes in paper tape (character format)	Paper tape reader	Character (byte)	Parallel
Written form (English language)	Teletypewriter	Character (byte)—serial	Parallel
Written form (English language)	Keyboard	Character (byte)—serial	Parallel
Magnetic tape	Tape deck	Character (byte)—serial	Parallel
Written form (English language)	Optical character reader	Character (byte)—serial	Parallel
Holes in cards (binary format)	Card reader	Part of a computer word—serial	Parallel
Holes in cards (Hollerith)	Card reader	12-bit byte—serial	Parallel

Switch Input

All digital computers have control panels which allow manual control of the computer. The control panel, as described in Chapter 2, not only supplies power controls and indicators but also allows direct accesss to the registers of the computer. Switches select each bit of a computer word separately, so that *any* computer word desired may be established and placed into the computer. Instructions may be established, data placed in memory, addresses selected, etc. Control panel switches are the simplest of all input devices, but since they do communicate directly with the computer, the user requires an *intimate* knowledge of the computer and its very basic machine language. Programmers who work at the machine language level and engineers/technicians who must troubleshoot malfunctions at the most detailed level would be the most common users of control panel switches. The everyday user of the computer depends on the computer to internally translate easier-understood inputs. User-oriented input devices such as keyboards, cards, paper tape, etc are discussed in the remainder of this chapter.

A General Approach

Like the control panel switches, any device that supplies input to the computer directly in machine language code is the most efficient in terms of computer compatibility. Unfortunately, the world external to the computer is seldom oriented binarily. Furthermore, each computer has its own binary coding scheme, and little commonality among computers exists. Finally, information representation in the computer is not compatible with the character set (letters, numbers, etc) used in the real world. Additional logic must be provided to accommodate these inconsistencies.

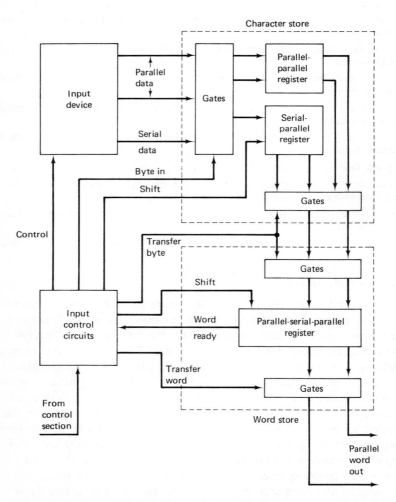

Figure 10–1   General input section block diagram.

Practically all input devices convert user-oriented information into computer-usable information. However, in many cases, the input device may be able to input only one character at a time, while the unit of information in the computer is the computer word. Within the INPUT section some means must be provided to convert the input device information into computer words. The functional block diagram of Figure 10–1 is a typical approach. (More detailed diagrams of selected devices appear throughout this chapter.) Under the direction of the CONTROL section, the input control block enables the input device to supply one unit of information (*byte*)* to the character store. While the character store is transferring the first byte to the word store, the input device supplies another byte to be retained. This cycle continues, under cognizance of the input control, until sufficient bytes have been supplied by the input device and placed in the word store. Input control then signals the word store to transfer its data to memory via the Memory Buffer Register.

The character store is simply a parallel input-parallel output shift register (Chapter 5). The number of stages in the register are determined by the number of bits used to represent an input character. More versatility can be furnished if the character store also has serial input capability, since many computer applications require the use of serially received information, such as from a remote terminal.

Word storage is accomplished by accepting each character from the character store and shifting the bit associated with that character to the end of the register making up the word store. Enough stages are included in the word store to accommodate all of the bits in a computer word.

10–2 PUNCHED TAPE INPUT

Information Representation

Punched tape is a common input medium. A *tape punch*, operating in conjunction with a keyboard device (Figure 2–12) or directly computer-controlled, accepts the blank paper or plastic tape† and delivers a *punched* tape. Information appears on the tape in the form of punched holes to represent a binary 1 and the lack of a hole to represent a binary 0. Codes used to represent information on punched tape may be actual binary or any of the alphameric codes discussed in Chapter 6. (Common applications seem to favor the 8-level code of Figure 6–7.) Whether actual binary or alphameric

---

*A byte is a unit of information consisting of a fixed number of bits, usually eight. An 8-bit byte is commonly used to represent an alphameric character or control function.

†Tape dimensions vary, but modern punched tape standards dictate one inch width and 0.0030 to 0.0043 inch thickness. Lengths vary, limited only by the requirements for information on the tape and the diameter of the tape reel.

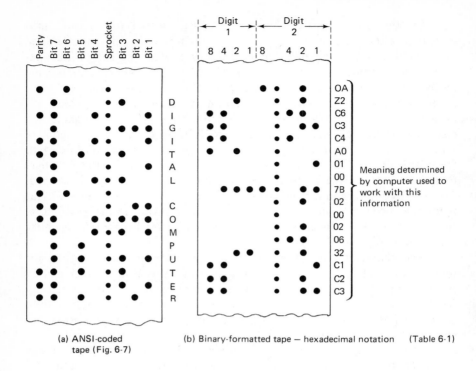

(a) ANSI-coded   (b) Binary-formatted tape — hexadecimal notation   (Table 6-1)
tape (Fig. 6-7)

Figure 10–2   Punched tape samples; (a) ANSI-coded tape,—Fig. 6–7,
(b) binary-formatted tape, hexadecimal notation—Fig. 6–1.

coded, each byte is punched across the width of the tape as shown in Figure 10–2.

The Tape Reader

Information contained in the punched tape is "read" by sensing the presence or absence of holes in the tape. The sprocket holes in the tape are engaged by a mechanical sprocket wheel which moves each byte position into place under a *read station*. A sensing device for each bit in the byte detects the presence of a hole and develops an electrical signal indicating that a binary 1 is on the tape at this position. The lack of a hole is assumed to be a binary 0. With a typical 8-bit code, eight sensing devices are provided, and all eight bits in the byte are "read" simultaneously to furnish *parallel* input to the computer.

Sensing devices may be either mechanical or electrical. Although some tape readers still employ mechanical fingers or brushes that complete an electrical circuit when a hole in the tape is present, more modern readers detect tape holes with photoelectric devices. Typically, a light source illuminates the tape as it passes the read station and light passes through only where holes are present. Photodetectors are mounted at each bit position on the tape and develop an electrical signal when they are illuminated. Figure 10–3 shows the concept of a punched tape reader. Details vary from manufacturer to manufacturer, and no attempt is made in this text to explain the mechanical operations.

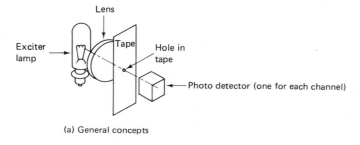

(a) General concepts

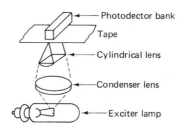

(b) Practical punched tape reading device

Figure 10–3   Reading punched tape; (a) general concepts, (b) practical punched tape reading device.

The Data Formatter

As far as the computer is concerned, it is much less time consuming to have its input supplied in binary form such as with switches. From the computer viewpoint, then, it would be desirable that the punched tape provide the full number of computer word bits each time information was made available. If a 16-bit computer word is considered, the tape must supply 16 spaces across its width, which has not been feasible with standard tape sizes. Therefore the most common approach has been to use two positions of the tape with eight bits assigned to each position. The controller assumes the responsibility for "packing" the two 8-bit bytes into a computer word prior to transfer of the word to memory.

Binary formatted tapes are not commonly employed except in initial computer startup or when maximum efficiency is required. Preparation of such tapes is usually the province of computer-controlled tape punches. Figure 10–2 shows typical punched tape samples with information entered in different formats.

Since it is easier to visualize how the computer can work with actual binary information, the flow of information from binary formatted tape through the input function is approached initially. With binary formatted tape, a computer word (assuming a 16-bit word) occupies two byte positions on eight-channel tape. In order to transfer the complete computer word to the computer, the two 8-bit bytes must be packed into a 16-bit word. The concepts required to perform this function are shown in Figure 10–4. As the first byte position passes the read station, the detectors sense the appropriate holes and develop electrical signals which are stored in a register as binary ones. Binary zeros are placed in all other stages of the byte storage register. The 8-bit byte is transferred to the word storage register while the tape is advancing to the next position and is then shifted serially into the lower eight positions of the word storage register. Detection of the second byte follows a similar sequence, except that upon transfer to the word storage register, it remains in the upper 8-bit positions. When two bytes have been transferred to the word storage register, word transfer is initiated, and the complete 16-bit computer word is passed to computer memory. The input registers are again ready to process the next package of input information.

To take care of differences in punched hole alignment due to tape skew and punch misalignment, data outputs are gated with the output of the sprocket channel. The sprocket hole is smaller in size than the data holes, thereby providing a "window" which *opens after* and *closes before* the data outputs occur.

When the punched tape is supplying information in other than actual binary format, operation of the input section is identical to binary input. Information on the tape is still in 8-bit form, but is in a format that represents an alphameric character or control function at each byte position. Therefore, with a 16-bit computer word, two characters may be placed in memory at a time. Information is stored sequentially as it is punched on the tape, and the assembler assumes the responsibility for converting this information to machine language. The usual operation is to feed the complete computer program and data to the memory via the INPUT function and then allow the assembler to convert and re-store the information in machine language form.

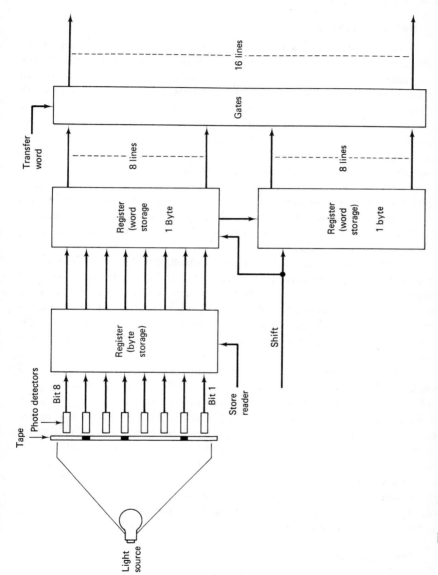

Figure 10-4 Punched tape data formatter requirements.

10–3   TELETYPE INPUT

Basic Concepts

Another common input device is the Teletypewriter* (abbreviated Teletype, or TTY) discussed in Section 2–5 and seen in Figure 2–12. The typewriterlike keyboard makes it an ideal, although slow, input medium due to the common use of the typewriter in everyday life. A direct outgrowth of early wired-telegraphy, the Teletype was designed to use single-pair wired-line communication lines. In order to employ only a single pair of lines, Teletype information is represented as a *serial sequence* of ones and zeros (marks and spaces). Initially a 5-level, 7-unit code was employed, where information was represented in the Baudot code of Figure 6–4 and a start bit and stop bit were added to assist in synchronizing the system. At the then common 60 word per minute speed, the start bit and five information bits each occupied 22 milliseconds of time, while the stop bit used 31 milliseconds. A total of 164 milliseconds was thus required to transmit a single character, as shown in Figure 10–5(a).

As explained in Chapter 6, a 5-level code simply does not allow representation of enough characters, operations, etc, and it has been necessary to expand the Teletype code to an 8-level, 11-unit code. ANSI 7-level code plus parity (8-level) has been selected for the intelligence portion of the character. The 11-unit code is organized as shown in Figure 10–5(b), and the designed timing results in a speed capability of 100 6-character words per minute.

The more common parallel form of information representation used in computers makes all bits (ones and zeros) available at the same time, but it can be seen that such a method would not be cost effective over long distances. An 8-bit character would require eight separate pairs of lines. The actual mechanics associated with forming the binary representation of characters is unimportant, as long as it is recognized that the *code* used may be valid *either* in serial or parallel form. For example, the ANSI representation of the number five is just as valid as the eight binary digits 01101010 (even parity), one following the other, as it is with each of the bits on separate lines. The actual output of the Teletype, then, is a serial train of pulses which must be converted to parallel form for use in the computer.

The Controller

When the computer memory can accept information in groups of bits which are smaller than the computer word length, input control is much simplified. For example, if a 16-bit computer can accept "half-words" of

---

*Trademark registered by The Teletype Corporation.

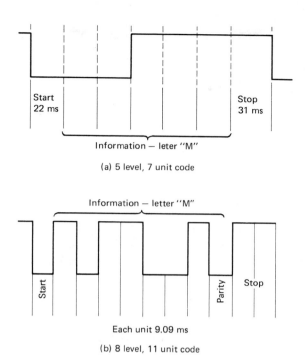

(a) 5 level, 7 unit code

(b) 8 level, 11 unit code

Figure 10–5 Teletype character formats; (a) 5-level, 7-unit code, (b) 8-level, 11-unit code.

eight bits each, no reformatting of input is required. Half-words may also be called bytes when specifically speaking of the 16-bit computer word. In the case of an input device using 8-level ANSI code (such as a Teletype), each 8-bit character is entered in memory via the buffer register. The internal computer program performs the necessary conversions.

A block diagram of a typical Teletype controller and Teletype are shown in Figure 10–6. Instructions from the computer to the controller are decoded in the *command decoder*. The decoded instructions then enable the appropriate controller circuits. When, for example, a character is to be supplied to the computer from the Teletype, the decoded command would enable the *read interrupt* circuit. Upon completion of character movement from the *keyboard* through the *data I/O logic* to the *Teletype buffer register*, the *input ready detector* causes the read interrupt signal to be generated and the character is transferred to memory. The *shift control* supplies control signals that shift data in and out through the Teletype buffer register. Note that the information from the keyboard is in serial form but is restructured to parallel form by the Teletype buffer register.

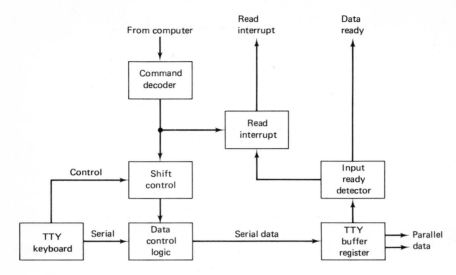

Figure 10–6   Teletype controller block diagram.

Operation of the Teletype input is under direct control of the computer program. The following sequence of events is representative of the instructions required to load a Teletype character into memory.

1. The computer program sends a *read interrupt enable* command to the Teletype controller. Decoding of this command enables the read interrupt and shift control circuits.
2. When a character has been shifted into the buffer register, the input ready detector supplies an input to cause generation of the *read interrupt* signal to the computer. This signal allows the computer to perform other operations while the much slower Teletype is transferring data.
3. The *data ready* signal is checked to determine if the buffer register has a character stored. If a character is stored, the data on the eight output lines is loaded into memory. If not, the computer returns to its other functions and returns later to check data availability.

It is interesting to note that the difference in speed of operation between the Teletype and the computer itself allows the computer to perform many of its own operations just during the time that the Teletype is transferring one character from its keyboard to the controller. At 9.09 milliseconds per bit, it takes 99.99 milliseconds for the keyboard to generate a single character. During this approximate 100 milliseconds, the computer, operating at perhaps a 2-microsecond cycle time, could perform 5000 functions. It is up to the programmer to take maximum advantage of these time differentials and gain maximum use of the computer's time.

After all information is loaded, one character at a time, the computer program translates the newly stored information into machine language so that the computer can process the data.

10–4 KEYBOARDS

One of the most common input devices used with today's computer is the keyboard. Although special-purpose keyboards such as found in cash registers and small pocket calculators are seen in profusion today, the type-writerlike keyboard shown in Figure 10–7 is typical of computer input keyboards. Most often the keyboard is associated with an output device, such as a cathode-ray tube (CRT) in a graphic display terminal or with a printer (see Chapter 11) to provide "interactive" communication with the computer. Note that the computer input keyboard, however, contains many special function keys that are not found on the common typewriter. Further-more, the computer input keyboard supplies an electrical output (in a pre-selected code format) rather than directly printing the character depressed.

Keyswitches

The heart of any keyboard is the switch associated with each key. As noted so many times before in this text, all information in the computer is represented as groups of ones and zeros arranged in unique orders for each

Figure 10–7 Typical computer input keyboard (courtesy of Cherry Electrical Products, Corp. Waukegen, IL)

character, number, etc. If the keyswitch is to feed information directly into the computer, then sufficient numbers of contacts must be provided on each switch so that the correct numbers of ones and zeros can be generated. For example, if the ANSI code is recognized as the means of manipulating information in the computer, seven sets of contacts are needed for each switch. Such a requirement is not only restrictive from a physical standpoint but also presents many electronic problems. Each time an electrical contact is made or broken, a strong tendency exists for the contact to "bounce," generating additional makes and breaks which may be interpreted by the computer as ones and zeros. Much effort has been expended to prevent or reduce this problem, and many innovative designs have resulted. Magnetic reed switches, mercury-wetted contacts, special gold alloy contact configurations, capacitive and photoelectric non-contacting switches are but a few of the methods of switching seen in modern keyboards.

Much of the "bounce" problem has been removed in modern keyboards. Each keyswitch now merely selects a specific digital encoder action, and the switching action is effectively isolated from the actual code that the computer sees. Although any desired code may be established, keyboards commonly supply the EBCDIC code for devices used in data preparation (such as card punches, key-to-storage units, etc.) and the ANSI code for data entry or communications applications. The keyswitches are arranged in an array format so that each switch merely shorts a row and a column line. The resulting shorts are scanned periodically, and either deliver a direct coded output or supply an address to a ROM which supplies the code stored at that address. Each time a key is depressed, then, one 7-bit ANSI character, plus parity, is made available at the computer input.

Encoder

Figure 10–8 is a block diagram of a keyboard encoder based on the scanning techniques mentioned above. The heart of the encoder is a 7-bit counter, a multiplexer, and a 4-to-16 line decoder. Encoded keys form a crosspoint matrix with each key connected to a decoder output and a multiplexer input. The decoder is addressed by the four least-significant bits of the counter and the multiplexer by the three most-significant bits. When a key is depressed, a matrix connection between the decoder and multiplexer is accomplished. When the counter reaches the appropriate ANSI code for the depressed key, the decoder and multiplexer outputs are both active, and the counter is stopped by the action of a one-shot triggered by the same clock pulses that are operating the counter. The seven outputs of the counter are gated through additional logic to accommodate upper case data if the shift key is depressed. Parity logic is used to establish an 8-bit ANSI coded character complete with parity.

The clock operates at a very high frequency so that all possible codes are scanned in under 250 microseconds. Further controls are provided to

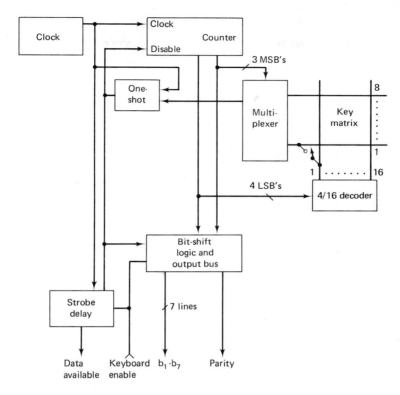

Figure 10–8 Keyboard encoder block diagram (courtesy of Cherry Electrical Products, Corp. Waukegen. IL)

signal the computer that data is available and to synchronize the operation of the keyboard.

Keyboard matrix operation can be explained by use of the logic diagram of Figure 10–9. Referring to the block diagram of Figure 10–8, the 4-to-16 decoder consists of gates G_1 through G_{16}, while the multiplexer function is performed by gates G_{17} through G_{25}. The counter of Figure 10–8 operates continuously, counting the output of the clock in a simple binary fashion until disabled by the one-shot. Detection of a depressed key on the keyboard provides the one-shot disabling signal. Assume that the "1" key on the keyboard has been selected. The counter continues to count until bits 1, 2, 3, and 4 of the counter are 1, 0, 0, and 0, respectively, and bits 5, 6, and 7 are 1, 1, and 0, respectively. In conventional notation (most-significant bit, bit 7, first) this translates to 0110001, which is the ANSI code representing the digit "1." The four least-significant bit combinations of 0001 enable G_{15}, which provides an activating input to G_{18} via the interconnection made when the "1" key was depressed. The other inputs to G_{18} become active when the three

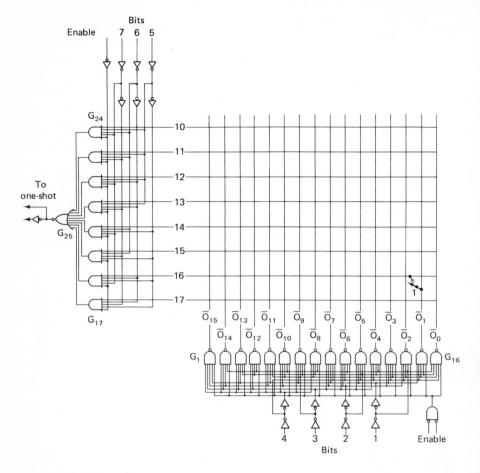

Figure 10–9 Keyboard matrix logic.

most-significant bits from the counter become 011. G_{25} is activated by the active output of G_{18}, and the one-shot receives an activating input, stopping the counter at the count equivalent to decimal digit one. The reader is encouraged to investigate other combinations of ANSI represented characters.

10–5 DIRECT CHARACTER INPUT

Magnetic Ink

Perhaps it has been noted by this time that the major effort in inputting information to the computer is that of supplying some coded version of an alphameric character to the computer for storage. Most of the time is spent in preparing the medium that carries the information. Punched tape and cards must be punched, switches must be actuated, keyboards operated, etc. Much effort has gone into development of machines that accept information in everyday form and convert it directly into computer input. Initial attempts at direct character input used special characters printed in magnetic ink (Figure 10–10). Most of us are familiar with these characters as they appear on bank checks.

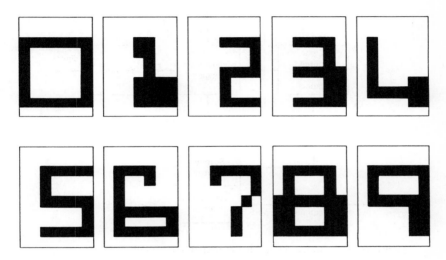

Figure 10–10   A magnetic ink character set.

Each character occupies a given number of squares in a 7×10 matrix (note that the characters resemble actual numbers). The device that reads a character examines the matrix and develops electrical signals for each square that contains magnetic ink. The composite electrical signal is then compared with an internally stored replica of each character, and the sensed character is identified.

Optical Character Reader (OCR)

More recently, *optical character readers* (OCRs) have been developed that do not require the use of magnetic ink. OCRs require, as a minimum, the functions shown in Figure 10–11. The *optics* convert the black-on-white printed or handwritten characters into a video signal which the *converter* changes into digital pulses. *Recognition logic* accepts the digital pulses from the converter and outputs a digital signal which represents the OCR code corresponding to the character in the read position. An *encoder* then converts the OCR code into a computer-compatible code which is made available to memory and the remainder of the computer. Controls are provided to actuate the scanner and/or document transport as required.

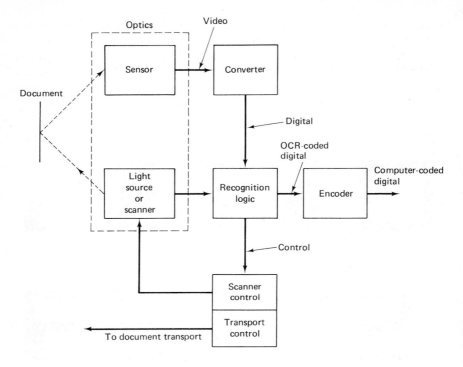

Figure 10–11   Optical character reader (OCR) block diagram.

The configuration of the optics depends on the technique used to change the character being read into digital pulses. Two methods are in common use. One approach uses lenses to focus a character's image onto an array of photosensors, while the other uses a scanning approach similar to that employed in television systems. Photosensor arrays are either one or two dimensional. One-dimensional arrays have a number of sensors in a single vertical line and the character is moved through the system while different horizontal components of the character are sensed. A register stores the electrical signals corresponding to the black and white field being sensed. Figure 10–12(a) shows a simplified version of one-dimensional scanning. Two-dimensional scanning focuses the complete character on a large array of photosensors, and its associated register stores the same type of information acquired by the one-dimensional method. Figure 10–12(b) shows a simplified two-dimensional system.

One of the most popular (although most expensive) methods of optically reading characters is the flying-spot scanner. A cathode-ray tube (CRT) such as employed in television systems is used as a point source of light, and deflection circuits move the spot in a predetermined pattern as it scans each

(a) One-dimensional
      sensor array

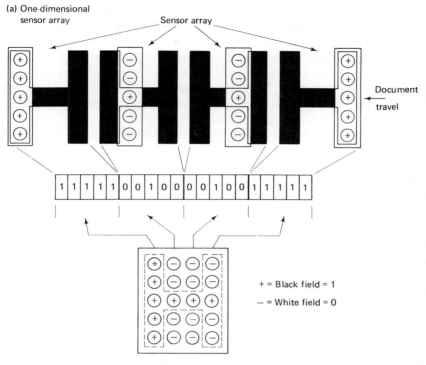

(b) Two-dimensional sensor array

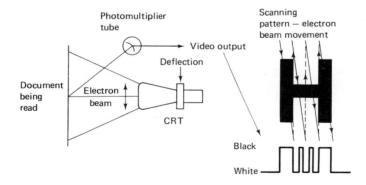

(c)   Flying spot scanner

Figure 10–12   OCR character scanning methods; (a) one-dimensional sensor array, (b) two-dimensional sensor array, (c) flying spot scanner.

character. A single photosensor picks up the light reflected from the character being read and converts it into a video signal. Figure 10–12(c) shows the concept of the flying-spot scanner.

The *converter* accepts the video information from the *photosensor* and converts it into digital form. Amplifiers, wave-shaping circuits, and registers are found in the converter. *Recognition logic* accepts the digital pulses from the converter, in either serial or parallel form, and compares them with prestored register patterns to determine the nature of the information recognized by the photosensors. A unique digital code is fed from the recognition logic to the *encoder* when a character is recognized. If recognition does not occur, quite often the optics will be instructed to read the character again, and another attempt is made. If recognition does not occur after the preprogrammed number of readings, the document is rejected. When recognition does occur, the optics and mechanics are instructed to move on to the next character. The *encoder* changes the OCR code into computer code. A Read-Only memory is commonly employed in this case, where the address to the memory is the OCR code and the output is the computer-compatible representation of the character. Scanner and transport control are provided to move either the scanning circuits or the document at the rate necessary for optimum reading.

OCRs commonly use a special type font (Figure 10–13(a)) to optimize reading speed and accuracy. Hand-printed characters (Figure 10–13(b)), when carefully constructed, may also be read by modern OCRs. On-going research is providing more versatility to the field of direct character input and is sure to ultimately free the user from stringent character format requirements.

Voice Input

Many of the techniques of pattern recognition developed for OCR applications are being applied to direct voice input to the computer. The

1234567890

ABCDEFGHIJKLMNOPQRSTUVWXYZ

(a)

(b)

Figure 10–13   OCR formats.

general concept of speech recognition is one of storing a pattern of word characteristics in a computer memory and comparing the spoken word input with stored information to cause the computer to react accordingly. Such systems are in use for baggage handling and routing, automobile assembly line inspection, and cathode-ray tube inspection and quality control. Efforts are under way to develop voice-data-entry systems that allow a paraplegic to use such devices as typewriters, calculators, and telephones. Another application that shows great promise is in the field of aircraft crew member operations. The use of direct voice input to gain access to various aircraft systems and displays would free the already overburdened crew members so that they could more effectively perform their functions. Dialog between computers and human beings is not far off.

10–6 PUNCHED CARDS

Information Representation

The "IBM" card is one of the oldest computer input methods. Although initially conceived much earlier, Herman Hollerith originated the idea of using punched cards as the prime source of data input for the 1890 census. Today's punched cards are mostly of uniform shape and size* with information presented according to a predetermined code by punched-out locations on the card. Figure 10–14 is a punched card showing letters, numbers, and characters entered.

Each of the 80 columns on the card carries one digit, letter, or symbol. Punch positions are arranged horizontally in 12 rows—the bottom ten for digits 0 through 9 plus two rows numbered 11 and 12 along the top of the card for *zone* punching. The digits 0 through 9 are each coded with a single punch, while alphabetical characters require a single row punch plus a zone punch. Special characters use multiple combinations of row and zone punches.

Reader and Controller

Punched cards are read by passing the card through a *read station* (part of the card reader). Holes may be sensed electrically, mechanically, or optically, and the same general reading techniques discussed with punched tape apply for card reading. Since the actual mechanism that moves the card is a mechanical device, it is not discussed in this text. From an input standpoint, the important characteristics are those of the electrical signals generated by the read operation.

Information on the card may be read column by column (row serial, column parallel) or row by row (column serial, row parallel). Each method

---

*A standard size is $3\frac{1}{4} \times 7\frac{3}{8} \times 0.007$ inches. Other sizes and shapes are used, but the most common type is described here.

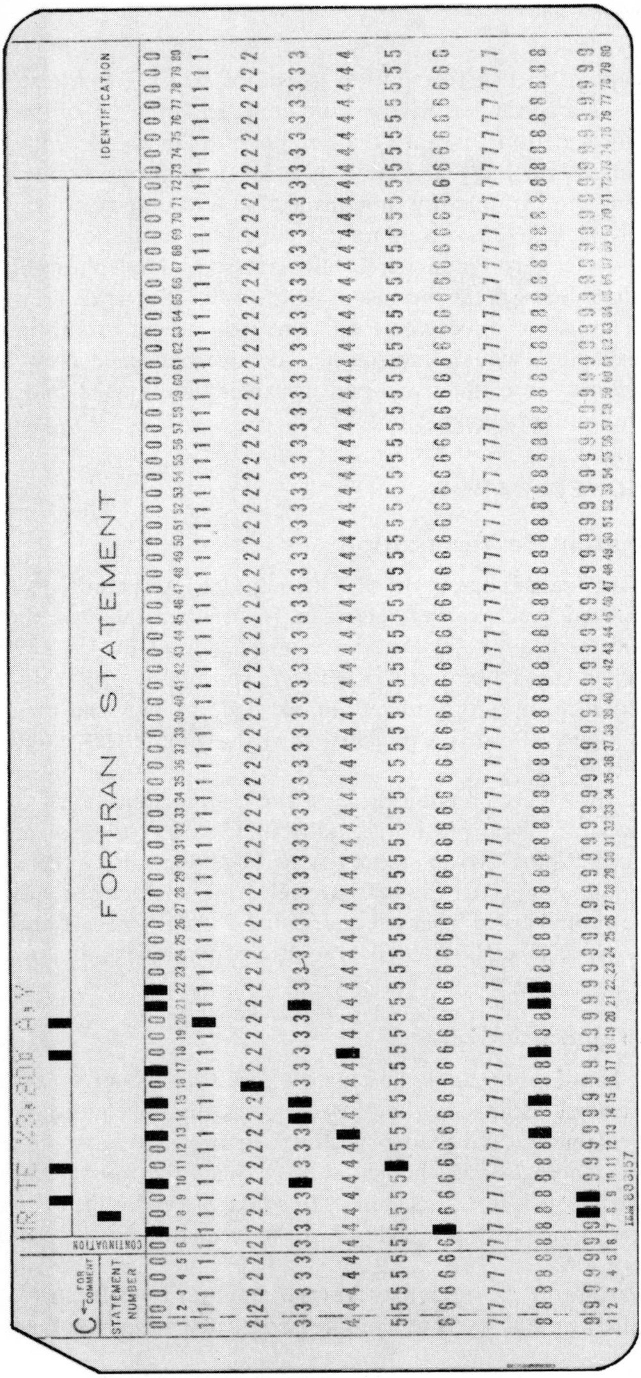

Figure 10–14 Punched card.

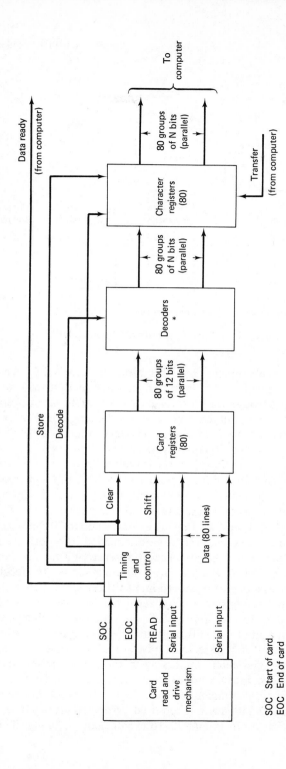

Figure 10-15 Card reader controller; (a) block diagram

SOC Start of card
EOC End of card

* Decoders may be
   time-shared by individual
   card registers

N Number of bits in
   character oriented
   output

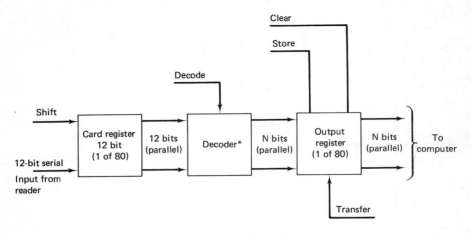

(b) Details of one stage of controller

Figure 10–15 (Continued) (b) details of one stage of controller

has its advantages and disadvantages, and the information handling techniques vary only slightly. The column serial, row parallel method will now be discussed. Cards move through the card reader (row 9 first) face up and edgewise. A fixed distance is maintained between the leading edges of two consecutive cards, and this distance is divided into equal timing periods (cycle points). For example, assume that 20 equal cycle points (timing periods) are used to read a punched card. The timing starts at the leading edge of a card, and row of the card represents one timing period. Thus only 12 timing periods are used to read a card, and eight timing periods are allowed to convert, check, and transfer the information to the computer's memory.

Each column is read by a separate sensing device, so up to 80 characters per card may be supplied to the computer. A card is moved into position so that the sensing devices can detect the presence or absence of a hole in each column on the bottom row (row 9). If a hole in a column is sensed, the resulting electrical impulse causes a one to be stored in a shift register for that column; if no hole is sensed, the register stores a zero. The card then moves to row 8, detects holes, and stores the appropriate ones and zeros. Each new row advances the information in the shift registers (see Figure 10–15). When all 12 rows have been read, all 80 registers will have stored the pattern of ones and zeros representing the characters appearing in the corresponding card columns. Figure 10–15 shows the concept of a card reader and its controller.

Investigation of the total number of characters to be inputted from a punched card shows that 12 bits are not required. Properly arranged, a 6-level BCD code such as shown in Figure 10–16 is sufficient. Actually, if the

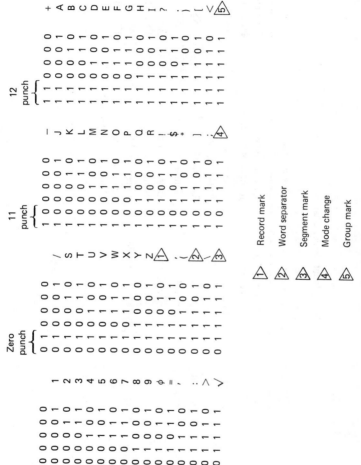

Figure 10-16 6-level code correlated with punched card codes.

315

Table 10–2 Input Device Characteristics

Input Device	Input Medium	Speed (Characters per Second)*	Input Capacity	Character Set
Switches	—	Operator skill dependent	Determined by number of switches	Determined by number of switches
Punched paper Tape reader	Paper tape	10–500	Determined by length of tape	ANSI
Teletype	Written data	Up to 10	Unlimited	ANSI
Keyboard	Written data	Up to 10	Unlimited	ANSI
Card reader	Cards	Up to 1300	Determined by number of cards	ANSI EBCDIC
Magnetic tape deck	Magnetic tape	1000 to 600,000	Determined by length of tape (200–1600 bits per inch)	ANSI EBCDIC
Optical character reader	Written data	Up to 360	Determined by number of pages	Alphanumeric
Voice	Sound	Experimental	—	—

*Values are nominal.

01 column in Figure 10–16 is considered equivalent to the zero punch, the 10 column as the 11 punch, and the 11 column as the 12 punch, it can be seen that the 12-bit Hollerith code easily converts to a 6-level BCD code. Therefore the 12-bit code may be decoded and reformatted to a 6-bit code prior to transfer of each character to the word register or directly to the computer if operating in BCD mode. In fact, any type of reformatting may be accomplished, and the 12-bit Hollerith code may be converted to any of the commonly used computer codes.

Cards may be advanced through the read station a row at a time or in one smooth, continuous motion. If "stepped" through, timing must be provided by the computer so that the location of each row is maintained. Continuous feed often uses an encoder attached to the feed mechanism to identify the row being read by relating the card position directly to feed mechanism rotation.

10–7 SUMMARY

Any of the common large-scale data storage devices such as magnetic drum, disc, and tape also fit into the classification of input devices. Chapter 8 discusses these items in detail. Interface between the device and the computer is via controllers, which are also discussed in Chapter 8.

Comparison between various input devices tends to be somewhat meaningless unless some common ground can be established. For example, it is misleading to try to compare the number of bits per second inputted by a binary formatted paper tape to the number of pages per second read by an optical character reader. In the final evaluation, the number of operations that the computer can be programmed through per second is the important parameter. But, since most of today's inputs to the computer are related to alphameric and control characters, perhaps the best point of comparison is the number of characters per second that can be inputted. Table 10–2 provides this comparison, along with other pertinent data concerning common input methods.

QUESTIONS

1. What is the primary function of the INPUT section?
2. List the major advantages and disadvantages of switch input to the computer.
3. List the major advantages and disadvantages of punched tape input to the computer.
4. How is information represented by punched tape?
5. How does the tape reader recognize and store a binary 1; a binary 0?
6. What is the major problem that the Teletype must overcome so that it is an effective computer input device?

7. What happens to the start and stop bits on the 11-unit Teletype code?

8. Define the term "byte."

9. Describe the computer's role in obtaining information from the Teletype keyboard.

10. What is the difference in operation between the Teletype keyboard and a typical computer keyboard input device?

11. Speculate on how a computer keyboard could be used to activate a Read-Only memory to furnish ANSI input to the computer.

12. Discuss the operation of a device that will read magnetic ink characters and convert them to ANSI computer input.

13. What do *you* think will be future developments in optical character readers?

14. What do *you* think will be the future of voice-entry systems?

15. Speculate on new types of computer input devices that you think are necessary or practical.

11

The OUTPUT Function

The OUTPUT section is the interface between the computer and the outside world, just as the INPUT section is the interface between the outside world and the computer. Information received from the computer's memory is converted by the OUTPUT section into a form that is easily interpreted by the user. Most OUTPUT devices are oriented toward standard codes, and as with the INPUT section, conversion from internal computer codes to standard codes must be accomplished. Either the computer's program must perform this conversion or the controller serving the OUTPUT device must have such capability. Unless otherwise stated, output information conversion is assumed to be a function of the computer's programmed operations. Chapter 12 will discuss computer programming in more detail.

11–1 FUNCTIONAL REQUIREMENTS

Concepts

Computer output may be viewed as a three-part operation similar to computer input. Of course, since the requirement is *from* computer *to* the outside world, the technique used in Chapter 10 must be reversed. First, control circuitry is needed to change the information from the computer into a form that the output device is capable of using. Second, a mechanism is required to convert digital information into a form that people (or perhaps other computers) can use. Finally, some visual display of human-oriented information must be provided. Complete computer output requirements and typical solutions are summarized in Table 11–1.

Table 11-1   Computer Output Requirements

Input from Computer	Output to Converter	Converter Mechanism	Output Information Representation
Bits	Electrical impulses	Panel lights	Visual
Part of computer word	Parallel	Tape punch	Binary tape
Byte	Parallel	Tape punch	Character tape
Byte	Parallel	Card punch	Binary card
Byte	Parallel	Card punch	Hollerith-coded card
Byte	Parallel	Direct character display	Visual
Byte	Parallel	Character printer	Hard copy
Byte(s)	Serial-parallel	Line printer	Hard copy
Byte	Parallel	Plotter	Graphical/hard copy
Byte	Parallel	Graphic terminals (CRT)	Visual

Panel Output Indicators

The simplest output provided by the digital computer is the indicator lights on the control panel. The control panel displays, *bit by bit*, the contents of various registers, just as the control panel provided a capability to insert addresses, instructions, and information bit by bit. As with switch input, lamp output requires intimate knowledge of the internal operations and machine language of the computer. Such output information is normally used by machine language programmers and those performing troubleshooting and repair of the computer. The control panel described in Chapter 2 is an excellent example of this level of detailed information display.

A General Approach

The OUTPUT section faces the same problems that confronted the INPUT section. Binary codes vary from computer to computer. Output devices seldom are binarily oriented and therefore are not efficient from the computer's viewpoint. Their character sets, furthermore, are not compatible with the computer's internal information representation. As in the INPUT section, additional logic must be provided to compensate for these discrepancies.

A block diagram of the major functional requirements for an OUTPUT section is shown in Figure 11-1. The *output control* block oversees the complete operation of the OUTPUT section. It receives directive signals from the CONTROL section and in turn enables and disables the remainder of the functional blocks as required. During a typical operation, the *word storage* block receives and retains a complete computer word from storage upon command of the output control. Assuming that the computer word has been

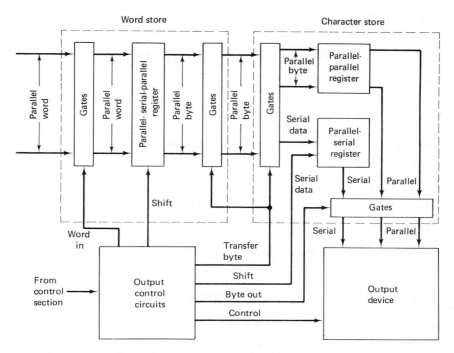

Figure 11-1 General output section block diagram.

reformatted to an output device-compatible form by the internally stored program, it will contain one or more bytes of information, depending on word length. Each byte is transferred to *character storage* and then to the output device for actual display. If a 16-bit word is considered, then two 8-bit ANSI characters could be contained in each computer word, and two transfers from word storage to character storage would be affected before the typical operating cycle was repeated.

The word storage device is, in simplified form, a parallel-to-parallel register which accepts the computer word 16 bits at a time and releases 8 bits of the word at a time to the character storage device. An 8-bit parallel-to-parallel or parallel-to-serial register will perform the required operations of the character store. Output control contains the necessary gates and flip-flops to implement the direction of the CONTROL section.

11-2 COMPUTER-ORIENTED OUTPUT

One general grouping of output devices consists of equipment that prepares input media for future computer input. Typical examples are tape punches and card punches. These devices accept information from the computer and actually punch holes in tape or cards so that they may be later used as computer input. Both punched tape and punched cards may also be pre-pared "off-line" using tape perforators and keypunches, respectively. A tape perforator and a keypunch are devices which resemble typewriters from a keyboard standpoint, but they output punched tape or punched cards instead of printed matter.

Punched Tape

Tape punches use mechanisms very similar to those used for tape readers. A functional block diagram of a tape punch is shown in Figure 11–2. Note that the major functions already discussed in the general output section also appear here. The *output control* sequences loading and unloading of the *word store* and the *character store*. Furthermore, tape advance and punch control signals orginate in output control. Only two major differences appear in the diagram of Figure 11–2. First, a new block called *character drivers* appears. This new block is necessitated by the type of mechanics used in the *punch and drive mechanism*. Each potential bit position in a column on the tape has associated with it a pin which must punch a hole in the tape when a binary 1 is to be entered. The pins are driven by electromagnets and require additional power for motive force. Hence the character drivers are needed, one for each position. The *drive mechanism* may be either friction or sprocket-hole driven, depending on equipment design. The output control provides "advance" information to the drive and receives feedback to indicate that advance has taken place. Such feedback is needed so that the output control realizes that it is time to proceed with the next punch operation.

The electromechanical nature of tape punches limits their capabilities to the range of 100 to 150 characters per second. Figure 11–2 is conceptual in nature and does not necessarily represent an existing tape punch. Electrical, logical, and mechanical details of a specific tape punch should be

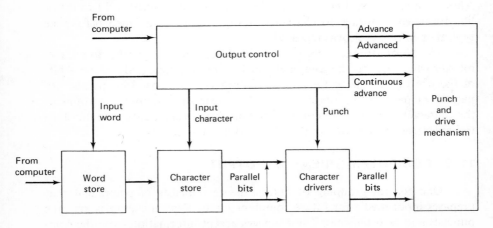

Figure 11–2   Tape punch block diagram.

obtained from the appropriate manufacturer's instruction and maintenance manuals.

If the tape is to be used directly on the machine performing the punching, then quite often the tape will be punched in binary format. No conversion hardware or software is required. More often, however, the tape must be compatible with other computers. In such cases, the binary code of the computer must be converted to the predetermined code before actuating the punch. A complete computer word is read from the memory and placed in word storage (see Figure 11–2). A character at a time is moved to the character store and then to the output device (the tape punch in this case) via the character drivers. As soon as all characters in the word are removed from word storage, a new word is retrieved from memory for storage in the output device and subsequent punching.

Punched Cards

Punched card preparation is very similar to punched tape procedures. The same mechanical requirements exist; that is, holes must be punched and the medium (cards) must be moved. Electrically and logically, however, some additional requirements exist, especially with cards moving through the punch row by row. First of all, since up to 80 characters may be placed on a punched card, a block of 80 parallel punches must be provided. Secondly, most internal computer codes are not directly compatible with the 12-bit information representation on punched cards and may not be easily software compatible for conversion. Internal decoding is often used. Finally, since row by row punching is not oriented toward character representation (only one bit of each of 80 characters is punched per row), all 80 words have to be retrieved from storage and placed temporarily in buffer storage in the punch.

Punched cards may also be prepared under computer control by punching a column at a time instead of a row at a time. This reduces requirements for number of punches and greatly reduces complexity. However, speed suffers unless special designs are undertaken to take advantage of columns where no information is to be recorded. (The card movement may be speeded up if no information is to be recorded in a column.)

After the card is punched, it is usually routed to a "read" station within the card punch. Here the newly punched information is compared with the information stored in the buffer register for verification of correct punching. Cards which pass the test proceed to a stacker for removal from the machine, while improperly punched or read cards are routed to a "reject" area.

11-3 DIRECT CHARACTER DISPLAY

Often the computer must output letters, numbers, or symbols, but a printed copy is not required. Some sort of alphameric display is thus called for. The cathode-ray tube (CRT) is used when large volumes of data must be displayed (see Section 11–6), but when smaller amounts of information are required (up to 256 characters), other alternatives exist. This section discusses various small-scale character display devices.

The NIXIE Tube

The "old standby" in numeric display is the NIXIE* tube (Figure 11–3). It is classified as a cold-cathode, gas-filled glow tube. In simple terms, it may be compared to the neon bulbs seen in small orange-colored night lights. Each of the "neon bulbs" is shaped like one of the ten decimal digits, and when properly activated, only one character glows at a time. The individual characters are so arranged inside the tube that there is a minimum of masking of characters which are in the rear. When one character is illuminated, it is difficult to see any of the nonilluminated numbers.

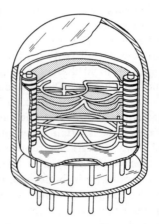

Figure 11–3   NIXIE Tube. (Courtesy of Burroughs Corp., Plainfied, NJ)

The major advantages of the NIXIE tube include long life, the capability to quickly change from one character to another, and relatively low power consumption. High voltage is required to operate the NIXIE tube, but recently developed integrated circuit decoder/driver combinations perform the job quite satisfactorily. If there are any major disadvantages, they would fall in the area of decoding complexity. Regardless of the internal code used by the computer, it must be converted to a 1-of-10 output. Such a decoding requirement usually results in the need for many additional gates.

---

*Registered trademark of The Burroughs Corporation.

Segmented Displays

It is unnecessary to use ten separate elements to display the ten decimal digits. A close approximation of digits 0 through 9 may be had by breaking the digits into *segments* and activating only the segments necessary to display the digit. Seven segments quite adequately synthesize the decimal digits (plus 14 alphabetic characters), as shown in Figure 11–4(a). When complete alphameric display is required, 16 segments are used (Figure 11–4(b)). The 16-segment display is capable of over 65,000 patterns, which allows great versatility in information display. Typical configurations of segmented display devices are shown in Figure 11–5. Directly viewed, incandescent filaments are used in the unit of Figure 11–5(a). A small incandescent lamp may be placed at the source end of a "light pipe" with the viewing surface of the display at the receiving end (Figure 11–5(b)). Vacuum fluorescent devices (Figure 11–5(c)) use individually activated fluorescent segments to form the desired characters. Furthermore, solid-state, light-emitting diodes (discussed shortly) using reflection of the multidirection light produce an easily viewable numeric display.

Another type of increasingly popular information display device is the *liquid crystal readout*. The basic principle behind the liquid crystal readout is simple. It consists of a thin layer of transparent liquid crystal placed between

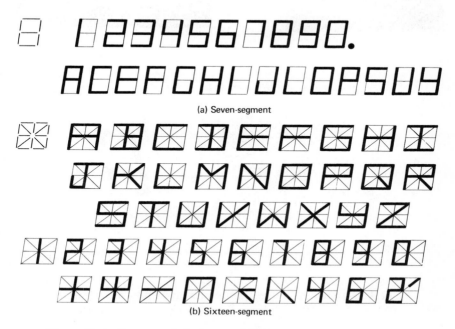

(a) Seven-segment

(b) Sixteen-segment

Figure 11–4 Segmented display capabilities.

two sheets of glass which are coated with an electrical conductor. The front electrode is transparent. The rear electrode is shaped in segments to form the desired character.

The display may be operated in either a *reflective* or a *transmissive* manner. In *transmissive* displays, the rear electrode is transparent, while in the *reflective* unit, the rear electrode is opaque, having a mirror-surfaced film. When voltage is applied between electrodes of either type, the liquid becomes

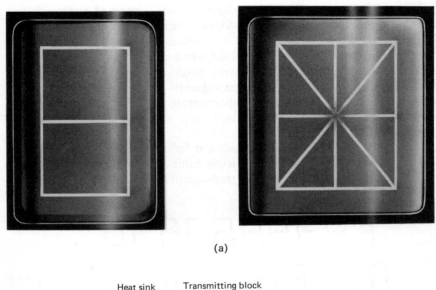

(a)

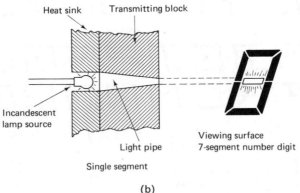

(b)

Figure 11–5 Segmented displays; (a) incandescent filament (courtesy of Pinlites, Inc. Caldwell, NJ), (b) the "light pipe" concept (courtesy of Tung-Sol Division, Wagner Electric Corp.), (c) vacuum fluorescent segments (courtesy Tung-Sol Division, Wagner Electric Corp.), (d) a liquid crystal display (courtesy OPTEL Corp., Princeton, NJ).

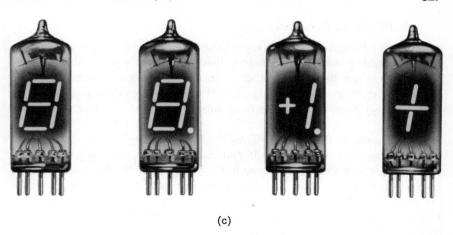

(c)

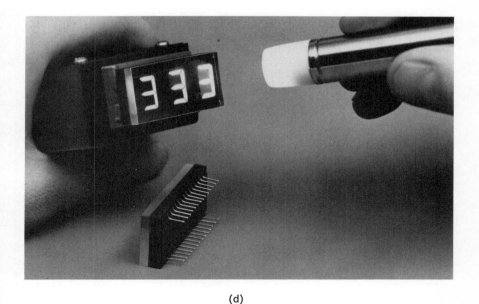

(d)

Figure 11–5 (Continued)

turbulent and scatters ambient light in the form of the rear electrode pattern. A source of local light or sufficient ambient light must be present for this type of display to operate. Figure 11–5(d) shows the general concept of liquid crystal display devices.

Solid-State Displays

In ever-increasing applications, *solid-state display devices* are beginning to dominate the information display field. Whether in segmented or dot-matrix form, the basic concept of operation is the same. Semiconductor diodes made of certain materials such as gallium-arsenide-phosphide (only one of many) possess the property of emitting light when proper potentials are applied.

For numeric display only, 27 of the light-emitting diodes are arranged in a 5 × 7 matrix (not all of the 35 matrix locations are occupied by diodes); a 28th diode is offset at the lower left to serve as a decimal point. Figure 11–6(a) shows a typical solid-state numeric indicator, which includes decoding capability. The block diagram for the complete assembly appears in Figure 11–6(b). BCD input signals are decoded on the IC chip into ten signals, representing digits 0 through 9. These signals are then encoded into signals that drive an encoder that selects the proper combination of light-emitting diodes to display the required digit. The decimal point is activated by a separate input.

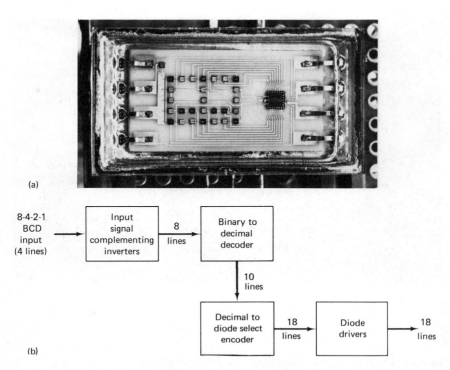

Figure 11–6 Solid-state numeric indicator diagram; (a) LED chip and decoder, (b) block diagram (courtesy Hewlett-Packard, Palo Alto CA).

When complete alphameric display is required, a full 5×7 matrix of light-emitting diodes (LEDs) may be employed (Figure 11-7(a)). The 5×7 matrix of LEDs which makes up each character is X-Y addressable. This allows for a simple addressing, decoding, and driving scheme between the display module and the computer logic.

To form alphameric characters, a method called *scanning* is used. Information is addressed to the display by selecting one row of LEDs at a time, energizing the appropriate diodes in that row, and then proceeding to the next row. After all rows have been excited (one at a time), the process is repeated. By scanning through all rows at least 100 times a second, a flicker-free character composed of discrete illuminated LEDs can be produced. Information may be moved from row to row of the display (*vertical scanning*) or from left to right (*horizontal scanning*).

Figure 11-7(b) indicates how (with vertical scanning) letters A and B would be formed by sequentially selecting the rows and energizing the cor-

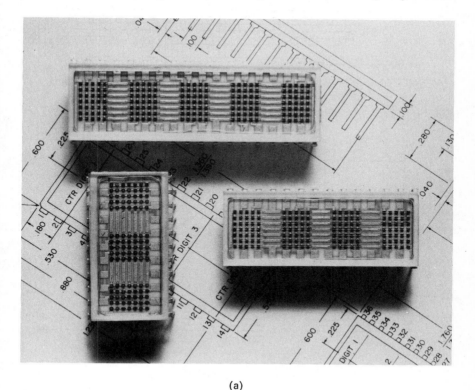

(a)

Figure 11-7 Alphameric LED display operation; (a) assemblies (courtesy Hewlett-Packard Co., Palo Alto, CA)

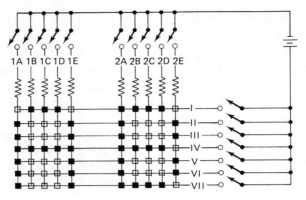

(b) Formation of letters A and B with vertical scanning

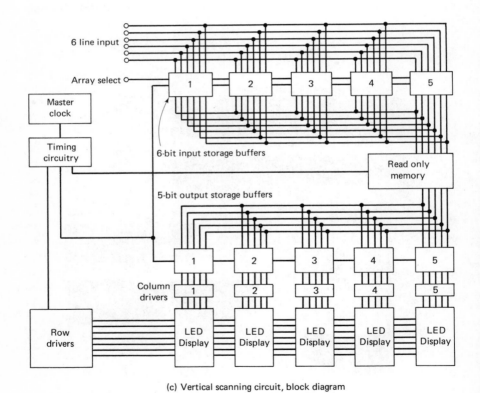

(c) Vertical scanning circuit, block diagram

Figure 11–7 Alphameric LED display operation (Continued);
(b) formation of letters, (c) vertical scanning circuit block diagram
(courtesy Hewlett-Packard Co., Palo Alto, CA)

rect diodes in each column. When row I is selected, only columns 1B, 1C, 1D and 2A, 2B, 2C, and 2D are energized. When selecting row II, columns 1A, 1E and 2A, 2E are energized. The process is continued, as indicated by the solid squares in Figure 11–7(b), until all appropriate LEDs have been lighted. The cycle is repeated at a high rate, so the eye sees a continuous *flicker-free* character.

A typical vertical scanning circuit for addressing the display is shown in the block diagram in Figure 11–7(c). This particular scheme contains five display characters. Operation for other numbers of characters is similar. Circuit operation is as follows.

1. Coded 6-bit alphameric information is sequentially entered and stored in five 6-bit input storage buffers.
2. Next, with the input information stored in the input buffers, timing circuitry enables the ROM and input storage buffer number one, so its stored 6-bit code can be read by the ROM. (All other input storage buffers are disabled.)
3. The 6-bit input is decoded by the ROM, and the first row of character information is stored in the 5-bit output storage buffer number one. In other words, if the character *A* is being written, diodes 1B, 1C, and 1D of row I will be lighted (see Figure 11–7(b)); and this information is stored in the first output storage buffer.
4. Having completed the first loading operation, the timing circuitry now activates input storage buffer number two. (All other input storage buffers are disabled.) The coded character is read into the ROM, decoded, and the row information fed into output storage buffer number two. This operation is repeated until all five characters stored in the input storage buffers are sensed by the ROM character generator and the first line of character information is stored in the output storage buffers.
5. Next, the timing circuitry connects the top row driver, so current flows through and lights up all of the appropriate LEDs in the top rows of the five display characters.
6. The complete cycle is then repeated to decode and display row II of the LED matrix characters, then row III, on through row VII. Since the time to decode and load the output storage buffers is short in comparison with the time the display is lit, repeating the character scanning at a rate above 100 times per second gives a flicker-free alphameric character.

Plasma Panels

Cold-cathode, gas-filled display techniques have been modernized, and these improved techniques have resulted in some very versatile display devices. *Segmented displays*, using 7, 9, 13, and 15 bars, have been produced to meet the requirements for alphameric display. *Multicharacter assemblies,* using gas discharge techniques, have also been developed and are being used.

One of the most interesting gas-discharge displays is the so-called *plasma panel.* Characters are displayed in a dot-matrix form, one of which is the familiar 5 × 7 form discussed earlier. The physical construction of one version of this type of display (SELF-SCAN* panel) is shown in Figure 11–8(a).

Although the following explanation is grossly simplified, enough of the general concepts are presented to determine its basic principles of operation. When the panel is energized, sufficient potential difference is established between the keep-alive cathode and the keep-alive anode to establish a glow discharge in the keep-alive grooves located in the rear glass cover. The physical construction of the keep-alive cathode and anode are such that charged particles can diffuse into the area of the reset cathode.

The scan anodes are maintained at a high dc voltage, and when the reset cathode is grounded, complete ionization of the partially ionized gas that has diffused from the keep-alive area occurs. A glow is then established in the seven rectangular areas of this single cathode, defined by the intersection of the rear of the cathode strip and the seven scan grooves in the rear glass cover. (This area is not visible from the front of the panel.) The first character-forming cathode is then grounded, immediately following removal of the ground from the reset cathode, and the glow is transferred. Each character-forming cathode has seven tiny holes (0.030 inch in diameter) called *glow-priming aperatures.* (These holes are small enough that the glow from the rear of the character-forming cathode does not show through, yet charged particles can diffuse through them into the display cavities.) The ground is removed from the first character-forming cathode and transferred to the second cathode. Glow discharge is transferred in this manner until the end of the display is reached. The reset cathode may then be grounded again and the scan process started over. Thus *the glow discharge is started at the left and transferred one cathode at a time along the entire length of the panel.* Actually, the logic circuitry needed to perform the scan may be simplified by using a "3-phase" drive circuit and grounding every fourth cathode. Glow transfer occurs only between adjacent cathodes, so this technique still allows transfer of only one cathode at a time.

As the glow is scanned down the panel, a phenomenon called *glow priming* occurs. Figure 11–8(b) shows a cross-sectional view of a panel, depicting one cathode with a glow discharge on the rear (scan side). The scan glow covers the rectangular portion on the scan side of the cathode located beneath each display cavity. The priming aperatures have allowed

---

*Registered trademark of The Burroughs Corporation.

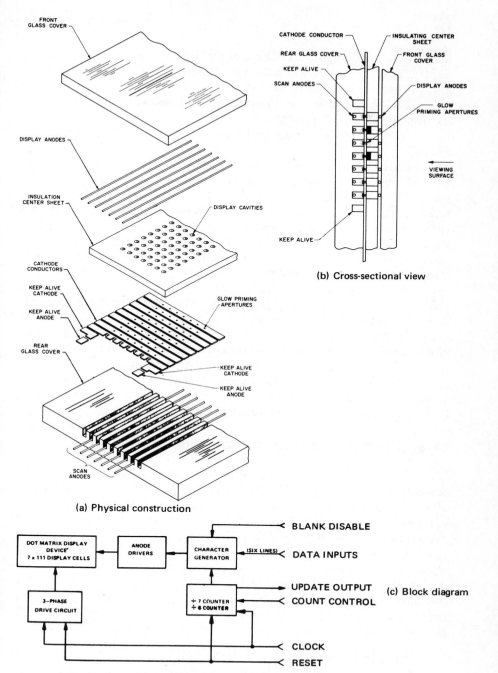

Figure 11–8 Plasma panel; (a) physical construction, (b) cross-sectional view, (c) block diagram (courtesy Burroughs Corp., Plainfield, NJ)

the partially ionized gas to diffuse into the display aperature. If any of the display anodes are placed at a sufficiently high dc voltage, the partially ionized gas will become completely ionized, and a glow will occur in the display cavity. Characters are written on the viewing side of the panel by addressing the display anodes in synchronism with the glow-priming ionization present on the scan side of the cathode that intersects the point where the dot is to appear.

Figure 11-8(c) is a block diagram showing the general concept of "writing" information into the display panel. The clock input, which occurs at a frequency that allows the overall panel to be scanned approximately 60 times per second, feeds the *3-phase drive circuit* to sequentially ground the cathodes that form the characters. A reset input is also provided to return the panel scan to the left side. The *character generator* converts six bits of primary information and a clock pulse into a dot matrix character format made available column by column, seven bits in parallel. A *counter section*, using the count control and clock inputs, establishes the spacing between characters. The actual character information is provided by a *read-only memory*. *Anode drivers* are provided to interface between the logic level of the character generator and the high-voltage dc levels of the display panel. If information is to remain on the panel for display, external circuits must be provided to refresh the input to the character generator.

Panels using this or similar techniques may be used to display as few as one and as many as 256 characters. Display size of characters ranges from 0.25 to 0.5 inch in height. The future will surely see these heights extended.

11-4 SHAPED CHARACTER PRINTERS

The principal output of the digital computer is a "hard-copy" display, something that gives a permanent record of the results of the computer's efforts. It can range from something as simple as a column of numbers to a complex graphical plot of a spacecraft's flight to the outer planets. Initially our explanations will be limited to those output devices that provide printed information such as number, letters, and symbols. In the later stages of this chapter, interactive output devices and plotters are discussed.

"Hard-copy" devices tend to be strongly oriented toward mechanical functions (much more than input devices), so a certain amount of mechanical detail must be included to explain their operation. However, mechanics will be kept to a minimum, and the associated electronics will be stressed.

Electric Typewriter

Perhaps the most common output device that provides printed copy is the electric typewriter. Properly interfaced, the electric typewriter is able to accept output from the computer and supply printed copy. The electric typewriter fits into the category of serial impact printers, supplying a single

Table 11–2 Printer Characteristics

Printer Type	Character Set	Speed	Characters per Line	Special Paper?
Character serial (full)	48–128	10–30 cps	1–132	No
Character serial (dot)	64–128	30–165 cps	74–132	No
Drum	28–128	200–9000 lpm	32–160	No
Train/chain	16–128	125–2000 lpm	80–136	No
Electrostatic	64–123	275–3600 lpm	80–210	Yes
Thermal	51–96	10–30 cps	80–140	Yes

cps: characters per second
lpm: lines per minute

character at a time. Speed limitations exist with typewriters, however, as may be seen in the comparative data table (Table 11–2). Mechanical design of different methods can greatly improve speed performance.

Print Wheel Printers

One common approach places all numbers, letters, and symbols around the periphery of a *print wheel*. As the wheel spins, a hammer drives the paper momentarily against the wheel just as the selected character moves into alignment. Thus the print wheel printer prints "on the fly." Character-by-character printing occurs for every column position across the paper, one character printed per print wheel revolution. Figure 11–9(a) shows the simplified mechanical details of a typical print wheel and character printing sequence. Note that the print wheel characters are arranged spirally so that the wheel may move continuously across the paper while the character set remains aligned with each column for complete print wheel revolution.

Actuation of the printing hammer must be accurately timed with the position of the character to be printed if proper printing is to occur. A *shaft encoder* is attached to the print wheel shaft to indicate drum position. The functional system shown in Figure 11–9(b) uses a magnetic encoder, but photoelectric and direct commutative encoders are also used. In a magnetic encoder, a "gear tooth" for each character position on the print wheel is provided. As the "gear tooth" passes a magnetic pickup, a pulse is generated, signaling a specified position of the print wheel. One "tooth" is left out at the arbitrary beginning point of the type font, and this special pulse is used to reset a counter. The *counter* counts each tooth as it passes so that the output of the counter represents the actual character under the hammer at the time. Counter output is compared with the computer's representation of the character to be printed (stored in the *line register* with the rest of the characters), and when the *coincidence detector* determines that the print wheel is at that position, it supplies an activating signal to the *hammer solenoid* through a *driver amplifier*. Upon detection of the next reference position, the next

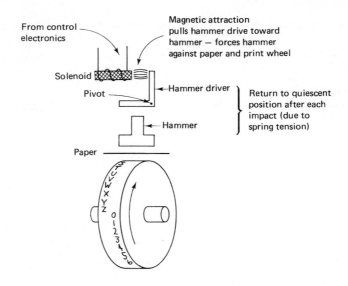

(a) Print wheel mechanical details

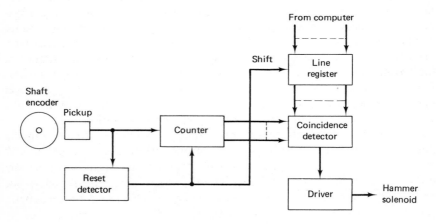

(b) Print wheel electronics block diagram

Figure 11–9   Print wheel printer; (a) print wheel mechanical details, (b) print wheel electronics block diagram.

character to be printed is moved into position in the line register, the counter is reset, and the cycle repeats. Additional circuitry, not shown, is required to detect the end of a line, move the paper, etc. However, the basic concepts of on-the-fly character printing has been shown, and no difficulty should be experienced as more complex printing arrangements are discussed.

Most print on-the-fly machines using print wheels are limited to about 30 characters per second due to mechanical limitations. One approach, using the 64 ANSI character set, arranges the characters in six 32-character segments around the print wheel. Six print hammers are used, one for each segment, giving each hammer a half print wheel rotation for stabilization to overcome one of the major speed difficulties. Speeds up to 100 characters per second are realized using this method.

A modern takeoff from the print wheel technique is the *daisy wheel*. Radial spokes project from a plastic hub, with a raised piece of type on the flat side of each spoke. The wheel is spun in a horizontal plane, and when the desired type character is positioned in front of a hammer mechanism, the wheel is stopped and the hammer activated. This drives the type character into a ribbon and the ribbon into the paper. Sufficient force is applied to make up to six copies, and speeds up to 45 characters per second are not uncommon. Electronic requirements are similar to the print-on-the-fly systems.

Drum and Line Printers

Extending the print wheel concept results in the use of a *drum* with one character font and one hammer for each column in the printed information. Obviously much more electronics are required, since effectively a complete line of information can be printed for each drum revolution, but the same basic concepts discussed during the on-the-fly single-character print wheel still apply. Figure 11–10 is representative of a modern drum printer.

Another basic type of *line printer* uses character sets that move horizontally on a chain or train. In a chain printer the characters are mechanically

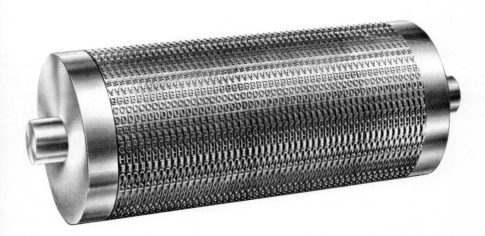

Figure 11–10 Typical drum printer

linked, while in the train printer each character rides freely around a track. The character set, in both cases, however, passes in front of a row of print hammers that strike the appropriate character as it passes the column. A chain-oriented line printer is shown in Figure 11–11.

Chain/train and drum printers, since they are printing a line of characters at a time, are faster (and more costly) than the single-character printers. Modern line printers have capabilities of greater than 2000 lines per minute.

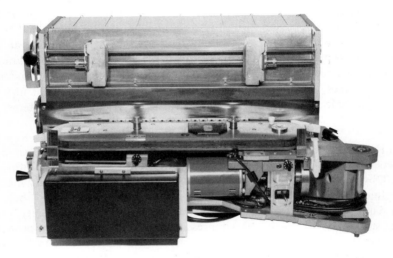

Figure 11–11 Chain printer mechanism (courtesy Mohawk Data Sciences Corp., Utica, NY)

11–5 SYNTHESIZED CHARACTER PRINTERS

Dot Matrix Format

It should be noted that all printing systems so far discussed have used shaped characters similar to those formed by a conventional typewriter, and printing has been accomplished by impact of the type font or an associated hammer with the printer paper. When character esthetics, that is, fully formed characters, are not a requirement, synthesis of characters may be used to good advantage. Characters may be synthesized using a dot matrix format of, typically, 5×7 dot dimensions. Figure 11–12 shows how some of the characters in the standard 64 character ANSI set are formed in a 5×7 matrix.

Print Wire Printer

When high-speed serial character printers are required (from 100 characters per second to 300 characters per second), but not at the expense of the line printer, an impact printing dot matrix method can be used. Printing is

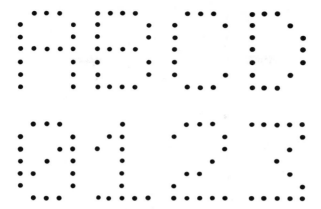

Figure 11–12 Dot matrix formation of characters.

accomplished by selectively energizing seven solenoids attached to print wires arranged radially around the print head (Figure 11–13(a)). Each solenoid can be energized independently up to five times for each character.

The free ends of the print wires pass through a wire guide at the front of the print head. The wire guide properly spaces the wires so that the correct wire passes through the correct hole in the print jewel. When the printing impulses are received, the print solenoids are energized to drive the print wires against the ribbon, paper, and platen to form the characters out of

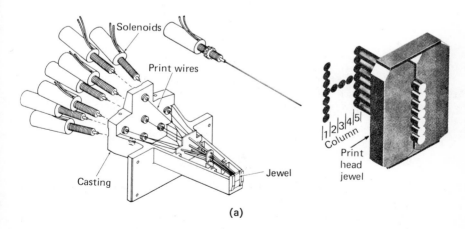

(a)

Figure 11–13 Print wire printer concepts: (a) print-wire mechanical details (courtesy of Centronics Data Computer Corp.), (b) print wire printer block diagram, (c) formation of letter "A" by character generator.

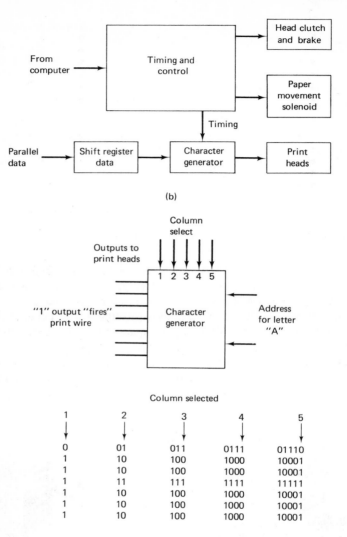

(b)

(c) Formation of letter "A" by character generator

Figure 11–13   (Continued)

the dots. When the print solenoids are de-energized, the print wires are drawn in flush to the surface of the print head.

A block diagram of the print wire type of impact printer is shown in Figure 11–13(b). Input to the printer from the computer is assumed to be in standard ANSI parallel form and is stored character by character in a *shift register buffer*. Controls from the computer initiate printer action via the *printer control circuits*, which include timing, paper motion controls, head motion controls, etc. The output of the shift register buffer serves as the address input of a *ROM character generator*. The Read-Only Memory (ROM) contains the desired displayable characters as five separate 7-bit words (35 bits), addressable in ANSI format. Each output word appears as seven parallel bits, since the printer generates the characters vertically, seven bits at a time. *Control timing* sequences write pulses to the print heads as each vertical column is selected. Figure 11–13(c) shows the development of the letter *A* using this method.

Non-impact Printers

Another complete "family" of printers has appeared in recent years. These printers operate without impacting the output medium and are almost entirely dot matrix character formation devices. Non-impact printers use various electronic and chemical techniques to create images of the characters on paper and to achieve higher speeds. Also, because images are formed by dots and points rather than solid lines, these printers may function as plotters to create graphs and other complex shapes. Appropriate software (computer programs) must be supplied, however, to accommodate graphic capability.

Electrostatic printers deposit an electrostatic pattern on special dielectric paper by means of charged wires or pins. The pins supply a charge to the paper in the desired pattern, quite often the conventional 5 × 7 matrix form. Other common matrix dimensions are 7 × 9 and 16 × 16. Dot resolution varies from 72.5 dots per inch up to 200 dots per inch. The large number

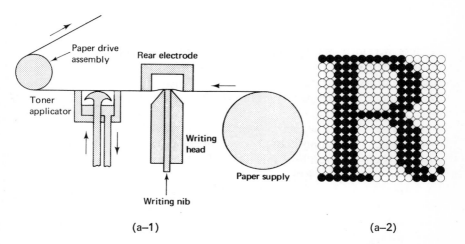

(a–1) (a–2)

Figure 11–14 Electrostatic printer; (a) principles (courtesy of VERSATEC).

(b)

Figure 11–14   Electrostatic printer (Continued); (b) typical printer (courtesy of VERSATEC).

of dots per inch make electrostatic printers, with appropriate software, readily adaptable to the production of graphs and other plotting tasks. Basic concepts of electrostatic printing are shown in Figure 11–14. Information is applied to the paper via the writing head and rear electrode, which place the desired charge on the paper. The characters become visible as the paper passes through a solution containing ink particles of opposite charge to the paper. The oppositely charged ink particles adhere to the charged spots on the paper, resulting in a visible image. An electrostatic printer may be seen in Figure 11–14(b).

Thermal printers use printheads that convert electrical pulses to heat. The image is created on heat-sensitive paper, by either the conventional 5×7 matrix one row or column at a time or by 35 heaters on each pad. Figure 11–15 is a typical thermal printer.

Another technique shoots a stream of charged ink drops toward the paper. The stream is deflected by electrostatically charged plates to sweep out an image of the desired character. The charged particles adhere to the paper to create a line of print. *Ink jet printers* require special paper to catch and hold the charged ink and also tend to be a bit messy. The concepts of ink jet printing are seen in Figure 11–16.

Figure 11–15 Thermal printer (courtesy Computer Devices, Inc., Burlington, MA).

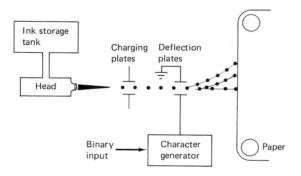

Figure 11–16 Ink jet printer concepts.

11–6 GRAPHIC COMPUTER TERMINALS

The Display

Since the appearance of the electronic digital computer in the 1940s, engineers and scientists have been diligently searching for better and faster man-computer information interface methods. *Interactive graphics*—a method of communicating with a computer through static or animated diagrams via some type of display terminal—shows great potential to solve this problem. The most commonly used display terminal is a cathode-ray tube (CRT) such as is used in television receivers. Capabilities range from simple character formats (numbers and letters) to complex electronic circuit design complete with symbols. Since the user *interacts* with the computer and the display, some method of *input* is usually included with the terminal. Keyboards and light pens* are common input devices used with interactive graphic terminals. Figure 11–17 is a typical graphic computer terminal.

Figure 11–17 Typical graphic terminal (courtesy of Tektronix, Inc., Beaverton, OR).

---

*A light pen is a hand-held device that detects light changes from the CRT and signals the computer with information concerning the location and nature of the intercepted data. The pen can be used either to enter information directly or in a "pointing" mode.

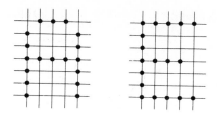

(a) Dot matrix character formation
(see also figure 11-12)

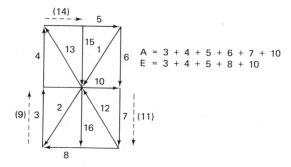

A = 3 + 4 + 5 + 6 + 7 + 10
E = 3 + 4 + 5 + 8 + 10

(b) Stroke character formation

Figure 11–18 Display formats; (a) Dot matrix character formation (see also Figure 11–12), (b) stroke character formation.

Information is displayed on the screen of the CRT in a number of different formats. Common information, such as letters and numbers, can be made up of either a series of dots in a 5×7 matrix (Figure 11–18(a)) or by a series of short lines with only specified segments displayed (Figure 11–18(b)). When lines or circles must be drawn, additional circuits must be added.

Operation

Figure 11–19 is a block diagram showing the major functional requirements for an interactive graphic display terminal. The terminal consists of a *display generator*, the actual *CRT display*, and *input devices* so that the user can interact with the display. Unless the display generator contains actual computing capability (often called a "smart" terminal), an external digital computer provides processing control. The electronics and logic associated with the terminal are in the display generator. *Timing and control logic* directs the operation of the display generator. It routes signals within the display generator, selects the appropriate input mode, develops CRT beam deflection

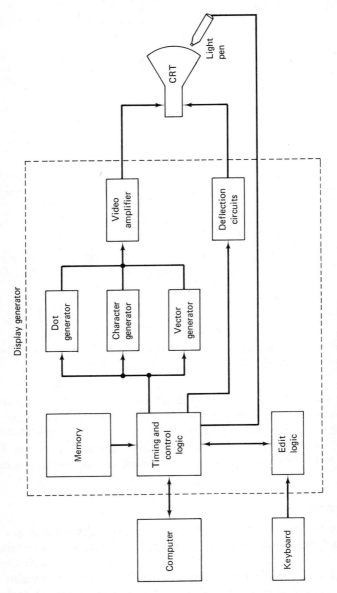

Figure 11-19 Interactive display block diagram.

voltages, etc. Information from the external computer, keyboard, and light pen is routed to and from *memory* via the timing and control logic. Processing sequences, information to be displayed, etc. are stored in the Random-Access Memory (RAM).* Keyboard input to the display generator passes through *edit logic*, which furnishes the capability to erase, delete, and insert information already in the display generator. The actual shape, size, and relative location of CRT displayed information are determined by the *dot generator*, *character generator*, and *vector generator*. With these three devices, practically any character, symbol, or shape can be synthesized and displayed.

Figure 11–20 is a possible means of implementing a 5×7 dot matrix character generator. The Read-Only Memory (ROM) contains the desired displayable characters as five separate 7-bit words (35 bits), addressable in

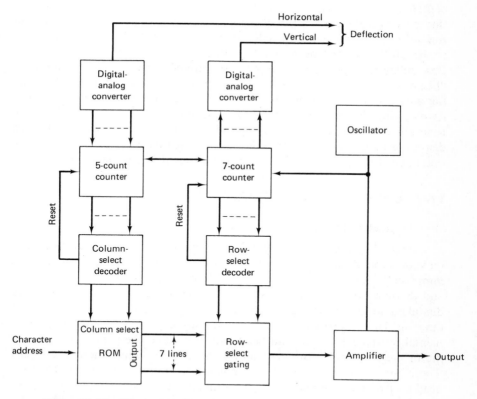

Figure 11–20 Character generator.

---

*When "smart" terminals are being used, the memory is often replaced with a complete microprocessor or minicomputer.

ANSI format. Each output word appears as seven parallel bits, since the display system generates the characters vertically, seven bits at a time. A specified character is selected using the *character select* inputs which serve as the ROM input address. Each column in the character is selected by the *column select* inputs. After five sequential binary column select addresses with the same character address, the complete 35-bit character will have been formed. Character formation, then, is similar to that seen in moving billboard displays and was explained in Section 11–5. Figure 11–12 showed the development of the letter *A* in 5 × 7 dot matrix form.

Since the beam of the CRT may be only one place at a time, it must be positioned precisely for each dot position in the 5 × 7 matrix as every character is developed. A *7-count counter* selects each of the vertical positions of the matrix, while a *5-count counter* determines which column is being displayed. Analog signals are required to actually position the beam, and *digital-to-analog converters* convert counter outputs to analog voltages for this purpose. *Decoders* select the appropriate row and column, while the *row-select gating* connects the individual ROM outputs through an amplifier to the CRT. The CRT beam is automatically blanked (shut off) at each position unless the appropriate output line selected is providing indication of "beam on" as the character is developed. Figure 11–20 is capable of developing only a single character, and much more logic is required to sequentially develop and display many characters. However, the concept of character generation has been shown, and should the reader encounter interactive display terminals, no difficulty should be experienced in comprehending their operation if the preceding discussion is thoroughly understood.

11–7 OTHER OUTPUT DEVICES

Digital Plotters

Digital plotters present a graphic presentation of the computer's output on some type of "hard-copy" material, such as paper. Common methods of impressing the computer's information on the medium are ink, electrostatic, and thermal printing techniques such as discussed earlier. The plotter uses digital commands from the computer via a controller to produce the plot or drawing. The commands typically actuate stepper motors* to produce incremental movement of the print head with respect to the paper. One stepper motor may control movement along the *X*-axis, while another controls *Y*-axis movement. Composite commands can be given to move the print head on two axes simultaneously, resulting in pen movement in any of eight directions. Lines, circles, numbers, letters, etc may all be plotted on digital

---

*A stepper motor converts an electrical pulse into a precise mechanical movement. The shaft of the motor rotates a fixed number of degrees for each pulse applied rather than the continuous rotary motion found in conventional motors.

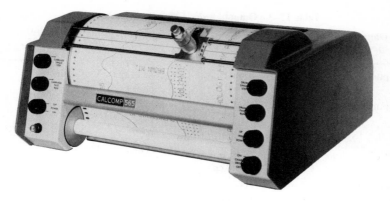

Figure 11–21   Calcomp 565 drum plotter (courtesy California Computer Products, Inc. Los Angeles, CA).

plotters. The plotter may operate at speeds up to hundreds of increments per second, with increment sizes in inches on the order of 0.002, 0.005, and 0.01. Figure 11–21 shows a modern flatbed plotter and a typical plot produced by this versatile type of machine.

Voice Response

Voice response units which allow the computer to respond to an inquiry with the spoken word are promising to become one of the most popular computer output devices. The typical voice response unit stores its prerecorded vocabulary on a high-speed, head-per-track magnetic disc. Complete words, sentences, phrases, or even parts of words may be stored and recovered when addressed. In fact, separate syllables may be stored and put together to form words. The magnetic disc drive is under control of a minicomputer in many voice response units. All of the advantages of computer control, then, may be applied to operation of voice response units.

On-going research efforts are investigating digital storage of synthetic sounds that may be combined to form words, random-access tape storage, and digital storage of phonemes (basic sounds of the English language). Combined with voice input capability, voice response units will perhaps soon see computers *talking* to computers.

11–8   SUMMARY

The continuing reduction in computer prices has caused a revolution in peripheral devices, particularly in the output field. As more and more users gain access to the computer, the requirement for easily interpreted, fast, and attractive output grows. It is difficult to keep up with the rapid

Table 11–3   Output Device Characteristics

Output Device	Output Format	Output* Speed	Output Medium	Capacity* per Display
Tape punch	Binary or character	25–150 cps	Punched tape	Variable
Card punch	Binary or character	60–200 cpm	Punched card	Variable
Character display	Character	—	Visual	Up to 256 characters
Typewriter	Character	60–100 wpm	Hard copy	Variable
Print wheel	Character	30–60 cps	Hard copy	Variable
Drum printer	Character	200–1800 lpm	Hard copy	Variable
Line printer	Character	200–1500 lpm	Hard copy	Variable
Print wire printer	Character	30–330 cps	Hard copy	Variable
Electrostatic printer	Character	up to 3000 lpm	Hard copy	Variable
Thermal printer	Character	10–120 cps	Hard copy	Variable
Plotter	Graphic	up to 18,000 lpm	Hard copy	Variable
CRT	Character	—	Visual	500 to 4000 characters
Voice response	Word	—	Aural	Variable

cps = characters per second   wpm = words per minute
cpm = cards per minute   lpm = lines per minute

*Values shown are nominal.

growth in this field, but Table 11–3 attempts to summarize *current* output
device characteristics. The reader is urged to update this table as newer
devices appear.

QUESTIONS

1. What is the primary function of the OUTPUT section?
2. List the major advantages and disadvantages of control panel light output from the computer.
3. Explain the function of the *character store* in a punched tape punch controller.
4. How does the tape punch controller know that it is time to advance the tape for punching of the next character?
5. Discuss the logic circuitry needed to punch cards in a column-by-column organization.
6. What type of output application would be most suited for use of NIXIE tubes; liquid crystal readout devices?
7. What is a light-emitting diode (LED)?
8. List five applications of LEDs as output devices.

9. Explain how an alphameric character is formed using LEDs and associated logic circuitry.
10. Discuss the principles of operation of plasma panel output devices.
11. How does a print wheel printer know it is time to print a specific character?
12. What determines the maximum speed of operation of an on-the-fly printing device?
13. Why are drum and line printers so much faster than electric typewriters, print wheel printers, etc?
14. What is the minimum size of dot matrix needed for printing of readable characters?
15. Explain how a print wire printer forms alphameric characters.
16. Explain how an electrostatic printer forms alphameric characters.
17. Discuss the relative advantages and disadvantages of print wire printers, electrostatic printers, thermal printers, and ink jet printers.
18. Show how the following alphameric characters would be formed using *both* 5 × 7 matrix and segmented methods (Figure 11-18): B, E, H, 0, 2, 8, and +.
19. Discuss the applications of interactive graphic terminals.
20. Discuss possible future computer output devices.

12

Computer Programming

12–1 INTRODUCTION

Basic Requirements

As has often been stated and more often implied, the digital computer is merely a collection of electronic circuits, which, by themselves, are entirely incapable of performing any useful function. Great capabilities exist with this marvelous collection of electronic circuits, though, and it merely remains to "instruct" the computer in order to realize its tremendous potential. Given an adequate list of instructions (called a *program*) and data with which to work, the computer becomes a virtual genius. Therefore, one of the requirements for computer use is that of supplying the list of instructions (program) to the computer.

Procedural Steps

A *computer program is an explicit sequence of instructions to instruct the computer in the solution of a task*. Writing computer programs (*programming*) is a demanding task. The *computer programmer* must understand the problem being programmed with great clarity; problem analysis must be complete; and no errors can be tolerated. The programmer's job can be separated into five separate tasks: (a) *analysis*, (b) *organization*, (c) *coding*, (d) *testing*, and (e) *documentation*.

During the *analysis* phase, the programmer must develop a concise statement of the problem, analyze the facts, and write the mathematical expressions for problem solution. The more efficiently a computer is used, the better planned must be the programs. The key to a good program is an *algorithm*, which is a fool-proof, step-by-step procedure that takes into account *all* possible situations, including exceptions. The algorithm, then, is an unambiguous procedure that always leads to an answer (or at least an identification that an answer cannot be obtained) in a finite number of steps. An algorithm can be likened to a receipe in a cookbook or the choreography of a ballet. All combine a number of individual small steps into a composite action.

The *organization* phase of the programmer's job is closely tied to the analysis phase. The algorithm constructed during analysis is now organized and sequenced into the operations required to perform the problem solution. Most programmers use *flow charts*, which are block diagrams of an algorithm, for the organization task. Flow charts use standard symbols (see Figure 12–1) and serve as a very good communications link between programmers, much as a blueprint does among engineers. The use of both algorithms and flow charts is demonstrated in subsequent sections of this chapter.

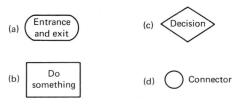

Figure 12–1 Flow chart symbols.

With the help of the flow chart, the computer program is *coded*. Coding is simply the process of converting the flow chart actions into instructions that will result in computer operations. Many different levels of coding are used, depending on program requirements. Coding at the machine, assembly, and compiler level is discussed later in this chapter.

After the coded program is prepared, it is first *tested* by comparing each step with the appropriate flow chart action. Often the coded program is flow charted by another programmer so that any errors may be detected. When these preliminary tests are completed, the program is prepared for computer input, and either an attempted solution is tried or more detailed testing accomplished. After *debugging* (removing all errors), the program is "run" and desired data obtained.

Documentation is the final, and perhaps the most important, step. The corrected flow chart, a printout of the final program, sample input and output data, etc are included so that future changes to the program may take advantage of the experience gained during the original program evolution.

Hierarchy of Programming Languages

The hierarchy of computer programming languages is shown in Figure 12–2. At the lowest, and most detailed, level is the machine language, the only language that the computer can really understand. A program at this

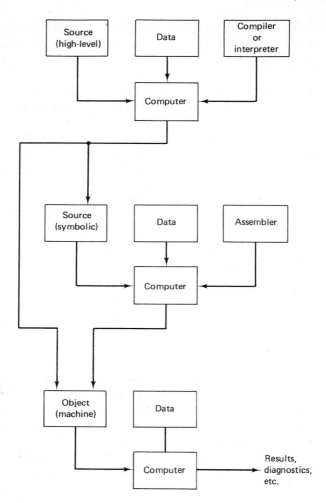

Figure 12–2   Hierarchy of programming languages.

level is called an *object* program (Section 12–2). The next higher level is a symbolic system of programming which uses a language that is mnemonically related to the operations to be performed. The symbolic language *source* program is converted to a machine language object program by a special program called an *assembler* (Section 12–3). At the highest level of programming is the *compiler-based* system. The source program is written in a language which very closely resembles the type of problem being solved, and it is translated by a special program called a *compiler* (Section 12–4). The computer outputs either a symbolic assembly language program which must be further converted to a machine language program or a machine language program directly. At the same level as the compiler, although slower as explained in Section 12–4, is the *interpretive system*. The language is problem related and in a conversational mode. An interpreter program converts each statement into either a symbolic or machine language program.

12–2 MACHINE LANGUAGE

Concepts

The most fundamental method of computer programming is at the machine language level. It may have been noted that all explanations of computer operation in previous chapters considered that the computer responded to binary codes only. It is with the use of binary codes that machine language programming takes place. Furthermore, it should be recalled that information within the computer is manipulated in groups of bits called computer words.

Only one computer word is stored at each location in memory, and there is usually no way of telling whether that word is a data word or an instruction word. Therefore it is imperative that the computer be told explicitly which locations contain instructions and which locations contain data. Imagine what would happen if a data word inadvertently were supplied to the CONTROL section as an instruction word. The results would be highly unpredictable but invariably catastrophic as far as program completion is concerned.

Throughout this text we have discussed the computer word and its makeup, and it is with this information that we approach machine language programming. In its simplest form, the instruction word contains a binary code representing an operation to be performed and an address indicating where the information to be operated upon is located. Consider first the operation code (*op-code*) portion of the instruction word. We will arbitrarily assign six bits of a 16-bit computer word to define operations to be performed. These are the bits that ultimately are routed to the instruction register in the CONTROL section and which establish control signals for the rest of the computer. Table 12–1 lists a few arbitrarily assigned op-codes, enough so that a simple programming example may be developed.* The remaining ten bits of the instruction word are assigned the function of defining the address of the data that is to be operated upon. Therefore, each 16-bit computer word (instruction word) carries a binary code representing the operation to be performed and the location of the required data.

---

*A more complete list of instructions is shown when an actual computer is investigated in Chapter 13.

Table 12–1   Simple Op-Codes Used in Machine Language Program

Instruction	*Meaning*
110000	Clear register A (accumulator); that is, all stages contain zeros.
001000	Add to the A register the data stored in the location in the address portion of the word.
010100	Compare the contents of the A register with the data stored at the location defined in the address portion of this word. If the two data words are not the same, go to the next instruction in the program; if they are identical, skip the next instruction in the program.
001010	Go to the location defined in the address part of this word to obtain the next instruction.
100001	Stop execution and await orders.
011110	Store the data in the A register at the location defined in the address portion of this word.

Problem Analysis

If we are to construct a program, we must have a statement of the problem, analyze the facts, write mathematical equations and the algorithm, construct the flow chart, and code the program. Testing and documentation, of course, depend on the availability of a computer, and we shall not perform these steps.

The problem to be programmed can be stated in the following manner.

Example 12–1.

As part of a larger computer program it is necessary to determine the relationship between two variables named X and Y. If X plus the constant 7 is equal to Y, then X is to be assigned the new variable name Z. If X plus 7 is not equal to Y, then Y is to be assigned the new variable name Z. The computer must then stop program execution and await new orders. Mathematically, the problem can be stated

$$\text{if } X + 7 = Y, \qquad \text{then } Z = X$$
$$\text{if } X + 7 \neq Y, \qquad \text{then } Z = Y$$

The method of solution is implicit in the mathematical statements as is often the case. Therefore it is merely necessary to devise a method of solution. It will be necessary, of course, to have available a value for X and Y, in addition to the constant 7. The $X + Y$ addition must be performed and the result compared with Y. Assignment of X or Y to Z follows the rules shown above. Upon completion, the computer stops and awaits orders for execution of the next program.

On the assumption that X, Y, and the constant 7 are already stored in computer memory, the flow chart in Figure 12–3 shows a possible method

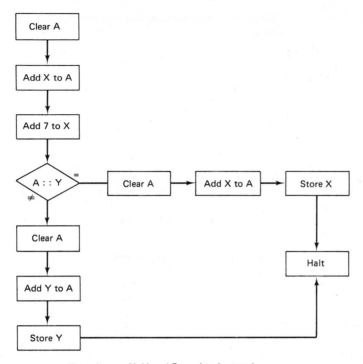

Note: Assume X, Y, and 7 are already stored

Figure 12–3   Flow chart, machine language problem (Table 12–2).

of solution to the problem. It should further be noted that neither the flow chart nor the attendant sample program has been optimized. Other solutions, perhaps using more sophisticated methods, are possible. However, this solution demonstrates the development of a flow chart to solve a specific problem and shows a possible machine language computer program written using the flow chart as a guide. Limiting factors in the computer program must of necessity include the minimal repertoire shown in Table 12–1, plus the limited capabilities of our simplified computer that we have been using throughout this text.

The Program

When actually coding (writing) the program, a format must be used that takes into consideration not only the op-code and operand address of each computer word but also where in memory each of the program words is to be stored. Likewise, all data used during execution of the program must have its location identified. Table 12–2 is a machine language program that will accomplish the number comparison problem.

Table 12–2   Machine Language Program

Location of This Information	Op-Code	Address
(32) 1 0 0 0 0 0	1 1 0 0 0 0	0 0 0 0 0 0 0 0 0 0
(33) 1 0 0 0 0 1	0 0 1 0 0 0	0 0 0 1 0 0 0 0 0 0
(34) 1 0 0 0 1 0	0 0 1 0 0 0	0 0 0 1 0 0 0 0 1 0
(35) 1 0 0 0 1 1	0 1 0 1 0 0	0 0 0 1 0 0 0 0 0 1
(36) 1 0 0 1 0 0	0 0 1 0 1 0	0 0 0 0 1 0 1 0 0 1
(37) 1 0 0 1 0 1	1 1 0 0 0 0	0 0 0 0 0 0 0 0 0 0
(38) 1 0 0 1 1 0	0 0 1 0 0 0	0 0 0 1 0 0 0 0 0 0
(39) 1 0 0 1 1 1	0 1 1 1 1 0	0 0 0 1 0 0 0 0 1 1
(40) 1 0 1 0 0 0	0 0 1 0 1 0	0 0 0 0 1 0 1 1 0 0
(41) 1 0 1 0 0 1	1 1 0 0 0 0	0 0 0 0 0 0 0 0 0 0
(42) 1 0 1 0 1 0	0 0 1 0 0 0	0 0 0 1 0 0 0 0 0 1
(43) 1 0 1 0 1 1	0 1 1 1 1 0	0 0 0 1 0 0 0 0 1 1
(44) 1 0 1 1 0 0	1 0 0 0 0 1	0 0 0 0 0 0 0 0 0 0
(64) 1 0 0 0 0 0 0	Binary representation of X	
(65) 1 0 0 0 0 0 1	Binary representation of Y	
(66) 1 0 0 0 0 1 0	Binary representation of 7	
(67) 1 0 0 0 0 1 1	Binary representation of Z	

Actual location of both the data and instructions is arbitrarily assigned and is indicated in binary form. The actual program occupies locations 32_{10} (100000_2) through 44_{10} (101100_2), while data is stored in locations 64_{10} through 67_{10}. Detailed explanation of each step follows.

Step 32.   Register A (the accumulator in the ARITHMETIC/LOGIC section) is cleared and contains all zeros as a result of this step. This is a common preparatory step at the beginning of a program to assure that no extraneous data is allowed to creep into the calculations.

Step 33.   Op-code 001000 causes the information stored in the location identified in the address portion of this word to be added to the contents of the A register. Therefore, recognition of this op-code retrieves the information at location 64_{10}, routes it to the ARITHMETIC/LOGIC section, and adds it to the previously cleared A register. Since the binary representation of X has been stored at this location, the A register contains $X + 0$, or X, at the completion of step 33.

Step 34.   Another addition occurs at this time. The information at location 66_{10} (7) is obtained and summed with the contents of the A register (X). Upon completion of this step the A register contains $X + 7$.

Step 35.   A comparison of the contents of the A register ($X + 7$) with the data stored at location 65_{10} (Y) is performed at this time. The results of the comparison will determine the next action. As defined in Table 12–1, op-code 010100 causes the program to continue sequential execution if the two data words are not the same; otherwise (if they are the same) the next step in the program is skipped before resuming sequential execution. This *branching* action may be seen in the flow chart of Figure 12–2. Initially assume that the comparison indicates that the two words are not the same and that the next step is executed. (We will return and investigate the other branch shortly.)

Step 36. The binary code 001010 causes the program to deviate from normal sequential execution and *jump* to the location defined in the address portion of the word for the next instruction. Therefore a jump to location 41_{10} occurs as a result of step 36.

Step 41. Clearing of the A register is accomplished.

Step 42. The data stored in location 65_{10} (Y) is added to the cleared A register. Thus Y is now available for processing in the A register.

Step 43. The information in the A register (Y) is transferred to memory and stored in the location defined in the address portion of the instruction word. Location 67_{10} has been reserved for storage of the variable Z, so as a result of this step, Y becomes Z.

Step 44. A "halt" occurs; the computer ceases execution of program steps and awaits new direction from either the operator or its *executive program* (discussed in Section 12–5).

We must now return to step 35 and determine what action would have been performed if $X + 7$ had been the same as Y. Recall that the next step (36) would have been skipped and sequential execution would have been resumed with step 37.

Step 37. The A register is cleared. (Same as step 32.)

Step 38. X is restored in the A register. (Same as step 33.)

Step 39. X is stored in location 67_{10} (same as step 43) except X is stored as Z instead of Y.

Step 40. Another *jump* occurs, this time to step 44.

Step 44. This is the "halt" step and has been explained previously.

Even though the testing step of program development is not discussed in detail, it should be mentioned that trial data should be "hand-carried" through the program prior to any attempt at actual execution on the computer. Computer time is expensive, and quite often working trial data through the program by hand will detect obvious errors that would prevent the program from working on the computer. The reader is invited to select some arbitrary values for X and Y and validate the program developed in this section. (Note that when X and Y are both 0, Z becomes 0; not exactly "cricket," but additional steps could be included to detect this special case if desired.)

Advantages and Disadvantages

Machine language programming possesses two basic advantages over other levels of programming to be discussed in this chapter: (a) it allows direct access to the computer memory and logic for troubleshooting and detailed program debugging, and (b) it is very efficient as far as use of computer memory and logic is concerned. However, the disadvantages are many.

1. Machine language programming is extremely tedious and time consuming. One must keep track of all used and available memory locations. Each op-code must be remembered, along with the many formats of special computer words and data words. Machine language programming turns out to be almost a clerical job.
2. It is easy to make errors when programming directly at the binary level. There are lots of ones and zeros that all have to be placed properly.
3. The programmer requires a very detailed knowledge of the computer's hardware.
4. The machine language program is good for only one type of computer and must be rewritten if the program is to be used on any other machine.

It can be seen that generally the disadvantages of machine language programming outweigh the advantages. The following sections offer a solution to the dilemma.

12–3 ASSEMBLY LANGUAGES

Concepts

One of the major disadvantages of machine language programming seems to have been the use of binary coding. It is obviously very difficult to work with long strings of binary numbers, remember binary representations of op-codes, etc. A possible solution to this problem would be to define a *new* language, one which is oriented more toward English-language operations, and let the computer translate that new language into machine language.

In order to maintain most efficient use of the computer, our new language should be closely correlated with the machine language. That is, there should be a near one-to-one relationship between each "word" in the new language and each machine language instruction. Furthermore, each "word" should be suggestive of what action is to be performed. Possible mnemonics (symbolic codes that are remindful of actual words) for the machine instructions used in Section 12-2 are shown below.

CRA Clear Register A.

ADA Add contents of Register A to contents of memory location defined in address portion of the word.

CPA Compare contents of Register A to contents of memory location defined in address portion of the word.

JMP Jump to memory location defined in address portion of the word.

STA Store contents of Register A in memory location defined in address portion of the word.

HLT Halt.

Of course, most digital computers have many more such symbolic codes, but these are sufficient to perform a simple program. A full list of symbolic codes for a common digital computer appears in Chapter 13.

The Assembler

Once the symbolic language has been decided upon, the next step is to determine how conversion to machine language is to take place. The conversion process is accomplished by a computer program called an *assembler*. The assembler consists of a number of machine language *routines* (separate small programs) which convert the mnemonic-coded program into machine language form. Each of the symbolic instructions is stored in memory in binary form along with its equivalent machine language instruction. In other words, the *assembler* includes a *table* of symbolic instructions vs machine language instructions. One of the assembler routines causes a comparison between this table and symbolic instructions provided by the program. When correspondence occurs, the equivalent binary value is taken from the table and stored elsewhere in memory as the op-code portion of the machine language instruction word. This routine is "called up" whenever an instruction word needs to be translated.

The programmer can also add his own symbols for such purposes as location definition of either instruction or data words. He may assign an address to this new symbol, or a separate routine of the assembly program may do so. From then on, the symbol may be used in the program as though it were a complete machine language address. Other routines are used to detect language errors, prepare listings of the assembled program, etc.

The Program

A symbolic-coded program in assembly language, performing the same functions as the machine language program of Section 12–2, is shown below. The symbolic codes mentioned earlier in this section are used, and each symbolic entry may be correlated on a one-to-one basis with the machine language program. It is further assumed that the assembler assigns addresses equivalent to those used in the machine language program.

32		CRA
33		ADA, X
34		ADA, C
35		CPA, Y
36		JMP, BR1
37		CRA
38		ADA, X
39		STA, X
40		JMP, BR2
41	BR1	CRA
42		ADA, Y
43		STA, Y
44	BR2	HLT
64	X	
65	Y	
66	C	
67	Z	

Using the Assembler

A detailed evaluation of the operation of the simple program just shown will provide considerable insight into the makeup and functioning of an assembly program. It is assumed that the assembler is already entered into the memory of the computer and that the computer is ready for operation. The *source program*, written in our new *assembly language*, is, for the purposes of this exercise, contained on punched tape. Many assemblers require more than one "pass" for the source program, and it is assumed that our assembler operates as a "two-pass" assembler, with an optional third pass. The first time the source program is entered into the computer via the tape reader all user-identified symbols, such as labels, addresses, etc, are defined and placed in the assembler's symbol table. Addresses are assigned, and any errors in format and/or language are identified. During the second pass, the binary machine language equivalents of each of the input source language statements are generated and a punched tape is prepared with the machine language program (*called the object program*). If desired, the third pass may produce a printed listing of the program's instructions with locations and generate binary codes and source codes for each program statement. However, this third pass is most often used for documentation and debugging purposes, and the program may be "run" on the computer by merely loading the binary tape produced in the second pass.

It should be noted that, on some computers with adequate memory capability, the second and third passes are automatic without reloading the source language tape. The first pass stores the complete source language program, and an *executive program* (Section 12–5) sequences the computer from pass to pass without interruption.

The sample source program is converted to a binary object program in the two-pass manner just described. During the first pass the assembler evaluates each statement. For example, when the assembler sees the first statement (CRA), it first looks to see whether such a mnemonic is an acceptable operation that is stored in its symbol table. If so, it moves on to the next statement, which is ADA, X. ADA is recognized as a valid operation symbol, but this time the assembler sees another symbol (X) which is not stored in its table. X is placed in the table and assigned an address, which we have assumed to be 64_{10}. Each of the symbolic source program statements is evaluated similarly, and each new variable assigned the appropriate address. Upon completion of the first pass, all symbols are accounted for and have a definition or address for use during the second pass.

During the second pass, each symbolic source program statement is again evaluated. This time, however, the operation symbol is matched up with its mate in the symbol table and the machine language equivalent is obtained. If an operand address is required, as in all but steps 32, 37, 41, and 44, its machine language equivalent is appended to the machine language opcode, and a complete machine language instruction word is developed. Upon completion of the translation and conversion process, a binary machine language tape has been produced, or the machine language program has been stored in computer memory. In either case, the machine language program is now ready for execution. The third pass, if used, merely matches up the machine language program with the source language symbolic program and provides a printed record for later use.

Advantages and Disadvantages

The advantages and disadvantages of assembly language programming may now be stated.

ASSEMBLY LANGUAGE ADVANTAGES

1. Produces most efficient code, similar to machine language.
2. Uses least number of locations in memory to solve a problem, similar to machine language.

3. Gives detailed control of hardware operations.
4. Reduces time needed to write programs, easier to learn and debug.
5. Eliminates need to keep track of memory locations in detail.
6. Allows programming tasks to be divided among programmers.

ASSEMBLY LANGUAGE DISADVANTAGES

1. Removed from common methods of stating problems.
2. Requires an intimate knowledge of hardware, since a one-to-one relationship still exists with machine instructions.
3. Coding detailed and laborious, takes a long time.
4. Machine dependent.

12–4 HIGH-LEVEL LANGUAGES

Concepts

Once the concepts of assembly language programming have been mastered, it should not be too difficult to conceive how higher-level languages may be used. The primary difference lies in the reaction of the computer to a programmer's statement. Whereas in assembly language programming the computer supplies machine language statements on a one-to-one basis, in the higher-level languages the computer may supply *many* machine language statements for a single high-level statement. Rather than dwell on the mechanics of *how* high-level languages accomplish their functions, we will discuss the capabilities of such languages. Each high-level language must have a repertoire of allowable symbols, plus some type of program that translates these symbols ultimately into machine language statements. The repertoire of allowable symbols, the language, closely resembles that normally used in connection with a specific problem or procedure. For example, COBOL (Common Business Oriented Language) uses terms associated with business problems, FORTRAN (Formula Translation) is oriented toward algebraic and mathematical problems, etc. These types of languages are usually independent of the computer's hardware and are usable on most computers with sufficient memory capacity. The program that provides the language translation (the *compiler*) is far more powerful than assembly language programs, giving the programmer far more latitude in program preparation.

A FORTRAN Program

The flexibility of a language such as FORTRAN may be demonstrated by showing a program that performs the same operations that both the machine language and the assembly language programs of earlier sections performed. Note that the program shown below consists of only five steps, whereas the machine language and assembly language programs each required 13 steps. The number of variable assignment statements are also reduced, since the appearance of the variable in a FORTRAN statement results in memory space being reserved for it.

$$\begin{array}{ll} & \text{IF } (X + 7 - Y)\ 100,\ 200,\ 100 \\ 100 & Z = Y \\ & \text{GO TO } 300 \\ 200 & Z = X \\ 300 & \text{STOP} \end{array}$$

The first statement in the program, the IF statement, makes the decision concerning the relationship between X and Y. FORTRAN recognizes the arithmetic signs such as $+$ and $-$ and, as in arithmetic and algebra, performs operations inside parentheses first. Thus 5 is summed with X, followed by the subtraction of Y. The numbers following the parentheses are *labels* of steps to be performed *next*, based on the results of the operations inside the parentheses. Rules are as follows.

1. First number—go to the statement with this label number if the numerical value of the arithmetic expression inside the parentheses is negative.
2. Second number—go to the statement with this label number if the numerical value of the arithmetic expression inside the parentheses is zero.
3. Third number—go to this statement number if a positive value results from the arithmetic operation inside the parentheses.

Statement 100, $Z = Y$, assigns the value of Y to Z if $X + 7$ is not equal to Y, while statement 200 assigns X to Z if $X + 7 = Y$. The GO TO statement is an unconditional transfer to statement 300, where the STOP command is a simple way of indicating the logical end, or termination, to the procedure. By following the rules just indicated for the FORTRAN statement used in the sample program, the reader should be able to substitute values for X and Y to verify that the program does indeed perform the same operations as both the machine language and the assembly language programs used previously. It should also be obvious that a higher-level language such as FORTRAN has many advantages. Such a problem or situation-oriented language is much easier to learn, and it is not necessary to study the organization of the computer in detail to effectively apply *compiler* languages. High-level languages allow the programs to become machine independent, therefore removing the stigma of program obsolescence. Compiler-oriented programs are easily written and debugged. The number of statements necessary to perform a procedure may be reduced by as much as 80 or 90 percent.

The less you have to write, the less chance of error exists. Finally, many programs are already available, since most of the high-level languages have been in use for many years. The lack of machine independence makes these programs applicable to any machine that has the language compiler.

The only major disadvantage of the higher-level languages is that they are inefficient. They take much of the computer's time in the translation process. Furthermore, they take considerable memory space, limiting the length of program that can be executed with a limited space computer. However, in recent years the cost of *software* (computer programs, etc) has reached and surpassed the cost of hardware, and it just might be more practical in many cases to use more memory and realize the reduced cost of software.

Other Languages

An even more powerful language than FORTRAN is in use in many computer installations. ALGOL (ALGOrithmic Language) has a structure that makes programs even closer to the natural way of stating a problem so that the user can see the logic of a program without having to fully evaluate it initially. One statement in ALGOL completely defines our sample problem in this chapter:

$$\text{IF } X + 7 = Y \text{ THEN } Z \longleftarrow X \text{ ELSE } Z \longleftarrow Y$$

As with any of the high-level languages, though, the ease of programming must be weighed against the cost of the additional hardware necessary to accommodate the translating program.

Another type of high-level computer language is found in applications where the user interacts on a "conversational" mode with the computer. This type of language is called *interpretive*, and the program that translates the language to machine language is called an *interpreter*. Although closely allied in terms of language capability, compilers and interpreters have one basic difference. Whereas the compiler performs its translating tasks on major sectors of a program as a unit, the unit of translation for the interpreter is a single statement. Each command is scanned by the interpreter, and when identified as a valid command, one of the appropriate *routines* of the interpreter is called into action. The interpreter is a relatively self-contained programming system, because it edits inputs from the user and identifies errors, translates the edited inputs, and finally executes the program. Interpreters are somewhat slower than most compilers due to the translation sequence but are extremely useful where conversational computation is required. Common applications are to educational systems, to business and scientific operations where many different types of problems must be solved, to timesharing systems, and wherever the need for a "super-calculator" exists. BASIC (Beginners All-purpose Symbolic Language) is one of the most commonly used conversational languages.

12–5 OPERATING SYSTEMS/EXECUTIVES

Concepts

Operating systems and executives are more a matter of computer organization and operation than of programming, but they are closely allied with the use of computer programs and are discussed for that reason. To this point only programs which cause the computer to perform information processing operations have been discussed. No mention has been made of the procedures necessary for program execution, or how programs might be made to work together. Perhaps the best introduction to the subject of *operating systems* is to consider the sequence of events that must be performed to obtain the problem solution when the problem has been programmed in a high-level language such as FORTRAN.

Many of the preparatory steps are common, no matter which programming language is used. That is, the problem must be analyzed, organized, coded, tested, and documented. Analysis, organization, and coding were discussed as various levels of programming were investigated. Testing was only slightly mentioned, but it should be realized that testing included "walking" through the program with sample data before submitting it to the computer and then running sample data through the program after the program has been accepted by the computer. Documentation, of course, includes an acceptable package of information so that some other programmer could use the program without redoing all of the preparatory steps.

Now consider the possibility of having to test and run a number of different programs, perhaps in different programming languages. In Section 12–3 the procedure for assembling a computer program written in symbolic (mnemonic) language was mentioned. Recalling that the procedures required at least two "passes" through the computer in order to define an answer should make it apparent that much time is wasted by loading and running program tapes, operating switches, etc. If a computer has an *operating system*, many of the manual steps can be eliminated.

Definitions and Functions

An *operating system* is a unified collection of *control programs* used to improve the overall operating efficiency of the computer. Actually, the operating system also includes *processing programs* that perform the language translations, but these have already been discussed thoroughly in this chapter.

Many different terms are used to describe the components of the control programs, so this discussion will be aimed more toward program functions than program nomenclature. One major function is that of input/output control.

The *input/output control* component of the control program supplies the statements necessary to read and write from or to peripheral devices such as card readers, punched tape readers, disc memories, etc. It also schedules the use of such peripheral devices so as to most efficiently use them, perhaps even operating more than one device in a given time period. A *system loader* program, also part of the control program, manipulates components of the object program, relocating them to more appropriate locations in memory, linking the object program with required subprograms, etc. Actual control rests with an *executive program*, which interprets system directives, calling upon appropriate programs for execution of the user's programs. Control will be relinquished to processor programs or other components of the control program as required; but upon completion of user program execution, the executive program again assumes control of the computer.

Numerous *support programs* also exist in the operating system, any or all of which may be called upon as needed. A complete library of mathematical routines, sorting and merging routines, etc may be called up and integrated with the user's programs. Editing of user-supplied input programs may be accomplished by another support program, while an error-detection program may be used to ferret out mistakes before they are allowed to get to the computer during program execution. Programs that do not operate satisfactorily may be investigated with the use of *debugging programs*. The number and applications of support programs are almost beyond the imagination. They are limited only by the capacity of the computer and the programmers.

A large-scale computer will typically have at least the control programs mentioned above, plus many more specifically designed for the computer's applications. Processor programs will include the basic assembly language for the computer (perhaps more than one), compilers, and perhaps even interpreters. When the computer is used for multi-user applications such as *timesharing*, a means for establishing job priority, clocks to keep time records on each of the users, and sequencing programs are also evident. *Timesharing* is the simultaneous utilization of a computer by users at multiple-access terminals. The terminals are often physically separated by thousands of miles and tied together by a telephone or microwave transmission link. As the state of the art advances, multiprogramming (the interleaving of two or more programs by the same computer) and multiprocessing (the interleaving or simultaneous execution of two or more programs by two or more processors) are becoming more popular. It should be evident that the only limiting factors on computer application are the cost of hardware/software and the ingenuity of the designers/programmers. People are talking to computers (and they are "talking" back), and the day of computer control may not be far off. But a word of caution—*the computer cannot control anything without a program written or initially conceived by humans or without inputs provided by humans.*

The complete interdependence of the components of the operating system may be seen in Figure 12–4. Control components of the operating system are shown as they relate to the overall operating system, hardware, and user programs/processing programs.

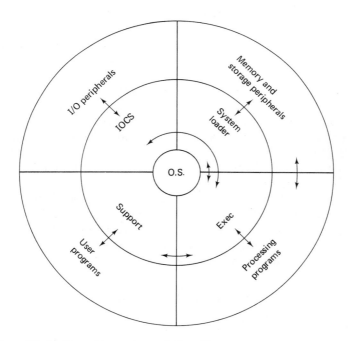

Figure 12–4   Operating system relationships.

12–6 MICROPROGRAMMING

Another form of programming, although it is not commonly accessible to most programmers, is that of *microprogramming*. It may be recalled from earlier discussions that even a simple operation such as addition requires numerous information transfers in order to complete the operation. In some cases this has been accomplished by segmenting the computer cycle into a "fetch" and an "execute" cycle, using the computer's clock to enable circuits as required. Many computer cycles are required when anything more than primitive operations must be performed.

The programmer usually writes a series of operations in his program. These operations occupy computer cycles, and time for execution of the series of operations can become restrictive. In microprogramming, *each* computer instruction carries out *many* information transfers in a single execution cycle. In other words, a simple instruction to the computer results in numerous operations rather than one operation per instruction. The individual control sequences are stored in a *control memory* (often of the Read-Only Memory form). A computer instruction acts as an address to the ROM, and the data output of the ROM is the series of commands necessary to perform the required instruction. Actually, the control memory and associated logic behave as a small *microcomputer* within the main computer.

Although many control memories have the capability of modification by computer instruction, most of them are contained in ROMs and can be modified only by changing the ROM. Thus, a new term has been generated to describe the instruction set of the microprogram. Since it is neither changeable by rewiring (hardware) nor by rewriting a program (software), the microprogram instruction set is called *firmware*.

Microprogramming concepts are being introduced in computers from as small as the "computer on a chip" calculator to as large as the multi-million dollar giants. The programmer may encounter situations where he must develop microprograms, and this task must be learned just as machine language, assembly language, and higher-level programming are learned. Microprogramming, since it is firmware, is more easily visualized when both software and hardware are integrated. Therefore, a more detailed coverage of microprogramming is discussed in Chapter 13, where a modern computer with microprogramming features is presented.

QUESTIONS AND PROBLEMS

1. List the five tasks entailed in writing a computer program and discuss each of them.
2. Why does a computer only *directly* respond to machine language programs?
3. Compare the advantages and disadvantages of machine language programming, assembly language programming, and high-level language programming.
4. List the types of problems most suitable to machine language programming.
5. List the types of problems most suitable to assembly language programming.
6. List the types of problems most suitable to high-level language programming.
7. What is the difference between a compiler and an interpreter?
8. Describe the characteristics of an operating system and discuss its component parts.
9. What is microprogramming?

13

The Computer Revisited

Chapter 13 presents another look at the digital computer, one that integrates all of the information from previous chapters. The computer selected for detailed discussion is representative of the present state of the art and, with certain projections, *should* represent future computer concepts. The integrated circuit field is expanding rapidly and more and more capability is being provided in less and less space. Computer functions now occupying a complete circuit card will soon be performed by a single, large-scale integrated circuit (LSI). Consequently, the total computer may shrink to single circuit card size, and the extra space may be used to greatly expand machine capability. Although a *minicomputer* in size, the computer discussed in this chapter uses many of the techniques employed in larger machines. Therefore, the concepts presented build a solid foundation for further study.

13–1 THE COMPLETE SYSTEM—SIMPLIFIED

Introduction

Trends today are away from the purely classical Von Neumann machine approach used throughout this book (see Figures 1–8 and 2–4) and toward a scheme that makes more efficient use of the computer's time and talents. The five basic functional sections are still used, but they are organized in a slightly different manner. Figure 13–1 is a block diagram of a *bus-organized* computer.

Although some names have changed, all of the basic functions are identifiable. The major difference between the classical organization and the bus-organized machine is the existence of a *bus*.* INPUT/OUTPUT

---

*A bus is merely a group of wires which connect all data, control, and power signals of one section to all other sections.

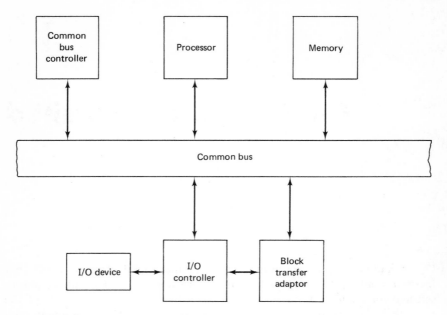

Figure 13–1   Bus-organized computer.

(I/O) devices each have a *Controller* that matches the I/O device characteristics to the rest of the computer. Each Controller contains a small amount
of MEMORY and a portion of the CONTROL section. The major portion
of the MEMORY section is just as previously discussed. A new functional
block called a *Processor* contains some MEMORY, some CONTROL, and
the ARITHMETIC/LOGIC UNIT. Finally, the *Common Bus Controller*,
which routes information between all other sections, contains MEMORY
and CONTROL functions.

Functional Sections

The functional sections of the computer are contained on plug-in
printed circuit cards. Each card has a 110 pin plug which mates with a
socket in the main-frame of the computer (Figure 13–2). A main-frame
may have up to 24 sockets and, with a few minor exceptions, any functional
section may plug into any socket. This is accomplished by connecting all
socket pin ones together, pin twos together, etc, up to and including connecting all socket pin 110s together. Thus all similar pins are "bussed," and
any signal on a specific pin number is seen by all cards on that same pin
number. Modern printed circuit technology provides the interconnects
without the maze of wires often seen in many computer main-frames. The
Common Bus, then, is merely a name applied to the *interconnection of the*

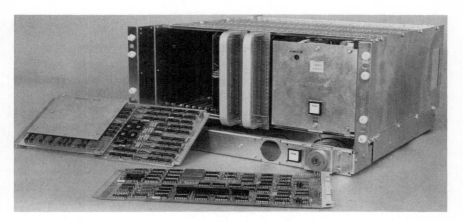

Figure 13–2 Computer mainframe showing cards removed (courtesy Lockheed Electronics Co., Inc. Data Products Division).

functional sections of the computer, and only those interconnections required for specific functions are used during any given operation.

All information transfers from section to section of the computer are under control of the *Common Bus Controller*. Each functional section of the computer has the capability to originate *and* to receive information. Furthermore, if a section desires to transfer information, it may request access to the Common Bus. It is the function of the Bus Controller to resolve device-request priority and to grant access to the bus. If another request occurs while the present request is being performed, the Bus Controller will store the information and act upon the second request as soon as possible.

Memory system modules used in the computer described in this chapter do not require additional discussion beyond that accomplished in Chapter 8. Either random-access core or random-access semiconductor (static or dynamic) memory organizations are used. The reader is referred to Section 8–2 for semiconductor and magnetic core memory organizations.

The *Processor* module is actually a small self-contained computer using modern technology to achieve its powerful capability in the small space of only two printed circuit cards. Two 16-bit computer words can be processed logically within 130 nanoseconds or arithmetically within 160 nanoseconds. Due to the internal organization, which is built around busses and registers, the Processor operates relatively independent of other system modules. The internal organization, in conjunction with its micropro-grammed capability for high-speed operation, gives the Processor the computing power of many large-scale computers.

Input/output Controllers are provided for each peripheral device used in conjunction with the computer. Each Controller performs functions similar to those discussed in Chapters 10 and 11. However, the organization of the computer in this chapter allows for more powerful input/output capability. Therefore additional logic circuitry is provided so that the Controller may communicate directly with other system modules (such as Memory modules). Each Controller actually performs some of the functions of the Bus Controller and Processor so that other system modules can be "tricked" into thinking they are talking to the rest of the computer.

A system module called a *Block Transfer Adaptor* is used in conjunction with input/output Controllers and other system modules to accomplish large-scale data transfers. Block Transfer Adaptors share the Common Bus with all other system modules. Their basic function is to convert character-oriented input/output Controllers to a capability for *block* transfer of information. The Block Transfer Adaptor must be inserted into the slot immediately adjacent to the input/output Controller to be converted. By external connection, it is then possible to transfer data to and from Memory without interrupting Processor operations.

13–2 THE COMPLETE SYSTEM—DETAILED

The Common Bus

The *Common Bus* consists of 82 lines (plus 28 power and ground lines) that are used to convey address, data, and control information to and/or from all system modules. Three major components, other than power and ground functions, comprise the Common Bus: the *Address bus* (A), the *Data bus* (D), and the *Control bus* (C). Figure 13–3 shows the organization of the Common Bus.

The Address bus consists of 16 bi-directional lines (labeled AB00 through AB15) that are time shared by all system modules. Sixteen more bi-directional lines (labeled DB00 through DB15) also are time shared by all system modules. For example, the Processor uses the D bus to read data from or write data into Memory, transfer data to or from an I/O Controller, etc. The C bus uses approximately 50 control lines which define the specific actions that a system module is to perform. C bus lines are subdivided into four broad categories:

> Data Access and Service (Direct Memory)
> Processor Access and Service (Instruction Stream)
> Interrupt Access and Service (Real-time Response)
> . System Control

Additional special-purpose control lines are used for adjacent module communication, memory options control, and miscellaneous functions. Table 13–1 shows all control lines (by function), while a definition of those

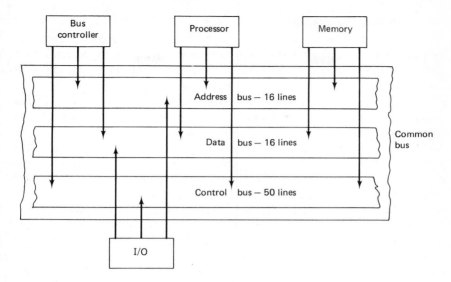

Figure 13–3 Common bus organization.

Table 13–1 Control Bus Lines

Data Access and Service	Processor Access and Service	Interrupt Access and Service	System Control	Others
SRLD	SRLC	SRC1	REPB	BT1A, B
SELD	SELC	SRC2	MRES	BT2A, B
		SRC3	PFIN	BT3A, B
		SRC4	PWST	BT4A, B
		SEL1	LFIN	KEYO, 1
		SEL2	LFRQ	PBLO
		SEL3	PRAL	PBHI
		SEL4	PRIN	HOLD
			ATLD	CLK1
	PCDA/B		MINH	RUNN
	SACK		EXAT	
	STRB			
	DONE			
	QUIT			
RITE				
BYTE				
HCYC				

control lines necessary to explain simple computer operations follows. Control lines are activated only when required by specific operations to be performed. Details are forthcoming in the following section.

The Bus Controller

Computer operation is based on the *Bus Controller* monitoring certain key communication lines to maintain knowledge of what the remainder of the machine is doing. In response to the activities on the communication lines, the Bus Controller also originates appropriate control signals.

Common Bus communication occurs in two overlapped cycles: *bus select cycle* and *bus service cycle*. In other words, a system module can request access even while another module is being serviced by the bus service cycle. The *requesting* system module (*master*) must acknowledge when selected and the system module being read out or written into (*slave*) must signal completion as soon as possible. The Bus Controller monitors requests, acknowledgements, and completions and disconnects system modules from the Common Bus if actions are not observed within predetermined times.

Four general types of communication use the Common Bus. *Data Access and Service* provides communication directly to and from Memory or other system modules (other than the Processor). Direct data transfer has the highest priority of all service requests and is initiated by activating a control line labeled *SRLD*. The next level of communication priority is for Processor *interrupts*. Four levels of interrupts exist: the *SRL4* line has the highest priority and indicates system faults; the *SRL3* line allows high data rate input/output devices (discs, drums, magnetic tape, etc) to interrupt the Processor; the *SRL2* line signals the Processor that data is ready for transfer from a slow data rate device such as paper tape readers or punches; and the *SRL1* line provides for manual system interrupts. Service Request C (SRLC) indicates a *Processor request for access to the Common Bus* and carries the lowest priority. *System control* signals also exist on the Common Bus but do not exist within the priority system. Descriptions of many of the Common Bus signals follow.

SELECTED COMMON BUS SIGNAL DESCRIPTIONS

SRLD	Service Request Line, Data. This line is used by a device to request bus access.
SELD	Select Module for Direct Data Transfer. In conjunction with the Precedence line, this signal is used to select the device for bus access.
PCDA/B	Precedence. A Precedence pulse is originated in the Bus Controller and is propagated from right to left through each device. The device requesting access traps the pulse and prevents further propagation.
SACK	Select Acknowledge. SACK is used by a device to signal recognition to the Bus Controller that it has been selected for the next bus service cycle.
STRB	Strobe. When activated, STRB signals that the Common Bus is busy in a service cycle and, when inactive, indi-

cates that the Common Bus is available to a selected device.

DONE Done. Done is used by a slave module to signal that the bus service cycle is completed.

QUIT Quit. QUIT signals the master module that the slave module did not signal DONE within 2 microseconds of the start of the cycle.

RITE* Write. When activated, RITE signals a write function.

HCYC* Half-cycle. HCYC specifies a half-cycle memory operation.

BYTE* Byte. When active, BYTE allows transfer of only DB00-DB07, that is, a byte only transfer of information.

SRLC Service Request Line, Computer. Processors use SRLC to request bus access.

SELC Select Computer. The highest precedence Processor requesting bus access is selected by use of SELC.

SRL1-4 Service Request Lines, Interrupt. Any system module generates system interrupt using SRL1-4.

SEL1-4 Select, Interrupt. The Common Bus Controller generates SEL1-4 in response to SRL1-4. SEL1-4 selects the interrupting device.

REPB Reset Push Button. The Bus Controller senses activation of the Reset Push Button on the Control Panel and generates a Master Reset signal, MRES.

MRES Master Reset. Master Reset to all system modules is generated by the Bus Controller upon occurrence of REPB, power initiation, or power failure. All modules are reset to an initial status condition.

RUNN Run. RUNN is generated by all Processors. It is used by the Control Panel to light an indicator displaying that any Processor is in the Run mode.

Numerous other control signals are used within the computer and on the Common Bus, but these examples are typical. Table 13–1 presented the complete list of control signals.

General Bus Controller controlled operation of the computer during a Data Service Request D (SRLD) can now be shown. When the select line (SELD) is inactive, any one or more master device(s) can activate the service request SRLD (Figure 13–4(a)). If no master device is waiting for the Common Bus, the Bus Controller will activate the SELD line and the Precedence Chain (PCDA/B). The Precedence Chain is merely a control line which

*Various combinations of these three signals allow both byte and word read, write, clear, and restore operations within any slave module.

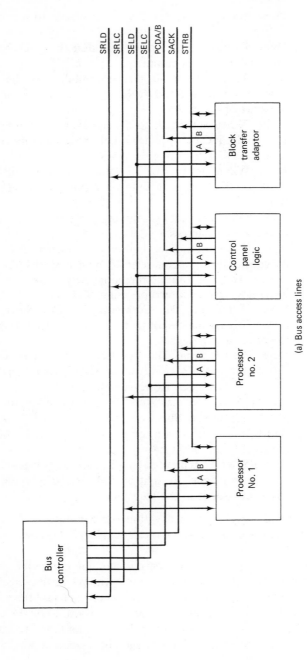

(a) Bus access lines

Figure 13-4 Bus access and service lines; (a) bus access lines, (courtesy of Lockheed Electronics Co. Inc., Data Products Div. Los Angeles, CA).

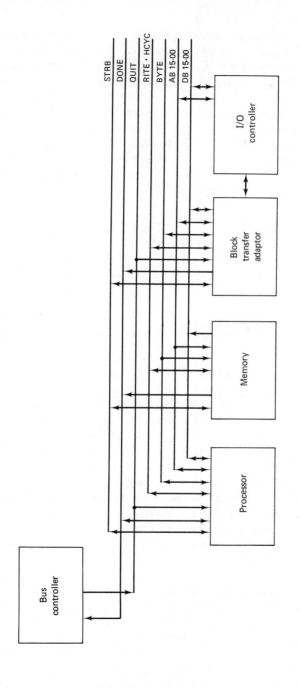

(b) Service lines

Figure 13-4 (Continued) (b) service lines (courtesy of Lockheed Electronics Co. Inc., Data Products Div., Los Angeles, CA).

connects all system modules in series (Figure 13–4(a)). A precedence pulse is generated by the Bus Controller and propagated through all devices until it reaches the first master device requesting use of the Common Bus. The requesting master device highest in the precedence chain, that is, closest to the Bus Controller, blocks further propagation of the precedence pulse. PCDA is the precedence pulse entering a system module, while PCDB is the same pulse leaving the module. Figure 13–5 shows the concept of PCDA/B propagation. When a master device receives the precedence pulse *and* the activated SELD line, it indicates that this master will be given the next Common Bus cycle. The master device must then activate Select Acknowledge (SACK) and remove its service request SRLD.

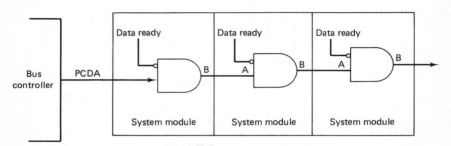

Figure 13–5   PCDA/B propagation.

Activation of SACK is recognized by the Bus Controller, which removes the precedence pulse (PCDA/B) and select (SELD) signals. The waiting master device now inhibits other attempts to gain access to the Common Bus by the presence of its SACK signal. A signal called Strobe (STRB), which indicates that the Common Bus is busy in a service cycle, is monitored by the waiting master device to determine when the Common Bus has been released by the previous master and has become idle. When STRB is removed, the selected master device activates the address and control lines and also activates the data lines if the operation is to be a write. The waiting master then activates the STRB line and removes SACK to allow the Bus Controller to select another master device.

All slave devices examine the address and control lines (Figure 13-4(b)). The slave device addressed must respond with the service completion signal DONE. If the transfer is a write (RITE) to the addressed slave device, DONE indicates to the master that the data to be written into the slave has been taken from the lines. When the DONE signal from the slave is recognized, the master removes strobe, address, data, and control. The write operation for this master has been completed, and the Common Bus is idle, unless a newly selected master activates its address and control signals.

Overlapped selection of a new master could have been enabled earlier when the current master removed its SACK.

In a read operation, the selected master activates only address and control lines when it recognizes that STRB has been removed by the previous master. It then activates its STRB for the addressed slave to place the data on the data lines, followed by a DONE signal. When the master recognizes the DONE signal, it samples the data and then removes its address, control, and strobe. The read operation for this master has now been completed. The Common Bus can be idle or a newly selected master can activate its address and control signals. Just as during the write operation, overlapped selection of a new master could have been enabled when the current master removed its SACK.

Receipt of DONE by the master device indicates successful completion of the bus service. If DONE fails to occur within a given period of time, the Bus Controller will activate the QUIT line, indicating a cycle abort. The occurrence of DONE or QUIT causes the master device to remove its activated lines and indicates to other devices that another transfer may begin.

Figure 13–6 defines Common Bus overlapped request and service timing. Note that the second request begins before the first request has completed the transfer. System timing is derived from the 25 mHz clock located on the Bus Controller module.

Operation of functional sections of computers are often explained using flow charts. Figure 13–7 is a flow chart depicting the implementation of Service Request priority functions in the Bus Controller. Such flow charts are used by system designers as guides during logic design, by programmers as they develop software for the computer, and by technicians (in conjunction with logic diagrams) as an aid to troubleshooting and repair activities. In many cases the flow chart may replace "wordy" explanations of system operation and complex logic diagrams. The reader is encouraged to develop flow charts of logic operations encountered in his computer experience and to become intimately familiar with their use.

I/O Controller

A general block diagram of a typical *I/O Controller* module is shown in Figure 13–8. *Line drivers/receivers* are provided for *each* output/input to the Common Bus that interfaces with the Controller. Since numerous system modules connect to each Common Bus line, *line drivers* are used to furnish sufficient signal power to the Common Bus so that signal degradation does not occur. *Line receivers* accept bus inputs, amplifying and reshaping them as required. In the typical modules shown in Figure 13–8, a line driver is required for each sending-only line, such as SRLD, PCDB, and SRL. Each receiving-only line requires a line receiver. SEL, MRES, QUIT, SELD, PCDA, and SACK are examples. Each *bi-directional* line requires

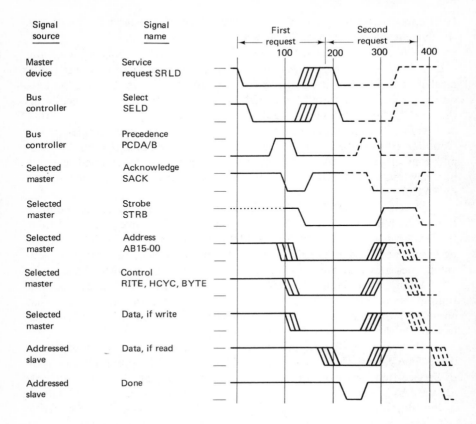

Note: Time in nanoseconds
First request and service signals in unbroken lines
Second request and service signals in dashed lines
Previous strobe condition in dotted lines

Figure 13–6   Common bus timing (courtesy of Lockheed Electronics Co., Inc., Data Products Div., Los Angeles, CA).

both a line receiver and line driver. Typical are all address bits, all data bits, STRB, DONE, and RITE. A quick count shows that the I/O Controller selected for discussion requires a total of 38 line drivers and 41 line receivers. This is just one more of the many examples showing that the computer's complexity is not because of highly sophisticated circuits but rather because of the existence of many simple circuits.

Every system module on the Common Bus must be able to operate in the slave mode—that is, recognize when it is being addressed. *Address recognition* circuits perform this function. A system module examines the address

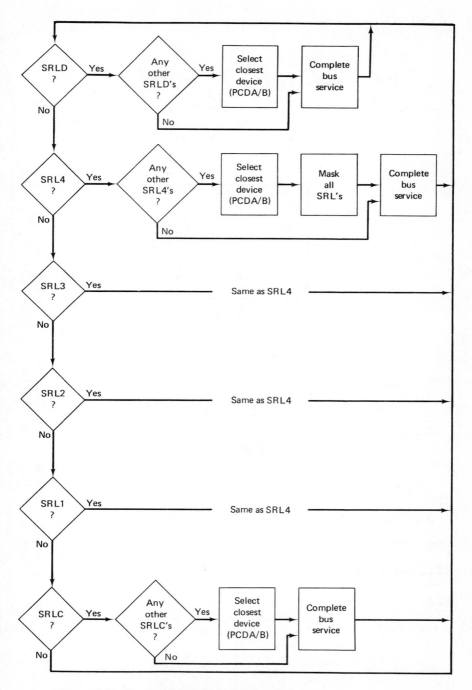

Figure 13–7 Service request priority flowchart.

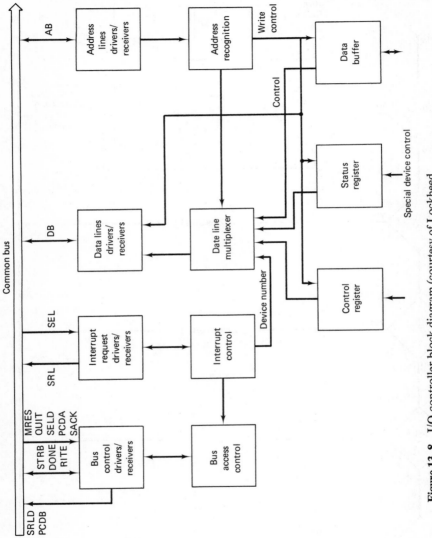

Figure 13–8 I/O controller block diagram (courtesy of Lockheed Electronics Co., Inc., Data Products Div., Los Angeles, CA).

lines when the strobe signal is activated on the Common Bus. When a module detects its address, it will examine the RITE line to determine if a read or write operation is required. If the RITE line is not activated, a register read operation is commanded. The module gates the contents of the selected register onto the Common Bus data lines. If the RITE line is activated, the data on the Common Bus is written into the selected register. In both cases the module signals DONE to indicate completion of the data transfer.

Three addressable registers are shown in the diagram of Figure 13–8: a *control register*, *status register*, and *data register*. The control register is loaded by the Processor instruction to start or stop the Controller's operation. Indications of the Controller's status are contained in the status register. Typical status information is *data ready*, *device not ready*, etc. The data register formats data during input or holds data to be output. It is capable of storing the complete package of information (computer word or byte) going to or coming from the I/O device.

The module's *interrupt logic* requests a bus cycle by activating a service request line (SRL1-4). Upon being granted access by the Bus Controller, the module places its device number on the data lines of the Common Bus and, after a short delay, activates the strobe line. *Bus access control* operates in conjunction with interrupt logic to form the required input and output control signals. A *data line multiplexer* offers a convenient method for gating several sources of data onto the Common Bus data lines. Note that in Figure 13–8 inputs to the multiplexer are available from many different sources, but only one source can be selected at a time. A simple multiplexer was shown in Figure 5–28.

Block Transfer Adaptors (BTA) are merely specialized I/O Controllers containing modified data handling circuits. All of the Bus Control, interrupt, and address capability must be included, since the BTA must communicate with the rest of the computer. The remainder of the BTA consists of reformatting logic circuits that prepare I/O information for storage or readout in the proper form. Registers and counters, along with control gates, perform the reformatting tasks. Under BTA control, then, data is transferred to and from memory and I/O units in large blocks of information, rather than as single computer words.

The Processor

Figure 13–9 is a block diagram of the 2-card Processor module. One Processor card contains an arithmetic-register unit and Common Bus interface logic; the second card contains a Read-Only Memory (ROM) organized *control* capability. The arithmetic-register unit contains a Register File of twelve 16-bit registers and six additional registers organized around a high-speed, parallel arithmetic/logic unit (ALU). MEMORY capability is implemented in the Processor using the Register File. Even though it consists of

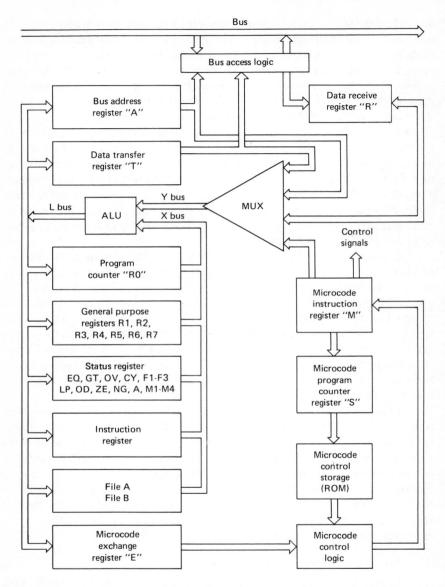

Figure 13-9 Processor organization (courtesy of Lockheed Electronics Co., Inc., Data Products Div., Los Angeles, CA).

only twelve registers, it still performs the classic memory function. INPUT/ OUTPUT functions are accomplished by the Bus Access block, plus the Address (*A*) register, Receive (*R*) register, and the Transmit (*T*) register. For the purpose of this discussion it is assumed that input/output information is available on the Common Bus. *CONTROL* functions are preprogrammed in the ROM control memory and cause activation of all necessary hardware during operation of the Processor. Note that all five basic computer functions (INPUT, OUTPUT, CONTROL, ARITHMETIC/LOGIC, and MEMORY) appear within the Processor.

Incorporation of its own internal busses allows the Processor to operate almost independently of other system modules and to minimize its use of the Common Bus. Once information is available to the Processor's internal storage, it then can perform its own internal operations under control of the ROM without constant access to the Common Bus. Furthermore, the Processor can operate in either the master or the slave mode. It may request a bus cycle from the Bus Controller and may command a read or write operation from any other system module that can operate in the slave mode.

Separation of the Processor into three subsections makes it easier to discuss its operation. The *Common Bus Interface* supplies basic bus drivers/receivers for all lines going out and/or coming into the Processor. Bus drivers/receivers are identical in all system modules. When the Processor is halted (not performing internal operations), all of the Processor's internal registers can be addressed by other system modules that operate in a master mode. Therefore the Common Bus Interface must recognize when one of these registers is being addressed and respond by receiving or transmitting the selected register's contents. Addressable registers include the seven General Registers, Program Counter, Status, Instruction, and two firmware registers. The Address (A) register holds the address that is placed on the Common Bus when the Processor is addressing a system module. The Receive (R) register receives data from the Common Bus, and the Transmit (T) register holds data for transmission on the Common Bus. All three of these registers may be gated to the ALU for logical or arithmetic combinations with the selected register of the Register File.

The *arithmetic-register* section consists of the ALU, the Register File, and a Multiplex Unit (MUX). The MUX is used to select an operand from one of three registers or a 16-bit input separated into four 4-bit fields. Each field is individually enabled or disabled as an input to the ALU under microcode control. The ALU responds to a command from the microcode word. These commands specify one of 16 logical functions or one of 16 arithmetic functions to be performed by the ALU. The functions are performed on the two ALU inputs, X and Y, and an arithmetic carry signal C that adds to the least-significant position. ALU output is via the L bus that provides the path to write the results of the microstep into the Processor A, T, and E registers or Register File.

One of the twelve registers in the Register File is selected by the microcode for input to the ALU via its X input. The twelve registers consist of

35	34	33	32	31	30	29	28	27	26	25	24	23	22	21	20	19	18	17	16	15	14	13	12	11	10	9	8	7	6	5	4	3	2	1	0
S		T		A			C			D			X			F		Y			M				L_2					L_1			Z		W

Figure 13-10 Microcode field format (courtesy of Lockheed Electronics Co., Inc., Data Products Div, Los Angeles, CA).

the Program Counter, seven General Registers, Status Register, Instruction Register, and two registers (File *A* and File *B*) that are used internally for microprogrammed execution of instructions.

ROM Microcode Control consists of 256 (expandable to 512) 36-bit words used for control of the Processor. The microcode control uses three registers. The *E* register holds the 16-bit programmed instruction that was received from MEMORY or other external source. Fields of this register specify the instruction code, addressing mode, General Register, Index Register, and occasionally a literal operand. The *S* register is an 8-bit counter that sequences microsteps. It addresses the Control Storage and is under control of the microcode. The *M* register holds the 36-bit microcode that specifies action of the current microstep as well as control of the next sequential step.

The microcode word format (Figure 13–10) contains 13 fields for specification of control functions within the processor and selection of operands. This large word size for microprogram control allows a number of useful functions to be specified in one microstep. It further minimizes the number of microsteps that are needed to execute a single instruction. The result is high-speed instruction execution with the flexibility of microprogram control.

Microcode fields are related to the organization and functions of the Processor. A variety of special condition test and skip or test and branch microsteps are provided to allow conditional coding to minimize microsteps. The microcode word format represents a three-address microinstruction. Detailed code functions follow.

The *X* and *Y* fields each specify an operand, and the *W* field specifies the destination for the result of the operation. The *S* field selects the microinstruction class. *T*, *A*, and *C* fields specify the operation code of the ALU. In combination, the M, L_2, and L_1 fields are used for either branch or jump addresses within the microstore, for literal operands, or special commands for housekeeping functions. Preparation for the next microinstruction is supplied by the *D*, *F*, and *Z* fields.

13–3 SELECTED COMPUTER OPERATIONS

No attempt is made in this chapter to explain the detailed, bit-by-bit, gate-by-gate, register-by-register operation of the computer. Such detailed explanations obviously belong in handbooks prepared for specific computers. However, some of the concepts of modern computer technology can be observed by examining the methods by which information is handled using the organization shown in Figure 13–1 and the details provided in previous sections of this chapter.

Teletypewriter to Processor Data Flow

Consider the transfer of information from a Teletypewriter to the Processor. Because of unique device and register identity on the Common Bus, special input/output instructions are not required. Input and output data transfers are accomplished by simple "move" instructions. Therefore, software controls movement of control commands, data, and status between *any* addressable storage location and an I/O Controller in the same manner that it would communicate with Memory.

As noted in Chapter 11, the Teletypewriter supplies an 11-bit serial code to the I/O Controller, and the Controller reformats the information into an 8-bit parallel ANSI character. The 8-bit character is then moved to the designated general-purpose register or memory location. Figure 13–11(a) shows the concepts of a single byte transfer from the Teletypewriter to a destination register.

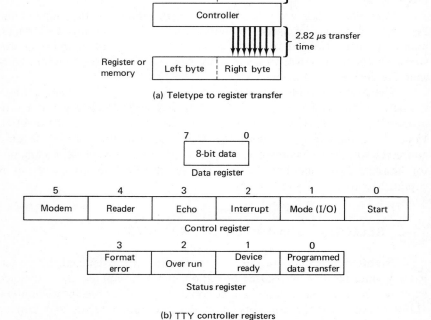

Figure 13–11   Teletype controller operation; (a) teletype to register transfer, (b) TTY controller registers (courtesy of Lockheed Electronics, Data Products Div., Los Angeles, CA).

Serial information read or written by the Teletypewriter is assembled by the I/O Controller for parallel transfer from the data register in the Controller to a general-purpose register. The I/O Controller uses three registers to accomplish the transfer function. Register organization and bit assignments are shown in Figure 13–11(b). An 8-bit *data register* manipulates the ANSI representation of the character to be transferred or accepted. It must be capable of both serial-to-parallel or parallel-to-serial operation to accommodate the serial organization of the Teletypewriter and the parallel organization of the computer. The 6-bit *control register* provides start/stop, enable/disable, and miscellaneous control bits to determine the operating mode(s) of the Teletypewriter and the I/O Controller. Status of the I/O Controller is located in the 4-bit *status register*. A typical operation with a Teletypewriter would enter information from a paper tape reader and automatically "echo" the information to the Teletypewriter printer.

A character is read from the low-speed paper tape reader by setting bit 4 of the control register, which, in turn, resets bit 0 of the status register, indicating that the Controller is busy. When the character bits start to enter the data register, the Controller de-energizes a relay in the Teletypewriter to release the tape feed latch. When released, the latch mechanism stops the tape after a complete character has been read and before the next character is started. Once the character is completely available in the data buffer, the PDT bit is set to indicate that the I/O Controller has data available for transmission and a bus access for an interrupt is requested. After the bus service routine (see Section 13–2) has read the data, the PDT bit is automatically reset, indicating a readiness for new data. Note that it takes less than 3 microseconds to actually make the register to register move, while it took 100 milliseconds to transfer the character from the Teletypewriter to the Controller. The Common Bus and all other system modules are free, then, to perform other operations almost all of the time. Only the I/O Controller associated with the Teletypewriter is busy for the full time.

Computer Instructions

As may have been noticed, much more activity than just single control line signals to request bus access, select system modules, etc is evident on the Common Bus. Addresses must be exchanged between modules, and data must be moved from module to module. Within the Processor, data movement and operations are controlled by a microprogram. However, the microprogram must be told what operations to perform, and other data movement operations throughout the computer must have direction.

During design of the computer, a *list of instructions* is developed. These instructions represent the basic functions that the computer must perform, such as data movement, arithmetic operations, etc. Instructions are designed to be accommodated in one or more computer word lengths

(16 bits in the case of the computer being discussed in this chapter). Each instruction contains the minimum amount of information necessary to accomplish one or more computer operations; and in the case of instructions that are oriented toward Processor operations, they select one or more microwords from the microprogram store to perform their operations. The complete instruction repertoire of the computer being discussed in this chapter is quite large, and it would serve no useful purpose to show it in its entirety. Selected samples are shown in Table 13–2.

Table 13–2   Selected Computer Instructions

ADDB	Add Byte	HALT	Halt
ADDW	Add Word	IORB	Inclusive OR Byte
ANDB	And Byte	IORW	Inclusive OR Word
ANDW	And Word	JSBR	Jump to Subroutine
BCYF	Branch if Carry False	JUMP	Jump
BCYT	Branch if Carry True	MOVB	Move Byte
BEQF	Branch if Equal False	MOVW	Move Word
BEQT	Branch if Equal True	MREG	Memory-to-Register
BGTF	Branch if Greater Than False	MSTS	Memory-to-Status
BGTT	Branch if Greater Than True	REGM	Register-to-Memory
BLPF	Branch if Loop Complete False	RETN	Return from Interrupt
BLPT	Branch if Loop Complete True	RSTS	Reset Status Indicators
BLTF	Branch if Less Than False	SETS	Set Status Indicators
BLTT	Branch if Less Than True	SLAO	Single Left Arithmetic Open
BNGF	Branch if Negative False	SLLO	Single Left Logical Open
BNGT	Branch if Negative True	SRAO	Single Right Arithmetic Open
BRUN	Branch Unconditional	SRLO	Single Right Logical Open
BZEF	Branch if Zero False	STSM	Status-to-Memory
BZET	Branch if Zero True	SUBB	Subtract Byte
CMPB	Compare Byte	SUBW	Subtract Word
CMPW	Compare Word	TSTB	Test Byte
DSBL	Disable Interrupts	TSTW	Test Word
ENBL	Enable Interrupts		
EORB	Exclusive OR Byte		
EORW	Exclusive OR Word		

As a minimum, each instruction must tell the computer hardware *what it must do* and, in some way or another, *what it must do it with*. Furthermore, the instruction format must agree with the manner in which the computer hardware is wired and the computer software is designed. The typical instruction words discussed in earlier chapters perform the same functions. In the case of the list of instructions shown in Table 13–2, however, considerably more information may be available.

The computer has 64 instructions in four basic groups. Each group has functions designated by class, and each class has associated operations. Relationships between groups, classes, and operations are shown in Table

Table 13–3   Instruction Groups and Classes

Class	Group	Function
0	Control	Control
1	General Register	Register to Memory, Auto-Decrement
2	General Register	Register to Memory, Auto-Increment
3	General Register	Register to Memory
4	General Register	Register to Register, Jump, Jump to Subroutine, and Data to Register
5	General Register	Memory to Register, Auto-Decrement
6	General Register	Memory to Register, Auto-Increment
7	General Register	Memory to Register
8	Branch	Branch if False or No Operation
9	Branch	Branch if True or Unconditional
10 (A)	Shift	Shift
11 (B)	Extended	Reserved
12 (C)	Extended	Reserved
13 (D)	Extended	Reserved

13–3. The *control* group includes load/store of multiple general-purpose registers, load/store of status conditions, and interrupt control instructions. A *general register* group performs the arithmetic, logical, compare, test, and data handling operations. The *branch* group includes the conditional and unconditional branch functions. Shift capabilities from 1 to 15 bits, in eight different modes, is provided by the *shift* group.

A typical *control* instruction is seen in Figure 13–12(a). This instruction disables any or all levels of interrupts by the presence of a "1" in bits 3, 2, 1, and 0 of the instruction word DSBL. The four most significant bits (15, 14, 13, 12) defined the *class* of instruction (Table 13–3). Bits 11, 10, 9, and 8 indicate the *gross type of operation* to be performed (interrupt control), while bits 7, 6, 5, and 4 *detail the operation* (disable interrupts). Many other control instructions exist, but in general they follow the pattern of the DSBL instruction.

Table 13–3 shows that there are seven *general register* classes. Instructions in these classes allow movement of information from registers to memory, memory to registers, registers to registers, data to registers, and various "jump" operations. Certain of the register instructions also include the capability of automatically increasing or decreasing associated addresses so that complete tables may be manipulated with a minimum of instructions. The general format for register group instructions is shown in Figure 13–12(b). Bits 15, 14, 13, and 12 once again define the *class* of operation as defined in Table 13–3. Since the computer under discussion is capable of operation with either 16-bit words or 8-bit bytes, bit 11 (B/W) defines byte (1) or word (0) mode. The actual operation to be performed is defined in bits 10, 9, and 8 and is listed in Table 13–4. Bit 7 (I/D) is used to indicate

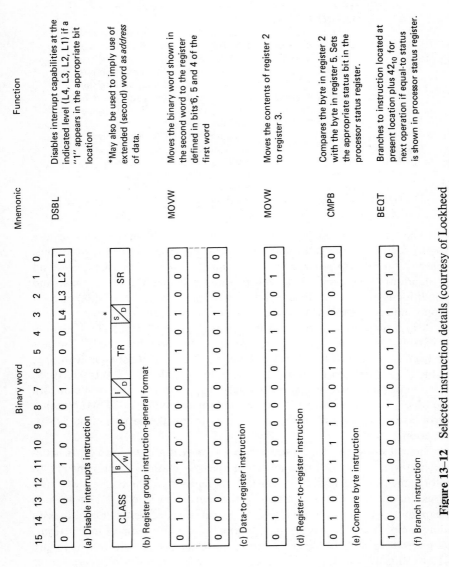

Figure 13-12 Selected instruction details (courtesy of Lockheed Electronics, Data Products Div., Los Angeles, CA).

Table 13–4   Register Operations

Operation	Description
0 MOVe	Transfer the source operand to the target operand.
1 SUBtract	Subtract the source operand from the target operand and store in the target operand.
2 ADD	Form the sum of the source and target operand and store in the target operand.
3 AND	Form the *logical product* of the source and target operand and store in the target operand.
4 Inclusive OR	Form the *logical sum* of the source and target operand and store in the target operand.
5 Exclusive OR	Form the *logical difference* of the source and target operand and store in the target operand.
6 CoMPare	Subtract the source operand from the target operand. The register content and memory content are not affected.
7 TeST	Form the *logical product* of the source and target operand. The register and memory content are not affected.

whether the address used in this instruction is to be assumed as the actual address (direct, 0) or whether the address is merely the *location* in memory or a register *of the actual address* (indirect, 1). The destination register (*target*, TR) is indicated in bits 6, 5, and 4, while the *source* register (SR) is defined in bits 2, 1, and 0. Bit 3 (S/D) indicates if this instruction is a single word (0) or double word (1) instruction. If a double word instruction is indicated, the next 16-bit word is to be considered part of the preceding word.

A class 4 general register instruction may be used to move a constant to a register. Figure 13–12(c) shows an instruction word that places the number 72_{10} in general register 6. Note the use of the double word format. An example of register-to-register information transfer is shown in Figure 13–12(d). The reader is urged to closely examine each of these examples and determine the actions that result.

Another often used operation in the general register class is the *compare byte* or *compare word* instruction. This instruction performs an arithmetic compare by subtracting the source from the target and indicates equal-to, less-than, or greater-than via status bits in the Processor status register. The compare instruction is useful in searching for known data. For example, a table termination character might be 11111111. As each character is moved into a register for output it can be checked against the termination character, and when the comparison results in an "equal-to" condition, the computer can perform the desired operation. A typical example of the compare operation appears in Figure 13–12(e) and in the sample program of Table 13–5.

An instruction that often follows a compare instruction is a *branch* group instruction. A branch instruction tells the computer to deviate from its normal sequence of taking the next instruction that follows and to go

Table 13–5   Sample Program

1.		MOVW	=72,R6	Place byte count in R6
2.		MOVB	=FF,R5	Place terminating character in R5
3.		MOVW	TABL,R7	Place TABL location in R7
4.		MOVW	=9,R3	Move input code to R3
5.		MOVW	R3,CONTWD	Move code to Control Register
6.	PDTSTA	MOVW	STAWD,R4	Move Status Register to R4
7.		BODF	PDTSTA	Loop until new data in Data Register
8.		MOVW	DATAWD,R2	Move data from Data Register to R2
9.		MOVB	R2,(R7+)	Move data into stack and increment R7
10.		CMPB	R2,R5	Compare data to terminating character
11.		BEQT	PDTEND	If yes, then exit
12.		SUBW	=1,R6	Decrement byte count
13.		BZEF	PDTSTA	Loop back until byte count goes to zero
14.	PDTEND	HALT		Halt after completion

somewhere else for another instruction. Figure 13–12(f) is a *branch if equal true* (BEQT) instruction. It includes the usual class designation in bits 15, 14, 13, and 12. Bits 11, 10, 9, and 8 define the actual test to be performed, such as equal-to, less-than, greater-than, odd, negative, etc. Up to 12 separate conditions may be tested. The address to which the program should go when the tested condition has been met is contained in bits 7 through 0. Branch instructions use a relative displacement addressing technique that allows a branch 128 words back or 127 words ahead of the location of the existing branch instruction. This is the maximum range allowable in the eight bits that remain after class and operation are defined, and maintains the branch instruction as a single word.

Teletypewriter to Computer Input Program

Table 13–5 is a segment of a program that inputs Teletypewriter keyboard data to the computer. It should be realized that this is only a *partial* program and, as such, does not fully perform *all* required operations. For example, the computer must be entered into this program by means of control console inputs or from other programs, address assignments must be made, etc. The purpose of this program segment is to help explain how the computer performs its operations, *not* how to program the computer. Numerous fine texts exist on actual programming, and these texts, along with the manufacturers' programming manuals, will provide the necessary programming background.

The program segment of Table 13–5 is shown in assembly language (mnemonic) form, as it would be coded for entry into the computer. As stated in Chapter 12, the assembler accepts each of the statements and converts them to computer word format prior to actual execution of the program. Machine language computer word formats of some of the typical computer instructions were presented in Figure 13–12, and the reader may wish to refer to them as the steps in Table 13–5 are studied.

As the programmer writes his program, he must restrict himself to certain statement format rules. In general, the assembly language statements used with this computer are written in the following format:

Label   Operation   Operand 1, Operand 2   Comments

Label is used when needed as a reference by other statements. Its use in a statement will result in an automatic assignment of an address by the assembler, so that every time the label appears as an operand in another statement, the program will go to that assigned address for the required information. The *operation code* is a mnemonic machine operation such as shown in Table 13–2. *Operand 1* and *operand 2* are the data or addresses of data that are to be operated upon by the mnemonic code used in the operation code portion of the statement. The *comments* portion of the statement is optional and is used to aid the programmer or user of the program in determining the rationale behind the program's construction, etc. Comments are not processed by the computer but are merely printed out for each statement as written originally.

The following comments apply to the step numbers of statement in Table 13–5 and are meant to further clarify the meaning of the steps and the symbology used.

1. No label is provided, since this statement is not referenced elsewhere in the program. Note that most of the statements in this program fit into this category. Also, the use of "=" in operand 1 is interpreted by the assembler as notification that data to be inputted follows. The number 72_{10} is placed in Processor general register 6 as a result of this step.

2. This is a move byte (MOVB) instruction, which places the hexadecimal character FF (binary 11111111) in Processor general register 5.

3. TABL, which is the label of the storage table, is entered into Processor general register 7. TABL must have an address assigned by the assembler before this program will successfully operate.

4. The binary equivalent of 9_{10} (001001) is placed in Processor general register 3 for subsequent transfer to the control register in the Teletypewriter Controller. Figure 13–10(b) shows that 001001 will result in echo of the keyboard input to the printer and will start keyboard operation.

5. Contents of Processor general register 3 (control word) are moved to the control register in the Teletypewriter Controller.

6. The contents of the Teletypewriter Controller status register are moved to Processor general register 4 so that the Processor can monitor conditions in the Controller. This step is labeled, since it will be referenced elsewhere in the program.

7. BODF is an instruction that monitors status and branches to the location of operand 1 as long as status is false. Statement 7 examines the status of the Teletypewriter Controller and, as long as data is not ready for transfer, branches to step 6. The status word is again transferred to the Processor, statement 7 monitored, and the "loop" is repeated until Controller status signals that data is ready. Status is then true, and the program continues to the next statement.

8. Data from the Teletypewriter Controller data register is moved to Processor general register 2.

9. The first character from the Teletypewriter (now in Processor general register 2) is transferred to the location called out by Processor general register 7 (starting address of TABL), and Processor general register 7 is incremented by 1 (R7+). The next character to be stored, then, will be placed in *one* memory location *higher* than the first character, etc, until all characters have been transferred. Character storage is thus in a "stack," with the first character received on the bottom and the last character received on the top.

10. Comparison (CMPB) of the character in Processor general register 2 is performed with the character in Processor general register 5 (the terminating character).

11. If the operation in step 10 is true, that is, both characters are the same, the program branches to PDTEND (step 14). This is the normal operation of the BEQT instruction.

12. If comparison is not true, the program continues, decrementing the byte count in Processor general register 6 by 1.

13. The byte count is monitored by BZEF, and as long as it is not zero, the program branches to step 6 (PDTSTA) and moves in another character by executing steps 6 through 13 again. The "loop" encompassing steps 6 through 13 repeats until the byte count reaches zero. The program then continues to the final step of the program.

14. HALT stops Processor operation and turns on the HALT light on the control panel. The computer has now transferred 72 characters from the Teletypewriter keyboard, echo printed them on the printer, and stored them in a table (stack) in memory for future use. The computer merely must ask for the information called TABL and the complete stack can be recovered.

Micro-operations

It should be further recognized that each of the statements in the program of Table 13–5 that required action by the Processor resulted in many operations within the Processor. The power of the Processor as a result of its microprogrammed capability was seen in Section 13–2.

A simple operation, MOVW, shown in Figure 13–12(d), demonstrates in general terms how many operations must take place simply to move a computer word from one register to another within the Processor. Microsteps are normally sequenced at 7.69 mHz rates, 130 nanoseconds per step. (Note: When microsteps that require an arithmetic function in the ALU are encountered, a step is given 160 nanoseconds to assure that any carries generated can propagate under worst-case conditions.) The MOVW instruction, however, takes 2.5 microseconds to accomplish. Therefore, at 160 nanoseconds per microstep, 15 microsteps can be accomplished, or at 130 nanoseconds per microstep, 19 microsteps can be accomplished. Processing speeds are limited by the ALU, since the microprogram store may be accessed in as little as 60 nanoseconds.

The organization of the Processor requires that all internal operations be accomplished using the ALU. This requirement can result in some additional steps above and beyond those which might be needed in other processor organizations. However, the use of microprogramming easily balances the added time required for ALU processing by reducing hardware requirements and increasing versatility. One merely needs to consider that the internal operation of the Processor might be unimportant. It is only necessary to consider the overall computer's response to instructions, and it will be seen that the microprogrammed, internally bussed computer offers many advantages over more conventional machines.

13–4 THE END

By the time this point is reached, the reader has progressed from an abacus to the sophisticated, highly complex digital computer: from a simple gate to the complex processor on a chip. There is no doubt that much has occurred in the field of digital computers from their beginning with the abacus to their present state of the art. No one is wise enough to predict the future of digital computers any more than Aiken, Mauchly, Eckert, and Von Neumann might have predicted the present state of the art in the 1940s and 1950s. After all, it was felt in that time period that 1K of core memory was adequate to expeditiously solve *any* problem. We will see the digital computer performing more and more routine, everyday operations. It will appear in the home and in our automobile. It will get larger for very complex operations, and it will get smaller for simple operations. The digital computer is strongly affecting all of our lives. You are taking the first steps on the way to understanding the device and to making it work for you, not against you.

QUESTIONS AND PROBLEMS

1. What are the major differences between the classical Von Neumann machine and the bus-organized machine?
2. List the functions of the Common Bus Controller.
3. List the functions of the Processor.
4. What is a Block Transfer Adaptor?
5. Describe the Common Bus.
6. Why must address and data lines be bi-directional?
7. Describe a typical bus select cycle.
8. Why are line drivers/receivers required in each system module?
9. What general type of system module requires address recognition logic?
10. What are the major attributes of the Processor in the computer discussed in this chapter?
11. Describe the functions of the General Register File in the Processor.
12. What controls the ALU in the Processor?
13. List the functions of the data register, control register, and status register in an I/O Controller.
14. Discuss the computer word organization of a *control* instruction.
15. Discuss the computer word organization of *general register* instruction.
16. Discuss the computer word organization of *branch* instructions.
17. Discuss micro-operations as used in the computer described in this chapter.

Postulates, Theorems, and Laws of Boolean Algebra

POSTULATES

$0 \cdot 0 = 0$	(P—1)	$0 + 1 = 1$	(P—6)
$0 \cdot 1 = 0$	(P—2)	$1 + 0 = 1$	(P—7)
$1 \cdot 0 = 0$	(P—3)	$1 + 1 = 1$	(P—8)
$1 \cdot 1 = 1$	(P—4)	$0 = \bar{1}$	(P—9)
$0 + 0 = 0$	(P—5)	$1 = \bar{0}$	(P—10)

THEOREMS

$A \cdot 0 = 0$	(T—1)	$0 + A = A$	(T—8)
$0 \cdot A = 0$	(T—2)	$A + 1 = 1$	(T—9)
$A \cdot 1 = A$	(T—3)	$1 + A = 1$	(T—10)
$1 \cdot A = A$	(T—4)	$A + A = A$	(T—11)
$A \cdot A = A$	(T—5)	$A + \bar{A} = 1$	(T—12)
$A \cdot \bar{A} = 0$	(T—6)	$\bar{\bar{A}} = A$	(T—13)
$A + 0 = A$	(T—7)		

LAWS OF BOOLEAN ALGEBRA

The Laws of Identity	$A = A,$	$\bar{A} = \bar{A}$
The Commutative Laws	$AB = BA,$	$A + B = B + A$
The Associative Laws	$A(BC) = ABC,$	$A + (B + C) = A + B + C$
The Idempotent Laws	$AA = A$	$A + A = A$
The Distributive Laws	$A(B + C) = AB + AC,$	$A + BC = (A + B)(A + C)$
The Laws of Absorption	$A + AB = A,$	$A(A + B) = A$

The Laws of Expansion $AB + A\bar{B} = A,$ $(A + B)(A + \bar{B}) = A$
De Morgan's Laws $\overline{AB} = \bar{A} + \bar{B},$ $\overline{A + B} = \bar{A}\bar{B}$

COMMON IDENTITIES OF BOOLEAN ALGEBRA

$A(\bar{A} + B) = AB$

$A + \bar{A}B = A + B$

$(AB)(A + B) = AB$

$(\overline{AB})(A + B) = A\bar{B} + \bar{A}B$

$A\bar{B} + \bar{A}B = AB + \bar{A}\bar{B}$

$(A + B)(B + C)(A + C) = AB + BC + AC$

$(A + B)(\bar{A} + C) = AC + \bar{A}B$

$AC + AB + B\bar{C} = AC + B\bar{C}$

$(A + B)(B + C)(\bar{A} + C) = (A + B)(\bar{A} + C)$

Number Tables

POWERS OF TWO

2^n	n	2^{-n}
1	0	1.0
2	1	0.5
4	2	0.25
8	3	0.125
16	4	0.062 5
32	5	0.031 25
64	6	0.015 625
128	7	0.007 812 5
256	8	0.003 906 25
512	9	0.001 953 125
1 024	10	0.000 976 562 5
2 048	11	0.000 488 281 25
4 096	12	0.000 244 140 625
8 192	13	0.000 122 070 312 5
16 384	14	0.000 061 035 156 25
32 768	15	0.000 030 517 578 125
65 536	16	0.000 015 258 789 062 5
131 072	17	0.000 007 629 394 531 25
262 144	18	0.000 003 814 697 265 625
524 288	19	0.000 001 907 348 632 812 5
1 048 576	20	0.000 000 953 674 316 406 25

Diodes and Transistors in Logic Circuits

While computer logic may be discussed and thoroughly understood without benefit of electronic background, many readers desire to correlate logic assemblies with electronic circuits. This appendix shows typical electronic implementation of common logic circuits in preparation for discussing the various logic "families" of the past, present, and future.

Modern digital computers consist of electronic assemblies constructed almost entirely using *solid-state* technology. Although the basic electronic circuits were known and used many years before development of solid-state electronics, today's equipment takes advantage of the low power and minimal space requirements of solid-state designs. Solid-state digital devices operate on the principle of electrical charge carrier control. The detailed fundamentals of semiconductor electronics (where the principles of electrical charge carrier control in solid-state devices are developed) are left to the many excellent texts already in publication. Only the simplified facts necessary to explain digital solid-state devices are discussed here.

The simplest of semiconductor devices is the *diode*. It consists of two types of semiconductor material (Figure C1(a)): one part (the *n* section, or *cathode*) contains an excess of negative electrical charge carriers (*electrons*); the other part (the *p* section, or *anode*) contains an excess of positive electrical charge carriers (*holes*). The electrical characteristics of such a device are shown in Figure C1(b) and may be summarized as follows.

1. When the *p* material (*anode*) is positive in respect to the *cathode* (Figure C1(c)), circuit current is limited mainly by the series resistance. The diode is effectively a "closed switch," exhibiting very low resistance.

2. When the *p* material (*anode*) is negative in respect to the *cathode*

(Figure C1(c)), circuit current is very close to zero. The diode is effectively an "open circuit," exhibiting very high resistance.

Diodes used in computer logic circuits are typically cylindrical in shape, on the order of 0.3 inch long and 0.1 inch in diameter. Modern computer logic circuits seldom use discrete diodes, since they are manufactured as an integral part of integrated circuits.

The property of one-way conduction allows diode-resistor combinations to perform as either AND or OR gates. Figure C2(a) is a diode AND gate and its equivalent symbol, while Figure C2(b) depicts an OR gate.

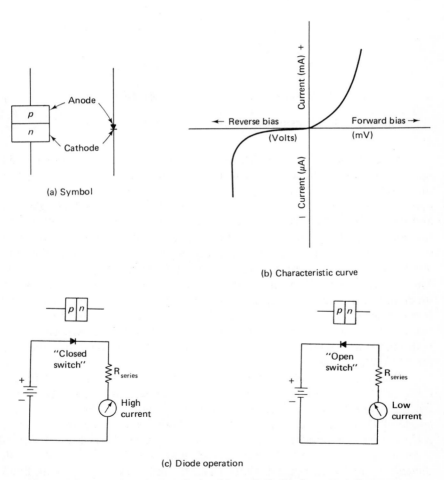

(a) Symbol

(b) Characteristic curve

(c) Diode operation

Figure C1 Semiconductor diode; (a) symbol, (b) characteristic curve, (c) diode operation.

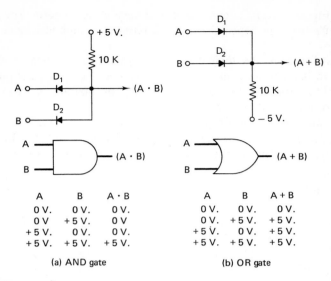

(a) AND gate   (b) OR gate

A	B	A · B
0 V.	0 V.	0 V.
0 V	+5 V.	0 V
+5 V.	0 V.	0 V.
+5 V.	+5 V.	+5 V.

A	B	A + B
0 V.	0 V.	0 V.
0 V.	+5 V.	+5 V.
+5 V.	0 V.	+5 V.
+5 V.	+5 V.	+5 V.

Figure C2   Diode gates; (a) AND gate, (b) OR gate.

When a diode conducts, it acts as a low resistance on the order of 50 ohms; when non-conducting, its resistance approaches 500,000 ohms. The diode AND gate of Figure C2(a) can be examined by the use of a table of combinations employing common voltage levels such as +5 volts (logic "1") and 0 volts (logic "0"). An equivalent circuit may be drawn for each row of the table and voltages determined. For example, row 0 shows that 0 AND 0 = 0. Both D_1 and D_2 have 0 volts applied to their cathodes, while the anodes are common, returning to +5 volts through a 10,000-ohm resistor. The output (A AND B) is also connected to the anodes of the diodes. Each diode has its anode + in respect to its cathode (forward biased), and there-fore acts as a small (50 ohm) resistor. The resultant equivalent circuit, with voltages, currents, and resistances shown, is seen in Figure C3(a). Therefore, with both A and B inputs connected to 0 volts (LOW, or logic "0"), the out-put is LOW, or logic "0."

When A is +5 volts and B is 0 volts, the equivalent circuit of Figure C3(b) results. D_2 is a low resistance (forward biased), and the voltage at the output is LOW, as shown earlier. Since the output is LOW (0 volts), the anode of D_1 is negative in respect to the cathode (reverse biased), and D_1 is a high resistance. Similar reasoning results in a LOW ("0") output for A = +5 volts and B = 0 volts. However, when both A and B are +5 volts, both diodes are high resistance (reverse biased), and very little current flows through R_1. The output is therefore near the +5 volt source, showing that +5 volts AND +5 volts = +5 volts.

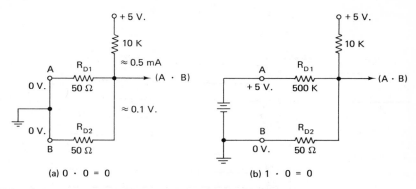

Figure C3 Diode AND gate equivalent circuits; (a) $0 \cdot 0 = 0$, (b) $1 \cdot 0 = 0$.

Diode OR gates (Figure C2(b)) also operate using the principles of high-resistance reverse bias and low-resistance forward bias. If both A and B are connected to 0 volts (logic "0"), both D_1 and D_2 are forward biased, and the output $(A + B)$ is effectively connected to 0 volts. Changing either A or B (or both) to $+5$ volts allows the appropriate diode(s) to route $+5$ volts to the output, and the other diode (if appropriate) becomes reverse biased. Thus if either A is $+5$ volts or B is $+5$ volts, or both are $+5$ volts, the output $(A + B)$ is $+5$ volts.

Although diode gates are simple, they do present some major disadvantages. Multiple input diode gates suffer performance degradation due not only to diode leakage but also to output loading as a result of connecting additional circuits to the output. Furthermore, diode gates do not provide the negation (NOT) operation. Modern computer logic circuits seldom use discrete diodes and resistors to perform gating functions. Gating is usually accomplished by using the integrated circuit techniques that are discussed in Appendix D.

Transistors greatly expand the capabilities of computer logic circuits. A transistor is a semiconductor device constructed from n and p materials similar to those used in diodes. Depending on desired characteristics, the transistor may be a "sandwich" consisting of n material between two p materials (PNP, Figure C4(a)) or p material between two n materials (NPN, Figure C4(b)). The center material is called the *base*, while the other materials are called, respectively, the *emitter* and *collector*. Input to the transistor is conventionally between emitter and base, which is operated as a forward-biased diode with resultant low resistance. Output is developed between the collector and base, which is operated as a high-resistance reverse-biased diode. Due to the principles of semiconductor physics and construction of the transistor, the change in input current as a result of input signal is almost

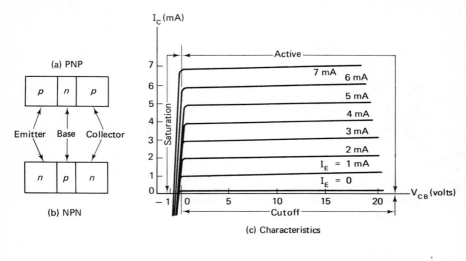

(c) Characteristics

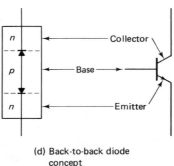

(d) Back-to-back diode
    concept

Figure C4   Transistor concepts; (a) PNP, (b) NPN, (c) characteristics,
(d) back-to-back diode concepts.

completely (99.5%) transferred to the output. The small change in current
at the input becomes "amplified" at the output because the output resistance
is so much greater than the input resistance. As an example, a 100 microampere change of current in an input resistance of 100 ohms results in a
voltage change of 10 millivolts. The same 100 microampere change in current
(less 0.5%) in an output resistance of 10,000 ohms results in a voltage change
of 995 millivolts. General operating characteristics of transistors are summarized in Figure C4(c).

When used in digital logic circuits, transistors can be considered as
two "back-to-back" diodes (Figure C4(d)). Since digital circuits require
identification of only two separate conditions, the "active" part of the char-

acteristics curve is often not used, and analysis of circuit operation is simplified. Only the *cutoff* and *saturation* modes of operation are discussed.

A typical *inverter* (NOT function) circuit is shown in Figure C5. Consider first the case where the base is connected to 0 volts. Since both base and emitter are connected to ground (0 volts), the base-emitter diode is reverse biased (non-conducting), and no return path from V_{cc} to ground exists through the transistor. Thus no current flows through R_c to ground through the transistor, and V_{cc} appears at the collector. The 0 volt input (LOW) therefore appears at the output as $+V_{cc}$ (HIGH), and logic inversion has been performed. When HIGH is applied to the input, however, the base-emitter junction is forward biased (conducting) and heavy current flows. The mechanics of transistor action cause this heavy current to also flow in the base-collector diode, and a large voltage drop appears across R_c. $\bar{A}$ is thus a LOW, and inversion again occurs.

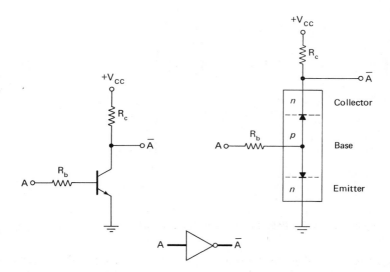

Figure C5 Inverter.

The basic concepts discussed to this point have all been based on the use of *bipolar* technology. As applications for logic circuits have grown, more space and more power have been required. These problems may be countered by using MOS (Metal-Oxide Semiconductor) technology, which allows higher packaging densities and lower power requirements. MOS logic circuits operate on *unipolar* principles. A bipolar device uses *both* positive and negative electrical charge carriers within the same device, while a unipolar device uses only positive *or* negative charge carriers. Furthermore, the physical location of the active charge carriers in a bipolar device is within the mass of the device, while in unipolar devices the charge carriers move close to the surface. Thus the charge carriers may be directed by external electrical fields and relatively little input power is required. In fact, the input terminal of an MOS formed transistor (called a *field-effect transistor*) is actually insulated from the rest of the transistor, and the polarity and magnitude of the potential applied to the input (gate) determine the amount of conduction that will exist from the output (drain) to the common point (source). Relatively small changes in input voltage cause large changes in output conduction.

A common symbol for an MOS field-effect transistor can be seen in the inverter diagram of Figure C6. The solid bar represents the semiconductor

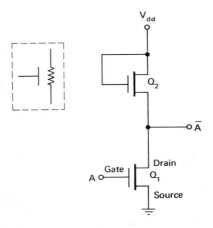

Figure C6   MOS field effect transistor inverter.

material which makes up the drain-source structure, while the unconnected line parallel to the solid line represents the gate. Either p or n material may be used to form the drain-source structure, which behaves as either a high resistance or low resistance, depending on the magnitude and polarity of the gate input in respect to the source. Q_1 represents the inverter element, while Q_2 functions as a dynamic load resistor. (The transistor's conductance characteristic is used to obtain a large value of resistance in a small area. Often the MOS dynamic load resistance uses the symbol shown adjacent to the actual transistor symbol to more adequately define its function.)

If the drain-source structure is constructed from n material, the charge carriers are electrons ($-$). With a 0 voltage (LOW) input applied to the gate, construction of the MOS device is such that very little current flows through the structure. A positive (HIGH) input "enhances" the current flow, and a relatively large amount of current results. In Figure C6, a LOW input to Q_1 becomes a HIGH output. (With little current flow, very little voltage drop occurs across the load transistor Q_2 and V_{dd} effectively appears at the output.) The relatively large current flow through Q_1 as a result of a HIGH input causes a large voltage drop across Q_2, and the output becomes LOW. Thus the logical NOT operation is performed.

The general fundamentals discussed in this appendix may now be combined to explain the most common logic circuits. See Appendix D.

Logic Families

As logic applications have grown in the past three decades, various "families" of logic circuits have evolved. Each of the most popular logic families is discussed in this appendix so that the reader may examine the numerous means of implementing basic logic operations. In general, the logic circuits are discussed as through they are constructed from discrete components (resistors, diodes, transistors, etc.). Actually, modern technology implements logic functions almost entirely with integrated circuit techniques.

Certain specified paramaters are used to evaluate digital logic circuits. Rather than discuss these parameters each time a new "family" is encountered, this appendix supplies comparison information in Table D1. This technique allows the reader to concentrate on circuit analysis without the interruption of strictly characteristics data.

Table D1 Logic Family Characteristics

Parameters	DTL	RTL	TTL	ECL	MOS
Average propagation delay (ns)	30	12	10	4	40
FF clock frequency, MHz (typical)	12	8	60	120	5
Power dissipation per gate (mW)	8	12	22	40	10 nW
Noise margin	Good	Poor	Good	Fair	Good
Power supply	5 V	3 V	5 V	5 V	3 to 18 V
Fan out	8	5	10	25	50

DIODE TRANSISTOR LOGIC (DTL)

By combining the characteristics of diode gates and the transistor inverter, NAND and NOR gates may be obtained. Diode transistor logic, as it is called, is one of the evolutionary families of logic circuits that have resulted in today's complex integrated circuit logic assemblies. A simplified DTL NAND gate is shown in Figure D1. D_1 and D_2, in conjunction with R_1, function as a typical diode AND gate, while Q_1 performs logic inversion. Both concepts have been previously discussed. D_3 isolates the AND gate from the inverter and effectively reduces noise sensitivity of the gating function. Circuit analysis may be simply performed by considering the gate and inverter separately, using already furnished information.

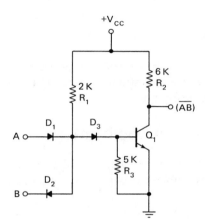

Figure D1 Simplified DTL NAND gate.

NOR gates may be formed by combining OR gates and inverters in a manner similar to the formation of NAND gates. More commonly, however, DTL supplies either NAND *or* NOR gates and constructs other types of gates using the techniques shown in Chapter 3. DTL circuits constructed from discrete diodes, transistors, and resistors are rarely encountered in modern digital logic applications. Integrated circuit versions of DTL may be encountered, and the theory of operation just discussed will enable the reader to better understand, evaluate, and apply DTL in digital circuits.

Modern implementations of DTL are more complex than the simplified gate of Figure D1. The DTL gate of Figure D2 is typical of IC units. Transistor Q_1 generally improves high-speed response and reduces input circuit requirements so that preceding circuits can drive more gates.

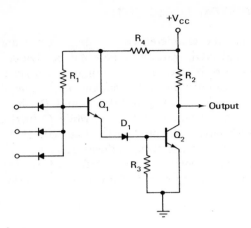

Figure D2 Modern DTL NAND gate.

DTL flip-flops appear in the usual forms, such as, *R-S*, *T*, *J-K*, in both direct and master-slave configurations. Figure D3 is a schematic diagram of a DTL master-slave *J-K* flip-flop.

RESISTOR TRANSISTOR LOGIC (RTL)

RTL (Resistor Transistor Logic) is another of the logic families leading to modern IC logic assemblies. It consists of the basic circuit of Figure C5, which performs the inversion operation (see Appendix C). The resistor in series with the base (R_b) limits the transistor input current and isolates the transistor from the preceding circuit. It is typically on the order of about 470 ohms. Output is taken from the collector circuit, which typically uses a load resistor (R_c) on the order of 680 ohms. Inversion in this circuit occurs for the reasons mentioned during initial discussion of transistor operation.

Gating functions are performed by connecting one or more of the circuits of Figure C5 in parallel, as shown in Figure D4. Since a + input to an RTL inverter causes the transistor to conduct heavily, the output drops to a voltage near 0 volts. Therefore if either *A* or *B*, or both, becomes +, the output becomes 0, and the NOR function is implemented. Within reason, a number of inputs may be combined by adding circuits such as shown by the dotted lines of Figure D4. AND, OR, and NAND operations may be implemented by the methods of Chapter 3.

Furthermore, flip-flops may be constructed using RTL techniques. As stated in Chapter 3, a simple *R-S* flip-flop requires only two 2-input NOR gates connected as shown in Figure D5(a). Replacing the logic symbols with discrete component symbols results in the circuit diagram of Figure D5(b).

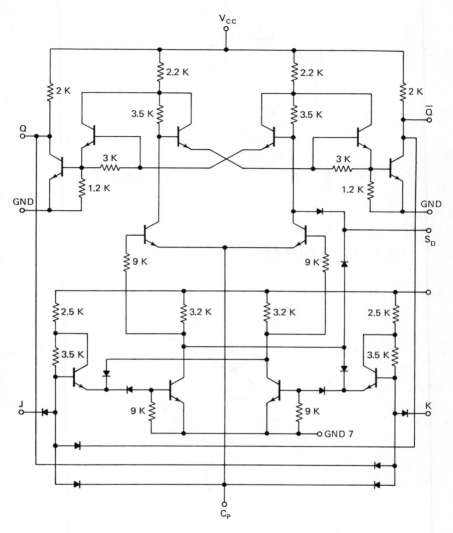

Figure D3   DTL flip-flop (J-K master-slave).

TRANSISTOR TRANSISTOR LOGIC (TTL OR T²L)

Transistor Transistor Logic is a logic system that has evolved from DTL. The concept of TTL gating is shown in Figure D6(a). Each DTL diode is replaced by a separate transistor, although the transistor inverter remains as in the DTL logic family. Consider first that both A and B are at a LOW level (0 volts). Both Q_A and Q_B will have their base-emitter junctions forward

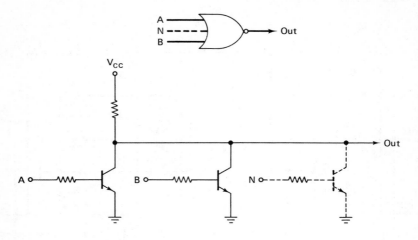

Figure D4   RTL NOR gate.

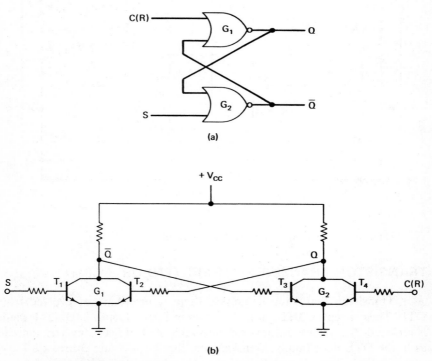

(a)

(b)

Figure D5   RTL flip-flop.

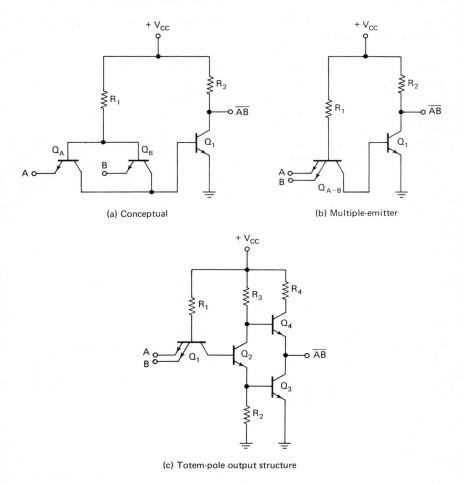

(a) Conceptual

(b) Multiple-emitter

(c) Totem-pole output structure

Figure D6 Transistor-transistor gate evolution; (a) conceptual, (b) multiple-emitter, (c) totem-pole output structure.

biased; both will be saturated, and their collectors will be near 0 volts. Q_1 will therefore be "turned off," (its base-emitter junction reverse biased); and since no current is flowing, its collector will be at a HIGH level (V_{cc}). In fact, if either A is LOW or B is LOW, or both are LOW, the same conditions exist. If, however, both A and B are HIGH, the transistors (Q_A and Q_B) are turned off, and their collector voltages rise. Q_1 turns on and the collector of Q_1 is near 0 volts. Thus if both A and B are HIGH, the output is LOW, and the NAND function is performed.

$\quad$ Q_A and Q_B are usually replaced by a single transistor with multiple emitters. Since the bases of Q_A and Q_B were connected, as were the collectors

(Figure D6(b)), the multiple emitter transistor functions just as though it were two separate transistors.

The more common TTL gate is more complex than those configurations shown in Figure D6(a) and D6(b). Conceptual TTL gates suffer from low drive capability, along with poor rise time characteristics. Figure D6(c) is a relatively standard TTL gate circuit, although recent advances have resulted in even more complex circuits. Base current for Q_2 is obtained from the multi-emitter transistor Q_1. As in the conceptual TTL gates, with both emitters of Q_1 HIGH, both base-emitter junctions are reverse biased. Under these conditions, Q_1's collector is HIGH, and Q_2 is saturated. Maximum current flows through Q_2, causing a large voltage drop across R_2 and R_3. Q_3 turns on, while Q_4 turns off, producing a LOW output. Thus the NAND function is performed.

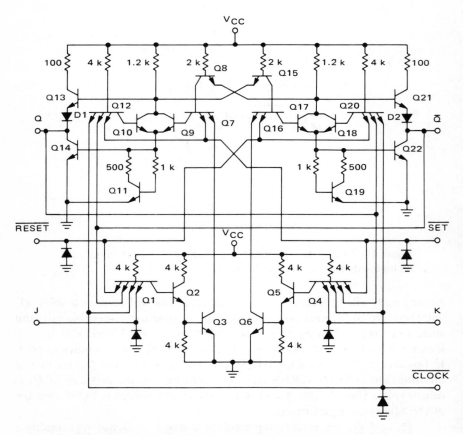

Figure D7   TTL J-K flip-flop (courtesy Motorola Semiconductor Products, Inc., Phoenix, AZ).

NAND gates are the common TTL logic package. Other logic operations may be obtained by the methods discussed in earlier chapters, although some manufacturers do provide separate AND, OR, NOR, and NOT packages. Flip-flops may be implemented by using cross-coupled NAND gates or by direct integrated circuit techniques such as shown in Figure D7.

EMITTER-COUPLED LOGIC (ECL)

Emitter-Coupled Logic (ECL) is a family of circuits characterized by high-speed, high-input impedance and low-output impedance. High speed is achieved by operating the input transistor in the "active" region of its characteristics (see Figure C4(c)).* High-input impedance is the result of the differential amplifier configuration of the input circuit, while the low-output impedance results from the emitter-follower output circuits. Figure D8 is the schematic diagram of a basic 2-input ECL OR/NOR gate. Transistors A_1 and A_2 are the input transistors, while B is the second half of the differential amplifier input circuit. C is the NOR output emitter follower, and D provides the low-impedance OR output.

A simple DC R-S flip-flop is shown in Figure D9. Dual inputs allow the OR function to be performed at the Set or Reset inputs. Note that both

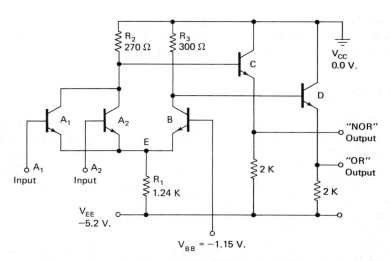

Figure D8 ECL gate (courtesy Motorola Semiconductor Products, Inc., Phoenix, AZ).

---

*When a transistor is operated in the "saturation" mode, charge carriers tend to remain in the saturated portion of the transistor and must be "swept out" before the transistor can be returned to the "cut-off" mode. The time it takes to remove the excess charge carriers detracts from the overall speed of the logic circuits.

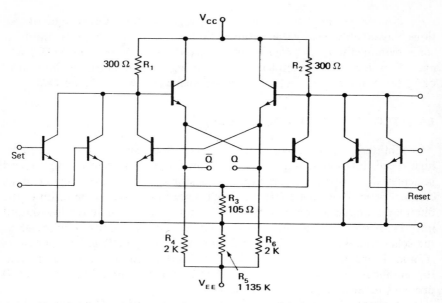

Figure D9 ECL flip-flop (courtesy Motorola Semiconductor Products, Inc., Phoenix, AZ).

the input OR functions and output amplifiers are emitter coupled. Thus the ECL flip-flop retains the same advantages as ECL gates—that is, high-speed, high-input impedance and low-output impedance.

MOS LOGIC

The basic logic functions implemented by DTL, ECL, TTL, RTL, etc may also be implemented using MOS technology. A logical NOR function is implemented by the MOS n channel circuitry of Figure D10(a). If either A or B (or both) is HIGH, conduction occurs and the output is LOW. If both A and B are LOW, no conduction exists and the output is V_{cc} (HIGH). The NAND function is shown in Figure D10(b). It is apparent that *both A* and B must be HIGH in order to obtain the LOW output, since the gating transistors are connected in series.

As in other logic families, flip-flops may be constructed from crosscoupled NAND or NOR gates. However, to take advantage of space-saving features, an MOS flip-flop is usually constructed as shown in the simple *R-S* example of Figure D10(c). The DATA lines are used for *both* input and output, depending on external gating circuitry for proper selection. Information is read into or out of the flip-flop with a HIGH level on the ENABLE input.

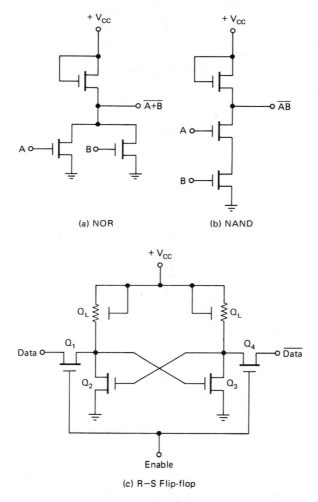

(a) NOR   (b) NAND

(c) R−S Flip-flop

Figure D10   MOS logic circuits; (a) NOR, (b) NAND, (c) R-S flip-flop.

During "read-in" the appropriate DATA/$\overline{\text{DATA}}$ line is pulsed to store information. After removal of the input pulse, the DATA/$\overline{\text{DATA}}$ lines may be examined when information stored in the flip-flop is needed.

MOS flip-flops (cells) such as shown in Figure D10(c) are often used as storage cells in larger arrays as discussed in Chapter 8. In addition, MOS circuitry is also found in the *dynamic* cell configuration of Chapter 8.

Another version of MOS is known as CMOS (Complementary Metal-Oxide Semiconductor). CMOS logic devices are constructed using both *n* and *p* type materials in the same circuit. MOS devices suffer from current leakage problems when in the non-conducting stage. However, if an *n* channel device is combined with a *p* channel device in the same circuit, both transistors are non-conducting when not enabled. Consequently, power requirements are reduced and more efficient operation results. Typical CMOS gates are shown in Figure D11.

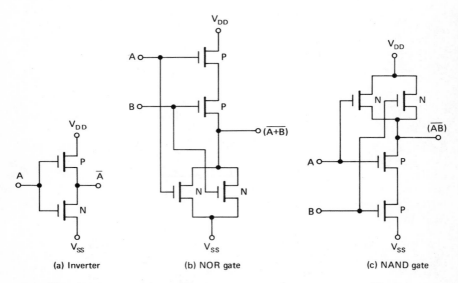

(a) Inverter (b) NOR gate (c) NAND gate

Figure D11 CMOS circuits; (a) inverter, (b) NOR gate, (c) NAND gate.

SUMMARY

Rapidly advancing semiconductor technology is quickly shifting the emphasis from one logic family to the next. Just a few short years ago, DTL and RTL occupied much of the computer equipment market. As TTL developed, it replaced DTL and RTL, only to be displaced by MOS circuitry. The future surely will find new technology supplementing and/or replacing MOS. However, the basic concepts presented in Appendices C and D supply adequate background for the reader to understand these new techniques as they evolve.

The relative characteristics shown in Table D1 compare important paramaters of various logic families. As new techniques evolve, it is merely necessary to add to this table to remain current with modern techniques.

Bibliography

BARON, ROBERT C., and ALBERT T. PICCIRILLI, *Digital Logic and Computer Operations*. New York: McGraw-Hill, 1967.

BARTEE, THOMAS C., *Digital Computer Fundamentals*, 3rd edition. New York: McGraw-Hill, 1972.

BOYCE, JEFFERSON C., *Digital Logic and Switching Circuits*. Englewood Cliffs, N.J.: Prentice-Hall, 1975.

BURROUGHS CORPORATION, Technical Training Department, Defense, Space, and Special Systems Group; *Digital Computer Principles*, 2nd edition. New York: McGraw-Hill, 1969.

CHURCHMAN, LEE W., *Survey of Electronics*. San Francisco: Rinehart Press, 1971.

DAVENPORT, WILLIAM P., *Modern Data Communication*. New York: Hayden, 1971.

DEEM, WILLIAM, KENNETH MUCHOW, and ANTHONY ZEPPA, *Digital Computers*. Reston, Va.: Reston, 1974.

DICKEY, LARRY W., *Introduction to Computer Concepts*. Englewood Cliffs, N.J.: Prentice-Hall, 1974.

DIETMEYER, DONALD L., *Logic Design of Digital Systems*. Boston: Allyn and Bacon, 1971.

KARNAUGH, M., "The Map Method for Synthesis of Combinational Logic Circuits," *AIEE Proceedings*, November 1953, p. 593.

KETCHUM, DONALD J., *Applications of Digital Logic*. Farmingdale, N.J.: Buck Engineering, 1966.

MALEY, GERALD A., *Manual of Logic Circuits*. Englewood Cliffs, N.J.: Prentice-Hall, 1970.

MANDL, MATTHEW, *Fundamentals of Electronic Computers: Digital and Analog*. Englewood Cliffs, N.J.: Prentice-Hall, 1967.

MARCUS, MITCHELL P., *Switching Circuits for Engineers*, 2nd edition. Englewood Cliffs, N.J.: Prentice-Hall, 1967.

PHISTER, MONTGOMERY, Jr., *Logical Design of Digital Computers*. New York: Wiley, 1958.

ROBINSON, VESTER, *Basic Principles of Digital Computers*. Reston, Va.: Reston, 1974.

SIGNETICS; *Application Memos*, Sunnyvale, CA ©1969 Sects. 3-4 and 4-10.

————; *Digital, Linear, MOS Handbook*, Sunnyvale, CA © 1972 Sects. 2 and 3.

————; *Digital, Linear, MOS Applications*, Sunnyvale, CA © 1973 Sect. 3.

VEITCH, E. W., "A Chart Method for Simplifying Truth Functions," Association for Computing Machinery, *Proceedings*, May 1952, 127.

————, *Application Notes*. Anaheim, Ca.: California Computer Products, 1974.

————, *Application Notes*. Palo Alto, Ca.: Hewlett-Packard, 1974.

————, *Application Notes*. Plainfield, N.J.: Burroughs, 1971–1974.

————, *Application Notes*. Phoenix: Motorola Semiconductor Products, 1969–1975.

————, *Application Notes*. Worcester, Mass.: Sprague Electric Company, 1970.

————, *SUE Computer Handbook*. Los Angeles: Lockheed Electronics, 1974.

Index